HUMAN RESOURCE MANAGEMENT

The New Agenda

PAUL R. SPARROW

Sheffield University Management School

AND

MICK MARCHINGTON

Manchester School of Management, UMIST

FINANCIAL TIMES
PITMAN PUBLISHING

FINANCIAL TIMES
MANAGEMENT
LONDON · SAN FRANCISCO
KUALA LUMPUR · JOHANNESBURG

Financial Times Management delivers the knowledge,
skills and understanding that enable students,
managers and organisations to achieve their ambitions,
whatever their needs, wherever they are.

London Office:
128 Long Acre, London WC2E 9AN
Tel: +44 (0)171 447 2000
Fax: +44 (0)171 240 5771
Website: www.ftmanagement.com

A Division of Financial Times Professional Limited

First published in Great Britain in 1998

ISBN 0 273 62823 2

British Library Cataloguing in Publication Data
A CIP catalogue record for this book can be obtained from
the British Library.

3 5 7 9 10 8 6 4 2

Typeset in Sabon by M Rules
Printed and bound in Great Britain by
Clays Ltd, St Ives plc

The Publishers' policy is to use paper manufactured
from sustainable forests.

To Sue, for doing her best to make me write English,
and for giving me the freedom to work.

To Lorrie, Jack and Lucy.

CONTENTS

Part One
CHANGING ORGANISATIONAL FORMS, PROCESSES AND CONTRACTS

Part Two
DEVELOPING PARTNERSHIP AND EMPLOYEE VOICE

Part Three
THE PURSUIT OF MULTIPLE AND PARALLEL FLEXIBILITIES

PART 1

Changing organisational forms, processes and contracts

1

Introduction: is HRM in crisis?

PAUL SPARROW AND MICK MARCHINGTON

Sheffield University Management School, University of Sheffield
Manchester School of Management, UMIST

CRISIS, WHAT CRISIS?

The 1990s witnessed a period of fundamental change in both the context and content of HRM. Despite the many recent prescriptions for the most appropriate HRM policies and practices, there are a number of underlying tensions and contradictions within the field. For example, delayering has led both to empowerment and to work intensification and redundancy. In managing the tensions between seeming opposites, searching questions are being asked by academics and practitioners alike and the word 'crisis' has been used by some to highlight the current state of the field and the need to stimulate new thinking. What is a crisis? It comes from the Greek word *krînein* meaning to decide, a decisive moment or turning point. Will decisions made today about the shape of HRM policies and practices prove to be a turning point in terms of what is feasible after the millennium? It is a moot point. There has certainly been a crisis of confidence in some quarters. The central purpose of this book, therefore, is to ask whether the crisis in confidence is justified. Does the field need to have, or need to be in, a state of crisis or is talk of crisis an unnecessary distraction, a useful ruse to get new issues onto the agenda? These questions have been at the forefront of debate over the last few years.

In order to address the debate, a joint academic–practitioner approach to articulating the key issues has been taken. A series of ESRC–IPD workshops brought together experienced researchers, practitioners and policy-makers with a view to developing practice which is informed by theory, contemporary research and leading edge practice. We feel that the seminar series, through this book, crystallises the emergent debates within the field, and enables constructive analysis of problems in the field and an identification of the most appropriate way forward. The workshops reveal that there is indeed a major set of problems facing the field in the form of a series of dilemmas to be resolved. However, experts prefer not to use the language of crisis, arguing that what we face is simply another evolutionary challenge to the role of HR practitioners. We must appraise objectively the major themes around which this book is structured, without 'talking up' yet another crisis and period of navel-gazing in the profession. However, put at their starkest, critiques of HRM suggest that the field faces a challenging new agenda in the context of having

3

handed significant power over to people who have low levels of competency, within organisations that are finding it difficult to implement existing changes, operating in an environment of much cloaked but nevertheless backward-looking and defensive thinking and analysis, and a political environment in which people prefer to use words which say one thing, but behave in ways that say something else. It is not surprising that HR practitioners find difficulty in maintaining their credibility or control over the agenda in such a context!

This is, however, too stark and cynical a view, and as many contributors to this book will demonstrate, crisis is an over-statement. Most of the issues to be faced at the millennium were apparent by the mid-1990s. For example, in 1994 the US Human Resource Planning Society set up a State-of-the-Art (SOTA) Council to consider what the main change drivers and challenges would be at the millennium (Eichinger and Ulrich, 1995). Not surprisingly, the tensions were felt to be around issues associated with globalisation and internationalisation. These issues were at that time seen mainly as 'soft' problems, as were the implementation problems associated with structural change and horizontal management techniques such as total quality management (TQM) and business process re-engineering (BPR). The need to build trust and confidence (so that individuals inside and outside the organisation believe what managers say) and the need to become boundaryless (with information and ideas moving across hierarchical, horizontal and external boundaries effortlessly) also featured in their analysis. Flexibility was seen as a problem, mainly in terms of there being potentially limited capacity for change. As we shall see, these issues are central at the millennium. Perhaps the main difference is that they are all now recognised as 'hard' problems, because it is time to deliver.

So perhaps there is not crisis as such. However, the time for decisive action still beckons. HR practitioners are faced with an increasing number of dilemmas, some old and some new, which are becoming clearer as they attempt to make the role changes prescribed for them in the mid-1990s. Practitioners are being forced to commit or react to a series of propositions which, from their perspective, contain many contradictory or naive intentions. If HR practitioners cannot resolve these dilemmas, then someone else will do it for them. If we look at the new agenda in the field, we can see a number of possible points of departure or new directions that may be taken over the next few years. Do organisations purposefully address changes in employee behaviour that are resulting from the pursuit of flexibility with new and distinctive policies, or do they maintain existing thinking? Should organisations pursue employee participation and involvement through institutional means or favour a direct and individual dialogue? Do we accept a social model of HRM under a European influence, attempt to replicate the American approach, or find our own way?

CENTRAL THEMES IN HRM AT THE MILLENNIUM

What is clear is that in trying to find an acceptable path through these dilemmas, the fields of knowledge that will carry weight in the profession are changing rapidly. What are the central fields of knowledge now needed to cope and does this knowledge reside within the gift of HRM professionals any more, or has it now been outsourced to line managers, consultants and external institutions? Clearly the basis of expert knowledge needed by HRM professionals now has to be reconsidered. Why do we say this? Many of the chapters in this book are concerned with the *breakdown* of work and traditional relationships and linkages. As we witness *a fragmentation of the employment relationship*, we see a breakdown of several linkages that have previously guided our thinking about HRM. Work is being reconstituted in totally new ways and this makes it difficult for practitioners to put their trust in knowledge based on the old relationships and linkages. We have to give renewed consideration to many relationships that are now being changed: our links with ourselves in terms of what we want out of work, how we maintain a sense of individuality in a world where we either increasingly subsume our life to more intense employment, or face no employment at all; our relationships with other individuals in a work process that can be altered in terms of social interactions, time patterns and geographical location; the co-operative and competitive links between different internal and external constituents of the organisation in their new more flexible forms; and the relationships between key stakeholders and institutions such as governments, unions and managers.

We believe there are three concepts around which HRM professionals need to gain increased understanding, and these recur throughout the whole book:

1 **New organisational forms and new psychological contracts.** How should organisations and HRM professionals cope with the pressures created by these changes? Is this the 'trust no-one' era of HRM and organisational life, or can we find ways of re-engaging individuals and HR practitioners, as well as all the stakeholders in the employment relationship? The central question therefore is **where is the trust?**

2 **The need for partnership in the employment relationship.** Can we build new structures and mechanisms to foster participation and involvement at work or is partnership 'a dead duck'? Will recent institutional developments and shifts in power within modern organisations enable us to create and sustain high levels of performance? The central question here is **who has the voice?**

3 **The drive for multiple and parallel flexibilities within organisations.** Is this drive inevitable and is it manageable? The central question here is **what is work**, i.e. what is it in which we now place our trust?

Although we have placed notions of trust, work and voice at the heart of the three issues of changing organisational forms, partnership and flexibility, they are of course intertwined concepts. Because of this, they appear repeatedly throughout the whole book and also *within each* of the three themes outlined above. In opening up this debate, we would note that it is perhaps politically incorrect to ask personnel management institutions to talk of crisis, but the context outlined in the next section must be considered.

THE CONTEXT: UNPLEASANT TRUTHS AND NEW REALITIES

An issue of work and society

Before we consider the main dilemmas faced by HR practitioners at the millennium and their ability to tackle the agenda created by changing organisational forms, flexibility and partnership, it is necessary to remind ourselves of the overall context within which their work is carried out. Many of the problems faced by HR practitioners today clearly reflect deeper issues that are linked to changes in *work and its role in society*. Ultimately the actions that will resolve many of the contradictions in the field of HRM *are* decisions about work and society. Derek Torrington notes in Chapter 2 that HR practitioners should not be blamed for the consequences of such changes, but as the tenor of this book shows, *they do have a role in getting the important issues of trust and voice on to the agenda in this societal debate.*

Therefore, while issues of work and society are not the central concern of this book, we cannot avoid situating the debate about the shape of HRM within the UK institutional context. For example, CEOs are under conflicting pressures from a range of stakeholders. They are often guilty of not telling analysts about the 'soft' side to implementing heightened performance expectations. This runs the risk of creating unrealistic performance expectations among institutions, because internal problems associated with creating the necessary changes in culture and systems are obscured and glossed over. John Monks considers this issue in Chapter 11.

It is necessary to do this because it is the HR practitioners who have to be the bearers of bad tidings to the CEO, without being seen as having 'gone soft' on the business issues! Sadly, the more tightly integrated HR practitioners become with the strategic process and environment of their firm, the more the limits to their power, knowledge and influence in managing such consequences are exposed, and the more obvious becomes the confusion over their identity. They can see themselves becoming *prisoners within* or *hostages to* their own national business system.

Changes in national business systems

In Britain the hope of post-industrialisation has become the reality of deindustrialisation and rationalisation. Moreover, there is an inevitable redefinition of the role that HRM can play in organisations. This is mainly because of a shift in terms of who has the power and consequently who has the most important stake in determining and setting the agenda for HRM. One of the phenomena of the 1990s has been a continued transfer of responsibility for social cost from organisations to either the state or the individual, and from the state to the individual. For example, in the USA it is calculated that if corporations were now to pay as much tax as they did in the 1950s, the US government would gain $250 billion extra revenue a year, enough to wipe out the entire budget deficit (Korten, 1993). Organisations will not pay for social policy. Within the EU estimates suggest that in the UK the hidden economy is now worth about £80 billion, or 12 per cent of GDP (up from 6–8 per cent of GDP in the mid-1980s). At a cost to the Treasury of £20 billion a year, it represents a third of all annual tax revenues. States will allow considerable degrees of 'self-help' as long as it does not siphon off too much revenue.

Consider some of the HRM implications of the recent shifts in power, and political and financial influence. After all the rationalisation, downsizing, delayering and process redesign, what we are really witnessing is a process whereby senior management roles are becoming increasingly divorced from those of middle managers and require a very different set of skills and competencies. Middle managers are essentially being designed out of the organisation and many of their roles pushed down to lower levels; and the distinction between junior managers and workers is being eroded as work teams are empowered and operate more on a self-managing basis under tight performance control. As a consequence, the power to shape the HRM agenda has shifted within organisations. Senior managers can make or break HRM systems as there is less formalised policy, but then so too can work teams. The same pattern of power shift has happened outside the organisation. National governments have increasingly become redundant – designed out of the process, the power and the influence – as we witness globalisation and the counteracting development of pan-national institutions such as the EU, both of which now set the pace for change in HRM policy and practice rather than national governments. Reflecting the empowerment of junior teams, we see the growth in power of regions and their relationships with organisations. Regions and their business infrastructure can create jobs far more powerfully than national governments. In a more deregulated environment, organisations also have more autonomy and power to shape the nature of their own HRM.

Moreover, an increasing strait-jacket of economic determinism is changing the political and economic context for HRM. Of course institutions such as the International Monetary Fund through its World Economic Outlook argue that globalisation merely accentuates the benefits of good national policies and that national governments are not redundant. There is still scope for intervention in the areas of corporate governance, the quality of investment (through financial intermediation, regulation and competition policies), the skills of the workforce (through primary education provision and vocational education and training networks), openness to the transfer of technology and innovation, and general macro-economic stability. The counter argument points to the process of globalisation in the 1990s as the greatest transfer of economic sovereignty in recent history, and to the removal of numerous 'degrees of freedom' for national governments in terms of their ability to finance changes in social policy and job creation programmes.

Tensions mount worldwide and everywhere we see a questioning of the status quo. In the first five years of the 1990s 3.1 million US workers lost their jobs through redundancy and reorganisation. The erosion of employment in its more traditional sense and the continued pressure on employers to maintain current staffing levels is expected to continue. In 1991 the American Management Association surveyed 1142 organisations that had downsized (Academy of Management Survey, 1995). The limited success and many negative side effects of the strategy were clearly evidenced. Sadly, the most recent AMA survey in 1995 saw 'a continuation, if not an acceleration of many of these trends' (Mroczkowski and Hanaoka, 1997, p. 58). Twenty-nine per cent of US organisations expect to further trim their workforces, the highest proportion since the surveys began in 1987. The use of alternative strategies to stave off redundancies (demotions, transfers, recruitment moratoriums) has declined from 70 per cent of organisations to 43 per cent. A recent survey of 400 US Conference Board organisations shows that 70 per cent expect to continue downsizing (Mirvis, 1997). It is seen as an essential way of maintaining cost control, profitability and improved productivity.

Disillusionment knows no national borders. Japan too has changed from being a role model for HRM policies and practices, to becoming a major target for those who argue for the break-up of national business systems (Wood, 1994). The Chairman of the Japan Federation of Employers Association (*nikkeiren*) today urges pay restraint in wage and bonus demands, and states that Japanese companies employ 1.2 million excess workers. There is evidence of convergence in practice between Japanese and US organisations. The Japanese process of gradual adjustment of employment levels (*koyochosei*) and the strategies pursued by 'best practice' US organisations attempting to pursue proactive downsizing and work system redesign (Mroczkowski and Hanaoka, 1997) bear many similarities.

Flexibility is an issue in Japan. Wage increases are flexible, but the annual wage bargaining ritual known as *shunto* (spring labour offensive) means that wages increase uniformly across sectors irrespective of productivity. Japanese Ministry of Labour data show that in 1996, although basic wages increased by only 3 per cent (accounting for 72 per cent of total compensation), average final monthly wages increased by 7 per cent. Such pay pressure has seen divergence from the uniform agreements, with profitable firms such as Toyota offering well above the average, but Nissan and Honda falling behind. Financial markets have dropped harmonious practices and share prices of internationally competitive exporters have increased while several organisations face bankruptcy. Within companies, the seniority-based wage system and employee dependence on high and virtually guaranteed twice annual bonuses (amounting to 23 per cent of total compensation) is under threat. Mitsubishi allows the pay of managers of the same age to vary by plus or minus 10 per cent. Sony and Honda run western-style performance-related, merit-based pay systems. Matsushita introduced the first tiered wage system in Japan which differentiates between those following a lifetime employment 'contract', newcomers who want to bring forward and forego the substantial retirement benefits, and those with specialist skills in demand who wish to contract out of most age- and service-related benefits.

In Europe we witness calls to break-up national business systems. In Germany there is evidence of significant change in some areas of the employment relationship, with the Bundesverband der Deutschen Industrie (BDI) arguing that enterprise is blighted by high tax, wages and welfare costs. To counter the export abroad of around 2 million jobs from manufacturing and an increase in unemployment to 4.5 million, Germany has attempted to balance cuts in pension funds, unemployment pay, redundancy protection, health insurance and sickness benefit, and more flexible work hours by positive attempts at job creation. There is pressure to break up the 40 000 *Tarifverträge* that regulate German pay and compensation negotiations. The recent trend has been to trade off reductions in take home pay by providing more time off work. In a complex deal, Ford Germany intends to save £74 million a year in costs through more flexible work levels, adjustment of shift times and reductions in overtime. The carrot for workers is that they end up with more time off. Working a 37.5 hour week with 30 days holiday and ten 'free' shifts a year when they can stay away from work, the deal provides an additional 15 free shifts a year, earned through work practice flexibility. Such a deal suits German work values. However, as both the welfare state and employer–works council consensus have come under pressure from new legislated changes, Germany is witnessing the largest public demonstrations since World War II.

A political economy and comparative perspective

It is the political economists, therefore, who now contribute to the analysis of obstacles facing HR practitioners. They argue that sustained developments to the HRM role become near impossible while there are 'financial systems that fail to reward companies making hard-to-measure investments in their workforce, and macroeconomic policies that penalise companies that try to provide long term commitments to their employees' (Levine, 1995, p. 2). It has become easy to argue that the nature of work and organisational life is best understood as a subset of the political economy and that this is where most of the new people management developments will be driven from. The HRM field has become disenfranchised. It is argued that we should not give too much attention to organisations and their HR practitioners, and the limited changes they may currently be able to make in their HRM systems.

Moreover, our understanding about the link between HRM and the national business system within which it resides is being built up on an increasingly international and comparative basis. As we break away from the American assumptions about high performance practices and look towards other parts of the world, such as Europe and the Far East, in order to gain insights into best practice, there is a growing understanding about the importance – and dominating rule – of national business systems in setting the context for people management. HR managers are becoming more international in many ways, acting as:

- home-based HR managers, but having a central focus on managers who are international, multicultural team members, and having to work on a series of international projects;
- internationally mobile HR managers making frequent but short overseas visits;
- expatriate HR managers working on lengthy assignments in a single country.

They are therefore increasingly aware that there is a competition between the different forms of capitalism and their associated mindsets, and that each of these systems looks at HRM and views its content and role in very different ways (Sparrow and Hiltrop, 1994; 1997). The role of the state and financial sectors, national systems of education and training, employment and tenure expectations, and national cultures combine to create 'national business recipes', each driven by its own 'dominant logic of action' (Whitley, 1992). Therefore, the development and success of specific managerial structures and HRM practices – such as ideologies about employee participation or commitment – is strongly determined by the degree of integration between and support from the institutional arrangements in a country (Lane, 1989). This stream of work argues that any progress that has been made towards a new territory and role for HR practitioners in the UK is at best fragile, and is subject to becoming 'unlocked' or 'dislocated' by the marked changes in markets and technology that we now witness (Knights, Morgan and Murray, 1992).

It also highlights the need to understand the different national frames of reference for HRM. At a recent Anglo-French British Council meeting, French HR directors and employment ministers spoke of the need to offer *employabilité*, defined as the creation of competitive competencies in the wider labour market, yet the British and French participants differed widely in terms of the means through which the creation of employability should be pursued, the employee relations strategy deployed and the pace at which they thought it legitimate that organisations should challenge the psychological contract of employees (MacLachlan, 1996). Although many of the factors, such as restructuring and downsizing, that have been seen to challenge the psychological contract within the Anglo-American literature have crossed national borders, there are clearly distinctive national trajectories in the individual and organisational response. Given the importance of these arguments, we bring in an overtly international and comparative perspective to the flexibility debate in the chapters by Chris Brewster and Alan Jenkins.

EVOLVING CONCERNS

Will economic determinism lead to the collapse of the HRM metaphor?

Has this economic determinism led to the collapse of the HRM metaphor? David Guest addresses this question in Chapter 3. It is an important issue. Do the recent changes in the nature and purpose of organisations imply that the field of HRM is dead, having itself been made redundant by developments in the way organisations are managed? If there has been a collapse in the metaphor, we need to know why. Is it because the HRM philosophy itself has failed, i.e. having gone down the HRM route in the 1980s it has proved not to be really linked to performance, or so marginally linked that organisational performance can never be significantly influenced? Is it because the HRM philosophy has never really been adopted, or because no amount of change in internal HRM policies can hold back the waves of change to macro-competitiveness? Is it because the agenda has always been to take out the unions and thereby gain control of the employment relationship? Or is it because of the weak national business system set-up in the UK, which has meant that HRM died on the vine through institutional neglect? Depending on the answer, we face very different tasks in changing the nature of people management at the millennium.

Optimistically it can be argued that the issue faced by HR practitioners in this environment is not one of crisis and lack of identity, but one of evolution towards a new set of business pressures and ethics. There is still the possibility that HRM can take on a new and more central significance to organisational life, especially if practitioners pursue a clear agenda. In times of rapid change and significant power shifts, the issue in the resultant face-offs (to paraphrase President Kennedy) is 'who blinks first'. It is never the institutions or organisation systems; they change last. It is the people. Therefore, although HR practitioners should not have to shoulder responsibility for society's transitions, they cannot avoid being the first to have to manage the consequence of changes in employee behaviour.

Echoes of the 1980s: divisions in work and society

In order to establish the new agenda, we need to consider recent history and identify the way in which HRM concerns have evolved. In particular, we should remind ourselves of the different foci of attention that followed the two UK recessions of 1979–83 and 1990–92. In terms of overall evolution, there has been a slow but clear change in the content and focus of HRM within most organisations. Personnel issues in the 1970s were principally concerned with industrial relations, performance and administration. By the 1980s responsibilities focused more on training and development, culture change and performance-related rewards. Research into the HRM implications of strategic change showed that organisations were only capable of implementing change by introducing a set of mutually reinforcing HRM systems aimed at creating, retaining and developing new skills, competencies and mindsets within the organisation (Hendry, Pettigrew and Sparrow, 1989; Hendry and Pettigrew, 1990). As we entered the 1990s, this debate was dominated by the need to redesign organisations, to resource a broader set of competencies that had by then been identified, and to adopt better human resource planning processes to tie the various HRM activities together (Sparrow, 1997a). Indeed, the 1990s were perceived both by researchers and practitioners as 'watershed' years. In many sectors the three stabilising pillars of employment levels, employee career structures and industrial relations came under simultaneous attack (Cressey and Scott, 1992).

The extent of this evolution becomes clearer if we consider the questions that were asked and the language that was used during and immediately after the recession of the early 1980s and that which became current after the early to mid-1990s recession. The two UK recessions rate among the top seven of *all post-war recessions* in *all* the G7 countries, so they were significant events. In the early 1980s personnel managers could have been forgiven for thinking their role was reaching the end of its usefulness (a familiar theme throughout their organisational history). The agenda was split between a deep consideration of the role of work and society, and an emergent regeneration of organisational power and renewed attention to what were called 'people-related business issues'. The role of work and its place in society became a significant issue again, although this time not with the idealism of the 1960s' consideration of a post-industrial society. New academic journals such as *New Technology, Work and Employment* or *Work, Employment and Society* rose to prominence and gave consideration to a number of issues relating to changes in the nature of work. There was a detailed focus on the problems created by the move towards an informal economy and the creation of productive households as the amount of formal employment shrank (Armstrong, 1984; Gershuny, 1983; Pahl, 1984). Consideration was given to general problems of 'employee well-being', with significant programmes of research to consider the psychology of unemployment and its impact on people, particularly among blue collar workers in manufacturing occupations (Warr, 1987). The agenda also included not just the loss of employment, but the pauperisation of many sectors of remaining employment, as jobs were deskilled, working hours were reduced, and terms and conditions were deregulated. Society had to provide basic incomes and accept that we have to pay people not to work, and therefore shift the funding of public welfare from taxation of income to taxation of indirect expenditure and consumption, it was argued (Sparrow, 1986). The agenda in the mid-1980s could be restated today: the rise and fall of unemployment, an exchange of free time for consumerism, increasingly productive households, jobless economic growth, deindustrialisation, limitations of monetarism, unrealistic targets for job creation, a pauperisation of employment, increased social divisions, and the need for work sharing, new forms of wealth distribution, alternative forms of work organisation and fundamental changes in work values.

Management history often shows us that what people predict for themselves generally comes to pass, but perhaps a generation later than we forecast! This first part of the 1980s' agenda is actually still very relevant at the millennium, either in terms of dealing with issues of pauperisation at work (*see*, for example, Kossek, Huber-Yoder, Castellino, Heneman and Skoglind, 1997) or in terms of once more addressing issues of work sharing (*see*, for example, Blyton and Trinczek, 1997). In Chapter 19 Karen Legge asserts similar arguments, drawing attention to the problems of the degradation of work and the distribution of high quality jobs across the workforce, as employees are enticed to shift their attention away from their role as producers to their role as consumers. The formal numbers associated with labour costs, productivity equations, levels of unemployment, prevalence of atypical forms of employment, size of the hidden economy, and other aspects of the societal context may have changed since the 1980s debate on work and society, but the implications have not. Employees do not behave in a social vacuum, nor do consumer markets. Across the whole of the EU, changes in the way unemployment is counted distort the apparent impact of current changes in work. If those of working age who are no longer seeking jobs are included in the statistics, then, according to the Hong Kong and Shanghai Bank estimates, UK unemployment is 14 per cent, not 6 per cent, and the OECD estimates of unemployment in the Netherlands increases by a factor of 2.7 to a similar figure (Naudin, 1997). In the late 1990s in the UK, 25 per cent of households have no one in work. The number of non-active people outside the organisation, or people active in the hidden economy is substantial. Employees meet these people, and their expectations of their employer and its behaviour are set in this context.

Despite some change in the context, therefore, many still see the issues facing HR practitioners at the millennium as part and parcel of the broader redefinition of work and its role in society, accompanied by a need to ask some deep and searching questions about the role of organisations. Pascale (1995) notes that in the unfolding drama there are three facets to the problem.

- We are looking for a painless way out of dealing with the changes in self-esteem, community and social identity that work is now creating, yet this is inescapably painful.
- The individual and the organisation cannot resolve these issues themselves.
- A new social context is necessary to legitimise and accept the experiences associated with the loss and change to our working lives.

As Ryland (1997, p. 301) bluntly puts it:

> *If corporate social responsibility is inefficient in a global marketplace, then the problem and the solution lie in adjusting corporations, not the rest of society.*

The HRM movement: historical blip or source of regeneration?

Seen in a longer term perspective, was the HRM movement a historical aberration? Back in the 1980s the work and society theme was, if truth be told, superseded when we all began to think again about growth, entrepreneurialism, consumption, money and the individual. A new lease of life was given to the role of people management in organisations and there was a regeneration of the role of personnel management under the twin drives of competitiveness and flexibility. Therefore, attention was given to the contrasting need to create a 'flexible organisation', focused initially around the need for functional flexibility and multiskilling (Atkinson, 1984). This drew attention to the tensions between the existing industrial relations framework and the pressing need for rapid human resource development within organisations, and led to a debate about the consequential retitling and/or restructuring of personnel departments around these new roles, and the loss of influence or actual removal of people with industrial relations backgrounds. Not surprisingly there were arguments about the consequences of a shift towards 'macho industrial relations' under Thatcherism (Marchington and Parker, 1990). Within the emerging field of HRM, the focus was on technical and territorial issues. On a technical note the issue was how to demonstrate the importance of linking HRM with business strategy and the various ways in which integration of strategic planning processes could be achieved alongside greater devolvement of HRM implementation to line managers. On a territorial note, the debate was about the true nature of HRM, what it entailed and whether or not the phenomenon was just 'old wine in new bottles'. These debates still resonate today (Gennard

and Kelly, 1997; Truss, Gratton, Hope-Hailey, McGovern and Stiles, 1997), but they originally took place in a society that was emerging from its deepest post-war recession and
was trying to learn about the new economic realities.

Yet within a decade, professional and management journals were talking about 'downsizing', 'rightsizing', 'delayering', 'recession fatigue', or the retrograde sounding
phenomenon of 'downshifting'. Reflecting the 'human resources' versus 'resourceful
humans' critique of HRM, there has been an increasing tension between the human
resource requirements of a flexible organisation and the organisational requirements of a
flexible human resource. The wheel has turned very quickly, and it now presents HR practitioners with some difficult dilemmas.

CHANGING ORGANISATIONAL FORMS AND NEW PSYCHOLOGICAL CONTRACTS

The end of jobs and the redesign of organisation co-ordination systems

One of these dilemmas has arisen because of broad changes to the shape and form of
organisations. The dilemma this has created concerns the need to change the *level of
analysis* at which HR practitioners operate. At what level of intervention should they
design and aim their policies, tools and intervention techniques? Should they direct their
attention to mediating the impact of change on the individual and their skills and attitudes?
Do they focus instead mainly on the design of jobs and on the issues raised in fitting the
person to the job? Should they become involved in understanding how jobs are best fitted
together and co-ordinated? Should they be the architects of organisational competitive
advantage? Depending on the answer, there are very different implications for the sort of
'armoury' they should bring to bear in terms of HRM policies, tools and techniques.

The link between changes in technology, how these affect the organisation structure, and
the impact that structural changes and new organisational forms have on the integration,
organisation and distribution of tasks, lies at the heart of the level of analysis dilemma.
There are two dimensions to this change which raise difficulties for HR practitioners:

1 the shift away from jobs-based systems to person-based systems;
2 radical changes in the location and nature of co-ordination within the organisation
  structure.

The task facing HR practitioners at the millennium is made all the more difficult because
much of their armoury is based on and targeted at jobs-based systems (Lawler, 1994).
These include the pay systems that compare different jobs in terms of their complexity and
place labour market valuations on jobs by comparing like with like, and selection systems
that match the person to the job based on assumptions of predicted performance. But the
rhetoric from the management gurus is that the end of the 'job' is nigh. Organisations, for
example, are experiencing high levels of rewards failure because most of their pay systems
do not reflect strongly enough strategic thrusts towards quality, teamworking, and competition based on time. The rewards systems – and most of the other jobs-based personnel
management systems – break down under pressure from technological change and downsizing. These changes have combined to reduce the 'half life' of the technical and functional

skills associated with a task-based view of the job and therefore the job evaluation systems. This distorts appraisal systems and leads to a break down of the pay-for-performance relationship. As organisations reallocate knowledge, information, power and rewards in response to this failure, a shift to person- as opposed to job-related performance management systems becomes inevitable because the evolving set of tasks and activities built into internal roles can no longer be accurately priced in the labour market. According to this argument, it is no longer jobs which have value, but people.

This also raises questions about the most appropriate organisational form and system of co-ordination at the millennium. Under the burden of economic and competitive pressure, a range of organisational strategies is aimed at competing not just on cost, but on quality and speed of response. These horizontal and vertical management philosophies generally involve offering more diverse products and services, greater customisation in design and production, and more rapid response in the design and delivery of production and services. New organisational forms are being created through these horizontal processes of re-engineering, as well as changes to the vertical structure of organisations, through processes of rationalisation, delayering and downsizing.

The key challenge to HR practitioners at the millennium is how to get more from less, i.e. how to create more added value, and not just more effort. HR practitioners have to accelerate this process of creating added value if they are to free up resources in the organisation to deliver the more positive aspects of restructuring – the autonomy, the challenge. Therefore the role of HR practitioners needs to be one of directing the change process, by drawing upon the principles of their functional knowledge and technical insights into the problem. Their business process insights carry more weight now than does their knowledge about organisation structures, systems and cultures.

This has led analysts to question the relevance of formalised concepts such as HRM, which are based largely on the need for a set of people–management functions designed for organisations that employ over 200 people. Yet, as we have seen, the context is now one of national business structures that contain far more small and medium-sized enterprises, and organisational designs and business philosophies that bear witness to the break up of large units into small self-managing units and teams.

Jobs-based flexibility

The forces that are changing the nature of the actual work that is done fall into three clusters:

- 'informating' of the workplace
- speed of manipulation and the production of data rather than products
- communications as a multiplier (Bridges, 1994).

Information technology inserts data between the worker and the product or service s/he is delivering. For example, in a traditional industry such as steel, employees no longer manipulate the steel itself but instead manipulate *data* about a sheet of steel. Work is increasingly seen as a tangible sequence or pattern of information that can be handled and changed. Each business service or product triggers a chain of data events, which may now require a minimum of human intervention, or at the very least a major redesign of the discrete work elements, tasks and duties that are needed. Several work functions along the production delivery route have been strongly 'informated' in recent years, such as purchasing, logistics and dispatch, process control, accounting, and sales management. It is this process of 'informating' work that means that our views about jobs-based flexibility should not be based on current narrow conceptions of functional flexibility, such as multi-skilling. These debates, while relevant to much manufacturing work in highly unionised environments, form only part of the large-scale changes to jobs that are being witnessed. As information is pushed down the organisation, it transforms the underlying decision-making process, and therefore the level of jobs-based flexibility. The most radical changes are being seen in white collar occupations, where the mental elements of the job are being redesigned. Moreover, the changes to the nature of jobs are not necessarily dictated by an automation of things past, but by the creation of totally new work elements.

Technology has also rendered many jobs obsolete because of the speed of manipulation that is now necessary and possible. The concept of what constituted a job fitted task patterns that were dictated by an old division of labour, where things had to be assembled or processed from raw materials before being stored, the specification of discrete tasks (which could be bundled up into jobs) was possible. Where data form the basis of work, they require minimal space in which to be maintained by users and can be replicated quickly and manipulated individually. The nature of duties changes in relation to the interests and expertise of the individual. The speed at which data may be manipulated or worked upon means that there is more work to be done than the individual is capable of, and so the role of choice and purpose in the selection of appropriate tasks that may be deemed to constitute a job has become more important.

In reaction to the primary changes of work informating and ease of data manipulation, communication technology has created a 'multiplier effect' interlocking the new groups of transformed workers so that time and distance are no longer an automatic constraint on the design of jobs. The volume of information and the interactions that need to take place around it has exploded, again requiring considerable flexibility in the nature of jobs.

This agenda has brought with it difficult and intractable problems concerned with the problem of competence, commitment and trust. HR practitioners face major problems when they consider the sort of people needed to manage in the new organisations, the depth of available talent and the ability of organisations and society to resource the appropriate competencies.

Reality soon outpaces rhetoric and the magnitude of the gap between the hype and the hard work that still has to be done in organisations has been borne out of practitioner experience. For example, despite the significant advances in the level of UK management development over the last decade (Storey, Mabey and Thomson, 1997), as many organisations look at the capabilities and competencies of their staff through the results of assessment centres they still see a yawning gap between the hoped-for levels of competency and current reality. Talk of organisational learning and leaders with 'generative' frames of reference (Senge, 1990) seems a far cry from both the average level and the type of existing competence in most employees or managers (Sparrow, 1996b; 1997a). Even the management gurus, when they look at the sort of managers needed to see through such changes, ask, 'Where have all the leaders gone?'.

Not only are the competencies of existing managers frequently put in question, so is the quality of the logic that guides their decisions. Many organisations seem to be operating according to defensive routines (Allcorn and Diamond, 1997). Those who are responsible for shaping the new systems often drag the cloak of the old business into the new. The managers on the BPR teams are often guilty of attempting to design outward-facing processes by applying an inward-looking and cost-saving mindset, and so many opportunities are missed. Mike Oram enters this debate in Chapter 5. We recreate in the new systems a microcosm of the very mentality that caused the problem in the first place, only now it can be actually designed into the very architecture and process of the organisation. A cartoon by Roger Beale in the *Financial Times* comes to mind. An employee is confronting his manager about problems resulting from a recent change to outsourcing, to which the manager blithely responds: 'It is no good moaning to me – we've outsourced the blame on this one!'.

The phenomenon of job insecurity and the individualisation of HRM

At the same time that HR practitioners are being asked to assist in the radical redesign of organisations and jobs, an issue that has come to the fore is the dilemma about the impact of all this on the *individual*. Considerable attention has been given to the phenomenon of job insecurity and the impact on the productivity and performance of those who survived the downsizing and delayering, i.e. the problems of 'survivor syndrome'. Smith (1997) conducted a computer trawl of articles in British national newspapers and found that in 1986, when unemployment was higher, there were 234 stories on insecurity and just ten on job insecurity, while ten years later in 1996 there were 2778 stories on insecurity and 977 on job insecurity. Within the UK, MORI opinion polls show that the proportion of people who feel secure in their jobs fell from 65 per cent to 54 per cent from 1990–95.

New psychological contracts and the refragmentation of HRM

A related issue, therefore, has been the arrival of a 'new deal' and talk of a changing 'psychological contract', a term which is used to capture a very wide range of changes around the nature and process of the employment relationship in organisations, has received much attention (see Ehrlich, 1994; Herriot and Pemberton, 1996; Morrison, 1994; Rousseau, 1990; 1995). The 'contract' is portrayed as an open-ended agreement about what the individual and the organisation expect to give to, and receive from the employment relationship. Psychological contracts represent a dynamic and reciprocal deal. New expectations are added over time and the contract changes as perceptions about the employers' commitment evolves. These unwritten individual contracts are therefore concerned with the social and emotional aspects of the exchange between employer and employee. The Conference Board (1997) report based on 92 US and European organisations including IBM, Amoco, Fiat, and Philips found that while 27 per cent denied that an implicit deal had ever existed and 6 per cent believed that they still offered a paternalistic relationship, 67 per cent acknowledged that they no longer had a contractual or tacit understanding with employees that promised a secure job in return for dedicated service. The majority of firms, after a period of denial, perceive that there is low morale, a trust gap, and a desire for a new set of HRM tools, practices and priorities at the millennium.

PARTNERSHIP

We therefore must also consider the theme of partnership. Questions about voice, power, conflict and consensus cut across most of the chapters in this book, but in recent years there has been an increasing bifurcation in the management of employee relations. Some employers are derecognising unions while others are establishing new co-operative partnerships with them. Developments in partnership can be set against a backcloth of individualism and free market enterprise promoted by governments and some employers, which can be contrasted with European Union and other proposals for a stronger institutional base through which social partnership arrangements and works councils can become effective.

The cynic could say, 'If employee involvement and partnership is so good, why is there so little of it about?'. The ability to provide 'voice' in the UK through *institutional arrangements and trades unions* remains questionable. In June 1997 only 31.3 per cent of the UK workforce were members of unions, the lowest proportion for 60 years, 37 per cent of employees have their pay and benefits agreed by collective bargaining, and only 6 per cent of workers under the age of 20 belong to unions. Set against this, days lost to strikes only accounted for 0.03 percent of potential working time. The partnership debate reveals a long history to these sorts of issues.

So, is partnership capable of delivering the goods for employees and employers at the millennium? The second part of the book covers a number of elements within this debate, including the collectivism and individualism debate, issues around the future of trade unions, shared responsibility for HRM and the impact of European Union initiatives in the field of partnership. HR practitioners also have to confront the *trust* dilemma when they consider partnership (Kramer and Tyler, 1996). If workers share ideas with a non-co-operative management, they may just be faced with business process intensification and harder work for less pay. But then if management grant autonomy and rewards to workers who restrict output because their psychological contract has been breached, profits plummet (Levine, 1995).

In order to rebuild trust HR practitioners are being asked to manage the 'social contract' that governs the employee–organisation exchange and mediates the intensity of any perceived violation. Clearly, new HRM structures and systems are needed to re-engage employees: to rebuild trust, and to involve, motivate and empower them. This requires organisations to make deep internal changes, as well as changes to the way that their HRM is subjected to or indeed acts as a point of influence on the way people are managed the whole way down the entire supplier and customer chain. But can the HRM professionals be trusted to have the technical competence to make these changes?

PURSUING MULTIPLE FLEXIBILITIES

Not surprisingly, then, flexibility is an issue of interest to many people. Exactly what is meant by flexibility, as the section on changing organisational forms and new psychological contracts shows, is still a concept in transition, even though it has been discussed now for nearly 20 years within the HRM literature. What is meant by flexibility seemed a little clearer in the mid-1990s. At that time there was a proliferation of business philosophies, such as total quality management (TQM), just in time production (JIT), advanced manufacturing technology (AMT), cellular manufacturing, and manufacturing resource planning (MRP II) which were all intended to improve the efficiency of operations. They all required new ways of linking work horizontally. Experience also showed that these initiatives risked higher levels of failure if the job design and work organisation implications were not considered properly. However, in many cases these philosophies still required limited jobs-based flexibility because the changes wrought were driven by an internal focus. The improvements to operational efficiency through productivity improvements, reduced lead times, product inventories and cost of quality were localised to small parts of the organisation. The information systems and performance management systems that surrounded jobs were still designed along functional lines, and therefore the focus was to 'optimise' individual functions. Traditional flexibility concerns of multiskilling, financial flexibility or time flexibility were felt sufficient to handle the changes to the content of jobs in the early 1990s.

This is now no longer the case and HRM professionals are having to pursue multiple and parallel forms of flexibility. Where jobs are concerned, changes to their content (traditionally seen as a need for functional flexibility best achieved through multiskilling) cannot be introduced without parallel flexibilities in structure, information systems, rewards and so forth. It is recognised that organisations cannot achieve one form of flexibility without tackling the others. As a consequence of broader attempts to create jobs-based flexibility, organisations seem to be seeking *seven* discrete but parallel flexibilities. They may chose to pursue one of the flexibilities for one job, a combination for another, or be attacking the whole organisation across a series of fronts. Each flexibility tends to be associated with a different type of 'battle' or struggle between interested parties.

1 **Numerical flexibility**, where the battle is around who owns (and therefore has some legal obligation towards) the employment relationship. Does the job need to be one within the internal labour market, or can it be sufficiently controlled through outsourcing, peripheral forms of employment, or the use of various associate relationships?

2 **Functional flexibility**, where the battle is around the roles and competencies deemed appropriate for the job. When the new package of elements, tasks and duties is considered, does the job need to be staffed by a multiskilled individual, are there new core competencies that must be delivered, or are there important cross-business process skills that must be acquired?

3 **Financial flexibility**, where the battle is around the reward–effort bargain to be struck with the job holder. What is the best balance between the type and nature of reward and the delivery of performance? Would a more efficient wage–effort bargain be struck by the use of performance-related pay, gainsharing, or cafeteria benefits?

4 **Temporal flexibility**, where the battle is the need for continuous active representation on the job. What time patterns should the job be fitted into and will employees be able to switch themselves onto the highest levels of customer service and performance throughout these time patterns? What is the role for instance of flexitime, nil hours, or annual hours?

5 **Geographical flexibility**, where the battle is around the ideal location of the job and its constituent tasks. Does the job need to be carried out in specific locations, or is there latitude for homeworking, or even operating through virtual teams?

6 **Organisational flexibility,** where the battle is around the form and rationale of the total organisation and its design, into which the job may be fitted. Does the organisation operate as an adhocracy, a loose network of suppliers, purchasers, and providers, or a temporary alliance or joint venture?

7 **Cognitive flexibility,** where the battle is around both the mental frames of reference required effectively to perform in the job and the level of cognitive skills required. Does the job require people with a particular sort of psychological contract? How must the impact of national culture be mediated? What sorts of strategic and cognitive assumptions cannot be tolerated?

The focus on flexibility in Britain is understandable given that it is easier to dismiss employees in the UK than elsewhere in Europe. In an OECD study (Lehrman Brothers, 1994) EU countries were scaled in terms of how difficult it is to dismiss employees. Countries such as Portugal, Spain and Italy scored above 14 on a 16-point scale. Germany, Finland and Sweden scored around 10. The UK scored 2. There are also major developments towards flexibility across Europe, with, for example, labour reforms in Spain in May 1997, and the IG Chemie trade union in Germany finally agreeing in June 1997 to allow Hoechst, Bayer and BASF to cut wages by up to 10 per cent in difficult periods. However, the 1997 EU Joint Resolution on Growth and Employment avoided using the word 'flexible' when describing labour market plans, adopting alternative adjectives such as 'adaptable', 'responsive' and 'employment-friendly' (Naudin, 1997).

Resolution of the HRM agenda associated with this state of affairs is not easy. Flexibility is a complex issue, and one that will dominate HRM across Europe for many years to come. Chris Brewster shows in Chapter 16 that the stereotype that Britain has led the way towards flexible labour markets in Europe and that European labour markets are inherently unproductive and over-regulated is a little naive, while Alan Jenkins provides some insights into the French situation in Chapter 17. Despite the jobs predicament in France, its labour markets are more flexible than often portrayed. On the one hand it has tenured public sector jobs, tax disincentives to return to employment and a minimum wage. On the other hand employers have failed to reinvest enough of their retained profits in new plant and equipment to create sufficient jobs (Naudin, 1997) to counter demographic population growth (preferring to invest in high yield government bonds). Attitudes to flexibility are understandably ambiguous in France, given that:

- wages have lagged behind growth in productivity for more than a decade;
- wages have only grown by an average of 0.2 per cent a year throughout the 1990s;
- the 1997 minimum wage is lower in real terms than it was in 1985 and is widely by-passed by 50 percent of French industry through subsidised contracts and branch agreements;
- for more than 40 per cent of the workforce significant pay rises are tied to individual performance.

Therefore, in helping organisations pursue these multiple and parallel flexibilities HR practitioners find themselves facing an *ethical dilemma* – not surprisingly directed at the failure of either their practices or their systems to control or influence the impact of economic and technological determinism. Derek Torrington reminds us of the long history to this identity crisis in the next chapter while Karen Legge picks up some of the ethical issues raised by the pursuit of flexibility in Chapter 19.

Ethical issues have become more potent, in part because discussion about the HRM function has become more honest and, sadly, more cynical. This discussion reveals the many tensions that exist between the rhetoric and the reality of practice. Korten (1993) notes that in the USA there are 40 000 more paid public relations employees than journalists, all paid to reinforce the myth of advancing corporate power. This creates tensions between the language used in organisations and the reality as perceived and experienced by employees (Legge, 1995). Psychologists (Beer *et al.*, 1990) discuss this tension in terms of what they call 'representational learning' (words, concepts, constructs and language) and 'behavioural learning' (changes in values and actual patterns of behaviour). We have all learned the new words, we all accept the new language, but we are happy to use the words merely as a way of making difficult decisions sound politically more acceptable and legitimate, and we fail to find ways of converting the words we use into any substantive or actual changes in behaviour. The challenge to HR practitioners is how to make the change from being seen as 'reinforcers' of what sounds *politically correct*, to becoming 'engineers' and architects of the *behaviourally responsible*. For Bartlett and Ghoshal (1995, p. 2) this requires both a new moral contract and a fundamental revision of the HRM management philosophy:

> *What is emerging from this dilemma is the very difficult contract between the individual employee and the corporate employer . . . the new moral contract of guaranteeing employability is not a new spin on a company's human resource policies to legitimize involuntary redundancy. It implies a fundamental change in the basic philosophy of management. Over the past five decades, under the mantra of 'professional management', companies have created and institutionalised a management doctrine in which people are treated as little more than another factor of production. Employment security is an essential element of this doctrine for it is the quid pro quo for the depersonalisation of organisations and the resultant narrowing of the individual skills and options.*

THE CONTRIBUTION OF HRM AT THE MILLENNIUM

This brings us to the final dilemma that cuts across all the chapters in the book. Coping with the various ethical issues that are raised by some of the changes already introduced (i.e. in organisational form, the pursuit of flexibility and the institutional arrangements to ensure voice) is made all the more difficult because of questions about the *contribution and competence* of HR practitioners. Jibes about the function having a 'big hat, no cattle' (Skinner, 1987) or better being titled the 'human remains department' still resonate today. This, of course, presupposes that everyone agrees what HRM is – a question which has distracted many from the more important issue of contribution. The *contribution dilemma* is being examined and questioned through three streams of investigation:

1 a questioning of the technical validity of many central HRM tools and techniques;
2 attempts to demonstrate a link between HRM practices and organisational performance; and
3 a growing theoretical sophistication about the role of HRM as part of a resource-based understanding of organisational strategy.

First, HR practitioners are clearly faced with a *technical dilemma*. In 1994 one of the critical skills needed by HR directors was what Eichinger and Ulrich (1995) not too explicitly called 'deep HR technology savvy'. The problem is that they also need to sell this savvy! There has been an increasing tension between what one UK HR director recently called the need for a 'WOW factor' (the need for line managers to exclaim "WOW" at first glance when presented with the latest offering from the HR department!) and the requirement for ever-more sophisticated, detailed and complex techniques that actually work and provide solutions to what are very complex organisational problems. The field of HRM has to plot an uneasy course between sets of internal customers who could be criticised for having the attention span and technical sophistication of a goldfish on the one hand, and, on the other, the increasing academic awareness of either poor and misguided technology, or misguided application when the internal customer has to be kept sweet without becoming truly competent.

In many functional areas of HRM there is an increasing loss of confidence in core tools, techniques and technologies. These concerns focus around the view that many tools have become blunted in their motivational power, have been by-passed by shifts in managerial competence, have become too cumbersome, bureaucratic or complex in their language, or simply are no longer valid. Recent years have witnessed a questioning of job analysis techniques (Campion, 1994), performance management systems (Hendry, Bradley and Perkins, 1997), competency-based pay systems (Sparrow, 1996d), recruitment and selection systems (Herriot and Anderson, 1997), psychological testing (Blinkhorn and Johnson, 1991), and teamworking interventions (Stevens and Campion, 1994), among many others. Do HR managers still have sound technologies, or are they just quacks, using pseudo-science and misselling 'sexy' but ineffective medicines?

Technical competence apart, to respond to the jibes about limited influence, there is a continued search for the *business case* that good people management is also good business management. This is evidenced through progressively more sophisticated tests for a relationship between 'bundles' of 'high performance work practices' and organisational performance (Arthur, 1994; Huselid, 1995; Huselid and Becker, 1996; Huselid, Jackson and Schuler, 1997; MacDuffie, 1995). David Guest picks up this challenge in Chapter 3. It is also evidenced in the development of resource-based theory (RBT) and the attention now given to understanding *how* the platitude that 'people are our source of competitive advantage' has a basis in reality. The human resource strategy (HRS) movement is another source of attack on the *level of analysis* at which HR practitioners should be operating. Throughout the late 1980s and early 1990s cost and quality advantages lost their potency, product lifecycles shortened and skill development lifecycles lengthened. As a consequence, there is now a growing realisation that external market-driven descriptions of strategy have limited value for most organisations. Indeed, the premise that strategy can be planned in an environment of rapid and discontinuous change and intense competition no longer makes sense (Grant, 1991). Strategists now focus their attention on the need to understand and mobilise the *strategic capabilities* of the *organisation*.

A number of writers stress the importance of exploiting and actively managing the internal resources or 'capabilities' of the organisation (Amit and Schoemaker, 1993; Barney, 1991; Coff, 1997; Hamel and Prahalad, 1991; Klein, Edge and Kass, 1991; Pfeffer, 1994; Reed and DeFillippi, 1990). They argue that *human capital*, under limited organisational control, *can* have the potential to generate 'economic rent', i.e. people are an asset, not just a cost. Therefore the need to understand these sources of advantage and to convert them into practical contributions has become paramount.

The last few years have seen our understanding about *how* the total pool of human capital provides competitive advantage advance considerably. Patrick Flood develops these arguments in Chapter 4. As strategic change is a learning process (Whipp, 1991), it is the concept of learning that is seen to be the best link between HRS and the process of competition. Clearly, only the ability to learn faster than the competition and to reconstruct and adapt the organisation's knowledge base (skills, structures and values) is a sustainable source of competitive advantage. To the extent that jobs are designed in a way that builds the system around the individual (rather than simplifying or designing out the human component) then the single best predictor of organisation performance has become the rarity of the individual who possesses a behavioural repertoire capable of bringing the best out of that system.

However, human resources (and their individual competencies) only become a source of true competitive advantage because of their value, rarity, inimitability and non-substitutability (Wright, McMahan and McWilliams, 1994). Because the value of human resources is felt to reside increasingly in its possession of *organisation-specific* and *organisation-level skills*, HR practitioners now have to downplay their expertise in managing human resources as individuals and stop focussing only on HRM practices and tools that align individual behaviour with strategic goals. As human resource strategists they have to focus on the competency of the *total pool of human capital* within the organisation, as this is now the resource that makes up competitive advantage. The HRS places a premium on developing the skill sets and cognitive capabilities of all those managers *involved in the strategic management process* (Sparrow, 1994; 1995). This may be seen in a fully empowered organisation as comprising all employees, or it may be viewed as a small elite. As research on top team diversity in the banking industry has shown, once the abilities of the top team are sorted out, more than a third of the organisational performance (in terms of innovations) of the top 150 US banks can be explained. HR practitioners are therefore torn increasingly between the twin objectives of creating advantage *through* people, and creating advantages *for* people. Does HRM have anything to do with the individual any more? How can the message that 'people are our source of competitive advantage' be made meaningful again? Such questions lie at the heart of the agenda for HRM at the millennium.

2

Crisis and opportunity in HRM

The challenge for the personnel function

DEREK TORRINGTON

Manchester School of Management, UMIST

For at least thirty years there has been a theme running through academic writing about personnel management that it is rather feeble. This has been matched by a feeling among personnel professionals that they are undervalued and unappreciated. The aim of this chapter is to suggest that both of these patterns of belief are ill-founded and that it is only their persistence that impedes the further effectiveness of personnel specialists in the overall activity of human resource management. The basis of the chapter is partly long experience and partly a result of research undertaken at UMIST on the development of the personnel function (*see*, for example, Hall and Torrington, 1997; Torrington and Hall, 1996). The suggestion is that any crisis for personnel specialists in human resource management stems from one or more of three uncertainties:

- confidence
- identity
- direction.

A CRISIS OF CONFIDENCE: DISPARAGING ACADEMICS AND PARANOID PRACTITIONERS

Personnel managers and, crucially, their academic commentators seem to spend more time agonising about their lack of effectiveness and influence than those in other management functions, and always have done. Before its present reincarnation as *People Management*, the monthly journal of the Institute of Personnel and Development was published for many years as *Personnel Management*. Scanning copies of that journal published 30 years ago, every second or third issue you find a letter or an article asking 'Is there a future for us?', 'Why doesn't anybody pay attention?', 'we are all crying in the wilderness', and so on. This is a continuing theme for people who are interested in that aspect of company affairs, but is not found elsewhere in management. You do not see marketing specialists writing about the sickness of marketing. They believe that what they are doing is important and acknowledged to be important. Nor do we come across accountants endlessly asking themselves how they can become more influential and effective in their businesses. TQM specialists have no doubt at all that their activity is the surefire passport to the promised land and that they themselves are little lower than the angels.

In contrast, heart searching and paranoia continue to be a dominant theme among personnel people. In a single issue of *People Management* (January 1997), you find the following at intervals throughout the copy:

> *human resource specialists should now see themselves as the facilitators of major organisational change. How realistic is this? . . . The authors do not see much of a future for the personnel function.*

> *The City of London is the world's premier financial centre, yet its personnel and training policies leave much to be desired, and their failure has been identified as a factor in a number of scandals.*

> *Some personnel officers want to abdicate responsibility for the outcome of tests . . . There seems to be no curiosity or ability to question . . . among the younger professionals . . . Bad handling of tests and data has been the root cause of many errors.*

Why should there be this lack of confidence and an almost masochistic interest in finding fault? Part of the answer may lie in the constant disparagement by academic commentators. It is worth examining some of the comments over the last 30 years.

A landmark piece was by Keith Thurley (1981), who had the distinction of being the first professor in a British university to incorporate the term 'personnel management' in his title, although it came second: he was Professor of Industrial Relations and Personnel Management. Much of the uncertainty was expressed in the title of his article, 'Personnel management in the UK: a case for urgent treatment?'. There was the inevitable reference to the comment of Peter Drucker (Drucker, 1955) about the personnel job:

> *partly a file clerk's job, partly a housekeeping job, partly a social worker's job and partly 'firefighting' to head off union trouble or settle it.*

This has been repeated so often it is sometimes forgotten that this was how personnel managers themselves saw their role. There were also Allan Flanders' criticisms from 1970 that the function was *ad hoc*, reactive and without sufficient planning, Legge's (1978) assertion that personnel managers lacked credibility and Watson's (1977) comment that they were seen as 'would-be reformers with long term ideological views' (*see* Thurley, 1981). If this type of comment were occasional it could be construed as all part of healthy debate and uncertainty, but the theme has been unremitting, contributing to a feeling among personnel practitioners that is verging on what can only be described as an 'introspective neurosis' (Guest, 1991).

In the 1990s the criticisms have altered, but disparagement remains an integral feature of the commentary. Academics have recently focused on two specific grounds for dissatisfaction:

1 Personnel management should be replaced by human resource management (HRM).
2 Personnel managers should be more interested in strategy than operational aspects.

When the HRM concept was adopted from the USA in the mid 1980s, it seemed so much more progressive than traditional personnel management that academics readily consigned personnel management to the trash can that Peter Drucker had described for it 30 years before. HRM was strategic with a long-term outlook (Storey, 1989), unlike personnel management which was condemned as merely operational (Gennard and Kelly, 1994). HRM used planning and was proactive, whereas personnel was reactive and downstream (Miller 1987; Schuler, 1989). HRM added value, but personnel was welfare oriented (Storey, 1989). HRM would be integrated with the rest of the business, while personnel managers were simply picking up the pieces (Guest, 1987). HR managers would be architects, whereas personnel practitioners were often administrators and clerks.

These wide-ranging theoretical propositions were duly set forth in the ivory towers and on the conference circuit before some academics moved on and spent time in the early 1990s looking for evidence of the HRM phenomenon, what it was and how it was performing. There were three main research projects with this aim. Storey (1992) completed case studies of 15 organisations and questions about HRM were incorporated in two well-established surveys, the Workplace and Industrial Relations Survey (Millward *et al.*, 1992) and the Warwick Company Level Industrial Relations Survey (Marginson *et al.*, 1993). The conclusions drawn from these surveys and other studies show that few organisations meet the neat academic formulations.

The overall conclusions followed a familiar theme. Personnel managers were less effective than they should be (Guest 1990), they are not as strategic as they should be (Monks, 1992; Storey, 1989), and seem 'to have taken refuge in a more reactive stance'. (Storey, 1992). They were only implementing strategies which had been formulated in other functions (Storey, 1989). They were not 'architects' but 'clerks and contract managers' (Sisson, 1995). In general 'the picture is hardly flattering' and 'extremely disappointing' (Guest, 1991; Sisson, 1995).

Sisson concludes that personnel managers are 'working against the grain' (Sisson, 1995). If they are, then arguably it is a grain that academics have created for them. In setting out an agenda that involves solving some of the endemic problems of working life in an advanced industrial society, and doing it pretty quickly, they have created a false and unattainable image for personnel practitioners to aspire to, and now grumble at them for not achieving it.

The influence of academics on the activities and the self-image of personnel and HR specialists should not be underestimated. More management academics are working in the general area of people at work than in any other area of management activity, and they dominate the pages of the research journals. The bulk of practitioners go through the IPD qualification process, which is closely related to a network of universities and colleges, including the leading research schools in the country.

Academics dominate the training and development of personnel professionals to an extent that is not found in other professional institutions such as accounting and banking. If academics tried to determine the syllabus for the professional training of accountants they would get very short shrift. In professions such as engineering, banking and law it is the professionals who determine the syllabus content, whereas as far as the IPD is concerned it is the academics who largely determine what the syllabus is and how it is taught. The stock in trade of research-oriented academics is critical debate, and there is a tendency for them unwittingly to undermine the confidence and effectiveness of practitioners by setting idealised agendas that are theoretically sound but practically inappropriate in terms of what can be achieved and what may be desirable in the setting of an organisation working in a commercially competitive environment.

Personnel managers have not converted workplaces into places of utter equality, fairness and straightforwardness. They have not produced an agreed and universally accepted model for training and development. They did not succeed in reaching a constructive, socially accepted accommodation with the trade unions, and they have not found the definitive answer to employment insecurity, work-related stress, or the ethical dilemmas of our post-industrial society. For an extreme version of this point of view, see the critique by Hart (1993).

In contrast, other management specialists have simpler expectations placed upon them. Marketing people have to understand, create and predict consumer demand. Accountants have to balance the books and avoid paying too much tax. However challenging these responsibilities may be, they are limited. Personnel people appear to carry on their shoulders all the problems of the human race. They repeatedly 'fail' only in terms of lofty ambitions that other people have suggested for them, which really are a bit tricky for ordinary human beings to attain.

A CRISIS OF IDENTITY: PERSONNEL MANAGEMENT AND HUMAN RESOURCE MANAGEMENT – WHAT IS THE DIFFERENCE?

One of the most tedious and unproductive of academic debates has been trying to figure out the difference between two concepts: personnel and HRM. Much of this discussion is of a strictly academic nature, similar to arguments about how many angels can balance on the head of a pin, but there is little disagreement that HRM is an activity of all managers, rather than just the personnel specialists.

HRM arrived in the UK in the mid-1980s as a fully formed set of values and prescriptions that had been formulated at Harvard Business School. In the USA personnel management had never achieved the degree of recognition that it had in Britain, even though British personnel practitioners spend so much time deploring their lack of influence. The first formulation to receive any widespread exposure on this side of the Atlantic was that of Fombrun, Tichy and Devanna (1984) who set out the proposition that HRM had four generic functions:

- selection
- appraisal
- development
- reward.

At first sight this seemed like elementary personnel management, but they added the comment that all of these were directed at performance. Although obvious, it was this emphasis that gave the concept a different spin on the ball: this was not administering employment, it was deploying performers.

There is always an interest in pursuing new ideas and HRM rapidly became the smart thing to do and to talk about. For some while personnel specialists had maintained their place in the organisational pecking order because of their prominent role in trade union relationships. The perceived power of trade unions was a bogey with which to frighten their managerial colleagues. Coupled with the growing complexity of employment law, it enabled the personnel people to say 'just leave it to us'. By the early 1980s it became apparent that the position of unions was altering. The raised level of unemployment had the effect of reducing staff turnover, thus reducing the amount of activity in recruitment and selection. Here were two salient features of the personnel manager's world that were worrying their managerial colleagues less than they had previously. Personnel people had good reason to worry about being misunderstood, unloved and not listened to.

Another feature was the impact of the change in industrial relations practice in academia and on research. This has been significant in the area of people management since personnel specialists first looked to social science for ideas in the interwar period. By the 1980s universities had departments of organisational behaviour, occupational psychology, labour economics and industrial relations. Quite quickly the industrial relations academics found that their research money was drying up and students were beginning to desert their classes. Looking for a new area of expertise, they latched on to HRM.

Practitioners and academics together heralded HRM as the new wagon onto which to hitch their star. There began an extraordinary litany of disparagement that included almost every criticism of personnel managers that had been made in the previous 100 years, and taking very little account of any evidence other than opinion. The overall message was always the same: everything to do with HRM was good, and anything associated with personnel was bad. The most pernicious undercurrent in all the debates was that HRM was *new*, while personnel was *old-fashioned*. In contemporary management thinking, nothing is more important than to latch onto the latest fashionable idea and to attend a couple of conferences on how it is going to change the shape of the world. That is so much more agreeable than trying to face up to the real problems of working life, demoralised employees and dissatisfied customers.

One of the things we can be quite clear about is that whatever academics call them, the people actually doing the job still call themselves personnel managers, personnel directors, personnel officers and so forth. Roughly two thirds of the 214 respondents to the UMIST questionnaire had the word 'personnel' in their title rather than the words 'human resource'. Also three quarters of the functions or departments were described in that way.

What is even more significant is that the label rarely bears any relationship to what is found inside. The difference between the two approaches remains a largely abstract debate on definition. What matters is what is taking place on the ground; how personnel management, or human resource management, or people management is actually being carried out. When you look at practice in human resource departments it is very difficult to say that they are doing something much different from what is done in all personnel departments. This is one of the points that John Storey has made rather tellingly. In our UMIST research we found departments where little had changed in a decade, except that they were now called 'Department of Human Resources'. Also, some of the most impressive and strategically influential of our respondents were quite clear that they were engaged in personnel management. It would almost be possible to say that the firmest rhetoric about the change from the old to the new was associated with the least change in practice. One cannot go quite that far, but there are certainly examples.

HRM may be a set of initials, but it is not a neat package like TQM, IIP or NVQ. It is an aspect of the way in which the personnel contribution is made, and there is no clear, pre-determined and agreed formula of what it is or should be.

A CRISIS OF DIRECTION: STRATEGY OR OPERATIONS?

Full-timers in the personnel world – whether academics or practitioners – have been seduced by the concept of strategy because it is sexy. It is not surprising that personnel practitioners identify strategic involvement as a way of clarifying the value and contribution of a function often perceived as marginal and ambiguous (*see*, for example, Legge, 1978; Watson, 1977). As Purcell and Ahlstrand (1994) express it, 'strategy presupposes importance'. Guest (1990) and Kamoche (1994) are among the many who have noted the attraction of strategy in the function's quest for status, and Schuler (1989) predicts an increase in status for the function if it can successfully link personnel/HR practices with the organisation's strategic goals.

An extensive literature has developed to prescribe the content of HR strategy and how this can be fashioned to meet the needs of the business. The recommended characteristics of HR strategy are that it should be externally integrated with business strategy; internally integrated and complete; proactive; and developed in collaboration with general management. A defining point in the development of HRM is undoubtedly the book edited by Fombrun, Tichy and Devanna in 1984. It is interesting to revisit that work as its significance was largely that it introduced the concept of *strategic* human resource management. The simple idea that people management issues could be strategic as opposed to operational was novel, and in a stronger vein some, for example Purcell (1995), describe the scenario of HR strategy as being proactive and determining organisational strategy.

Wherever the driving force is located, the integration with other strategic activities is seen as essential to its effectiveness. The two forms of integration advocated in the literature are internal and external. First, the different components of the HR strategy need to be mutually reinforcing and consistent, so that the strategy is integrated within itself (Baird and Meshoulam, 1988). Second, the HR strategy needs to be integrated with organisational strategy as emphasised by Baird and Meshoulam (1988), Guest (1987), Lengnick-Hall and Lengnick-Hall (1988), Peters and Waterman (1982) and Tyson (1995a), among many others.

We therefore begin to see a picture of minimal involvement by personnel practitioners in strategy. Monks (1992), in an Irish study, identified only nine out of the 87 organisations surveyed in 1989–90 as having personnel functions which were regarded as important and which had long-term plans. Storey (1992) reported on 15 case studies of large organisations carried out between 1986–8 and identified four distinct types of personnel function roles. He found that in only two of the case studies did the personnel function approximate to the strategic and interventionist role of 'changemaker'. However, in a more recent article reporting further work with the case study organisations (Storey, 1995, p. 10) he comments that 'we were impressed by the extent to which by 1993–94 the case companies had begun to take a strategic view of HR management'. This comment, however, gives no indication of who is involved in developing the strategic view, and line management involvement in HR strategy has emerged as a key theme. Storey (1992) found that the personnel function was often overlooked in the development of HR strategy in favour of line management involvement. Guest (1990, p. 378) argues that the implication of the concentration on the importance of people in organisations is that 'HR is too important to be left to personnel managers but is instead a key strategic issue demanding the attention of all managers.'

The HR dimension of strategy is becoming more important at the same time as it is 'not being left to the personnel people'. They may be ignored, they may be involved, but only occasionally do they lead. The UMIST research, however, showed that the personnel function was involved in strategy to a significant extent. Table 2.1 shows the results of a question which asked respondents to identify the type of strategic involvement of the personnel function in a range of different areas of HRM. Putting aside the differences between the content areas, there are two clear messages in this table. First, apart from quality initiatives and work design, very few senior personnel practitioners felt they lacked any strategic involvement. Second, if we follow Mintzberg's (1994a) division of strategy and planning and compare the two choices which clearly focus on strategy development (columns 1 and 2) with those which focus on implementation of strategy and on information input (columns 3 and 4), then the emphasis is on strategy development as opposed to implementation. In all content areas, except for work design, the combined percentage from columns one and two exceeds the combined percentage from columns three and four.

THE REALITY OF STRATEGIC INVOLVEMENT

Evidence for this level of strategic involvement was largely confirmed by the interviews, although some respondents clearly interpreted the word 'strategy' very loosely, so the figures in Table 2.1 may be a little optimistic. Most interviewees were able to cite examples of unequivocal strategic involvement, but this does not mean they had an integrated HR strategy. Strategic involvement focused on those issues identified within the business as requiring a strategic contribution from the personnel function. It was a piecemeal rather than a holistic approach, generally reacting to issues identified by others, rather than having a proactive, open-ended approach; i.e a reactive strategy. Although the choices made had long-term consequences for the business, and were an integral feature of business strategy, they did not represent an integrated HR strategy. For example, a typical response to the question of whether there was a holistic integrated HR strategy was:

> *I think, if I'm honest, it would be very much on an issue basis – broadly we're saying that the three areas we're looking at are reward, performance and training and development . . . but they've all been picked because they're the concerns of the Trust, rather than me saying we should have an umbrella strategy.*
>
> (Director of Personnel in a NHS trust)

and:

> *Currently we're just responding to changing circumstances. We've no integrated HR strategy.*
>
> (HR manager, electronics)

The second quotation is from an HR manager who responded in an apologetic way, before going on to explain how the product strategy had changed from a small number of

Table 2.1 Personnel roles in HR strategy

Answers to the question 'Which of the following most closely describes the nature of the personnel function's involvement at a strategic level in each of the areas listed below?'

	Develops strategy alone	Develops strategy with the line	Provides information to inform strategic decisions	Implements strategic decisions	None
HR planning	9%	49%	26%	6%	10%
Recruitment and selection	15%	49%	14%	16%	5%
Work design	2%	25%	24%	13%	35%
Performance management	7%	44%	23%	10%	16%
Quality initiatives	4%	38%	17%	11%	29%
Training	10%	60%	12%	7%	11%
Management development	10%	57%	10%	7%	16%
Career planning	7%	50%	16%	6%	22%
Communications	10%	53%	17%	10%	10%
Employee relations/ involvement	16%	56%	15%	7%	5%
Health and safety	13%	38%	15%	14%	21%
Reward	8%	45%	17%	14%	17%
Redundancy and dismissal	11%	46%	23%	14%	6%

generic products to a larger number of customer-specific products. The outcome of this would be more production teams, with more team leaders needing different types of skills than in the past. The HR team was involved in developing the new organisational structure and the development programme to make sure that the line had the team leaders with the appropriate skills when needed. The irony is that this major activity, which would clearly be a determinant of success or failure in the marketplace, was seen by the interviewee as only second-best, necessitating an apology for 'not doing it properly'.

Over half the interviewees felt that they should be doing more in terms of strategy and had plans to increase their involvement and 'do it better' in the future. After answering a question about the strategic involvement of the personnel function, one manager went on to say:

> *Is this really strategic? – the answer is that hitherto, it was 'not as strategic as it could be'.* (Head of retail HR, building society)

Only five interviewees were able to give any indication of anything like an integrated HR strategy. There is a clear indication that HR strategy is co-determined with the line rather than being the province solely of the personnel people. In every content area shown on Table 2.1 the percentages in column 2 (showing strategy development in partnership with the line) is always greater than that in column 1 (showing the personnel function developing HR strategy alone). In the most extreme case column 2 was over 12 times column 1 (for work design), but was more typically around six times that in column 1, as for example in performance management and training. The smallest multiple was health and safety with just under three times that in column 1. Here is another irony, as many would feel that there is a more powerful argument for personnel people to take a low key role in health and safety rather than in, for instance, recruitment, selection, training and reward, where they are likely to have crucial skills and expertise.

The interviews provided many illustrations of how this works in practice. Many interviewees reported that line colleagues were involved from the outset in discussing HR policy/strategy decisions, in order to incorporate their critical input. Other organisations had formed cross-functional semi-permanent groups where key personnel issues would be debated. Some businesses organised away days and policy conferences involving line managers where HR strategy would be discussed. In others the process was less formalised and less focused. In these cases senior personnel staff would use political and campaigning skills with senior and line managers to develop a joint understanding of facets of HR strategy that needed to be developed, anticipating that this process would take years rather than months. Personnel managers spoke positively of a partnership approach, while recognising it as demanding. As one commentator had it:

> *I would like to be influential, but I think we should be less solely responsible, and I think the way to achieve things is to get a much closer partnership with line managers . . . that is going to make my job and our job more difficult but it is bound to be beneficial in the long run.* (HR director, pharmaceuticals)

To some extent the idea of partnership reflected a tendency across the business to operate in a more cross-functional way.

> *In the past it would have been a case of somebody somewhere would be charged with drawing up a policy document – they would have gone into a cupboard somewhere and emerged back six months later and said 'here's a fully formed policy', two weeks before it came into action . . . Now . . . there's a more cross functional approach to it. So whenever there's a major strategic issue being debated you're more likely to find multi-function teams being put together to take it forward.* (Personnel manager, police force)

In another establishment a more ambitious project was underway, where a cross-functional team, including the personnel manager, was brought together for 18 months to work on overall strategy for the establishment, operating as an adjunct to the executive board. Yet in this establishment, the personnel function was currently not represented on the board, and indeed was not party to the ongoing discussions concerning redundancies.

The process of formulating strategy has a clear impact on the nature of the strategy that results. In practice, those that are jointly developed across functions are more likely to integrate HR and business issues, and the personnel function was sometimes seen as the integrating factor across all functions. No crisis here.

SO DOES BOARD REPRESENTATION MATTER?

If the HRM dimension is to be integrated at the outset of strategy development, a further traditional conviction has always been that the personnel function needs to be represented on the board of directors. This was a theme of the Donovan Report as long ago as the 1960s (Royal Commission, 1968), and Sisson (1995) argues that if personnel specialists are not there when the key decisions are taken then 'personnel issues are almost inevitably condemned to second-order status' and the personnel contribution is limited to 'dealing with the implications of implementing such decisions' (p. 97); although he also acknowledges that representation on the board is not sufficient in itself to ensure the strategic management of human resources.

In a survey in 1983, Mackay and Torrington (1986) found that in 21 per cent of cases the function was represented on the board. Higher figures have since been found by other researchers, for example Millward *et al.* (1992) found that in 69 per cent of establishments the personnel function was represented at board level. Similarly, Brewster and Smith (1990) found 63 per cent of corporate personnel functions were represented on the main board. These figures suggest increasing levels of board membership, but Purcell (1995) found declining board membership in his nine longitudinal case studies. The figures produced by Millward had changed little since 1980 and included non-personnel specialists representing the personnel function. Doubt has been cast on the relationship between board membership and strategic involvement by, for example, Brewster and Bournois (1991) and Purcell (1995) who, finding that the most influential HR directors in his research cases were those with a close personal working relationship with the chief executive, argued that corridor power was more in evidence than functional authority. Tyson (1995a) concludes that those with HR responsibility are exercising a much more political and flexible role. Our own research showed 63 per cent of respondents reporting the presence of a main board director representing the personnel function. This is a three-fold increase on the 21 per cent reported in 1983. Table 2.2 shows board representation from the UMIST research.

One striking feature is that only 20 per cent report no representation at all at the establishment level board, a figure which was even lower for boards at the national level. Put another way, over 80 per cent of the sample had personnel representation in some form on both boards. This may be because we did not confine our question simply to specialist personnel representation and because our analysis included the variety of roles which the professional might play on the board rather than just formal attendance. But it seems clear

Table 2.2 Board level representation of the personnel function

	Establishment-level board	National-level board
Decision-making role	43%	64%
Non-decision-making role	8%	8%
Other (includes irregular attendance at meetings)	29%	16%
No place on board	20%	12%

that personnel has a substantial presence at board level, even if those present are not always full board members.

Further light was shed on this issue during the interview stage of our work. One important point which came out of the interviews was that not having a formal board presence did not necessarily impede personnel's influence. In a number of businesses where there was no personnel presence on the board, the head of the function found other more informal ways to exert influence. If they had no formal place they often attended board meetings on an *ad hoc* basis, or were brought into meetings when any new initiative had an impact on the human side of the business.

One HR director of a training and enterprise council was not a member of the board but attended about a third of all meetings on a regular basis, claiming that as he could not effect a structural change he had 'a political way of dealing with it'. Interestingly the formal personnel voice on the board was through the strategic director, which overtly demonstrates the company's commitment to human resource issues.

Conversely, having personnel representation on the board did not necessarily increase personnel's influence. In some cases when there was a direct voice on the board, the function did not have much of a say in the decisions but dealt mainly with the implications, implementation and flowdown of the strategic initiatives. For example, the human resource director of a large building society sat on the board, but the department still very much dealt with the 'back end' of the planning process. Another interesting example was that of a publisher where the 'company and HR director' formally voiced personnel issues at board level, but it was the personnel manager who had a lot of the real influence.

Generally therefore, formal positioning on the board, or the lack of it, did not seem to make much difference to the extent of personnel's influence. They often found ways round it by informal networking, political interplay and old-fashioned expertise and hard work, which in some cases may have been more successful than if they had formal board status. Interestingly though, most non-board members did seem to aspire to this status and were either fighting for it or expressing discontent that they did not have it.

IMPLEMENTING STRATEGY: LESS VISION AND MORE CRAFT

Numbers are not enough. We also need to consider the quality of the representation. There are undoubtedly still some 'Old Joe' problems. The following is a comment by the managing director of a company that had recently taken over another:

> When we merged the two companies I obviously wanted my own team, so most of the pre-existing board took up the same roles in the new business. I clearly also needed to keep one or two of the directors from the company we had bought. There was a very good operations guy, who was glad to take on that function in the merged business and a marketing man, who was very shrewd and experienced. We made him Director for Personnel and General Affairs, so that he can now fill in for any of the others who are away for a spell.

A presence on the board may have a symbolic significance, but too many Old Joes could mean misrepresentation in practice.

Although the literature abounds with material on strategy formation (sometimes formulation) and development, there is very little indeed on its implementation. This may be partly due to the difficulty of finding a way of testing the effectiveness of implementation, although it is also undoubtedly due to academics finding greater interest in intellectual questions than in practical problems. It may also be due to the general instability in management careers. The high-flying, lantern-jawed executive with an MBA, a skills portfolio and a liking for the business class lounges of international airports may be moving so quickly that there is over-emphasis on the vision, the creativity, the networking and the personal exposure of style and image, rather than on actually making things happen. If, however, a finely tuned strategy is to be worth anything it has to be implemented, and has to be shown to 'work'.

All the textbooks say you have to have an integrated HR strategy. But how many integrated HR strategies can you actually find? What you find in practice is that there is a significant HR contribution to strategy, but HR's contribution is essentially reactive. Other people determine what the strategy should be and the personnel people are involved in modifying it and tweaking it. It seems ludicrous to suggest that there should be a separate HR strategy, a distinct entity, which is an input into the corporate plan or strategy. You do not find many examples of this, and those who claim to have got one might find that it would not stand up to close scrutiny. There are plenty of examples of aspiration: working papers, memoranda to the chief executive, agreed statements of principle by the personnel people, and even fully worked out HR strategy documents, but what actually happens is usually quite different.

The argument of this chapter is that personnel people are deeply involved in strategy and have a major influence on it, but they are usually, and most usefully, deployed in a reactive mode. During his time as Foreign Secretary, Douglas Hurd made an interesting comment on Britain's role in the European Union. He said that statesmen from other countries had very grand ideas and were very good at vision, but the British preferred to act like craftspeople, worrying away at the details and getting things to work. That may be a useful analogy for the personnel professional. An HR strategy cannot exist as a separate entity.

The direction of the business has to be in terms of finding the market niche and meeting customer demand within financial capabilities. The HR strategy will then be in two forms:

- a close examination of the proposals and their implications in human resource terms, with possible alternatives;
- a series of strategic initiatives to help get the show on the road.

Concern about not being reactive is as unrealistic for personnel people as it is crucial for marketing people. In marketing you have to be proactive and constantly changing things to find a competitive advantage. In HRM you can only react to proposals and then find specific strategic initiatives to help deliver the overall strategy.

FINDING EFFECTIVE OPERATIONAL ROLES

There then comes the question about the place of the operational level of activities in contrast to the strategic development. The literature on the operational role of the HRM function is very thin: that is all left to the consultants. In the main the literature assumes that operational aspects should be devolved to other people – the line managers. The enthusiasm with which personnel people have delegated or devolved operational aspects to the line may have been throwing the baby out with the bath water. If personnel people really continue to abdicate everyday responsibilities and create a vacuum of no operational or technical contribution at all, then it all would seem rather trivial. The contribution to strategic thinking would be gradually devalued if it had no operational weight and responsibility behind it. Bright ideas from people who also have to deliver are much more realistic and more welcome than bright ideas from people who do nothing else but dream up clever schemes for other people to implement. The future of strategy as the sole focus for personnel people must now be limited.

It is quite clear that the actual involvement – effective involvement – is based far more on the personality and skills of two people than it is on any kind of structural system. We have this fabled person called the chief executive whom personnel people have always wanted to influence. The research shows how important that working relationship is. Chief executives value the independence of the personnel perspective, as well as its human dimension, and many personnel specialists feel that they can achieve more by working in a way that is different from other functional specialists. This is risky. If your chief executive moves on, as they regularly do, what happens if the replacement does not have a 'people mindset' and if you have kicked out all the operational side of personnel work? You might involuntarily be looking for another career.

CONCLUSION: RE-ESTABLISHING CONFIDENCE, IDENTITY AND DIRECTION

There may well be a crisis in HRM as we approach the millennium. It has been in crisis for at least a century, so it would be very strange if things were not that way now. However, it helps to cope with the crisis if some of its dimensions are understood.

There is a *crisis of confidence* among personnel specialists, as there always has been. Their results are almost impossible to measure and their successes and failures are largely the successes and failures of other people. Furthermore, they operate in a field – how people behave – in which everyone else is an expert with a personal point of view from which they will not depart. The difficulty for personnel people is that they know how intractable some of the people problems really are. They are not helped by the persistent disparagement of HRM academics, who go to considerable lengths to explain how badly their job is done.

There is then a *crisis of identity* because of the HRM dimension, which is probably the most significant innovation in people management practice in the last 50 years, but which is not a complete toolkit of how to do things differently. It represents a change of emphasis which is defined differently by every academic commentator making a contribution to an increasingly sterile debate.

Third, there is a *crisis of direction* because of the preoccupation with strategy at the expense of operational personnel work which has been a dominant feature of discussion in the wake of HRM.

Personnel specialists can take some comfort from the fact that their field of work has been disparaged for as long as most of us can remember. In the face of the criticism, the number of working personnel specialists continues to grow. HRM is not a magic recipe making everything that preceded its announcement redundant. Most personnel people eschew the term as a description of themselves and their departments, at the same time as acknowledging that if it raises the importance of people management issues among their managerial colleagues, it can stay as long as it likes. Personnel people have a clear role in strategy development and its implementation. Their expertise and their authority in strategic discussions derive from their activity at the operational level. Abandoning operational activity and specialist knowledge is a high-risk strategy. First you get encumbered with consultants, then you wonder where your next job is coming from.

A final observation is that the whole of HRM is built on the assumption that what you are doing is making the organisation work effectively and that that organisation is some huge entity. It is the organisation that we are losing pretty rapidly. Business process re-engineering (BPR) was another set of initials that was going to save the world from extinction, and has had some vilification recently, but its core message was valid. BPR said never mind the structures, systems and cultures because they are things that make *organisations* operate and often interfere with how the *business* operates. What we have to move away from is a preoccupation with organisations and towards a preoccupation with methods whereby the business operates effectively and the people part of the business operates even better. That does not presuppose a structure – it presupposes an involvement in the process whereby people are employed, deployed, motivated, empowered, stimulated and paid.

The Japanese word for crisis means 'opportunity' as well. The crisis for personnel people entering the new millennium is not to get the right degree of involvement in strategy, or to work out what HRM means, but to make sure they remain closely involved in the process of the business rather than in the structure, culture and systems of the organisation.

3

Beyond HRM: commitment and the contract culture

DAVID E. GUEST

Birkbeck College

BEYOND HRM: COMMITMENT AND THE CONTRACT CULTURE

Some years ago, in a paper reviewing developments in the 1980s, and giving some prominence to the emergence of human resource management (HRM), I argued for the end of orthodoxy (Guest, 1991). The paper was directed to an audience of industrial relations academics and the orthodoxy in question was the pluralist Donovan tradition in industrial relations which had provided the conceptual framework and the empirical focus for much of the research and writing on employment relations in the UK. Whether writing from a Marxist or managerial perspective, whether offering a radical critique or a set of prescriptions, the pluralist perspective provided the conceptual focus, the point of departure.

In that same paper, I suggested that HRM might be emerging as a new orthodoxy. Now, with a series of seminars on 'HRM in Crisis', there is the implication both that HRM is an accepted orthodoxy deserving of special attention and that like pluralism before it, it is in some trouble as a central organising focus for our analysis of the employment relationship.

In this chapter I want to consider first, whether HRM has in fact developed to the point where it can be considered as the prevailing orthodoxy, in other words the dominant framework for conceptual analysis and policy considerations in employment relations; second, whether it is in crisis; and third, whether there is evidence of any competing new orthodoxy emerging to take its place. In doing so, I will pay particular attention to the concept of organisational commitment, which lies at the heart of some analyses of HRM and to the challenges presented by what might be termed the emergence of a 'contract culture'. The first sections explore the case for and against HRM as the current orthodoxy.

THE CASE FOR HRM AS THE CURRENT ORTHODOXY

Setting the agenda

One of the achievements of HRM has been to alter the debate and set the agenda. This lies at the heart of establishing its case as the dominant orthodoxy. At the very least it has become fashionable in academic circles, reflected in titles of departments, professorships and journals. No self-respecting publisher is without an HRM series. At the very least, as Karen Legge (1995) has somewhat cynically noted, it has provided a reasonably comfortable home for dispossessed industrial relations academics. Some even use the term 'the new industrial relations' instead of HRM, perhaps to provide familiarity. However it is more than this. It also provides an agenda for a range of disciplines and a focus which extends beyond the traditional manufacturing and public sector organisations that once dominated the work of those interested in the employment relationship into the hitherto neglected non-union sector.

In this respect, HRM is the focus of issues of implementation, of forms of practice or of radical critique. The starting point for analysis of employment relations, at least in the UK, is the concept and the agenda of HRM. We may not like it, hence the basis for the radical critique (*see*, for example, Legge, 1995); we may not think much of it, leading to debates about its pervasiveness and effectiveness (*see*, for example, Sisson, 1993; Storey, 1995b); but we cannot easily ignore it. Part of this shift in emphasis can be attributed to the external environment and to the political climate. It also reflects a shift in power towards a concern for the management of employment relations. But part of the shift is attributable to the coherence of the HRM agenda and the promise it offers.

HRM as new metaphor

It is important to remember that HRM was a product of its times. In the USA, this means the political era of Reaganism (Guest, 1990) and the managerial era of *In Search of Excellence* (Peters and Waterman, 1982). It was an era of growing optimism and of the USA's rediscovery of its self-confidence after the trauma of Vietnam. HRM, and the idea of commitment to progress for the individual, the organisation and the nation neatly captured the spirit of the times. For Americans faced with growing international competition and in particular growing competition from the Japanese in their domestic market, it was very tempting to look to an approach which could be presented as a distinctively American response. In the UK, too, Thatcherism at work was changing the agenda and helping to shift the focus of ideas for innovation towards the USA. As Stephen Dunn (1990) notes, the metaphor shifted from the trench warfare of pluralist industrial relations to the journey of the wagon train, boldly going forward to the new frontier. In short, HRM offered unitarism in place of pluralism, optimism in place of uncertainty and progress in place of retrenchment. This analysis can be developed much further but the key point is that this metaphor, with its powerful champions, captured the imagination and does present an attractive and in a sense comforting, if illusory, view of the world.

The role of strategic integration

HRM is, of course, much more than metaphor. One of the reasons why it holds a wide appeal is that it offers a strong focus around which to integrate a number of ideas and approaches. In particular, it provides a more powerful framework than had previously existed around which to integrate concern for people into the mainstream of business thinking. One key indication of this was its take-up by leading business schools as an essential subject for the aspiring top managers of the future. In all this, the idea of strategic integration and of the need for coherent linkages (Truss and Gratton, 1994) has become central in a number of ways. Although Mintzberg (1994b) among others has done an impressive destruction job on the idea of rational strategy, it nevertheless remains an attractive basis for understanding and in particular making post hoc sense of choice (Boxall, 1991). What strategic integration emphasises is the importance of acting consistently. The idea of strategic integration also provides a framework for action to which HR practitioners can aspire, a framework within which consultants can integrate a range of techniques into a more coherent whole and an interdisciplinary framework which is amenable to analysis by economists, by experts in strategy and by organisational psychologists. This also provides a framework for empirical or conceptual critique of HRM of the sort which has been powerfully mounted by, for example, Purcell (1995). Finally, it has become a major basis for some of the more contemporary research into the impact of HRM.

An alternative policy framework

The development of a new orthodoxy takes on more significance in a country such as the UK in the context of the pressures created by the former Conservative government's desire to let the market rule and to help this along by constraining the power of unions and law. If government dogma, as reflected in the policies and practices it imposed on the public sector, were to be followed throughout industry, then that orthodoxy of pluralism, which still informs the European Union, would have been replaced by the orthodoxy of the market, with many more people on fixed-term contracts and even greater concern about the changing nature of the psychological contract. Instead, HRM offers an alternative means to achieve high performance and competitive advantage. Our evidence from choices in greenfield sites indicates that although some firms opted for a form of market-driven, management-dominated approach – the bleak house or black hole where no unions and HRM practices may enter – others chose HRM as the core of their policy. It clearly is a viable and effective alternative (Guest and Hoque, 1996). In a difficult political and economic climate, we should recognise and be grateful for this alternative approach. While its critics identify shortcomings, these are of a different order to those forced to endure low pay and limited rights in the sweat shops of the 1990s. This point has now been recognised by the trade union movement and one of the signs of how far the prevailing thinking has shifted and how far HRM has moved into the mainstream is its attraction as a framework which trade unions can use to counter the harsher pressures of market-driven approaches to management of the workforce. As a policy framework, HRM presents coherence, a break with the past and an approach which is robust enough to stand up to the less palatable alternatives that are sometimes promulgated.

HRM pays off

One of the most compelling positive claims for HRM is that it is associated with higher performance. First, HRM practices – the so-called high commitment or high performance practices such as single status arrangements, an emphasis on job security and internal promotion, design of jobs to make full use of abilities, extensive training and considerable two-way communication – are associated with HRM outcomes such as higher quality of staff, higher flexibility and higher commitment, although the data supporting this remain weak, mainly because of the lack of clear evidence of cause and effect (Guest and Hoque, 1994a; 1996). Second, HRM practices, particularly when occurring in bundles, are associated with higher performance as measured by standard productivity indices (Arthur, 1994; Ichniowski *et al.*, 1994) and by higher profits (Huselid, 1995). The important point behind the idea of 'bundles' is that it is the combination of practices that matter rather than adoption of specific practices in isolation. It may well be possible to achieve good results through different combinations of practices or different bundles, although just how the practices combine is still a subject of continuing research (Becker and Gerhart, 1996). The amount of variance explained by use of different HRM practices is small but it is significant and for large firms it could have considerable financial implications. This gradually accumulating body of data, although not without its problems, is encouraging news for advocates of HRM. It also, incidentally, provides a challenge in that it is invariably based on complex statistical analysis of large data sets, an area of interest to labour economists and perhaps organisational psychologists operating within a strongly positivist paradigm. This has the benefit of making HRM a more attractive topic for research and theory from a wider range of disciplinary perspectives. Those less comfortable with this positivist, highly quantitative perspective may, however, feel concern that the subject area is being colonised (Legge, 1995).

In summary, HRM has provided a new agenda, a new metaphor, an alternative policy framework, an integrative framework for interdisciplinary research and an approach which is beginning to show positive outcomes. On this basis, we might conclude that HRM does represent the current orthodoxy and that within this framework policy and research are progressing smoothly and encouragingly.

THE CASE AGAINST HRM AS THE CURRENT ORTHODOXY

It is always easier to be critical. However it should be noted that many criticisms also reflect an advance in understanding and a sharpening of focus which can equally be construed as a sign of progress. Nevertheless there are a number of issues which cast doubt on any claims for the conceptual coherence or the impact of HRM.

There is no consensus on the definition of HRM

After all this time, we still cannot agree what we mean by HRM. I used to think that after the initial debates this did not matter. Now I am not so sure. If we wish to debate on common ground and to find out whether HRM works, we do need to know what 'it' is. Elsewhere (Guest, 1994) I have outlined three major perspectives on HRM. The first emphasises HRM as strategy, highlighting a strategic perspective as its distinctive feature. However, we still do not know whether to build our strategic perspective around a Porter-like model, as Schuler and Jackson (1987) have done, or a Miles and Snow model (1984), or a Tichy, Fombrun and Devanna model (1982); or do we start from an analysis of type of organisation as a means of determining the relevant locus of strategy? Indeed, how far does the choice of strategic categories matter given that they all emphasise the 'situational contingencies' (Hendry and Pettigrew, 1990) perspective? The second perspective looks inwards, focusing on the content of HRM, and arguing that its distinctiveness lies in a set of practices designed to develop commitment, quality and flexibility. This approach has been promoted by Walton (1985) and Guest (1987). However even if we could gain consensus about the HRM objectives, we still cannot agree about the key practices that promote them. The growing interest in bundles of practices cannot hide the variety of content of these bundles (Dyer and Reeves, 1995). The third approach is deliberately broad and claims as its distinctive feature the development of a framework to link HRM issues into general management. It is reflected in the models of the Harvard (Beer *et al.*, 1985) and MIT (Kochan and Useem, 1992) groups. But again we need to recognise that they are rather different in emphasis.

In addition to these three approaches to HRM, we have perspectives which emphasise hard versus soft and European versus American versions as well as the overlapping concern for the new industrial relations. It is possible to seek some common themes across all these approaches to HRM but beyond general statements about the importance of human resources and about the need to consider them strategically, they are quite hard to find. For example, the inherent unitarism is challenged by the stakeholder perspective of the Harvard type of approach and the commitment that lies at the core of some versions is challenged by the emphasis in others on strategic choice. All this provides fertile ground for critical debate but not for the underlying coherence that is required of a dominant orthodoxy.

The collapse of the metaphor

Part of the early promise of HRM was that it offered a new approach to the management of the workforce. Peters and Waterman (1982) helped to focus attention on the 'soft' 's'. In practice, this meant the promotion of organisational culture as a mechanism to win the hearts and minds of employees. Commitment to the organisation lay at the core of this approach and it was considered more effective to use a values-driven approach than, for example, money to gain commitment. As a result, the 1980s was a period when most large organisations tried to alter their culture and they did so by adopting a normative re-educative strategy. In practice, this meant a combination of the development of a mission statement, more two-way communication and lots of training. Human resource management lay at the heart of this approach.

By the beginning of the 1990s the economic climate had changed: instead of economic boom, there was recession. In place of growth and progress and commitment the language had altered, first to a focus on performance and then to retrenchment, downsizing and efficiency. Some of the champions of HRM, notably some of the computer companies such as IBM, started to perform poorly. The metaphor of the journey and the frontier was replaced once again by, if not trench warfare, the image of the stockade or even the dangerous free market world of Mad Max. The strategy of change shifted from normative re-educative to power-coercive with a hint of the empirical rational. The greater the cut-backs in staff, the better the stock exchange liked it. A new macho era had emerged. The new rationality was one of efficiency and its champions were the appropriately named Hammer and Champy (1993) with their process re-engineering and the rediscovery of the spirit of Taylorism. Organisational culture may have changed, but it changed through the use of power. The pretence of winning hearts and minds had gone. Instead a financial imperative had come to dominate and in the boardrooms the language of HRM had become a distant echo.

The lack of application

The results of the 1990 *Workplace Industrial Relations Survey* (WIRS) (Millward *et al.*, 1992) and the parallel *Company Level Industrial Relations Survey* (Marginson *et al.*, 1993) were probably a surprise to many people. Although neither was comprehensive in its coverage of HRM, both showed a rather limited uptake of HRM across a representative sample of industry, commerce and the public sector. These surveys certainly indicated that the academic rhetoric had run far ahead of the reality. Furthermore, people at work were less eager than academics to embrace the language of HRM. Less than one per cent of those responsible for personnel issues at establishment level used the HRM title (Guest and Hoque, 1993) and only at corporate headquarters was it taken up with any enthusiasm and even then by only about 17 per cent. Set against this, there is evidence from our own work on greenfield sites (Guest and Hoque, 1994b), that when starting anew, many firms do use a wide variety of HRM practices. Somewhat similar findings have been obtained by Hoque (1996) in his study of the hotel and catering industry. Despite such evidence, the weight of the comprehensive surveys implies more talk than action.

The failure to change commitment

The concept of organisational commitment lies at the heart of any analysis of HRM. Indeed, the whole rationale for introducing HRM polices is to increase levels of commitment so that other positive outcomes can ensue. The culture change programmes that became so popular in the 1980s were predicated upon assumptions about their impact on commitment. Yet there is little evidence that they succeeded in changing commitment (Marchington, Goodman, Wilkinson and Ackers, 1992; Wall, Kemp, Jackson and Clegg, 1986). Put bluntly, HRM as part of a strategy for change seems to have failed. We can debate the reasons for this and one likely cause is the failure to adopt a serious approach to strategic integration. Instead, most change programmes were partial and piecemeal.

A second factor is a failure to understand enough about organisational commitment. It was first introduced as a more robust and resilient concept than job satisfaction and the research evidence confirms that it is a relatively stable construct. Indeed, nothing seems to change commitment. There are virtually no published studies showing that any kind of intervention has any kind of impact on levels of commitment to the organisation (Guest and Peccei, 1996). There are a variety of possible explanations for this including the weakness of training and employee involvement focused interventions, the failure to concentrate on the main antecedents of commitment and the failure to change what Schein (1992) describes as the primary levers of organisational culture such as leadership behaviour and the significant reward systems, resulting in a major research headache and challenge. For the time being we need to accept the point that one of the core elements of HRM that provides the basis for a set of policy guidelines may not after all be susceptible to these policies. Alternatively, theories about how to introduce HRM are wrong.

HRM as rhetoric and ideology

Critics have always suggested that the rhetoric of HRM has run ahead of the reality (Legge, 1995; Chapter 1, this volume). The point about the use of rhetoric is that it helps to construct a view of reality. Yet it seems that academics have bought the rhetoric more readily than the rather more sceptical practitioners. This suggests that even as rhetoric HRM has failed. There are counters to this view. One position might be that HRM has helped to weaken opposition to a more aggressive management, if only by marginalising unions. Another is that its link to culture change has provided a cloak behind which new and more subtle forms of control have been introduced – the idea of surveillance. Yet the lack of successful application does not lend weight to these perspectives.

At the very least the research on lack of application suggests that we must be a little cautious in accepting the criticism that HRM is mainly about rhetoric and presentation. Nevertheless, it is certainly at least in part about ideology. One argument is that it uses unitarism in an apparently reasonable way either to obviate a felt need for trade unions or to let them wither on the vine. Certainly the imported American form of HRM is generally unfavourable to trade unionism. A more serious criticism, often advanced from within a post-modern perspective, is that HRM promises freedom and autonomy based around commitment while practising alternative forms of control and surveillance. The control may operate through the group or through the performance targets emanating from goal setting. The surveillance may come from new technology and the opportunity it provides, in all sorts of ways, to monitor our lives as workers and as citizens. Finally, returning to the rhetoric, it can be argued that HRM is part of a platform on which a pattern of false optimism can be created. The language of concern for the individual, the ideas of progress and growth, the notion of the organisation as a team or family and the idea that everyone has a part to play in the organisational adventure of challenging the competition can cloak a less pleasant reality. That reality may include a surrender of autonomy and a loss of power to respond when times are hard – when it is time to move beyond HRM.

In summary, after more than a decade, it can be argued that we still do not know what HRM is. Despite much talk, there has been relatively little action in terms of uptake in industry. If anything its focus seems to have shifted away from its original concerns, yet even these were dubious since they offered an ideology and a rhetoric that seem to provide an alternative to pluralism but one which industry, despite flirting with it, seems to have managed without.

BEYOND HRM: THE SEARCH FOR A NEW ORTHODOXY

The analysis to date has suggested that there is a choice of perspectives in evaluating the current state of HRM. A positive view presents a picture of coherent development of a flexible integrated approach which has altered our way of thinking about management of people at work and which is beginning to show evidence of encouraging pay-offs. A negative picture reveals an approach which has promised more than it has delivered, which lacks coherence and which has never been seriously adopted by most practitioners. Inevitably, both pictures are partly right and partly wrong. The key point is that HRM as a coherent orthodoxy is manufactured rather than empirically derived. At its core is the issue of commitment, yet we have known for some time and conveniently neglected the problems of changing commitment through the kind of interventions associated with HRM. HRM is, in particular, an academic construction. Equally, the idea of a crisis in HRM is manufactured on the back of assumptions about its coherence and application. It follows that we need to address the question of crisis with the same scepticism with which we approach the question of orthodoxy and coherence.

One way in which it might be useful to consider the issue of crisis in HRM is to accept the view that HRM has attained the status of a dominant orthodoxy and consider whether any new orthodoxy, any new integration and synthesis is emerging which might challenge the centrality of HRM in our analysis of the employment relationship. With this in mind, the remainder of this chapter will consider possible current challenges to HRM.

Beyond HRM: the emergence of the contract culture

Alan Fox, in *Beyond Contract* (Fox, 1974) anticipated some of the developments in HRM in his analysis of the development of trust. He was eager to move beyond the negative relationships emerging from a pluralist perspective without in any way returning to the law of the marketplace. In this respect there is some overlap between his work and that of writers such as Ouchi (1980) and Kalleberg and Reve (1993) who have sought to build a political economy of the employment contract by developing and moving beyond the work of Williamson (1975; 1985) on transaction cost economics.

Where Williamson sought to explain and, it might be argued, prescribe (Ghoshal and Moran, 1996) the circumstances under which contracts should be based on market or hierarchy, both Ouchi, and Kalleberg and Reve build on the common criticism of Williamson's work by seeking to incorporate a social and political/institutional dimension acknowledging the role of social norms in the national, and to a lesser extent in the organisational, culture.

Williamson and other transaction cost economists are interested in the kind of contracts that will maximise efficiency. If we follow Kalleberg and Reve and restrict our focus to employment contracts we can draw crude parallels with market-based contracts and hierarchy. In shorthand, these can be redefined as short, fixed-term contracts, often for a specified piece of work, and long-term, more permanent employment contracts within a more conventional organisational framework. Williamson predicted that hierarchy would emerge where there was greater asset specificity, greater frequency of exchange and higher uncertainty. Uncertainty in this context means that it is costly to monitor the quality and quantity of goods and services produced. Using this type of framework, we can see why bureaucratic organisations emerged as a cost-effective means of co-ordination and control as organisations grew larger and more complex.

Ouchi (1980) noted that the Japanese had very informal but long-term contracts both between employers and employees and with suppliers. This had advantages in lower transaction costs, especially the costs of control. Instead the control was achieved through the culture and the strong social norms leading to commitment and high trust. This approach, which Ouchi labelled the clan approach, provides one kind of theoretical basis for HRM based around concepts of commitment and contract. Control based on commitment built through both national and organisational cultural norms is more efficient than elements of hierarchy, and certainly than markets, because of the lower transaction costs and the reduced drift to opportunism. Based as it is on strong social norms and long-term relationships, this approach also implies long-term secure employment contracts.

Following this logic, we can see a pattern of development from the cruder disciplines of the market and control based on explicit contract, through the use of hierarchy, with the rule-based systems of control outlined by Mintzberg (1983) and others as a means of obtaining compliance, to the advanced state of clan or organisational cultures where the role of ideology is central to control. HRM, closely linked to an organisational culture designed to elicit high commitment to the organisation, is the most advanced, the most sophisticated and the most efficient basis for organising and for eliciting high performance from the employees. It is based on concepts of reciprocal commitment and high trust. While the pendulum may swing back occasionally, for instance in process re-engineering, to sweep up other type of efficiency gain, the logic of the analysis suggests that this use of internalised, commitment-based control will dominate.

The problem with the preceding analysis is that we may be at fault in adopting too linear an approach with all its optimistic assumptions about development and progress. Instead reality may conform more to a circular model. For those committed to the ideology of HRM with its roots in the idea of progress, this may seem uncomfortable. Yet a circular model in which we move from clans, culture and HRM back to markets seems to fit with the popular view of reality and with the shift from secure, long-term employment to insecure, fixed-term contracts; in short, to the emergence of the 'contract culture'. Indeed, following this logic, there seems to be no reason why we cannot carry on around the cycle; no doubt the move to a market perspective and control through contract will highlight the inefficiencies generated by high transaction costs and low commitment, prompting renewed interest in hierarchy. Yorkshire Television seems to be one example of an organisation that has gone through this cycle, first moving staff onto short-term contracts and then moving them back onto the permanent payroll. Beyond HRM now becomes 'Back to the Future', as illustrated in Fig. 3.1.

What a superficial analysis indicates is that hierarchy/bureaucracy is out of fashion and that in some sectors, the market, with its emphasis on contracts, is back in. Perhaps here we can find a new orthodoxy, allowing a particular version of economics to invade the employment relationship. There have certainly been political pressures for this. However once again we need to distinguish between rhetoric and reality. Undoubtedly, years of being bombarded with the market rhetoric has left its mark in the UK. It implies that we have moved beyond, or perhaps have side-stepped HRM. An interesting feature of the last year or two is that, after 15 years or more in the limelight, Japan has ceased to be so fashionable a model to emulate. The national culture that highlighted commitment has been replaced in the popular imagination by . . . what? One answer is that the USA, the traditional advocate of the market perspective, despite its dalliance with HRM, is back in fashion. Another more alarming thought is that the latest model may be the UK. It was certainly promoted by the British government as a model of excellence and received some echo in the response of European industrialists and bankers. However one suspects that the

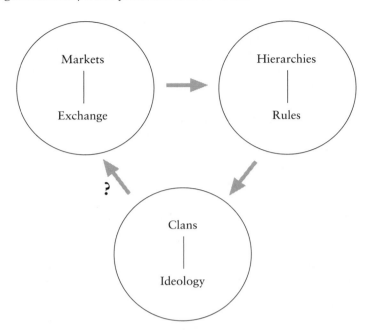

Fig. 3.1 Culture, control and contract

UK is of interest rather in the way that Chile was of interest when attempts were made to apply the policies of Milton Friedman. We were interested to see what happened but rather glad it was not happening to us.

Although the 'contract culture' and the growth of the UK as a model of flexibility has been extensively promoted, the reality is rather different. There has been a move towards more people who could be described as flexible workers in the UK. But the growth has been mainly in part-time workers, it has been restricted to a few industrial sectors such as retail and it is not an accelerating trend. The number of fixed-term contracts has grown but far less dramatically than we might expect (Beatson, 1995). There has been a public sector-driven growth of contract-based exchange, often confirming Williamson's premises in demonstrating high transaction costs and high opportunism.

It is fashionable to believe in the end of hierarchy, in the flattening of organisations and the end of the career. Yet 30 years ago Bennis (1966) was writing *On the Coming Demise of Bureaucracy* and it is still alive and fairly well. Similarly 30 years ago, writers were predicting the end of the career as an apparently growing number of executives sought to opt out of the rat race (Williams and Guest, 1971) Despite the fashion for HRM in high-commitment clan cultures or for markets and fixed-term contracts, the dominant organisational form remains the bureaucratic hierarchy (Guest and Mackenzie Davey, 1996). True, it is more nimble – the giants have learnt to dance – but it continues to dominate, despite the growth in the 1980s, now largely halted, of new small firms. For these large firms the challenge of HRM and high commitment remains. We know from WIRS3 that they still have a long way to go in implementing HRM. And we know from various surveys that the search for a committed workforce is still a priority for many companies. They are not adopting market-modelled employment contracts and relationships to any great extent. WIRS3 clearly shows this. Our research in greenfield sites (Guest and Hoque, 1994b; 1996) also indicates that many firms, when they have the choice, still opt for an HRM-driven, high commitment approach to the management of their workforce.

Although we may deny the spread of market-based contracts in much the same way as we challenge the extent of HRM practices, it may nevertheless be possible to discern the beginnings of a new orthodoxy based on the idea of contract. There is a core ideology in the concept of markets. There is a widely recognised analytic framework built around transaction cost economics. There is the potential for innovative application of ideas about new technology and its capacity to reduce transaction and interaction costs and therefore challenge the importance of traditional long-term supplier relationships. There are also assumptions about human behaviour, albeit pessimistic ones in the focus on the cash nexus and opportunism. There are some compelling employment issues such as job insecurity and the end of the career. Above all there are two attractive constructs which have already captured the imagination:

- flexibility
- psychological contract.

There is clearly a large and challenging research agenda built around these concepts. However, there are major problems in using them to construct a new orthodoxy. First of all, flexibility is already subsumed within HRM. Second, the extensive empirical and conceptual critique of the flexible firm concept has already been played out and although there are interesting links to debates on flexible specialisation and post-Fordism, the issues are not sufficiently wide ranging to embrace a framework for the employment relationship (Hunter *et al.*, 1993).

The problems with the psychological contract are of a slightly different order. This concept has an instant appeal by focusing on vaguely defined but clearly important concerns affecting most people at work. In particular, its current attraction lies in its ability to shed light on the wider issue of employment insecurity. Another major strength is that it focuses attention on, and gives primacy to individual concerns and individual well-being. However, this strength is also a potential limitation. To understand the influences on the psychological contract we need to examine it in context. That context is social, political and economic – it is that same context that concerned Kalleberg and Reve in their consideration of the employment contract. As the concept of the psychological contract has moved centre stage, it has evolved from a concern for the employment exchange to a concern for employee perceptions about expectations, inducements and obligations (Rousseau, 1995). In so doing, it has arguably become too one-sided. We need to consider the policy perspective and the factors which shape the contract as offered as well as the way in which it is perceived. If this approach is to be developed, we need to adopt a broader framework which embraces the work on employment contracts and extends to the employment relationship. Only then will this sort of perspective give us a fuller understanding of the dynamics of individual commitment, motivation and performance which lies at the heart of the concept of the psychological contract.

A final but possibly important point about using concepts built around the market, flexibility and contracts is that the ideological messages are muddled and they do not indicate any sense of progress. In this respect, an orthodoxy based on contracts is a backwards step – as noted earlier, it is back to the future. It is also an approach which had a particular resonance in the UK of the mid-1990s with its distinctive political and economic climate. As such it is unlikely to be a recipe which captures the imagination, even if in the UK it did reflect the rather depressed spirit of the times.

The new Utopia? Commitment, control and community

If a new and different synthesis is to emerge, it needs to be built around a concept which has all the necessary hallmarks of a successful fad or 'movement'. One such term is community, closely linked to the longstanding concept of stakeholder (Hutton, 1996). This well-established idea appeared in some of the main models of HRM, it has been adapted for use in organisations in the form of the balanced scorecard (Kaplan and Norton, 1993) and it fits well with the European notions of 'partnership'. It was, for a while, adopted as a central element in the political platform of the Labour Party in the UK. Ironically, given its rural overtones, it offers the idea of 'Vorsprung durch Technik', progress through the technology of the computer. It is now recognised that technology increases the choice of controls. Where in the past control was an extension of simple supervision, predicated upon physical presence in the workplace, now it can be exercised from a distance through monitoring processes or through measurable outcomes. As post-modernists have highlighted, technology permits forms of sophisticated surveillance of people at work. Increasingly, that surveillance can be extended to wherever they may be. More crudely, the portable telephone and the fax permit distanced contact and monitoring. This creates a new fragmentation, a new opportunity and a new challenge for organisational commitment. We can look at each in turn.

The new fragmentation, which is only now being spotted, lies in the distinction between those who need to be physically present in the workplace and those who can choose where to work and have the opportunity, for at least part of their working time, to work from home or at least away from the office or factory (see the outline of geographical flexibility in Chapter 1). Superficially, it appears that those with the choice have most to gain. In practice, they may experience a new constraint by being forced to work from home, with consequent economic, social and emotional costs and benefits. While those who fall into the broad class of knowledge worker will have more opportunity to choose the place of work, those engaged in certain kinds of production and service will need to be physically present. The division will not be based solely on hierarchy. There is likely to be a new challenge in developing personnel policies to manage this new division of labour.

The opportunity provided by the freedom of technology has been widely recognised as the chance to rediscover community. The choice of community to live in will become less constrained by the proximity of the workplace; the relationship to and the stake in the community may therefore change in character. Indeed, communities may wish to exercise more choice about whether to admit certain kinds of workplace. This means that organisations will need to give more primacy to environmental and quality of life issues. It will require new commitments on the part of the firm.

The challenge of the concept of community is that it reinforces the idea of multiple commitments. Technology allows membership of many communities simultaneously. Employing organisations therefore face even more strongly the challenges of competing commitments that gave rise to the concept of commitment in the first place. Yet there are a number of contradictory currents in this rather muddy water. On the one hand it is possible to dream of the kind of Utopia described by Huxley in *Island*, with half the day spent working and half the day spent in other more elevated pursuits. On the other, the ever present nature of work can become a new tyranny. For many knowledge workers, academics among them, the blurring of the boundaries of work space, far from liberating, act to imprison. Work becomes an addiction from which there is no physical escape. No European edicts restricting working hours can prevent this kind of addiction. In Japan, of course, addiction to work based on strong normative obligations is already recognised as a form of illness and the resulting physical illnesses and suicides receive publicity and occasionally financial compensation. In the western world, we worry more about reduced commitment while observing people in managerial and professional jobs working ever longer hours. Do people work the hours out of a sense of obligation or fear or challenge? If it is a sense of insecurity, what sort of insecurity since it is often those who are young, well qualified and highly marketable who work the ludicrous hours? Pahl (1995) offers some interesting insights into why this is happening but we badly need further research on this addiction.

I have tried to outline the parameters of a potential new orthodoxy. The idea of community and partnership is old but compelling. It resonates with nostalgia but retains the capacity to seem modern and progressive. Indeed the new frontier is no doubt located in the sunny community of Silicon Valley where home, work, organisation and career are all blurred in the heat haze or the barbeque smoke. It has the ability to operate at the political and ideological level, to point to policy prescriptions and to offer competitive advantage at least in the employment market. Before we get over-enthusiastic, we should recognise that it is easy to 'talk up' community as a new orthodoxy. The reality remains very different. The shift to working from home has not yet begun to happen in large numbers. We neglect, to our potential cost, the power of the traditional bureaucracy and the exercise of traditional control mechanisms. There is plenty of life yet in the dancing elephants.

Fracturing the future: fragmentation and integration

The search for a compelling orthodoxy will inevitably continue. If we step back and review the available empirical evidence what we see is a fracturing of practice (Chapter 1 talks about this). While it is tempting to identify or even to create movements and fashions and while industry, and indeed academics, will continue to be highly susceptible to anything which promises a shift of competitive advantage, it seems that what we are witnessing around us is a fragmentation of approaches. In analysing approaches to employment, it is not a matter of markets *or* hierarchy *or* clans/HRM, but of *and/and*. We may see variety of approach across sectors – for example, private industry has been slow to ape the contract culture of the public sector – as well as within sectors. We can also see diversity within organisations. The idea of the flexible firm offers the possibility of several kinds of contract and several kinds of commitment within the same enterprise. However we also know that very few firms adopt this strategy and it is easy to see why. The challenge of managing the complexity is just too great.

Another key aspect of fragmentation which is widely discussed though less often clearly demonstrated is the changing nature of the personnel role. After gaining in prominence over several decades, personnel specialists have been placed once again on the defensive, partly as a result of process re-engineering which potentially affects and constantly disrupts several functions. But in the case of personnel management it is also seen as something more. First, HRM advocates giving more responsibility for managing human resources to line managers. Second, the fashion for sub-contracting has been directed at the personnel function and perhaps training in particular. Third, as purveyors of bureaucratic control systems, in an era where debureaucratisation is fashionable, personnel departments are especially susceptible. Having said this, while there is some evidence of change in the organisation of personnel management, this does not amount to a crisis for the function. There has been some devolvement of personnel activity from the centre to the local management but this is usually from one personnel specialist to another. Numbers of personnel specialists have not consistently reduced, nor has their apparent influence. However, while some organisations have decentralised personnel activity, others have not – and still others are considering whether more needs to be drawn into the centre. What we see is a variety of approach rather than a clear consensus about the appropriate way to organise the function. Personnel specialists have a propensity for navel-gazing and neurosis about their role but on this occasion it seems ill founded. No doubt however, observers will continue to tell the healthy patient that he or she is ill.

While all the research evidence points to continuing and possibly to increasing fragmentation of perspectives on HRM and in the organisation of personnel departments and content of personnel activities, it is nothing particularly new. As ever, the role of academics, echoing elements of chaos theory, is to understand that fragmentation by mapping it and by seeking a new synthesis or integration. Within the subjects related to the employment relationship we can see a variety of possible integrative frameworks. We should also bear in mind the elements of continuity. One, of course, is the impetus of the continuing academic discourse. Another, and perhaps the core of any continuity in relation to HRM is, as Karen Legge (1995) has argued, the continuing need to do personnel work. Irrespective of who does it and with what aim in mind, selection, training, pay arrangements and design of jobs are tasks that must be undertaken. This core remains a legitimate area of study, analysis and prescription whatever framework is adopted for its analysis.

All this suggests that the challenges which led to the development of HRM are still there. The context in which it emerged has changed, but the new context simply means that the character of the challenges has altered somewhat. We should by now have more realistic expectations about what can be achieved through HRM and we should realise that application of a specific version of HRM is not appropriate in every organisation, a point some of us have been making for many years. The issue of commitment lies at the heart of these debates and in any new orthodoxy seems likely to continue to do so; the nature of commitment may have altered but the challenge of improving our understanding of commitment remains.

CONCLUSION

In summary therefore, this analysis implies the following conclusions. Is there a crisis in HRM? Probably not, or certainly no more than there has been at any other point over the past ten years. But constructing a crisis does help to stimulate our thinking about the topic.

Does the fragmentation of employment and the growing interest in the psychological contract present a challenge to HRM? Possibly, but only on the margins since it deals with an issue which has been around for some time. Are there lessons for HRM in this analysis? Yes, in the need to recognise the dangers of imposing a spurious uniformity of practice or in reconstructing a uniform past. It seems that HRM has always been a minority activity, therefore the surprise in its limited application is only a surprise to those who have swallowed the rhetoric of its more enthusiastic advocates. There is some evidence that those who can apply HRM can achieve significant pay-offs; but we also know, from the analysis of attempts to change organisational commitment, that it is very difficult to introduce the kind of changes associated with HRM. Finally, things are happening in employment that are neither a cause nor an effect of HRM but which could have some impact on it. These include the intensification of work, the choices of work location provided by technology and the divisive nature of a society in which many are idle and impoverished while many others are seriously over-worked.

4

Is HRM dead?

*What will happen to HRM when
traditional methods are gone*

PATRICK C. FLOOD

Department of Personnel and Employment Relations,
College of Business, University of Limerick

INTRODUCTION

In the previous chapter David Guest argued for a new orthodoxy in HRM, having first clarified the arguments for and against the HRM metaphor. We are currently witnessing a major transformation in the way in which business is organised and conducted. The business press reports on a daily basis the plethora of corporate restructurings which are taking place: mergers, demergers, strategic alliances, consortia, privatisations and attempts to create network organisational structures both within and between companies. These corporate restructurings frequently entail massive jolts to organisational memory, processes and routines including the human resource management systems within organisations.

The search for lean and mean competitive forms which can simultaneously deliver goods and services which are 'right first time', quickly, on time, cheaply and flexibly (Slack, 1991; Stalk *et al.*, 1993) has generated a management consultancy boom in the change management area. Futuristic competitive organisational forms, such as the much vaunted 'hollow corporation' dedicated to minimising internal and external transaction costs (including human resources) are regularly featured in the international business press as exemplars of how to structure the modern corporation. However, frequently the rhetoric outpaces reality. As Goffee and Hunt (1996) point out:

> what is remarkable about the language of modern organisational analysis is the extent to which it describes a world which literally does not exist . . . with the 'Virtual Organisation' the disappearing act is complete.

Delayering, downsizing and lean production can create a range of organisational pathologies including corporate anorexia, burn out and plummeting levels of trust and commitment among employees. The fallout of these organisational restructurings on human resource management is enormous and threatening. Organisational routines and memory become disrupted and even carefully planned human capital development plans become waylaid.

What challenges do these restructurings pose for the appropriate configuration of human resource management within the organisation? How can the HR function demonstrate the pay-off to careful investment in training and development and slow human capital formation when disruption and short-termism are omnipresent? What set of attributes is likely to be associated with the successful personnel manager of the future? What configuration of the human resource function is likely to be the most successful delivery mechanism in the 21st century? These are some of the themes which are explored in this chapter.

I begin by considering the two key questions posed in the title of this chapter: Is HRM dead? What will happen to HRM when traditional methods are gone? I approach the first question by reviewing some recent research which threatens to further fuel the fires of extinction of the specialist human resource function. This research is particularly associated with the work being carried out by David Metcalf and colleagues at the Centre for Economic Performance (CEP) at the London School of Economics, which suggests that there is little pay-off to maintaining a specialist human resource department.

However, there is some USA-based research which suggests that there is a pay-off to investing in human resource management of the 'high performance work systems' genre. The apparent gap between the UK and US research findings presents two challenging questions:

- How can we theoretically reconcile these divergent results?
- How should HRM be configured to create and embed high performance work systems within organisations?

I utilise the resource-based view (RBV) of the firm, introduced in Chapter 1, to attempt to answer the first question and as a mechanism theoretically to integrate these seemingly contradictory findings. The resource-based view of the firm has become an important theoretical perspective on the interface between strategy, human resource management and economic performance (Flood, Fong, Smith, O'Regan, Moore and Morley, 1997). The prescriptions of the RBV suggest that sets or 'bundles' of innovations in HRM be put in place in a direct shift away from traditional modes of organising. I then consider one particular set of human resource innovations, enumerated in Flood *et al.* (1995), which include managing without traditional strategic planning; owners; unions; personnel managers; supervisors; quality boundaries; and a full-time workforce. My treatment of a selection of these highlights both the costs and benefits of shifting away from traditional to non-traditional methods, and the associated set of change barriers presented to HR departments that are intent on creating a more effective reconfiguration.

Lastly I consider the implications of all of these research findings on the effectiveness of strategic innovations in HRM and consider what types of role are required by future 'would-be' successful HR managers. Paradoxically I find a combination of same old roles co-existing alongside the new although I envisage a considerable shift in emphasis from old roles to new ones. These new roles will also require particular sets of behavioural competencies and orientations and I question whether many HR professionals currently possess these attributes. I close by suggesting a possible TQM based focus for restructuring the HR function.

IS HRM DEAD?

Some UK research suggests that it should be. 'Big Hat – No Cattle' is the phrase famously used by Wickham Skinner (1987) in his polemic on human resource management. According to Skinner, grandiose HRM policies and practices developed by the specialist HR function often fail to demonstrate a performance pay-off at the organisational level. This taunt assumed renewed importance in 1994 due to the findings of Metcalf, Fernie and Woodland (1994) (using the authoritative third *Workplace Industrial Relations Survey* (WIRS3) reported by Millward *et al.* (1992)), which suggested that specialist personnel functions appeared to detract from both economic and industrial relations performance rather than enhance it.

In an attempt to rescue the valour of personnel management in the UK, the Institute of Personnel Development (IPD) then commissioned a further analysis of WIRS3 reported in Guest (1994). Guest begins his rebuttal by taking issue with the classification schemes used by Metcalf, Fernie and Woodland (1994) and argues that even on an *a priori* basis one would not expect to find any simple linear relationship existing between measures assessing the presence or absence of the HR function and organisational performance. This, Guest (1994) argues, is due in part to the fact that:

> *The contribution of personnel specialists [is] hard to identify because they work in partnership with line managers and succeed by exercising influence. In many cases, line managers take personnel decisions, perhaps within a framework established by the personnel department. Therefore, although we may be able to identify the impact of personnel decisions, we cannot always be sure whether the personnel specialist contributed towards them.*

Guest (1994) questions the negative findings of Metcalf, Fernie and Woodland (1994) and demonstrates that the presence of specialist directors spending more than half their time on personnel issues, with support staff, are likely to ensure that a wide range of 'positive' personnel policies and practices are in place. These policies and practices include performance appraisal, employee involvement schemes, problem-solving/quality circles, team briefing, merit pay for some categories of staff, job evaluation, sick pay and pension benefits. However the link between the presence of these policies and practices and organisational performance remains largely unproven. While specialist HR directors (presumably in an influential position) do result in the creation of 'better' HR practices, the pay-off to investment in such schemes (several of which are mandatory under statute in any case) is unclear.

This ambiguity of cause and effect presents difficulties for the specialist HR function. HR managers can establish policies and practices but ultimately the line manager is the predominant activator of these policies and practices in their daily encounters with employees. As a result, any direct linkage between the presence of a HR department and organisational performance is likely to be tenuous. The study of HR strategy, policy and performance in the National Health Service carried out by Guest and Peccei (1994) further bears testimony to the tenuous nature of the link between the presence of a specialist personnel function at unit level and various ratings of personnel effectiveness. Their research did find that the presence of an HR director at board level was associated with greater personnel influence over major organisational decisions which in turn predicted personnel effectiveness.

However, such results viewed from the perspective of a hard-nosed line manager provide a less than convincing rationale for further investment in the specialist HR function.

Rather more positive evidence has been amassed in the USA concerning the link between high performance work systems and organisational performance. How are we to resolve the apparently contradictory results of the US and UK research? One way of resolving this dilemma may lie in the argument presented by the 'resource-based' view of the firm which suggests that organisational processes – including the human resource system widely defined – can in certain circumstances provide a source of sustainable competitive advantage to the firm.

In the resource-based view (RBV), physical, organisational and human resources represent the opportunities available to the firm for the attainment of a sustainable competitive advantage. According to Barney (1991), a prominent exponent of the RBV, four criteria must be attributable to the relevant resource if it is to provide a source of sustainable competitive advantage (Wright *et al.*, 1994). These conditions are that the resource must:

- add positive value to the firm
- be unique or rare among competitors
- be imperfectly imitable
- be non-substitutable with respect to other resources available to competitors.

To the extent that the human resource management systems of the firm fulfil these four conditions we can argue that the configuration of the HR system may be a source of sustained competitive advantage. It is my contention that high performance work systems fulfill at least the first three of these four conditions. The term 'high performance work systems' has been defined by the US Department of Labour (1993) as the use of extensive recruitment, selection and training procedures, formal information sharing, attitude assessment, job design, grievance procedures and labour management participation programmes, performance appraisal, promotion and incentive compensation systems that recognise and reward employees. The use of most of these schemes has been positively linked to organisational level outcomes by a number of researchers. Huselid's (1995) study provides further evidence of this. In the most careful test to date of the impact of HRM practices of the high performance genre he demonstrates that there is an

> *economically and statistically significant impact on both intermediate employee outcomes (turnover and productivity) and short- and long-term measures of corporate financial performance.*

In the next section I argue that high performance work systems affect this impact on performance through their effect on the development of particular 'organisational capabilities'.

HRM AND THE CREATION OF COMPETITIVE CAPABILITIES[1]

In this section I examine the process through which 'high performance' HRM adds value. As Koch and McGrath (1996) point out, 'the way in which a firm manages its human resources is increasingly recognised as centrally important to its executives and has attracted academic attention in recent years'. HRM is a source of competitive advantage to the extent that HRM systems are aligned with critical capabilities (Flood and Olian, 1995). This is because HRM input, throughput and output processes that focus and stimulate employee behaviours that advance the goals of the business represent strategically aligned HRM systems. HRM processes which are appropriately aligned create and support adaptive efficiency (Hage and Atler, 1993) – i.e. the capacity to combine quality, speed, dependability, cost and adaptability. I consider each of these capabilities in turn.

Quality capability

The creation of quality capabilities involves selecting, developing, motivating and retaining a critical mass of talent that is customer focused but also able to quickly adapt to the delivery needs of tomorrow's products and processes (Flood and Olian, 1995). Numerous HRM systems are involved, including recruitment and selection, training and development for continuous learning, cross-functional teams and job rotations to develop multi-talented employees, and performance incentives for investment in learning and quality performance. Schneider and Bowen (1993) have demonstrated, in a series of studies, that HRM practices inside organisations are significantly correlated with customer perceptions of the service quality provided. The HRM practices which contribute to such customer perceptions of service quality include task design, supervisory feedback and reward practices, career growth and development opportunities, and employee orientation and training practices.

Speed capability

Bureaucratic HRM practices can affect speed to the extent that they create barriers to organisational responsiveness. Responsive HR systems involve pushing the HRM function down to line management and creating incentives tied to speed which do not compromise quality. Stalk, Evans and Shulman (1993) attribute Honda's competitive edge in the mid- to late-1980s to its ability to reduce cycle time, from design to testing to production. This took three years for Honda's new Acura division. By contrast General Motor's (GM) Saturn division needed almost six years to produce less than a third of the car volume. Honda relied on an existing, cross-functionally trained workforce that was sufficiently agile to shift toward a new product line. GM, however, had to create an entirely new customer-oriented workforce. A capable workforce can reduce time to market significantly. The latter point is borne out by a study in the steel industry concerned with the impact of four distinct HRM systems on cycle time (Ichniowski *et al.*, 1994). The HRM systems varied along a continuum at one end emphasising flexibility and participation (labelled system 1) to the other end of the continuum where narrowly tailored, quantitative production systems (system 4) characterised the approach taken. System 1 work practices push accountability and responsibility down to the line managers and also advocate the empowerment of teams and individual workers. Within system 1 there is a strong emphasis on the development of problem-solving skills, frequent worker management consultation and discussions, gainsharing compensation, valid selection procedures, and employment security. In contrast, system 4 HRM practices were characterised by infrequent problem-solving strategies or teams, rare worker management discussions or gainsharing procedures, unsophisticated selection procedures and low employment security, and a strong emphasis on the use of job classifications. The relationship between up-time (frequency of production shifts that met schedule) and a wide range of work practices was documented in the study.

This was reflected in significant productivity differences associated with each of the different HRM systems. System 1 had a 98 per cent achievement record on up-time compared to an 88 per cent hit rate under system 4 approaches. Interestingly, simultaneous bundling of a wide range of HRM practices (consultation, empowerment, utilisation of tacit knowledge, etc.) was critical to the overall productivity results since specific work practices, in isolation, were found to have little or no effect unless they were part of a larger systemic change. The latter finding is also supported by the work of Macy and Izumi (1993).

Dependability capability

This involves both engineering production systems and HRM systems. The production of a product consistently and reliably, that unfailingly satisfies customers' expectations is at the core of the dependability concept. Certainly, the quality movement has emphasised statistical process control systems to provide information on manufacturing variability, in the interest of systematically reducing the variability of a process. Machines and technology are frequently the source of some variability; however, ultimately most performance variability is man made. This is where HRM systems come into play. The other driver of dependable production (Flood and Olian, 1995) is a performance management system that:

● 'rewards the "right" kinds of employee behaviours'
● has a performance monitoring system sensitive to the level of performance consistency ('what percentage of customers received a follow-up call within the first five days of delivery of the product?')
● contains a reward system that is impacted in a meaningful way by the level of performance reliability (e.g. defect rates factored into quantitative measures of performance)
● has performance improvement systems designed to systematise performance processes and attack sources of unreliability (e.g. computerised form letters to provide one of five types of responses to job applicants).

The design process is the initial driver of dependability as this is where the process or product is designed to be right from the start, even if it costs more initially. Vesey (1991) argues that the incremental costs of correcting a product or process at later stages of the service or production chain is far in excess of original production costs. At each successive phase of the production process (e.g. from planning to product design, from product design to process design, from process design to production), the cost of defect correction increases exponentially. Vesey advocates concurrent engineering processes, relying heavily on multidisciplinary teams comprised of heterogeneously skilled individuals to eliminate unreliability at the source. Selection and training systems play a key part in creating this benchmark capability.

Cost capability

A further element in achieving incremental cost reductions is the involvement of workers in boosting productivity and eliminating waste through the use of continuous improvement, high involvement teams (Flood and Olian, 1995). Decentralisation produces better decisions because individuals with greater tacit knowledge are involved in decision-making, and can eliminate unnecessarily costly and non-value added tasks at the source.

Levine and Tyson (1991) reviewed some 29 studies on the effects of workplace participation on the costs of production to investigate this relationship further. Fourteen of the studies demonstrated that workplace participation had positive effects on production costs, two showed negative effects, and in 13 cases results were inconclusive. The authors concluded that the introduction of team-based participation was more likely to have a significant and durable impact on productivity when frontline employees were involved and when there was substantive and frequent participation in decision-making by shopfloor employees at the point of production. However, when organisational arrangements such as quality circles occurred in which information sharing was the focus rather than meaningful participation in actual decisions, the benefits were short lived. While quality circles draw on the tacit knowledge and creativity of workers, enthusiasm can often wane because the team lacks implementation authority. Other HRM practices that support a cost capability are gainsharing plans that reward employees for cost savings. Kaufman (1992) conducted a review of 112 gainsharing plans in manufacturing, observing the impact on labour hours input into a given product. Workers under IMPROSHARE plans (where bonuses equal half the increase in productivity) reduced defect and downtime rates by 23 per cent in the first year, and increased productivity over 15 per cent in three years.

Perhaps the most convincing evidence is provided by Macy and Izumi (1993) who conducted a meta analysis examining the relationship between 44 work practices, and productivity, quality and costs. Work practices were divided into three main categories:

● structural work practices (for example, job design and team work)
● human resources work practices (training and communications)
● technological work practices (computerisation, robotics).

This meta-analysis of 75 studies contrasting performance before and after introduction of new work practices indicated that practices were strongly related to increased productivity and reduced costs. In a selected sample of the field studies, introduction of new practices was associated with a 30 to 40 per cent improvement in performance. The larger the number of new work practices, the greater the increase in productivity and decline in costs. In the NUMMI study cited earlier (Pfeffer, 1994b), the new HRM practices in the Freemont California plant resulted in higher quality products with significantly fewer labour hours than was true for any other GM plant, achieving almost the same levels of performance as the benchmark Toyota plant in Japan.

The evidence demonstrates that HRM practices create key capabilities by eliminating non-value added processes and by stimulating process innovations. Key HRM processes in this regard are employee involvement strategies, incentive systems through gainsharing, and the development of a workforce capable of process improvements.

Adaptive capability

HRM systems can be rules bound, confining organisational players to the status quo, they can be benign – neither encouraging nor discouraging innovation, or they can provide the capability and incentives for experimentation and innovation (Flood and Olian, 1995).

Adaptive capabilities can be facilitated by the appropriate cross-functional skill building, incentive structures (e.g. tying rewards to suggestions and new improvements) and work structures such as teams which facilitate creativity and effective problem solving. The MIT study and related studies on auto assembly plants (Oliver *et al.*, 1993; Womack *et al.*, 1990) identified HRM 'buffers' (e.g. additional rules or layers of hierarchy) that impede agile adaptability to the needs of the market. In contrast, HRM systems that have created readiness for switches in product and process directions, and incentives for employees to welcome such changes, position the firm to be first to adapt in its market. This becomes a source of competitive advantage. While these studies suggest that 'high performance' HRM underpins the creation of these key capabilities it creates a very challenging agenda for HRM, particularly when we consider the countervailing pressures on HRM systems presented by the trend towards non-traditional modes of organisational structure.

MANAGING WITHOUT TRADITIONAL METHODS: COUNTERVAILING PRESSURES ON THE HRM FUNCTION

Do strategic innovations in HRM contribute to value enhancement of the value chain within organisations? This is a central issue for practitioners concerned with transforming the configuration of the HR process within organisations in an attempt to create greater linkage between human resources practices and processes and both the short-, medium- and long-term goals of the business. In the book, *Managing without Traditional Methods* (Flood *et al.*, 1995) this issue was addressed by focusing on a particular set of innovations in HRM which include managing without traditional: strategic planning; owners; unions; personnel managers; supervisors; quality boundaries; and a full-time workforce. In this section I consider four of these non-traditional innovations and discuss some of the HRM implications.

Managing without traditional strategic planning

Much has been written concerning the need to achieve strategic integration of the specialist HR function at board level, but the rhetoric has outpaced reality (*see* Legge, 1995 and Chapter 19 of this volume). In part this is due to the difficulties cited earlier in demonstrating an organisational level pay-off to maintaining a specialist HR function. Additionally, some premises associated with traditional approaches to HRM have been less than helpful. Smith (1995) has argued that the traditional approach to strategic human resource management (SHRM) is predicated upon three main assumptions:

1 that strategy has been decided;
2 that the role of SHRM is in strategy implementation; and
3 that even though the environment within which SHRM is enacted may change, the same central questions must be addressed concerning manpower flows, performance management, development and retention. Only the answer is deemed to change as strategic conditions change.

However, Lengnick Hall and Lengnick Hall (1988) argue that this is an inappropriate set of assumptions and suggest alternatives for the following reasons.

> *First . . . that the choice of strategy has not been made. Second . . . the management of human resources should contribute directly to strategy formulation and to strategy implementation . . . Third . . . that as strategic conditions vary, the fundamental [human resource] questions that must be addressed also vary because strategic issues reflect strategic contingencies.*

These authors are in fact recommending an emergent strategy approach to strategic human resource management which is much more attuned to changing business conditions and more experiential as distinct from algorithmic in emphasis (Gomez-Mejia, 1992). Flood and Olian (1995) distinguish between these two forms of HRM as follows:

> *Algorithmic (rules oriented) HRM systems emphasise behavioural control systems based on standardised operating procedures in the areas of recruitment, selection, rewards, work organisation and employee influence. Experiential HRM systems are more ad hoc and opportunistic in focus, dealing with informal and adaptive performance management feedback and response patterns.*

The experiential approach is increasingly being portrayed as an ideal model of a flexible approach to creating a close integration between the firm's business strategy and human resource strategy. However, it is extremely difficult in practice to accomplish skilfully this linkage. Research carried by the Leading Edge consortium at London Business School (Gratton *et al.*, 1996) suggests that creating a consistent linkage across HRM policy levers to create a closer fit between business strategy and human resource strategy is far from simple. This derives from the fact that human capital formation is a slow process and that the nature of the adjustment process is frequently in terms of downsizing and headcount reduction, which brings its own set of internal inconsistencies.

Additionally, the Lengnick Hall and Lengnick Hall (1988) prescription ignores the fact that most firms' strategy formulation process frequently does not involve the human resource director or manager (*see* the comments made by Guest in Chapter 3). This presents a formidable challenge to the HR director. However, as Carroll (1991) points out, HRM participation in the development of corporate strategy can take a number of forms, ranging from total strategic integration where the HR director is a full member of the planning board, to the design of implementation plans for the delivery of strategic goals. The latter in its most benign form involves an iterative process where the commentaries of the key HR personnel on the strategic plan become the basis for further discussion at board level or perhaps special presentations by the HR professional on an invited basis only. However, the exclusion of the senior HR manager in the strategic planning process seems an unbelievable waste of managerial resources particularly where the tendencies for low levels of co-ordination between functional areas within the top management team are already high, emphasising the need for the inclusion of boundary spanning staff, such as support personnel (Flood, Smith and Derfus, 1996; Hambrick, 1994).

The trend in managing without strategic planning in itself does not pose a threat to the human resource specialist. Rather it should be seen as an opportunity whereby the human resource manager actively manages the 'bottom-up' emphasis in emergent strategy formulation. This could include facilitating away-days, conducting customised diagnoses of the organisation's human resource capabilities to support the strategic intent of the business and recommending plans to ensure that any resultant human resource development gap is minimised.

Managing without traditional structures

A range of recent developments is breaking down traditional structures; downsizing, restructuring and rationalisation have characterised the late 1980s and early 1990s. In many industries the globalisation of competition, product markets and information has ratcheted up standards of productivity and quality. Ownership groups arising from corporate mergers, acquisitions, alliances and privatisation place new performance demands upon managers and employees in restructured firms. Advances in information systems and production technologies have facilitated the outsourcing of many operations traditionally carried out within the boundaries of the firm (Pinnington and Woolcock, 1995). Additionally many firms have attempted to outsource non-core competency areas and create satellites of sub-supplier and co-operating firms to cut operating costs. Many of these restructurings have also involved repeated waves of redundancy.

The impact of this organisational level restructuring on the HRM function is considerable. Restructuring typically results in a leaner organisation form without necessarily a proportionately reduced workload for the survivors of the restructuring. Therefore, for productivity to be at least maintained the survivors have to exert maximum effort levels and the human resource sub-systems have to be aligned with the strategic ambition of the business. As Wally *et al.* (1995) point out:

> in addition the quality of human resources has to be much higher to the extent that the organisation decreases its use of formalistic guides such as imposed procedure . . . research indicates that as an organisation becomes less formalised or less bureaucratic, the quality of managers becomes more highly correlated with performance (Gillen and Carroll, 1987). Also decentralisation and increased delegation require human resources to be much more competent than in a more centralised organisation.

Many of the restructurings taking place involve a greater emphasis on teamwork and team-based production and service routines. This is particularly so in the case of collaborative organisational forms such as strategic alliances and network-oriented organisations. There is a resultant increased stress on team behaviours – difficult to learn for some employees who perhaps have served much of their working lives in a perfunctory bureaucratic environment. Obtaining new employees with the requisite team orientations requires the redesign of many HRM selection, socialisation and development tools.

Restructurings have engendered considerable fear and distrust in management, particularly on the part of lower level employees (Hay Group, 1990). This has not been helped by the divergence between CEO pay and corporate performance witnessed in both the USA and the UK prompting some commentators to speak of 'the end of loyalty' (*see* Herriot, this volume, for a discussion of the consequences of this decline in loyalty on the psychological contract). The restructurings typically result in more decentralised organisational forms with increased use of delegation, teamwork and fragmented core–periphery workforces as covert control mechanisms.

Ironically, as O'Neill and Lenn (1995) point out, many restructurings involving downsizing simply do not result in a healthier organisation. The experience of middle managers is particularly relevant to this failure. Frequently middle managers are ignored in the planning process and are often the recipients of headcount reductions. Their experiences and perceptions of inequity are vividly captured by O'Neill and Lenn (1995) and include anger, anxiety, cynicism, resentment, resignation, desire for retribution and faltering hope. The anger of middle managers stems from the broken psychological contract based on loyalty and the jargonistic language which they are urged to adopt in restructuring – 'work smarter, not harder', 'rightsize, don't downsize', 'change is our friend', etc. Middle managers studied were angry at this language because it violated their sense of justice and implicitly glorified the downsizing process. Cynics might rephrase these exhortations as: 'downsize, rightsize, capsize'. The anxiety of middle managers stems not only from their fears for their own job security but also from the damage inflicted to the long-term capabilities of the company in terms of employee commitment. Cynicism is widespread among middle managers and is frequently directed at the CEO. The following quotation is typical of the frustrations experienced (O'Neill and Lenn, 1995):

> *I've never seen you in training sessions, like some of the CEOs I've read about. I've never seen you on my floor. The only time I see you is as a 'talking head' in some well rehearsed video. Those videos never answer the right questions.*

The resentment of middle managers towards downsizing stems from the gap between rhetoric and reality manifested in the urge to cut costs while maintaining – sometimes even increasing – CEO remuneration. Additionally, negative symbolism associated with maintaining executive dining facilities and corporate transportation fleets including company jets assume monumental proportions in the eyes of endangered middle managers. Demands for retribution frequently single out the CEO as a focus for blame. Finally, faltering pleas of hope were found by these researchers to exist among middle managers in the midst of downsizing as they clamour for leadership and vision to return them to the path of corporate salvation.

Managing without unions

The role of unions is discussed throughout Part Two of this book. However, at this point it is important to note that non-unionism has become increasingly common as markets deregulate and industrial restructuring moves occupations away from traditional union heartlands. Trade union membership suffered precipitous losses in the 1980s (Flood and Toner, 1995) in many countries. In the UK, debate has focused on the extent to which different shades of non-unionism are evident (Guest and Hoque, 1994a; Millward *et al.*, 1992). This debate began with Millward and colleagues' analysis of the third *Workplace Industrial Relations Survey* (WIRS3) which took place in 1990. The evidence from WIRS3 suggested that employees in the non-union private sector were considerably disadvantaged when compared to their unionised counterparts. On average, non-union employees in the UK were found to:

- have access to fewer information/communication channels
- receive less information from management
- work in organisations with fewer health and safety representatives
- record higher accident and injury rates
- have more dismissals of a non-redundancy nature
- have access to fewer grievance and disciplinary procedures

than union employees.

While non-union workplaces experienced virtually no strikes, they did record more compulsory redundancies and higher levels of labour turnover. Additionally, pay within the non-union sector was more often determined by market forces. Pay dispersion was higher for this sector and low pay a frequent occurrence. The non-union workplaces recorded higher usage levels of contingent workers and fewer personnel specialists than in unionised workplaces.

Some Catch-22s are associated, however, with union avoidance. Flood and Toner (1995; 1997) argue that even for the so called 'best' non-union companies – the large, high wage, non-union employers – the benefits which might be expected to accrue from union avoidance in terms of wage costs and flexibility are considerably constrained when there is a strong external union presence in the local labour market. They found that the fear of triggering a potential unionisation drive considerably restricts the exercise of unfettered managerial prerogative within large non-union firms. Their research indicates that large non-union companies must match the wages and benefits of similar unionised firms in order to avoid a potential unionisation drive. Additionally, they are frequently afraid to exercise unilateral change initiatives for fear of triggering unionisation. While unions are often accused of encouraging members to air trivial grievances, the non-union companies studied were also found to encourage the venting of these grievances in order to avoid a climate of discontent developing. Similarly, the non-union companies studied seemed unwilling to crack down on absenteeism or to dismiss unsatisfactory workers for fear of encouraging a unionisation drive. A considerable climate of indulgence existed in several of the companies studied, much more than might be expected to exist in non-union companies which are often seen as monolithic authoritarian regimes.

A rather broader conception of non-union companies to encompass the various shades of non-unionism – the 'good, the bad and the ugly' – has however recently been developed by Guest and Hoque (1994a). Flood and Toner's (1995) Catch-22 research suggests that HRM specialists in large high wage companies may find themselves on the horns of a dilemma. Their CEOs frequently cite the founding principles of the company in support of their union avoidance stance. According to these founding principles, unionisation is often seen by them to reflect a failure to manage the workforce properly. In practice, however, they allow more indulgent work practices to develop. A further Catch-22 is suggested by the recent study by the Institute of Work Psychology (1996) in relation to innovation in UK manufacturing. Their study of small and medium-sized companies indicates that unionised companies record the highest rates of innovation. Potentially, therefore, the absence of a union may mean that a tacit knowledge capturing mechanism is lost. There are echoes here of Freeman and Medoff's two faces of unionism argument (Freeman and Medoff, 1979).

The findings cited here and the research by Guest and Hoque (1994a) suggest that there is considerable variation between non-union workplaces. Those at the smaller end of the size scale are more likely to be of the 'no union – no HRM' genre while those at the upper end of the size scale are more likely to be of the 'no union – sophisticated HRM' variety. This variation in approach implies that no universal non-union HRM model is practised and that a contingency model of HRM is more appropriate.

Managing without traditional owners

This phrase is used by Van Neerven, Bruining and Paauwe (1995) in their discussion of HRM in management buyout firms. Many firms in their attempt to pare back to their core competencies are disposing of business divisions. This can lead to the phenomenon of management buyout where the existing management of the endangered division or branch pool their resources to mount an equity buyout of the company. In circumstances where employees participate in this buyout by contributing their savings and or redundancy payments the buyout is typically termed an employee buyout. A variety of researchers including Kaplan (1988; 1989), Bruining (1992), Wright and Coyne (1985) have recorded improved economic performance in the majority of buyout companies studied. Their research indicates that this improvement in performance derives at least in part from alterations made to the internal labour markets of the buyout firm. Overhead costs are often reduced, bureaucratic inertia is eliminated, decision-making at the top is frequently accelerated, partly as a reflection of the newly found autonomy. The buyout typically involves a more focused orientation in the firm's human resource policies and practices. In particular cases, share ownership structures are developed which allow employees to purchase shares in the company. This can, as Bradley and Nejad (1989) argue have positive effects provided sufficient numbers of employees purchase shares so as to avoid schisms developing between takers and non-takers. Their research at the National Freight Consortium (NFC) demonstrated that the buyout there had positive effects on motivation, commitment, cost-consciousness, self-supervision, self-monitoring and vertical monitoring. These results suggest that in the post-buyout phase tremendous attention is placed to reinvention of HRM policies and procedures in order to emphasise cost efficiencies and management of behaviour in line with the goals of the business. Managers will take advantage of the momentum associated with the buyout to restructure employment relationships and performance systems. Van Neerven *et al.* (1995) point out:

> *The event of a buyout provides a cornucopia of opportunities for management to be critical, to dot the i's, and to institute corrective actions where needed. A crucial advantage is the momentum for change that a buyout evokes. Under normal circumstances management tends to proceed slowly and is impeded by bureaucratic inertia, employee aversion to change and the opposition from labour unions and works council. During and immediately after a buyout such forces against change disappear or are minimal.*

HRM in buyouts typically covers three areas according to Van Neerven *et al.* (1995). First, more attention is directed towards improving the way in which leaders and subordinates interact. This typically involves greater decentralisation of decision-making facilitated by the introduction of team-based mechanisms and the introduction of performance appraisal at all levels of the organisation. Second, more attention is given to quality issues, training and consultation. In their study of Boekhoven-Bosch (a former Elsevier subsidiary) it was seen that employees received more training opportunities and an increase in the number of training courses at all levels. Personal responsibility for product and service quality became a key strategic implementation tactic. Third, the relationship between line management and the personnel department was altered. After the buyout the personnel department was transformed from a specialised, regulating and bureaucratic body to one with an integral task in management support. There was also a more prominent role for line management in the implementation of HRM policy. This brings me to considering HRM without HR managers.

Human resource management without human resource managers

Using a transaction costs (TCT) framework we can distinguish between the 'make' or 'buy' decision in HRM. These are two distinct alternative approaches through which HRM can be effected:

1 a decision to 'make' HRM within the boundaries of the firm
2 purchase HRM outside the boundaries of the firm through some outsourcing arrangement.

Taken to its extreme it is possible completely to outsource specialist HRM departments and services, leading to a scenario of HRM without HR managers. While there seems to be a generalised shift within organisations from 'make' to buy as organisations refocus on their core competencies, this shift has dramatic implications for the traditionally configured HR function, particularly in an era where the line manager is in the ascendant. Paauwe (1995) broadens the TCT framework to encompass this shift to line management by distinguishing between internalising (the shift from specialist staff to regular line management) and externalising (the shift from 'make to buy') where the possibility of effecting the personnel function from outside rather than inside the firm is considered.

The TCT framework suggests that organisations fundamentally revisit the issue of whether HRM is best effected within or outside of the organisation. The first and most important question is whether the HRM function/department is necessary and useful. If the answer to that question is positive the issue still remains as to how it should be effected within the organisation. This may be either through a partnership between the specialist HR department and the line managers, solely effected by the HR department or effected solely through the line manager. Should a 'buy' decision be made, then the HR function and the HR department's activities become candidates for outsourcing. Figure 4.1 outlines Paauwe's (1995) TCT framework.

I limit my discussion to quadrants B, C and D. When the line manager assumes full responsibility for personnel management activities then the specialist HR department is in theory unnecessary. In practice, however, line managers are often too busy fully to embrace HR techniques and practices and this results in a range of dysfunctional situations (Paauwe, 1995) including a lack of synergy arising from:

- a lack of opportunity to learn from personnel specialists
- inefficiency and duplication as each manager invents his/her own methods of HR management
- lack of uniformity in working conditions
- unstructured *ad hoc* personnel policies.

Another obvious option is using the outsourcing mechanisms in Paauwe's (1995) framework (see Figure 4.1 (B) and (C)). There he distinguishes between varying degrees of outsourcing the personnel function including partial outsourcing, contract management, specialised in-house units, internal consultancy/profit centres, agencies, leased employees and teleworking.

Partial outsourcing involves a core–peripheral approach to personnel management whereby certain activities are deemed to be more effectively carried out externally. Examples here might include executive search, graduate recruitment, temporary help and

Focus of change

	Internalising (shift from staff to regular line workers)	Externalising (outsourcing)

Minor changes	**A**
	• integral management
	• self-managing teams
	• core and peripheral
	  personnel activities
		B
		• outsourcing partially
		• contract management
		• specialised in-house units
		• internal consultancy/
		  profit centre

Major changes	**D**
	• personnel management
	  without personnel
	  managers
		C
		• agencies
		• leased employees
		• teleworking

(left axis label: Extent of change)

Fig. 4.1 Alternative HRM delivery: mechanisms found in practice

Source: Paauwe, 1995
(Reprinted by permission of Addison Wesley Longman Ltd)

outplacement services. The key decision criteria (Torrington, 1986) seem to include issues concerning cost efficiencies, quality, time availability and need for comparability.

Internal consultancy/zero budgeting is a situation whereby the HR department is not given a budget but must derive its revenue by contracting within the organisation to provide certain services to units/departments based on a fixed-term price contract.

Specialised in-house units can include internal HR consultancy-type services based on a project management basis. Occasionally these develop when executives create such units in anticipation of executive job loss.

External consultancies/agencies are another method of externalising whereby the bulk of selection, recruitment, training, payroll etc. is passed over to an external consultancy. Leased employees derive typically from core-periphery manpower strategies, whereby firms secure their manpower requirements directly from an agency that is the contracting party with the individuals concerned. The agency in turn acts as the individual's employer taking care of tax deductions, insurance etc. Dell Computers typically utilise this system for their manpower requirements.

Teleworking has become increasingly common and can include (Paauwe, 1995) lone tele-hunters, lone teleworkers and tele-outposts. The lone telehunters are freelancers/sub-contractors whose bond to the organisation is entirely monetisable. The teleworkers by contrast typically have both monetisable and relational aspects to their relationships with their companies.

Tele-outposts exploit regional availability of skilled workers at lower wages costs than are available where the work is produced. Information processing carried out in Ireland for insurance companies based in the USA is just one example of this.

All of the trends encountered, when coupled with the drive to eliminate or reduce transaction costs, present a difficult set of scenarios for the specialist HR function to respond to.

RESTRUCTURING THE HR DEPARTMENT: BEHAVIOURAL ROLE REQUIREMENTS

Ulrich (1995) argues that HR work deserves to be seen as work which has outcomes, knowledge, competence, codes of behaviour, and monitoring roles. As we have seen it is far from easy to convince line managers that they should share this perception. HR departments therefore face formidable challenges in reconfiguring their structures, roles and responsibilities. Yet changes are necessary. I shall now consider some salient issues surrounding the behavioural and knowledge requirements of HR executives who seek to be successful in the 21st century.

All the trends I have examined imply that stress will increasingly be placed upon demonstrating a link between HR activities and organisational effectiveness. The growing evidence on the pay-off to particular bundlings of HR activities in the form of 'high performance work systems' is particularly encouraging in this regard. However, it demands that HR professionals become conversant with issues of strategy and with explicating the HR – strategy – performance linkages. A new role emphasis on value chain enhancement is a pre-requisite for '21st century'-oriented HRM. Ulrich (1995) sets out some future key roles (see Fig. 4.2).

The successful HR manager must continue to embrace each of the four roles outlined in Fig. 4.2 but will need to shift the emphasis in terms of the time spent in favour of the strategic partner/change agent role. Administrative inefficiencies are a major irritation to busy line managers and information technology can now automate much of the mundane work

Fig. 4.2 Future HRM roles

Source: Ulrich, 1995
(Reprinted with permission from *Transformation*,
the journal of Gemini Consulting)

which has historically over-burdened HR managers and led to charges of administrative inefficiency. The behavioural requirements of HR managers who wish effectively to execute the roles of strategic partner, change agent and credible employee champion are interesting to consider. Carroll (1991) cites a fascinating study of the behavioural requirements of the HR managers carried out by Holder (1986). This delineated two types of HR manager: Type A and Type B. 'Type A' HR managers carried respect, credibility and influence within their organisations. 'Type B' HR managers are in the traditional HR mould. They focus primarily on their functional area of specialism, are reactive rather than proactive and typically wait for requests to become involved in problems rather than offering inputs first. They seek to please other HR specialists rather than top management and possess a 'bounded functional' view of their role. As Caroll (1991) points out:

> *Type A managers, in contrast [to Type B], eschew traditional HRM roles, viewing themselves first and foremost as business managers and strategic partners to top management. These managers develop a broad understanding of the entire business in all its functional aspects and take a deep interest in the firms overall strategy and goals. They actively search out problems that their HR knowledge and skills can address. They adopt an internal marketing orientation, viewing other functional areas as key clients whose needs must be met. In companies with Type A managers, HRM activities integrate business strategies with the need of key clients.*

On this basis, Type B managers would seem to fit in Ulrich's 'administrative expert' or Tyson's (1987) 'clerk of works' model. Type A managers would seem to fit within Ulrich's 'change manager/strategic partner' role set which is similar to Tyson's 'architect' model of HRM and Storey's (1992) 'changemakers'.

In view of the increased competitive turbulence and complexity which I described under the title of 'Managing without traditional methods' (*see* pp 59–67), it seems likely that demand for Type A HR managers will increase. However, an efficient administrative system – effected either through a clerical function or, more likely, an effective information technology management base – is paramount to free up time for the HR manager to operate as a strategic partner to line managers. The demand for Type B managers will decrease and is vulnerable to decreased unionisation of the workforce and to potential automation. The managerial values and personal orientations of the HR manager are also relevant here. A study by Miner (1976) cited by Carroll (1991) investigated the extent to which HRM professionals possessed the will to manage. It found dramatic results:

> *The data supports the hypothesis that the motivation to manage is relatively low among personnel and industrial relations managers. At the maximum, middle managers in the field appear to be at the same level as the average first-line supervisor in the other functional areas. Top managers appear to fall at a point roughly intermediate between lower and middle-level managers in other areas of the business.*

While it could be argued that the results of Miner's study are dated and that the managers at the millennium are a different breed in terms of motivation to manage, a definitive answer to this question requires further empirical study. However, it is the author's opinion, having taught many cohorts of IPD students, that the will to manage is a key behavioural predictor of the successful HRM specialist who is likely to become a regular member of the top management team in their respective organisation. It is, further, the author's estimate that this attribute is very unevenly distributed among students on IPD courses. It would be interesting to replicate this experiment in the 1990s using a large-scale survey including ratings of personnel effectiveness by line managers.

The lack of strategic orientation in the face of increasingly complex organisational structures does not augur well for the HRM department staffed by Holder's (1986) Type A managers. This will be particularly worrying if the profession continues to attract candidates who are weak on the will to manage and possess a limited perspective of business strategy. The responsibility for HR activities will also become less centralised as tasks are devolved to the line managers. However, a matrix-style HR function may also develop whereby (Carroll, 1991):

A generalist manager would oversee a particular plant or group of employees and co-ordinate the different specialists who handle specific HRM functions (staffing, training and so on) for that unit . . . in a sense, the generalist HR manager would function much as the product manager in other organisational units . . . this approach could suit particular units, while providing the integration of diverse HRM functions to ensure consistent and effective implementation of overall strategy.

Cardy and Robbins (1995) usefully summarise the major shifts in focus required by the specialist HR function by comparing and contrasting traditional HRM and total quality HRM (TQHRM). Their major differences are summarised as follows. First, in terms of the HRM process, traditional HRM assumes a unilateral role with an administrative focus, and high centralisation. In contrast, a total quality approach to HRM requires a consulting and developmental role and high levels of decentralisation. There are major changes too in the characteristic content of HRM policies (and therefore the skills and fields of knowledge needed by HR managers). Building on the comments made in Chapter 1, the shift is from the need for law-based knowledge to knowledge based on a pluralist set of customs, from compartmentalised policies and techniques to holistic methods, from worker-oriented to systems-oriented interventions, from performance measures to satisfaction measures, and from job-based to person-based tools and techniques.

Many of the behavioural requirements described are encapsulated by their TQHRM framework. This embraces a consulting role, decentralisation to line management and a 'market-in' (i.e. customer requirements focus) emphasis rather than a 'product-out' bias. The content emphasis is on designing HRM tools and techniques which adopt a pluralistic system-wide emphasis. A content emphasis requires more attention to the design of customer-focused metrics which are strongly person rather than job based. The emphasis on person metrics rather than job metrics reflects an increasing awareness of the importance of 'attitude' in creating a customer-focused workforce. HRM performance metrics have historically shied away from utilising behavioural measures because of their inherent subjectivity. Strongly customer-focused companies tend to include a battery of value-based metrics as well as the more quantifiable job performance metrics. Clearly, despite the shift away from non-traditional methods, there is a future for an agile human resource function but it will require a creative response to the restructuring initiatives which we have listed. In particular, successful HR functions will require leadership and vision to re-equip HR specialists with the requisite knowledge of competitive strategy and strategy implementation skills needed for success in the 21st century.

CONCLUSION

The challenge for HR specialists is to reconcile the different prescriptions lauded by writers on high performance systems within their own organisational contexts. On the one hand there is evidence that investing in participatory management systems actually pays off. On the other hand there is also evidence that shifting away from perfunctory HRM systems is by no means an easy task. The lessons of managing without traditional methods indicates that structural realignments are often necessary to reinforce the desired behavioural norms demanded by the shift to high involvement management. Structural form alterations which seem to be widespread include the new emphasis on decentralisation, the emergence of global matrix-based organisations such as the giant Asea Brown Boveri and the increased accountability inherent in profit-centred organisational arrangements. The emergence of network organisational forms and the increasing popularity of strategic alliances and joint ventures suggests a much more complex role for the human resource specialist in the information society. Innovative approaches and brokerage skills will be the hallmark of the successful HR specialist in the next decade, skilled in utilising information technology and adept at routinising and automating standard personnel tasks. One example of this is provided by Nortel in Ireland. It has placed all its personnel policies and procedures on a web page which is freely accessed by all employees and managers. Freed from the more mundane personnel tasks, the personnel specialist can concentrate on facilitating the introduction of organisational change. The increasing tendency of companies to dispense with more traditional management approaches implies that change management will be a key role in tandem with that of organisational innovator. More and more new businesses will be knowledge based and it will be especially necessary to understand how to manage professionals and to be creative in the design of compensation packages for such groups. Within the public sector, trade unions will remain strong for at least another decade. However, in the manufacturing sector the increasing amount of foreign direct investment emanating from North America suggests that the non-union sector will continue to increase. Additionally, many smaller service-based organisations will spring up as Internet-based business gathers momentum. For them non-unionism will be the norm. The personnel specialist of the future will need to be expert in organisational design as new and innovative organisational forms emerge. However, the standard issue of how to attract, induct, motivate and train employees suggests a continuing need for the personnel specialist. Computer-based training will become much more widespread and the role of some HRM specialists will be to quality audit the vast plethora of educational resources available through the Internet.

The qualifications mix of the next generation of top HR professionals is likely to include broader MBA-type degrees rather than specialist and narrowly defined programmes. This presents challenges for specialist providers such as the IPD to broaden their degree programmes. The more generalist business manager will also have an important role to play in the transformation of the human resource function. Clearly, the challenge is for the HRM specialists to broaden their business knowledge base, become adroit in enabling change management as required by the shift to managing without traditional methods and truly to become expert in organisational design. Those HR specialists who recognise the need to anticipate the knowledge requirements necessary to advance their careers not as narrow specialists but as broadly based business managers will thrive in the information society.

Notes

[1] I am intellectually indebted to Judy Olian, University of Maryland at College Park for her insights on the theoretical linkages between organisational capabilities and human resource management. I am also very grateful to my co-authors of *Managing Without Traditional Methods* for the many insights which they provided, particularly Martin J. Gannon and Jaap Paauwe.

[2] I wish to thank Stephen J. Carroll at the University of Maryland at College Park for kindly supplying various references on HRM roles and responsibilities.

5

Re-engineering's fragile promise: HRM prospects for delivery

MIKE ORAM

Strategic HRM Consultant and
IPD Vice-President, Membership and Education

INTRODUCTION

There is no news like bad news. As a nation, we seem to take delight in things going wrong so we can pick over the remains and pronounce our opinions on how the tragedy could have been avoided . . . if only the people responsible (hardly ever the commentator) had done 'this' or 'that' . . . But we then conclude, upon largely circumstantial evidence, that 'this' or 'that's' time was not of the hour, and we pass on to the next fad to be picked over, and so on *ad infinitum*. I would therefore like to start with some good news. Business process re-engineering (BPR) is alive and kicking and being successfully delivered in Britain. The bad news, however, follows, and it is that there are many more 'failures' than successes and that the prime cause of failure is inadequate attention to the human resource aspects. Conversely, where there has been 'success' the human resource issues have been central to the main issues being addressed, so there is scope for hope.

Before considering the various contributory and other factors, I would like to describe what I accept BPR to be, otherwise, there could be no rationalisation of my assumptions of 'success' or 'failure'. Some assert that re-engineering is the process that never was and to a large extent I agree. It is not in itself a distinct process but more a philosophy of rethinking the fundaments of an organisation and addressing the operating means as interconnecting and integrated processes rather than functions. But even as a concept, re-engineering is, some say, a non-event; nothing new over organisation development, TQM, socio-technical design and others (but *see* the outline of changes in organisational form in Chapter 1). However, Enid Mumford, who has been involved with organisational development and change longer than most, has grudgingly acknowledged BPR's existence as a *philosophy* as distinct from a *process* and at least on this we are in agreement (Mumford, 1995). I therefore have difficulty in accepting a recent assertion by Mumford and Hendricks (1996) that re-engineering has totally 'failed' or that it is 'dead'. These are blanket assertions that fly in the face of the evidence and, in my view, throw healthy BPR babies out with the proverbial bath water. We need to study healthy BPR babies as much as sick ones if we are to understand and to learn about the physiology and psychology of process re-engineering.

EXAMPLE RE-ENGINEERING PROJECTS

The following are a small sample of some of the outcomes of effective process re-engineering from five companies featured in a study by myself and Richard Wellins in a book called *Re-engineering's Missing Ingredient – the Human Factor* (Oram and Wellins, 1995).

- **Toshiba** in Plymouth undertook a fundamental rethink of its operations that increased productivity threefold, removed barriers and has stood the test of time, the company moving from number five in the UK colour TV league to pole position.
- Within two years **Bass** transformed its 'Cinderella' pubs operation, shunned at one time by all able and ambitious graduates, into one of its star performers, now one of the most popular spots for bright and aspiring people.
- **Rank Xerox** doubled its return on assets and met other targets including ratings on customer satisfaction, employee satisfaction and market share.
- **The Royal Bank of Scotland** went from near loss-making to £200 million incremental profit within two years.
- **The Leicester Royal Infirmary National Health Trust**, which has, for three years, continued to provide a model of what re-engineering can really deliver when properly conducted.

Examples of what has been achieved in Leicester in a remarkably short time include cutting diagnostic testing from 79 hours to 40 minutes. The time patients have to wait for diagnosis in one department is down from 8+ weeks and four visits, to two hours and one visit. Significantly improved teamwork has been achieved in the accident and emergency department, and an almost 50 per cent cut in waiting time for theatre. Everyone seems satisfied, not least the patients. And staff appear to have gained much: in job interest and satisfaction brought about by doing what they feel to be a better job and, in many cases, wider interest through multiskilling plus greater personal accountability. One staff member says 're-engineering has enhanced my working life.'

Comparing the approaches of these five cases one would be hard pressed to consider that they adopted anything approaching similar methods. Nevertheless there are remarkable consistencies when one compares methodologies. I use the word 'methodology' as distinct from 'method' to emphasise application of a set of principles that in any particular situation is reduced to methods uniquely suitable to the particular situation. The situation in nearly all circumstances will be very different. In the case of BPR, every BPR situation will be unique and the methods in each case will necessarily be different. What, therefore, can one observe that enables us to conclude that there is something consistent and uniform in the sets of principles and methodologies that have been applied? There seems to be seven consistencies, outlined as follows in no order of priority:

1 A combination of extensive 'project' scope and a relatively short timescale for delivery of the transformational change.

2 The adoption, organisationally, of something quite new and probably previously unthinkable.

3 A prime driving force and focus upon the attainment of super-ordinate goals.

4 Equal weight and attention given to operations, information systems and both internal and external people issues (typically 'customer' and 'employee' issues).

5 Issues are addressed with *holistic* sensitivity and attention.

6 Activities are generally founded on consideration of 'processes', being cycles of activity whereby inputs (resources) are converted into internal and external outputs (goods or services).

7 Resources (people and money), adequate to address all or most of the issues and difficulties arising, are made available.

These, to my mind, are consistently the issues that characterise successful re-engineering initiatives.

RISK MANAGEMENT

As suggested earlier, many people say that re-engineering's time has passed or that 'it' never really existed except in the imaginations of a few misguided or self-satisfying individuals; 'no coherent and consistent foundation; no supporting theory'. The points made here are not in support of re-engineering as a concept, for whether or not to reengineer in any particular case is wholly a matter for the stakeholders. Rather, for those who choose to reengineer the point is that to do so requires courage, preparation, resources in considerable measure and skills and sensitivities of a particular kind, especially as regards HRM matters. Re-engineering can *only* be safely delivered if certain issues, including the HR issues, are addressed. Re-engineering is unquestionably a risky business and risk assessment and management should be at its core. Management of the human resource risks is paramount.

MISSING INGREDIENTS AND BARRIERS

In a survey published in 1994 of 600 American and European companies, over 70 per cent believed they were involved in some form of re-engineering project (Oram and Wellins, 1995). A 1994 UK survey found 59 per cent of organisations planning or undertaking BPR activity (CSC Index, 1994). Far from being a 'dead' issue, re-engineering seems to be very much alive – whether it is healthy is another issue. I cannot deny that most BPR initiatives 'fail' in terms of not bringing about the hoped-for outcomes and I am interested to identify why this may be. But many *do* succeed, some far beyond original expectations. It seems logical to assess why those that 'succeed', do succeed, and why those that 'fail', fail. A gap analysis, in each case, identifies key ingredients necessary for success.

Of all the issues related to re-engineering processes, those that are obviously related to direct operations and the associated information systems seem to be the ones given most attention and investment. Yet, successful re-engineering depends essentially on building total workforce commitment to unprecedented change. In most 'failures', a lack of such commitment can easily be recognised. In all 'successes', considerable efforts, investments and skills have invariably been applied in bringing about commitment. These issues relate to the people in the enterprise. Inattention to the 'people bits' is the ingredient that is most commonly missing.

Enid Mumford (Mumford, 1995; Mumford and Hendricks, 1996) suggests that the success of a proposed change depends on the willingness of your employees to 'accept it with enthusiasm and implement it with care'. This may be an ideal if you follow a 'soft' approach to HRM but it is not, in my view, a prerequisite. For example, the commitment of Japanese workers, by common consent, is at a very high level. Evidence from comparative research done during the 1980s by the Metalworkers Union in Japan showed, nevertheless, that the satisfaction of Japanese workers with their lot was among the lowest in the world; yet their commitment and the care with which they exercised it is unquestioned.

More evidence of the difficulties of delivering effective re-engineering can be found from the work of Grint and Willcocks (1995). Out of nine critical success factors, six were related to human and political issues. Indeed, the collective response, when respondents were asked what they had learned from their BPR experiences, was summarised as 'pay much earlier, focused attention to the human and political issues inherent in BPR'.

In Fig. 5.1 the internal and external influences acting upon the physical/operational and behavioural influences, are illustrated. To transform an organisation, *all four quadrants* need to be addressed satisfactorily and each needs to take the others into account. The issues given the least attention are represented by the shaded area.

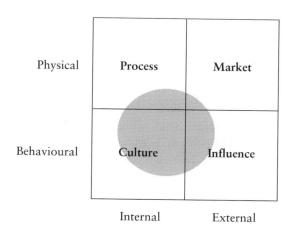

Fig. 5.1 The 'missing ingredient'

Grint and Willcocks (1995), who are information management and technology specialists, not HRM specialists, conclude: 'change management needs to be put at the core of BPR activity', and identify, 'the need for dealing with, rather than marginalising, human, social and political issues'. From all available sources of empirical evidence, and also from our experience, Oram and Wellins (1995) conclude that there are five main barriers to successful delivery of process re-engineering. Those barriers and their associated indicative solutions, are shown in Fig. 5.2.

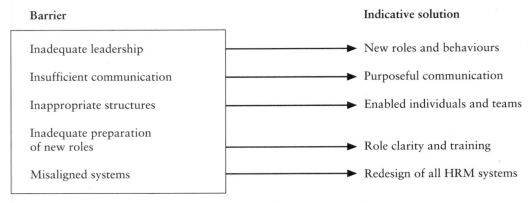

Fig. 5.2 Human delivery barriers and solutions

Inadequate leadership

Inadequate leadership is the first and fundamental barrier to successful re-engineering; virtually every study of the process has acknowledged the importance of leadership. Leadership is necessary at every level but is especially critical at the CEO level. For the HR practitioner, leading at a functional level is at least a prerequisite and gives him or her foundation credibility. Without offering strategic leadership of the HRM issues however, HR practitioners will inevitably be marginalised; leadership unquestionably begins at home.

In Chapter 1 the issue of trust was raised. Both Andrews (1994) and Handy (1995) emphasise the criticality of trust within empowerment programmes. In a recipe for success, lack of the smallest ingredient can make all the difference, especially face-to-face contact. Handy (1995) says 'Visionary leaders, no matter how articulate, are not enough. A shared commitment still requires personal contact to make it real . . . High Tech has to be balanced by High Touch to build High Trust organisations.' Andrews (1994) emphasises the extent to which *mistrust* by leaders and/or participants in empowerment and quality programmes undermines the capability for success. Trust is the adhesive required to hold all the leadership building blocks together.

A study by Howard and Wellins (1994) has identified specific new roles for those involved at all levels of leadership within high-involvement programmes. Figure 5.3 does not show *optional* elements. Increasingly, aspects of *all* of these are required in the roles that executives are adopting and despite 'empowerment' and apparent letting go of hitherto cherished powers and authorities, whatever new organisational and job structures evolve during a re-engineering programme, there is no doubt that the requirement for leadership in all its forms is enhanced rather than reduced. This is no less the case for human resource managers whose functional powers may seem to have been dispersed to line management. Wilson, George, Wellins and Byham (1994) identify the realities of moves towards empowered teams within organisations which have parallels with much of what goes on within re-engineering. These are summarised in Fig. 5.4.

Role	Role description
Delegator	Moves decision-making to lower job levels; sees that responsibility and authority accompany job tasks
Visionary	Visualises a more perfect future; expresses potential achievements of the work unit consistent with the organisation's vision
Change agent	Looks for better ways to perform work by challenging current paradigms and encouraging improvement ideas from direct reports and external stakeholders
Inspirer	Communicates the vision and inspires acceptance of and commitment to it
Model (trust)	Personally illustrates priorities and values; is both trusting and trustworthy
Coach	Helps others learn to be self-sufficient through personal development and arranging learning environments
Team builder	Establishes and supports teams that engage in self-managing activities
Supporter	Constantly expresses confidence in the self-sufficiency direct reports and treats their mistakes as learning opportunities
Champion	Visibly celebrates accomplishments of direct reports; promotes their best ideas to higher management
Facilitator	Provides resources (materials, information, etc.) for the work group; removes obstacles that impede the group's progress
Partner	Builds alliances with and communication bridges to other work units and external partners

Fig. 5.3 New roles for high involvement leaders

The transition to these new models is not easy for anyone. People get used to the order of things; it is rather like the grown up 'child' coming to advise and influence the parent on particular issues, but with the parent's overall wisdom and counsel still holding sway and being respected, and such respect increasingly having to be 'earned' rather than being blindly accepted. The challenges in rapidly changing organisations are immense and many who have spent much of their career 'controlling' subordinates cannot find new more egalitarian ways an easy fit. Likewise, those who have constantly been given directions may not

---

1 **Teams always need good leaders** – it is the nature of leadership that changes

---

2 **Leaders gain power in the transition to teams** – from enabling process improvements, attracting resources, removing barriers, making things happen outside the team, helping team members realise their potential

---

3 **Most leaders are capable of making the transition successfully** – 20% will survive whatever, 20% will not make it, 60% will make the transformation if given help.

---

4 **New leaders must be direct** – they need to loosen reins, not drop them; move from giving directions to providing direction

---

5 **Leaders need to relax** – it is OK to make mistakes – admitting and learning from mistakes will earn leaders respect faster than any other type of behaviour

---

Fig. 5.4 New realities of leadership

find requirements for self-direction always comfortable or easy. New skills and attitudes have to be developed. This highlights the need for training and support at all levels. Given such support, the realities begin to be at least promising.

Insufficient communication

Communicating the compelling case for change is an overriding task and one of the greatest barriers to be overcome. Many who are involved with transformational change say that you cannot communicate too much; that is true, so long as what is to be communicated is appropriate and the timing is right. The volume, content and manner of communication are all important issues and are considerable challenges to be faced. Communication at the 'wrong' time (both too early and too late) can, nevertheless, be as useless as no communication at all. Just in time communications are what are required. The link between the organisation's corporate strategy and its people is the initial bridge that has to be built. This requires multidirectional communication which involves significant two-way *listening*, again at the right time.

While most people will assert that communication is important, regrettably few of them can describe what they mean by 'good communication', or can even intelligently describe the process or purposes of communication beyond a few methods of communicating. Francis (1987) usefully breaks down the processes of communication into four main segments, each showing the different *purposes* for communications:

● communications for sharing the vision or mission
● communications for integrating effort

- communications for making intelligent decisions
- communications for sustaining a 'healthy' community.

For each of these purposes, there are three supporting elements:

- Communications for sharing the vision or mission:
  - persuasive management
  - compelling vision
  - sensitivity to the external environment.

- Communications for integrating effort:
  - integrating mechanisms
  - helpful geography e.g. workplace layout
  - downward flow.

- Communications for making intelligent decisions:
  - communications skills
  - apt administration
  - upward flow.

- Communications for sustaining a 'healthy' community:
  - high trust
  - lack of prejudice
  - supportive behaviour.

For each of the four segments and each of the supporting elements there are equal and opposite forces which can be described as 'blockages to communication'. So, for example, with regard to 'making intelligent decisions', the blockages would be as follows. First, inadequate communications skills – individuals do not have, for example, appropriate listening skills. Second, inept administration – information may be given out but may not be recorded or made available to those who need it. Finally, defective upward flow – the mechanisms are either not in place or are not used. Such 'models' are useful to organisations who wish to think intelligently about their own systems of communications. Against each 'blockage' a structured assessment can be made and appropriate countervailing actions taken. As an example, drawn from the case of Toshiba at Plymouth, in which I was involved, some of the facilitating actions to support *integrating effort* are shown in Fig. 5.5.

It should be noticed from these examples that the *mechanisms* underpinning communication are as much a feature as the *processes*. These mechanisms provide the means for the monitoring and control processes that are vital to ensure that the communications processes are continuously and appropriately applied. While it can be said that you cannot communicate enough in the 'right' way, the *what* and *when* of the communication can be critical. The scenarios illustrated in Fig. 5.6 certainly need to be avoided.

If dramatic change is to be brought about it is necessary, above everything else, to communicate the organisational/business reasons *why* the change is necessary. At the same time it is opportune to communicate what the alternatives to change are. The alternatives may well be wholly unacceptable. Without first gaining acceptance of the *need* for change, there

- A provision for formal and informal communication at various levels, e.g. daily 5-minute section meetings, monthly department meetings, monthly advisory board meetings, etc.

- Emphasis on the *total* system

- Explicit expression of an 'open' system

- Published framework procedures

- Immediate feedback on work performance (individual and group) and its effect on the whole

- Common workwear for everyone

- Open plan workspace for everyone

- Visibility and accessibility of managers and directors

- Small circle activity

- A *requirement* that the communication systems in place *will* work, e.g. obligatory attendance; no deferred meetings

- Noticeboards in work sections, managed by employees

- Logical workplace layouts

- Production managers' workspace and meeting space on the shopfloor

- Open circulation of minutes/notes within strict timetables

- Structured and participative report-back meetings

- Use of video for consistency of some messages

- Single-status facilities and terms of employment

- Half-yearly plenary meetings

Fig 5.5 Facilitating actions to support the integration of effort at Toshiba

will be no opportunity to effectively introduce or embed change. As someone once said, 'to bring about change you really need a crisis – if you don't appear to have a crisis, you'd better find one, or fail.' The absence of crisis, however, may be a sufficient indicator to review whether the change is really required and whether the effort towards change about to be employed might be wholly unproductive. Without a crisis, the influencing skills of a high order are undoubtedly required.

Who then should provide the lead in masterminding the communications process? If adequately prepared, the top HR practitioner is a natural choice. Without leadership and initiative, the roles of communication will not however be defined and necessary mechanisms considered and put in place.

Inappropriate structures

The structure of an organisation is a factor of its heritage often influenced significantly by the individual whims and idiosyncrasies of a succession of influential individuals. If processes change then structures required to support them will also need to change (*see* the discussion in Chapter 8). Structures which have developed in tandem with specifically defined job roles and hierarchies do not, for example, provide the framework to support flexible working, constant changes in production or new service level specifications.

	Example	Possible solutions
The right information given or received at the wrong time	● Information needed for 'design', received during implementation	Early representational involvement
	● Announcement of a change with no consequences yet available	Do not make announcements until the whole picture is known
	● When there is no time to consider what is communicated (information given or received), or resources to back it up	Plan and provide time and resources
The right information given or received in the wrong way	● Recipients hearing what they surmise and not what is being said	Repetition, multiple means of delivery. Ensure skills of corporate deliverers and listeners. Make time available
	● 'Bad' news or 'good' news received impersonally	Choice of appropriate means. Selection and training of personal communicators
	● Presented by someone not fully understanding or 'committed', or without requisite skills	Only use 'converts' as communicators. Ensure they have the facts. Ensure they have the right skill
	● Issues affecting feelings communicated in 'unfeeling' ways, e.g. only by memo	Choose the means to match the need: people for feelings, paper or technology for facts (usually both)

Fig. 5.6 The wrong 'right' information

Manufacturing units earlier designed for long runs of the same goods, restaurants serving one type of customer, service organisations backing up only one type of product or customer, bank branches only dealing with lenders and borrowers, and hospitals hitherto serving the bureaucracy as much as the patient are now all in the process of change.

Fixed or inflexible structures, built around functional silos with multiple hierarchies competing for attention and power, and with individuals and groups trading information as if it were an internal commodity are usually, through successful re-engineering, in decline. With BPR, the need is often for dramatic change in the ways work is undertaken. Such change cannot be sustained without a change in the structures that support the processes. And it is now in that sequence: the structure reflects the process needs, rather than the structure determining the jobs or roles. Flatter structures with fewer functional and other hierarchies, jobs designed or organised flexibly around business processes, and the emergence of team-based activities, different in kind from earlier concepts of teams, are the main structural changes within re-engineered organisations.

The emergence of different kinds of job roles and the way these interact in a team sense in supporting business processes are the driving forces on structure. No longer is it standard practice first to define the top hierarchy and then cascade the organisational tree on the basis of reporting relationships, dividing up perceived tasks in line with the scientific methods of Frederick Taylor. Re-engineered organisation designs emerge more from the bottom up, but in line with higher level needs for appropriate co-ordination. Control and co-ordination will be effected in quite different ways than hitherto. There are some important words of warning on the subject of top-down organisational design. The following quotation from Caius Petronius, 1st-century strategist and author, is illustrative and should act as a alarm:

> *We trained hard – but every time we were beginning to form up into teams we would be reorganised. I was to learn later in life that we tend to meet any new situation by reorganising, and a wonderful method it can be for creating the illusion of progress while producing confusion, inefficiency and demoralisation.*

I cannot here even seek to attempt to cover any processes for developing an organisational design in a reengineered establishment; only to assert that if your business processes change, then your organisational design will need to change too.

In BPR, job roles emerge through 'process mapping'. Process mapping comprises identifying the required outputs and requisite inputs to best serve the super-ordinate goals. Focusing upon the goals rather than specific actions often delivers processes that will possibly cross a number of hitherto prescribed functional or organisational 'boundaries'. The more involvement there is at the analytical stage with participation of knowledgable individuals at all levels who may later be the 'operators' of the emerging processes, the better will be identification of the real issues. With greater involvement and greater comprehension through participation, individuals and groups will better understand the emerging new roles.

Processes are the building blocks of BPR. Analysis of the processes at one point in time will tend to show up new 'ways' that are available to deliver them. The nature of work (content, timing, sequence and who performs it) will therefore inevitably change. Without response to the emerging new job needs, these essential elements of an organisation's structure will be inappropriately aligned. With re-engineering, the nature of most jobs change. The means used to establish the new framework for work and the requirements for the people involved, requires management capability and resources of a high order. Effective HRM is central to the activity, not just in defining what needs to be new but in managing the ongoing operation and ultimately in making the transition.

Newly re-engineered processes do not often generate discrete job roles; they tend to show up the need for discrete processes that require support from *groups* of people. Operating within a re-engineered organisation is most typically a team-based activity. Bringing about cross-functional team-based activities, mainly of a self-directed nature, within an organisation still more structured around *individuals* operating in *functional boxes* under *top-down direction* is one of the great challenges of BPR.

Within a reengineered organisation, a process team is typically a group that is *'self-directed'* comprising employees who are together responsible for a 'whole' work process or segment that delivers a product or service to an internal or external customer (Oram and Wellins, 1995). They will typically have *authority* over their work, with individuals within the team and the team collectively being empowered to make judgements and take actions without prior agreement of anyone outside the team. This will extend well beyond what has been characterised, somewhat cynically, as 'authority to do what the procedures lay down'. The authority is typically 'enabling' for making judgements and undocumented decisions, albeit within limits. The group is typically also engaged in and accountable for the processes of subsequent continuing improvement – *kaizen* activities. Clearly, such new ways of doing things will contribute to the nature of the organisation, its structure and its style of working.

Reporting and control mechanisms need to be quite different. Within teams, the nature of teamworking will often be quite different from conventional models. The traditional model of leader, surrounded by team members looking for direction from him or her, might move towards much more egalitarian approaches, to situations where team leadership is a role that moves between members at different times or on different occasions, or even to where teams have no defined leader but truly share in all matters.

In the consideration of new structures, it is vital that the 'social' issues, the human aspirations and interfaces of individuals and groups, are taken into account as much as the technical aspects. Who will address these issues: will they be left to chance or will human resource professionals take a lead? Surely, without integration of all of the means (the operational aspects, leadership, communications, control and co-ordination aspects) there will be imbalance or even disharmony within the structure. The structure and the processes have to be compatible for both holistic working and heuristic development. Change the processes and the structure will assuredly need to change. Without aligning networks and structures to the new processes, the organisation will be in imbalance and the 'old' ways of doing things will tend to be perpetuated. But realigning the structures is only part of the required activity and on its own, though a powerful impetus for change, it is not enough.

Inadequate preparation for new roles

That new roles will emerge from re-engineering activities has been demonstrated in earlier sections. Getting people to adopt the new roles and put aside earlier preferred skills and approaches is a different kind of challenge. Achieving the required outputs will depend significantly on:

- selection (internal and external) of people with the qualities to be best able to perform the roles;
- preparation of those people for their 'new' roles.

In a situation where there has been a strong and established way of doing things, people will readily 'revert to type' and behave in ways they have been used to, rather like reversing a knife and fork between hands. The tendency will be to swap back again when the imperative that brought about the swap fades, even momentarily, from the mind. New skills and behaviour need to be introduced over an extended period in order to become embedded. This practice when combined with understanding, through involvement for instance, will only optimally combine with changes in 'attitude' when there is harmony between knowledge, skill, required behaviour and intellectual application. Behaviour may be the element that is visible, but behaviour will not become instinctive without some change in attitude.

Changing attitudes is possibly the hardest to achieve, but for re-engineered organisations such achievement is perhaps more than highly desirable. It may even be vital – the *difference that makes the difference*. Of course, it is possible for people to adapt their behaviour to particular circumstances and there are ample indications that people do this when moving to new organisations. The greatest synergy, and hence probably also natural efficiency, can be achieved, however, when attitude is appropriately aligned either by dint of selection or favourable change in attitude. One aspect of 'attitude' required in a situation of change, includes a predisposition to:

● think openly
● work flexibly
● learn new ways.

The extent to which the 'raw materials' (the people selected) match these qualities will condition the 'preparability' of the workforce. Having all not just most of the workforce with a 'positive' attitude is the ultimate aim. Fifty-one per cent of the workforce with a positive attitude will mean that 49 per cent have either a negative or less than positive attitude (Wellins, Byham and Wilson, 1991). The objective, therefore, is first, through appropriate selection, to get as many as possible willing, and preferably eager, members of the workforce to head more or less in the same direction; and second, to bring everyone else, *willingly* into line, in the 'right' direction. The more employees with an appropriate predisposition, the less difficult the process will be.

Starting with the best materials is a fundamental principle for any organisation, and will govern its selection from external candidates. Selection is, however, just as important for organisations going through change. In the Toshiba and Royal Bank of Scotland cases referred to earlier, 'internal' selection was a significant foundation on which much else was built. There is considerable time, effort and significant investment that can be made in refining selection processes, and much that can be wasted if the issues are not addressed appropriately. Unquestionably, professional knowledge and understanding are required to define the scope and nature of activity. This, for required effect, has then to be aligned with appropriate skills, knowledge and understanding more widely within the organisation.

While selection may start and end with considerations of 'attitude', there is much more work to be done related to defining roles and accountabilities and the requisite skills and motivations that will be required for them to be successfully performed. Role analysis (subtly different from job analysis, by virtue of more expression of the required outputs and related inputs; wider than fixed job elements) may lead more directly to a 'person specification' than going through the hitherto conventional route of first preparing a job description.

Self-selection can be a very powerful tool and self-filtering mechanisms are techniques routinely and effectively applied by many organisations. In the change situation individuals within can, from information provided, exercise their own judgement and decide that the job (or jobs) on offer are perhaps not for them. This can sometimes present problems for an organisation when key individuals with vital attributes decide this. For the organisation, the judgement is whether to make alternative longer term arrangements or to apply temporary 'golden handcuffs' by means of incentives to stay.

Strategic 'under-selection' is also a productive approach in some circumstances, where selected individuals fall short in some dimensions of the optimum but, more positively, their capability to learn and grow in a job is high. In this situation a better return on training investment can be gained.

1 Selection goes hand-in-hand with training and other preparation, and essentially provides the base materials on which to build.
2 Following selection, and before commencement of changed working methods, the nature of individual and team role preparation will need to span new technical and required process capabilities plus new behaviours needed for optimum performance (in relation to both internal and external interfaces). Technical needs will, of their nature, be organisation-specific and will therefore be addressed in no great detail here, but they must be addressed by organisations; however, multiskilling in technical and other matters is often a defined requirement and natural outcome of re-engineering.
3 Behavioural training needs are perhaps the least obvious and the most important. To achieve required process outputs, most preparation will need to be related to the achievement of required behaviours. Such behaviours may include, for example, group induction/getting to work effectively together, better listening skills, and speaking over the phone with a 'smile in the voice'.
4 Non-behavioural capabilities that are to a much greater extent required in a reengineered organisation, might include, for example, managing time, selection skills, quality monitoring methods, etc.
5 Role-dependent skills and sensitivities might include concepts and operation of just in time methods and health and safety issues, including, perhaps, stress management.
6 The priority and sequence of training needs to be considered on a just in time learning basis.

With major change, you can prepare to a considerable extent without training having any effect until the organisation adopts and is seen to adopt the new ways. Then the 'doing it' takes over and correct preparation will pay off. No preparation – no chance. Leave it too late and people will believe the action is not going to happen. The timing of 'go' is a matter of judgement. However, the 'go' point is really only the beginning of a stage which has no end.

Misaligned systems

For HR practitioners, misaligned systems are one of the most fundamental issues to be addressed. It is not so much that individual systems will have to change in order to be aligned with new requirements, it is that *all* human resource-related systems will need to change (at least in some way) and that the individual systems will need to be aligned with one another, so that they are not counter-productive, and are mutually supportive. Along with and including the operational and organisationally specific systems required for successful implementation of BPR, there are five groups of HR systems:

1 **people resourcing systems,** including role definition, resource planning, selection, performance management and release from the organisation
2 **reward systems,** including non-monetary as well as monetary rewards
3 **training and development systems,** including suitable conditions for learning
4 **employee relations systems,** including individual and collective communications systems and collective representation systems
5 **management of HR functions systems,** including team integration, organisational performance monitoring, management of the human resource functions.

These five sets of systems are not mutually exclusive, each to an extent, being *inter*-dependent with the others (*see* Fig. 5.7).

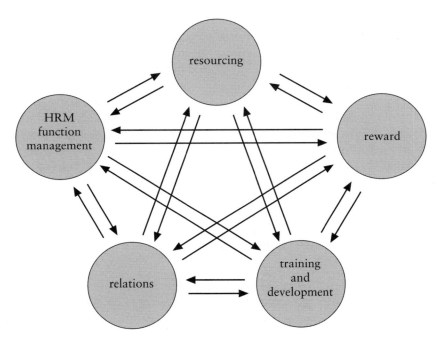

Fig. 5.7 Integration of HRM systems

If there were no integration of HR systems before re-engineering, there should certainly be such integration afterwards, otherwise there will be counter-productive forces from otherwise redundant systems. These points can be illustrated by the examples in Fig. 5.8. More comprehensive examples can be found in *Re-engineering's Missing Ingredient – the Human Factor* by Oram and Wellins (1995).

Illustrative systems	Indicative reasons why changes to systems are needed	Indicative system interdependencies
Resourcing systems changes		
Job analysis and job definition	Move from 'role inputs' to 'outputs' and competencies-type focus	Selection, training and development, team integration, reward, employee relations
Recruitment	Move towards more flexible use of resources; core (permanent), secondary (temporary/part-time), outworkers (sub-contractors, agency, consultants)	Human resource planning, selection, team integration, performance management, reward
Reward systems changes		
Monetary rewards generally	Changes to individual and team organisation and motivation leading to more team rewards, different roles and responsibilities, devolvement from central controls, focus on process outputs, methods of evaluation and comparison, different career patterns and expectations. Need for 'tailored' choice	Role definition, performance management, human resource planning, recruitment, selection, training and development, team integration. Employee relations
Rewards for encouraging new behaviours	Removal of 'old' systems designed for different motivations. Emergence of new patterns of work requiring different behaviours. Opportunity to respond to emerging wishes for greater individual choice	Human resource planning recruitment, selection, training and development. Employee relations
Training and development systems changes		
Identifying individual learning needs	Greater emphasis on strategic business requirements but *individual* learning needs and learning styles. Different people to do the identifying, e.g. line managers and team leaders, as well as greater individual ownership	Leadership, training and development, selection, performance management
Technological learning	Discontinuous and rapid changes in *technology* and the learning needs arising. Increasing needs for training and retraining. Greater goal-oriented conscious influence on development, i.e. *education*	Identification of training needs, human resource planning, selection, performance management
Employee relations systems changes		
Collective co-operation, involvement and participation	Emergence of new required ways of involving employees, feelings of loss of prominence by managers	Management development, behavioural learning, process learning, communications
Communications between individuals	Changed channels of communications for sharing organisational vision, integrating effort, making intelligent decisions and sustaining a 'healthy' organisational community	Management development, behavioural learning, team integration, collective co-operation
Management of HR function(s) systems changes		
Benchmarking	Possibly did not do benchmarking, need for internal, competitive and industrial comparators	Potentially all
Functional support	Moves towards more devolved HRM processes. Provision of professional functional *support* over functional *delivery*	Monitoring, performance management, training and development, human resource planning, recruitment, selection, employee relations

Fig. 5.8 Illustrative HR system interdependencies

THE DOWN SIDE OF RE-ENGINEERING: CONCLUSIONS FOR EFFECTIVE DELIVERY

The case has been put that with adequate attention to all of the factors involved and with adequate allocation of appropriate resources, a process of radical organisational change that incorporates the distinctive elements and philosophy of 're-engineering' can deliver dramatic and highly beneficial results. The problem is that few so-called re-engineering initiatives deliver what they were aimed to deliver and, as such, fall short of their goal or 'fail'. Further, some have disastrous outcomes for the companies involved. Re-engineering, its founding father Michael Hammer admits, 'is a high risk business'. Estimates on 'failures' range to as high as 80 per cent of all initiatives but most concede that failures are experienced by certainly more than 50 per cent. Re-engineering is nevertheless still very much an imperative of the corporate landscape in the 1990s that will probably carry over well into the first decade of the next century. Most major British organisations have attempted, or are in the process of attempting it in some form – the Grint and Willcocks (1995) survey in Britain found almost two-thirds of British organisations planning or undertaking BPR activity. If so many organisations are attempting BPR and if the success rate is so low, there seem to be considerable implications. A recent study about HRM effectiveness (Guest and Hoque, 1995) has concluded:

> *It is not so much human resource policies in general that have an impact on performance but a specific type of human resource approach that offers distinct advantages . . . **where the personnel/HR policies are integrated into a coherent philosophy and where this fits the business strategy, then superior performance results.*** (my emphasis)

Evidence of HRM practices that fall within the scope of that description is not widespread. Evidence gathered, again about HRM practices in general rather than those related to BPR in particular, gives little comfort (Tyson, Doherty and Viney, 1995):

> *employee skills, abilities and competencies are seen to be sources of competitive advantage . . . the personnel function's contribution to the development of these competencies is perceived at the 'tactical' level of recruitment, training and development practices. By implication any strategic contributions are not recognised.*

CSC Index (1994) and Grint and Willcocks (1995) have both concluded that the biggest barriers to successful re-engineering are people-related matters. Coupled with the apparent widespread scale of re-engineering in Britain, that offers a considerable challenge for HR practitioners.

There are some formidable realities for HR practitioners which they must accept:

1 The HRM aspects of re-engineering change are considerable and if not adequately addressed will almost certainly lead to 'failure'.

2 For a re-engineered organisation, probably *all*, not just some, human resource support systems will need to change; but it is the *attitudes* of all of the people in the enterprise, not support systems, that are the vital ingredients for difference.

3 Understanding *why* behaviours and attitudes in an organisation need to change, and how they can and will be changed, is as much a challenge to HR practitioners' *own*

behaviours, as it is for them to bring about wider understanding, acceptance and appropriate action.

4 Re-engineering human resource functions is, without doubt, an integral part of BPR. If HR practitioners do not address this, others will.

CONCLUSION

In re-engineered organisations, the practice of HRM will probably never be the same again. For some this will have been an on-going opportunity; for others, it will have been truly a crisis. The differentiating factor for successful delivery will undoubtedly be professionalism.

6

Building a new proposition for staff at NatWest UK

STEPHEN E. BENDALL, CHRISTOPHER R. BOTTOMLEY
AND PATRICIA M. CLEVERLY

NatWest UK Ltd

INTRODUCTION

NatWest UK, in common with most organisations of today, operates in a highly dynamic business environment of rising customer expectations, technological innovation, increasing regulation and new non-traditional competitors entering the marketplace offering products through a range of diverse distribution channels. To achieve profitable differentiation, new and innovative responses are required to meet these challenges. These responses have included product and delivery channel redesign, changing employee patterns and re-engineering of processes (*see* Chapter 5 by Mike Oram). However, they all have an impact upon how individuals perceive their relationship with the organisation. There is therefore an equally compelling need not only to manage our responses to the changing business environment but also simultaneously to understand and find responses to the changing nature of the 'psychological contracts' (Rousseau, 1990) which staff have with the organisation.

In Chapter 3 David Guest discussed the issue of falling commitment. This chapter outlines the development and implementation to date of what we have termed the 'Proposition for Staff' in NatWest UK. This represents our HR response to the changing nature of the relationship between staff and the organisation with the objective of refreshing and enhancing the commitment we need to sustain and make effective the internal changes needed to meet our business objectives.

The development of the 'Proposition for Staff' is summarised in the form of a model, which seeks to draw together the various stages in its development. This model proposes where potential linkages or interactions may exist between the achievement of business objectives and the psychological contract, and highlights some key considerations in terms of implementation. It is hoped that the model outlined in this chapter will provide a foundation for further discussion and debate about the potential effectiveness of such an approach and its appropriateness as an HR response to the needs of organisations undergoing significant change.

At this point, it is important to state that this is not regarded as a short-term HR initiative but a long-term development programme. It has at its heart a core philosophy of building a process to ensure that the best match is achieved at any point in time between the needs of an individual and the needs of the business. In addition to this, it also encompasses a series of short-term HR interventions which are intended to lay the foundation for the implementation of the core philosophy. Our objective is to ensure that every employee feels motivated to maximise his or her performance within a relationship that is mutually beneficial. The overall aim of this programme is to achieve our stated Vision, which is to be 'First Choice for Staff'. We must first explain the background to our initiative.

WHERE WERE WE?

At the beginning of 1994 the organisation was essentially one large operating unit known as UK Branch Business (UKBB) representing the largest sector of NatWest Group (*see* Fig. 6.1). It was characterised by a bureaucratic and hierarchical structure with the majority of decisions being taken centrally. There was a substantial head office presence, of which the personnel department accounted for some 350 people.

Historically, there was minimal line management involvement in people management. The majority of decisions affecting recruitment, selection and reward were taken by the

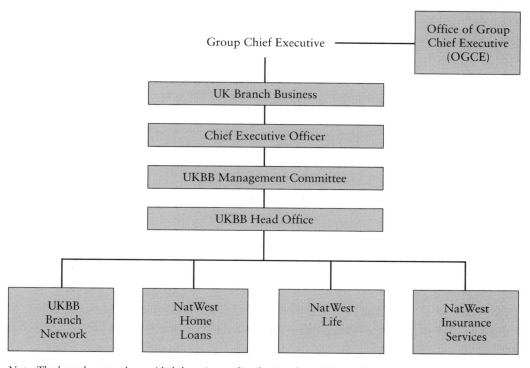

Note: The branch network provided the primary distribution channel for each business

Fig. 6.1 UKBB structure in 1994: 'One Business'

Centre through a policy of *'one size fits all'*. Significantly, the organisation was only impacted by the start of the material downsizing that had already been seen in other sectors in the early 1990s. Research undertaken by Manchester Business School in 1995 indicated that as yet there was no perceived impact on performance but staff were still in a period of 'denial' – 'aware that we are downsizing but it won't happen to me' (this issue is discussed in Chapter 8).

The organisation was also one year into a Vision programme, initiated by the Chief Executive, which had a number of core elements. These elements included core process re-engineering, process redesign, service improvement (a form of TQM), and a comprehensive change programme seeking to reverse the existing bureaucratic, risk averse and control culture. These culture change programmes were predicated upon assumptions about their impact on commitment (*see* David Guest, Chapter 3). The balanced business scorecard approach (Kaplan and Norton, 1993) was introduced as the primary measurement and management tool for the business. This aims to focus attention on the management of the business across four key dimensions, including organisational development, rather than the historic focus on financial performance only. An observation made by commentators at the time was that the organisation was embarking on the largest change programme in western Europe.

Past stability and success had engendered a paternalistic culture for staff where there was a 'job for life', the personnel department was their 'guardian', looked after their well-being and administered personnel systems and processes. The 'psychological contract' or 'deal' (Herriot and Pemberton, 1995a) between staff and the organisation is summarised in Table 6.1.

Table 6.1 The old psychological contract

Individual offers	*Organisation offers*
● Loyalty	● Security
● Steadiness	● Incremental progress
● Dedication	● Promotions for status
● Input focus	● Modest salaries
● Rule adherence	● Recognisable benefits
● Adaptation	● No choice – one size fits all
● Processing/functional skills	● 'Family' protection
● Safety	

There was little opportunity for the personnel function to influence the strategic direction of the organisation at this time. The function was not considered a key player in planning the development of the business, but waited for their 'task list'.

Why did we have to change?

The imperative behind the 'Proposition for Staff' began at the end of 1994 and was prompted both by a number of changes in the organisation's operating environment and the coming to fruition of many internal change initiatives. While the scale of profits continued to represent a competitive performance by the organisation, it was still facing increasing competition. The strong desire of our staff to provide outstanding customer service was leading them to question whether the organisation was serious in trying to help them better meet the needs of our customers.

At the end of 1994 NatWest UK was restructured into six businesses and a significantly smaller head office to produce a leaner, fitter structure (*see* Fig. 6.2). The imperative was to move decision making as close to the customer as possible and to create a focus on our key markets and our key competitors in those markets. It was vital to focus attention on the dynamics of each individual marketplace and to put in place an organisational structure that would not only reinforce this, but would enable us to respond rapidly to future changes, particularly where these enabled us better to meet customer needs.

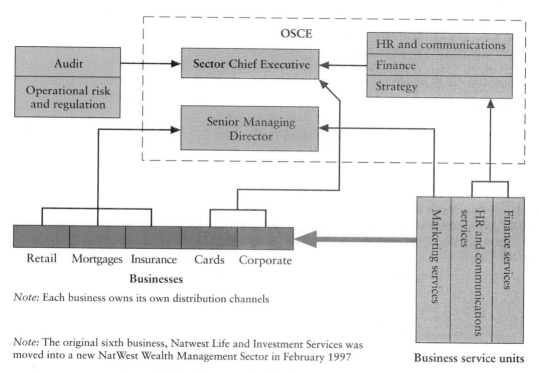

Note: Each business owns its own distribution channels

Note: The original sixth business, Natwest Life and Investment Services was moved into a new NatWest Wealth Management Sector in February 1997

Business service units

Fig. 6.2 NatWest UK structure, 1997

What did this mean for human resources?

The restructuring had implications for the operation of the human resources function at local, business and head office level. It provided an opportunity to 'step change' the function and move away from the personnel administration model towards an HRM model (*see* the discussion by Derek Torrington in Chapter 2). A new director of human resources was appointed to shape and drive the necessary changes and to develop a new vision for HR. The subsequent HR vision was founded on five principles which would underpin all future HR activity:

1 partnership with the businesses
2 champions and enablers of change
3 people management into the line
4 individual ownership and self-management of development and career
5 HR excellence:
   - operational excellence
   - personnel administration to consultancy.

Substantial re-engineering of the personnel function was undertaken in order to create:

- a small central HR function within the office of the Sector Chief Executive (OSCE)
- small head office functions in each of the six businesses
- two operations centres into which the majority of the personnel administration activities of NatWest UK were migrated, e.g. updating of personnel and sickness records, production of appointment and rise letters etc.
- an HR services arm to provide services to the businesses on a charged-out basis, e.g. graduate recruitment, job evaluation and employment law
- local, peripatetic HR advisers in each of the newly formed businesses to support line managers in undertaking their new people management responsibilities.

What does the centre do?

The role of the centre (OSCE) as a whole is broadly founded on the principles of '*parenting advantage*' described by Goold, Campbell and Alexander (1994). These principles outline that corporate parents should aim to 'create value' and not 'destroy value' through their influence on the businesses which they overview in their portfolio. In other words the businesses must be better off *with* a corporate parent than without one.

These parenting advantage principles required the OSCE HR team to ensure that activities undertaken were focused on adding value – looking for the synergy across the businesses, looking for tools, techniques, practices, insights and ideas to help provide a solution to issues that are of concern to either a particular business or across several businesses.

To support this change there was therefore a need to redefine the relative roles and responsibilities between the OSCE HR function and the HR functions within the businesses.

With the objective of mitigating against potential conflict or duplication, relative roles and responsibilities, with associated areas of discretion, were negotiated and encapsulated within a set of HR strategic and operational frameworks. This is a form of the 'decentralisation contract' referred to by Goold, Campbell and Alexander (1994). These frameworks provide clarity to support the relationship between OSCE and the decentralised HR functions. They act as a useful yardstick against which issues can be debated and resolved. These issues may relate to a specific business or to several businesses. They are raised and discussed at an HR forum, made up of the Director of Human Resources, NatWest UK and each of the heads of HR in the businesses. The forum also reinforces a sense of community across the HR function of NatWest UK, through collaboration and sharing of best practice.

Chapter 1 noted a series of dilemmas facing the HR function. We found that the need to fulfil the remit of 'adding value' and ensure that the centre does not 'destroy value' creates an interesting dilemma in practice. On the one hand, the centre acts as an internal consultant, advising a business on ways to address a specific business issue, commissioning internal and external research, encouraging the sharing of best practice and keeping in touch with external developments and the latest thinking in the HR field.

On the other hand, there are occasions when it is necessary to 'challenge' a particular business proposal which may be optimal for that business, but sub-optimal for another. A substantially differentiated reward structure, for example, in one business could potentially drive up rates and create salary drift across others.

Prior to the restructure there were 350 HR people in head office. After the restructure, and following the establishment of the business head offices, the OSCE HR team comprises 15, who report to the Director of Human Resources, NatWest UK. The function as a whole has been reduced by 30 per cent. Several key changes had taken place:

1 The establishment of the balanced business scorecard had created a focus on the management of the business beyond the financials and there was a growing recognition of the importance of effective people management.
2 The new Director of Human Resources was part of the new executive management committee of NatWest UK.
3 The enhanced role of OSCE HR enabled activity to be focused on key strategic people management imperatives greatly improving integration between business strategy and HR strategy.
4 Responsibility for developing HR policies and practices had been devolved in the main to the businesses to enable them to tailor policies to the specific needs of their market.
5 Line managers were given responsibility for managing and developing their people with the support of local HR Advisers.

How did all this affect staff?

Staff were faced with significant change, which was likely to accelerate. Morale and organisational pride indicators were in line with the financial services sector generally but were at a historically low level. The drive for overall reductions in staff numbers had led to significantly curtailed recruitment and the requirement for people to stay longer in their roles. This caused a significant change to the shape of the organisation. In 1990, 43 per cent of staff were aged 25 and under and 44 per cent were aged 26 to 45. By 1995 those under 25 represented 23 per cent of staff. Sixty-four per cent were aged 26 to 45.

There were clear implications for the development of people generally and for the organisation's ability to replenish its 'seedcorn' capability.

There were, of course, different expectations and changing staff aspirations to be managed and a great deal more uncertainty than people were accustomed to. Deskilling of jobs through, for example, centralisation and automation of transaction processing activity, potentially impacted upon the opportunity to capitalise on a better educated workforce and promotion opportunities were significantly reduced. Increasing use of part-timers was prompting the need for greater flexibility in contractual terms, e.g annualised hours and flexible working. Union membership was increasing to the extent that some 70 per cent of staff were members.

Research findings indicated that staff were experiencing a greater level of responsibility:

Responsibility has improved as has flexibility in changing jobs. Responsibility is moving lower down the ranks.

However, staff felt that the organisation now had the upper hand:

The balance has changed from the individual's favour to the organisation's.

The reaction of line managers to their enhanced responsibilities for people management was variable. Many embraced the changes with enthusiasm and quickly initiated changes locally. Some struggled under the weight of continuing changes to the operational nature of their roles. Although support was provided by HR advisers, there was a growing recognition that a greater skills gap in people management capability existed than had been anticipated (this issue was noted in Chapter 1).

Staff were also aware of the implications of the formation of the six business structure in terms of removing the historic 'one size fits all' approach to HR policies and practices (*see* next section). However, in the transitional period, while the newly formed head office HR functions were establishing themselves in the context of their own market demands, there was a fragmentation of the old relationship creating a weakened understanding of what the organisation was now offering its staff. The benefits that the organisation had previously offered seemed largely to have been removed from 'the deal', for example security, promotions for status (as summarised in Table 6.1). The delayering and structural change had led primarily to a shrinkage in middle management which inevitably weakened the communication channels between staff and 'top management'.

While there was an element of denial as to the potential impact of downsizing on individuals there was also evidence of survivor syndrome (*see* Chapter 8) and its attendant behaviours – reluctance to take on new responsibilities, or working to minimum standards particularly among older senior managers (discussed by Peter Herriot in Chapter 7, in managing transitions). These behaviours were in line with the findings from external research. This revealed a number of key issues for the organisation:

- dissatisfaction at the rate of driving out projected cost savings from initiatives such as process redesign, re-engineering, etc.
- the need to create a confident environment for innovation and development of new income streams was potentially undermined
- low staff turnover/wastage rates being more indicative of the difficulty in finding alternative employment than the desire to stay (i.e. potentially obscuring low morale rather than demonstrating high motivation and commitment).

The old relationship had been broken but there was a lack of clarity as to the nature of the new one. This manifested itself in weakened commitment by staff to the organisation at large, but much stronger local identification. Higher morale was primarily consequent upon the quality of local leadership.

HOW DID WE BEGIN TO MANAGE THIS?

There was a recognition that we could not go back to where we were or 'engineer' a new psychological contract. Any new 'deal' could not be a single package designed by the 'Centre' to be applied to all staff. The simplicity of the 'one size fits all' approach no longer had relevance or meaning to the changing nature of the business both internally and externally. The organisation was faced with a multitude of potential psychological contracts to understand and manage effectively. Outputs from staff focus groups held during 1995 highlighted that we needed to find a response which could accommodate any number of different deals. Two examples are shown in Tables 6.2 and 6.3.

Table 6.2 The 1995 deal for clerical staff

Individual offers	*Organisation offers*
● Performance	● Flexibility
● High quality	● Pay
● Hard work	● A job today
● More of your life	● Possible bonus and PRP
● Flexibility	● Perks, but fewer
● Responsibility	● Less beneficial staff mortgage

Table 6.3 The 1995 deal for middle managers

Individual offers	*Organisation offers*
● Specific skills	● Responsibility
● Limited commitment	● Autonomy
● Effort if rewarded	● Accountability
● Loyalty to colleagues	● Carrots and sticks
● Loyalty to career	● Confusion, constant re-structuring
● Flexibility of:	● Pressure for results
– job content	● Some opportunities
– career direction	
– training and development	

This reinforced the need to work out, in conjunction with our employees, the best match between:

● what they would ideally require in return for the commitment and performance being asked of them and
● what is commercially viable and acceptable for the organisation to provide?

It also started to highlight opportunities, on both sides, where something was on offer which had not previously been understood by the other party. For example – research showed that staff were more prepared to embrace change than the organisation had considered them to be. A more flexible approach was required to tailor deals to meet the different needs of the various groups of staff necessary to meet our business objectives, e.g. part-time evening staff in a telephone centre versus a corporate Managing Director in Corporate Banking Services.

As a consequence of many of the long-established roles having disappeared, and with the existence of fewer key roles, there was a need to re-establish clearly signposted career paths/themes. These would need to be based on skills competencies and development rather than hierarchical status, in order that they could stay robust and could further structural changes in the organisation. It was also important to give these new career paths credibility through supporting mechanisms such as reward and grading structures. There was a need to understand better the changing nature of the skills at an organisational level and to ensure that skills gaps could be identified and appropriate responses planned, for instance for recruitment or training and development. Part of this challenge was to shift to a culture where progress became charted against developing value to the business and growing individual competence, rather than being charted against grade/status and pay relativity.

To counteract the restricted communication channels, there needed to be a revised strategy for listening to and understanding the 'agenda' of employees and ensuring that these signals reached the executive. This would also help us to challenge ourselves about the apparent perception of 'lack of suffering at the top' versus what we were expecting the rest of the organisation to accept. Keeping our word throughout would be vital. While staff morale can be temporarily talked up with promises of new systems and better processes, if not delivered the resultant dissatisfaction could set back morale and motivation to below the previous starting point. It was important to keep promises realistic and manageable.

HOW DID THE 'PROPOSITION FOR STAFF' BEGIN?

We needed a different approach to people management. One which:

- was more flexible
- was wider than 'explicit' HR practices, e.g. would embrace communication and management style
- helped to reduce the emphasis on 'status' and 'job security'
- enabled us to accelerate culture change through a process of experimentation
- could be locally driven within a NatWest UK framework
- resulted in individuals perceiving their relationship with NatWest UK to be fair
- reflected individual needs as well as business needs.

We began two parallel streams of activity during 1995. The first was to build an appreciation and understanding of the meaning, relevance and importance of 'psychological contracts' and in particular the impact on organisational performance, not only among the HR community but also at executive level. The long-term strategy was to lay down a foundation of supporting frameworks, feedback processes, tools, techniques, and guidelines which could ultimately be placed in the hands of line managers to enable them to tailor packages with their staff (*see* Fig. 6.3).

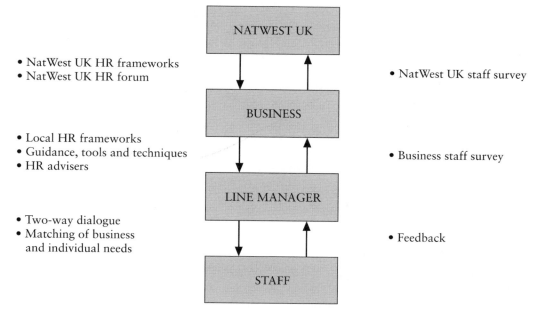

- NatWest UK HR frameworks
- NatWest UK HR forum

- NatWest UK staff survey

- Local HR frameworks
- Guidance, tools and techniques
- HR advisers

- Business staff survey

- Two-way dialogue
- Matching of business and individual needs

- Feedback

Fig. 6.3 Supporting frameworks for the Proposition for Staff

There was no timescale established for introduction as it was recognised that this was dependent upon:

- the capability of line management to use the increased flexibility effectively
- the complementary upskilling of the HR community to provide support to line management and increase their change management skills and strategic awareness
- the nature of each individual business and its market needs which would determine the overall pace of introduction
- building a more co-operative relationship with the unions.

This '*building awareness*' activity has been facilitated externally but with ownership resting firmly with the individual businesses. It has involved briefing sessions to the HR functions in each of the businesses, and in some cases the executive management team, coupled with local workshops where staff and managers could identify offers and wants from the organisation's and staff's perspectives, respective fit and areas which could form the basis for further negotiation.

The second stream of activity was shorter term and concerned with the review of all existing HR policies and practices to build in fairness, choice and flexibility. Figure 6.4 shows the activities that were linked to this approach.

Work undertaken to date has for example involved:

- The introduction of a more flexible reward structure providing the option for staff to elect to switch an element of their annual salary increment to bonus within the overall constraint of the reward pool allocated to their unit.
- A review of benefits, e.g. car scheme and mortgage assistance scheme.

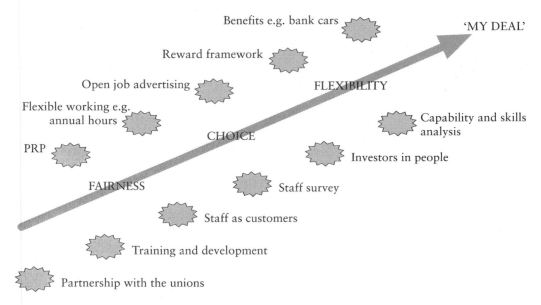

Fig. 6.4 Policies and practices linked to fairness, choice and flexibility

- A 'Staff as Customers' programme which establishes the principle that all staff should be treated in the same way as customers in terms of products and services while at the same time offering them preferential terms.
- The introduction of an enhanced staff survey, which has a NatWest UK dimension as well as business specific elements. This aims to remove information 'filters' and monitors key indicators drawn from the survey as part of the balanced business scorecard.
- The introduction of a more flexible approach to working hours, in particular a move to annualised hours, which for a full-time member of staff equates to 1826 hours a year. This enables staff, aware of business needs, to determine their own rosters within their team. It is this local involvement and a recognition that there must be a match of staff and business benefit which has been key to successful implementation.
- A move away from the traditional confrontational approach with the recognised unions to one of 'partnership' (*see* various chapters in Part Two). This is built on the premise that both NatWest UK and the unions have a common interest in the success of the business and that staff are best served by working together in a spirit of trust and co-operation. While there is mutual recognition that agreement will not always be possible on all issues, we have sought to bring the unions into the debates on key issues earlier and with greater access to information, to enable them to provide more meaningful input on behalf of the staff they represent.

As work progresses and the understanding and appetite of the businesses and their line managers grows, and information from the staff survey and focus groups is collated, the ability to 'trade' between component elements may need to be considered if this is required by staff. For example, we may need to provide the option for staff to elect to use their bonus for AVCs or school fees depending upon what stage they have reached in their life-cycle and their personal needs.

WHAT HAVE WE LEARNT?

Figure 6.5 captures the impact upon the approach to people management of two primary influences. The horizontal axis represents the extent to which line managers are skilled, capable and willing to directly manage the people for whom they are responsible. The vertical axis represents the extent to which the control and management of HR policies, practices and systems are devolved down into the businesses to enable them to be tailored to specific local needs. Clearly the degree to which an organisation has moved on each axis has a significant impact on the way people management is undertaken in that business. In the model we have briefly described the four basic scenarios that can be constructed from the variations in progress on each axis.

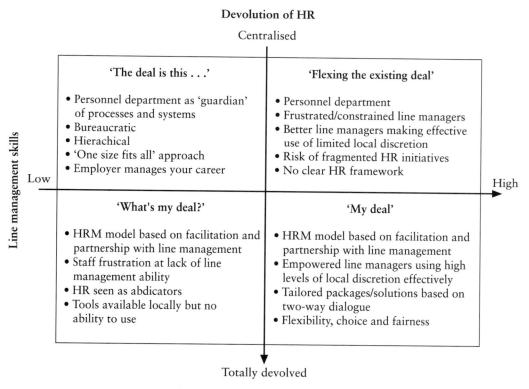

Fig. 6.5 Four contracting scenarios

Managing the balance

In moving towards the organisational model where each employee can say '*My deal is . . .*' there are a number of tensions that need to be understood and managed. The most critical is to manage successfully the balance between the rate of devolution of HR policies and practices and the rate of upskilling of line management. If the rate of devolution outpaces the growth of skills locally the effectiveness of the transition to the use of local tools and techniques is not only significantly diminished, but can give rise to confusion and frustration locally. In this scenario of *'What's my deal?'* there is the danger that:

- no one will be seen to be taking the lead in terms of managing and developing staff, giving rise to feelings of being undervalued and 'uncared for'
- the HR function may be regarded as having abdicated their historic role with no compensating uptake of that role by line management
- line managers may feel an unwarranted pressure on them, leading them to ignore or subordinate their people management responsibilities.

However, if line management capability in people management is high and HR responsibilities with supporting tools and techniques are not passed into their hands quickly enough, an equally discordant scenario can be created of *'Flexing the Deal'* where:

- line management become frustrated at the lack of local HR accountability and availability of tools and techniques which they recognise could help enhance the performance of their staff locally
- their frustration leads them to begin to act locally and unilaterally
- without a clear HR framework being in place there is an increased risk of misguided initiatives due to lack of understanding regarding employment law considerations
- good practice is not easily identified, captured and shared across the organisation.

To help mitigate the worst of these scenarios there is a need to ensure that effective local HR support is available and the revised responsibilities are clearly communicated and understood.

What needs to be devolved?

It is also important to identify what elements of HR should be devolved to line management. Moving away from a centralised personnel model does not imply that it is relevant or necessary to move the paperwork and administration locally. Our experience would suggest that this is not only ineffective but can severely constrain progress towards line managers' acceptance of their people management responsibilities. The overall objective of devolution is to put into the hands of line management the ability to manage and develop the skills and talents of their people more effectively to enhance business performance – not to make them expert in the upkeep of personnel records or the impact of European legislation on employment law in the UK. When putting in place the framework for devolution, options for dealing with particular HR components therefore need to be examined. It may be more effective to maintain a central expertise in areas such as employment law or reengineer administrative systems to enable them to be undertaken in HR processing centres. (*See* the discussion of future HR roles in Chapter 4 by Patrick Flood).

Corporate *v* business needs

Where the organisation has moved, as in the case of NatWest UK, to a portfolio management model there is also the tension between overall corporate requirements and business needs to be considered. The 'First Choice for Staff' aspiration is a corporate one. So, while recognising the importance of enabling businesses to manage and tailor policies and practices to meet their particular business needs, there is an equal acceptance that NatWest UK is one organisation, particularly in the eyes of our customers. Our staff, whatever business they happen to work within, are the face of NatWest UK to customers, and our most effective ambassadors. A balance must, therefore, be maintained between the desire of particular businesses to create a unique set of HR policies and practices which distinguish their business and the need to maintain sufficient 'corporate glue' to reflect the interdependencies between the businesses and the view that our staff are '*NatWest staff*'. It is crucial that HR policies and practices reinforce the NatWest brand to customers and do not act to create dissonance.

This balance has been of particular concern in taking forward the 'Proposition for Staff'. The corporate glue is reinforced through the establishment of the HR frameworks and HR forum. However, the scenario of '*My Deal*' is by its nature one of locally tailored packages and solutions which could easily lead to greater fragmentation and progressive pulling away from an overall corporate identity. The composite framework for its development is therefore critical: it must be sufficiently flexible to enable the businesses to 'package' the approach for their needs while retaining a *minimum or core deal* for all staff across NatWest UK.

Without this binding framework there is the potential for businesses to become so distinctive in terms of culture, and performance management structures that the transferability of staff across the organisation would be curtailed not only to the detriment of individuals' development but to the detriment of the performance of the organisation overall. The customers' needs must be paramount – our aim to become 'First Choice for Customers' can never be subjugated to our desire to be 'First Choice for Staff'. Rather they must be mutually reinforcing.

Engagement and communication

Keeping the concept on the executive agenda is also vital, not only to retain and reinforce the corporate perspective but also to champion the development in the eyes of staff. If the executive team is aware of the approach it will be able to reinforce the principles in communications to staff, enhancing awareness and overall progress of the programme. Derek Torrington reminds us of this central role for HR directors in Chapter 1.

The last key learning point has been the importance of aligning and integrating shorter term initiatives within the overall umbrella so that they are seen to build upon the core philosophy. For example the introduction of a staff survey was key to building feedback processes at NatWest UK and business level. This provided information on the effectiveness of existing policies and practices and helped identify whether changes were required, either at NatWest UK policy level or at business level, to help line managers better match needs locally. A past criticism among staff members was that initiatives appeared to be introduced in isolation and that there did not appear to be any overall coherent strategy or picture. In planning the work behind the 'Proposition for Staff' the initial focus was not only on building a holistic strategy for the implementation of policies and practices to support '*My Deal*', but also the programming in of the supporting initiatives along the way. It is vital that all changes are aligned with the overall stated goals. If this is not achieved staff will quickly spot the contradictions and gaps.

CONCLUSIONS: LOOKING AHEAD

There are a variety of options in going forward. The model we have developed could be regarded as a template which describes a number of scenarios an organisation may find itself in and against which different routes could be considered. We conclude by noting the most important considerations associated with each option.

Option 1 – Accelerate progress across the whole organisation to the scenario of 'My Deal'

- In a devolved business portfolio structure, how can this be managed as a central initiative without it being seen to override individual business autonomy and differing market conditions?
- How will momentum and engagement across the organisation be achieved and managed?
- How will line managers' capability be developed in line with the overall pace of the programme? What are the implications on training and learning investment and focus?
- What is the potential impact of aligning or developing new, more flexible systems and processes to keep ahead of the programme, e.g. salary budgeting and payroll systems?
- How will the relationship with the unions be affected and how ready and willing are they to embrace such changes?
- The role of HR would require rapid redefinition and potentially skills development. What is the new HR role?

Option 2 – Facilitate a 'staged' progress towards the scenario of 'My Deal' with businesses moving at different paces

- What different expectations will arise between different groups of staff and how can these be managed to avoid frustration or cross-business comparison?
- How can sufficient focus be retained on overarching organisational goals during the transition?
- What legal and other constraints would need to be considered and managed?
- What is the impact of changes to systems and processes at different levels and at different times?
- Line management skills development would be at different rates and priorities. What is the overall impact on training and learning programmes?
- Approaches to the unions would be fragmented as each particular business identifies its requirements. What is the potential impact on the overall relationship?
- Is there potential for cost drift and how could this be managed?
- The differing paces of implementation will generate learning. How should this be harnessed and shared?

Option 3 – Recognise that different businesses will adopt different scenarios within the model for managing the 'Proposition with Staff'

- What are the benefits of such a fragmented approach?

- Will those businesses who see their competitors adopt these more flexible approaches surrender advantage?
- How would we manage the permanent fragmentation of the organisation?
- What is the potential impact on the 'single view' that the customer has of the organisation?
- How will transferability of skills be maintained and managed, particularly in the key cadres?
- What is the impact on the overall HR community and its standing within the organisation?
- Society is changing regardless of whether parts of the organisation change accordingly. How will we acknowledge and meet individual needs and what is the impact of our ability to recruit, retain and motivate our staff?

We are still in the early stages of this development and recognise that changes may take place in our marketplace and/or internally which could either impact on the rate of introduction or indeed change the shape of the programme. Nevertheless, we have already seen significant benefits being delivered and are encouraged to press on with delivering the overall 'Proposition for Staff' programme.

7

The role of the HR function in building a new proposition for staff

PETER HERRIOT

Institute for Employment Studies

INTRODUCTION

The account of organisational change given in Chapter 6 highlights the ways in which the HR function can add value to a large organisation seeking to adapt to its rapidly changing environment. My purpose in this chapter is not to give an alternative account, but rather to seek to understand how the function in NatWest UK succeeded in playing such a leading role in the process of change. I will finish by pointing up the lessons for the future for the HR function implied by the NatWest UK experience. There appear to be four fundamental elements contributing to their success:

1 They used an overarching framework to express the principles underpinning the employment relationship they desired to establish with employees.
2 They ensured that that framework fed into corporate business planning and also into local business practice.
3 They adapted these activities successfully to the devolved organisational structure.
4 They evaluated their progress and planned for the future in the light of a clear model of what determines the successful application of the framework.

I will deal with each of these features in turn, while recognising with the authors that a great deal still needs to be done before the framework is universally understood and applied in practice.

UNDERSTANDING, NOT RHETORIC

The theoretical framework on which the 'Proposition for Staff' was based was the psychological contract. This concept was originally used by Argyris (1960), and subsequently developed by Levinson (1962), Schein (1978) and others. The psychological contract is defined as the beliefs of each of the parties to the employment relationship, the individual and the organisation, as to what their mutual obligations are.

The psychological contract is distinct, therefore, from the formal employment contract, in that it refers to beliefs about what the deal is rather than what is written down about it; it is a psychological rather than a legal construct. This does not mean, however, that the formal contract does not contribute to the psychological one. Clearly, legal terms and conditions will affect perceptions of obligation. Nor does the term 'psychological' imply that the psychological contract is all in the mind and never expressed. On the contrary, it may be explicit to varying degrees. To the extent that it is explicit, each party will have a clearer idea of what the other believes the deal to be, though such explicitness does not necessarily imply agreement.

However, the concept of the psychological concept as classically defined does have two very important implications. The first is that different individuals will have different perceptions of their psychological contract; there will be no universal notion of what 'the' deal is in any one organisation. This is for several reasons:

- different people have different perceptions, even of the same terms and conditions
- different people in the same organisation usually have different terms and conditions
- the psychological contract covers much more than perceptions of terms and conditions (for example, prospects of promotion, willingness to be mobile).

The second implication of the psychological contract is that the employment relationship is perceived to be one of exchange. The idea embraces the promissory exchange of offers by the two parties, and therefore the mutual obligation to fulfil these offers (Rousseau, 1995).

The psychological contract is essentially a content-based concept, however. It encapsulates what at any point in time is the perceived deal between the parties. It does not have much to say about how the deal was arrived at or about the origins of the perceptions of mutual obligation. A process model (Herriot and Pemberton, 1996) was therefore developed to enable the change implications of the concept of the psychological contract to be made clear. A simpler working model for organisational use was also developed (Herriot and Pemberton, 1997) (*see* Fig. 7.1). This contracting model emphasises the two fundamental implications of the contract, i.e. that it differs between individuals, and that it is a two-way exchange process rather than a unilaterally imposed one. It also stresses the importance of the business and social contexts, of information exchange, of equity and of monitoring and honouring the deal.

The original idea of the psychological contract was an attempt to understand employees' responses to the employment relationship, in particular such attitudinal responses as organisational commitment and motivation. It is not surprising, therefore, that the concept has gained in popularity as a consequence of the recent and continuing organisational restructurings typical of the last two decades, for it offers an explanation for the feelings and reactions of those made redundant and those who survive (Noer, 1993). Such an explanation is couched in terms of strong feelings about the perceived reneging of the organisation on the psychological contract that employees thought they had. For many, that contract contained the elements of security of employment for loyalty and hard work, and enforced redundancy was seen to break it. The need to renegotiate a new contract to replace the old one was seen as a logical consequence (Herriot and Pemberton, 1995a).

The HR function at NatWest UK selected the contracting model for those very reasons. They understood the consequences of the recent restructuring for the morale and

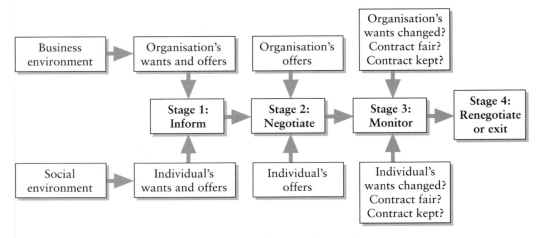

Fig. 7.1 The four stages of psychological contracting

commitment of its survivors, and they believed that the elements of individuality and mutuality were crucial to re-establishing the employment relationship on whatever terms met both the organisation's business and the employees' personal needs. Their use of the psychological contract was therefore entirely in accord with its original meaning and its use as an analytical concept to understand organisational change. Their further use of the model of contracting was a principled extension of the analytical concept to facilitate organisational change.

In this respect, the HR function at NatWest UK demonstrated an unusual degree of critical thinking. For in choosing to embrace the classical concept, they rejected its recent *rhetorical bastardisation*. One of the major difficulties faced by practitioners is that no sooner has an idea been seen to be useful in understanding a situation than it is perverted by opinion formers to mean something entirely different (Legge, 1995). The idea of the psychological contract has recently become a rhetorical device. The (bad) old psychological contract of loyalty in exchange for security has given way to the (good) new psychological contract of flexibility in exchange for employability.

Or so runs the rhetoric. The function of such rhetoric is to enable its users to get their way, in this case by pretending that what they want to be the case is in fact the case. The deal of flexibility for employability is new, good, and inevitable, they urge. Clearly, the rhetorical perversion of the idea of the psychological contract entirely destroys those two features of the original concept that were so attractive to NatWest UK's HR function, viz its mutuality and its individuality. For this supposedly inevitable new deal is unilaterally imposed and is the same for everyone.

The rhetorical perversion of the concept of the psychological contract is not the only such perversion currently being peddled. There is a general tendency among some gurus, consultants, and high profile HR practitioners to create or embrace new rhetorics. Their motives may be varied: to create a reputation for themselves, to market an associated product, or to exercise more power in their organisations. These rhetorics usually capitalise upon our tendency to think in binary categories (bad old versus good new), or in cataclysmic terms (the end of the job). It is one of the main functions of HR practitioners in such a fevered climate of ideas to review such rhetoric. Top management is often attracted by clear and simple analyses which appear to capture the essence of the problem. Critique, however, is not enough. HR practitioners have to come up with something better. The 'something better' is not necessarily something new. In the NatWest UK case it had been around for a generation.

To summarise, the first reason for the success of the NatWest UK HR function was that it chose a simple and clear practical expression of the values it believed should underpin the employment relationship. And the proper meaning was retained despite its subsequent rhetorical perversion.

BUSINESS PLANNING AND BUSINESS PRACTICE

The selection of a framework which embodies the values underpinning the desired employment relationship was only the start, however, albeit a necessary first step which many omit. The next task was to ensure that the framework, its values, and their implications for practice, fed into top-level business planning and grass roots business practice. Clearly this task is one of creating organisational change, not as in the past, 'waiting for a task list' to come down from on high.

However, the HR function was not fighting a lone battle. Top management had already embraced the concept of stakeholding. The balanced business scorecard was a recognition of two principles: first, that there were other interests to be considered in addition to those of the shareholders; and second, that in a finance sector organisation used to measuring everything that moved, indices of the degree of satisfaction of the stakeholders were essential for credibility.

Within such a context the ideas of the employees as customers, and of NatWest UK as their first choice as employer, sat well. The existence of an employee attitude survey permitted changes in their degree of satisfaction with their deal to be measured. It also enabled the three key elements of fairness, choice and flexibility to be elicited and concentrated upon.

As the previous chapter indicates, this treatment of staff as one of four sets of stakeholders was supported by a variety of policies and practices: Investors in People accreditation, increased flexibility in working hours, open job advertising, capability and skills analyses, and so on. While many other large organisations boast a similar quiverful of HR initiatives, not many of them have an underlying framework to justify, integrate and motivate them.

One of the major problems in discovering and understanding what is going on in organisations today is that outside investigators usually derive their information about HR interventions from one or two sources: HR practitioners and, perhaps, top management. They seldom hear from middle line managers, or from ordinary employees. Hence they only receive perceptions from one perspective, and not an entirely disinterested one at that. HR practitioners have a tendency to believe that the systems they have put in place (or to use more grandiose metaphors, the architecture they have constructed, or the programs they have rolled out) automatically get used. Yet the little research which uses a triangulated design (e.g. Hirsh and Jackson, 1996) discovers marked differences in the perceptions of those with different perspectives. Designers, users and recipients do not often agree about the value of HR processes.

The thorough and regular sampling of the attitudes of staff at all levels enabled NatWest UK to get a regular fix on attitudes towards HR initiatives and towards other elements of the employment relationship, however. As noted in the previous chapter, this evidence suggested historic lows in motivation and morale, in common with the rest of the sector. Also in common with almost every organisation known to the writer, attitudes were less favourable lower down the organisational hierarchy than higher up. This evidence suggested irrefutably that the principles of the psychological contract (the 'Proposition for Staff') had to be demonstrably put into practice at grass roots level. Unless this occurred, the initiative would become perceived as 'just another management fad'.

This feeding of the framework into the grass roots of the businesses was primarily accomplished through their HR directors. Some concentrated upon persuading their managing directors of its importance, others directly pointed to business units where the management team was likely to welcome such an intervention. The most noteworthy of such projects were in factory type environments, where a lot of the work involves routine processing of documents or data. However, one was with a functional unit (finance) and another with senior business managers nearing the end of their careers. This variety of projects demonstrated that the framework was not an HR process or system, but was rather a way of negotiating the employment relationship which could be expressed in different ways with different staff. The next task is to discover the best way of transferring the learning gained at the project sites to other parts of the organisation.

Thus the HR function succeeded in feeding the framework into business planning at the top level of the organisation; and it also succeeded in penetrating the grass roots at local level. Much has been written recently about the need for HR practitioners to get a seat at top table (Tyson, 1995b), and the appointment of the personnel director to the executive committee indicated success in this regard. Yet there is also a powerful research literature (e.g. Beer, Eisenstat and Spector, 1990) which insists that successful organisational change has to have local roots. NatWest UK HR function succeeded in achieving both sorts of leverage, and the next section explains how.

ADAPTATION TO DEVOLUTION

Many organisations have decentralised and devolved into separate businesses in order better to address different markets. Some have gone on to acquire other businesses in order to enhance their presence in these markets. NatWest UK is no exception. There have been varied consequences for HR in such organisations. In some, HR is structured as follows:

1 Corporate HR has been reduced to a very few senior staff who are concerned with corporate board succession and remuneration.
2 The businesses retain a few senior HR staff to deal with reward policy, performance management, management development, and employee relations.
3 They are likely, however, to have contracted out the routine HR tasks such as payroll and benefits.
4 The training function will probably have been contracted out or turned into a business unit which has to earn its keep outside as well as inside the organisation.

5 Line managers have been given responsibility for people management.

6 Staff have been told that their development is their own responsibility.

It is a common complaint in such organisations that line managers have neither the time, the skills, nor the inclination to fulfil their people management responsibilities unaided. Dissatisfaction with career is likely to be very strong in these organisations.

. Others, however, have begun to consider carefully the source of their competitive advantage, such as it is. For many, it is not now possible to compete on the basis of cost alone. Cost competitiveness is taken for granted, and real advantage is seen to derive from certain core organisational competencies (Hamel and Prahalad, 1994). These are based on the skills and knowledge of employees, who must therefore be enabled to enhance their existing skills and to acquire additional ones. This will both keep organisations ahead of the competition in their existing markets and also facilitate them to colonise new ones. Given that competitive advantage derives primarily from employees' skills, the enhancement of such skills in order to retain existing market dominance, and the acquisition of new ones in order to colonise new markets are both business requirements. Such a business stance requires a larger and different contribution from the HR function than is typical of many recently devolved organisations. The NatWest UK HR function adapted to devolution in such a way as to provide this contribution.

First, while the size of corporate HR was slashed, it nevertheless retained a fundamental role. The most important element of this role was the task of retaining 'the corporate glue', the 'NatWest brand', as the previous chapter puts it. In other words, the task of corporate HR is to ensure that the fundamental values which underpin the framework are adhered to throughout the different businesses. The knife-edge that corporate HR must tread is well expressed: 'The composite framework . . . must be sufficiently flexible to enable the businesses to "package" the approach for their needs while retaining a minimum or core deal for all staff across NatWest UK.' (Chapter 6, p. 103).

One of the dilemmas here is whether that core deal is about the content of the different deals, or whether it is about process only. In other words, are there elements, such as an explicit promise about length of notice of any redundancies, which should apply to all staff, or is it just the fair and explicit way in which deals are concluded that is crucial?

The HR function also ensured that there was an HR presence on the boards of each of the businesses. Each business had an HR director to enable its business plan to incorporate its own strategic skill needs. These are markedly different for the five businesses, first because of the different services they offer, and second because some are in an expansion phase, others in contraction.

The third way in which HR adapted to the devolution into the businesses was to send many of its formerly corporate-based practitioners out into the businesses as consultants. This met the complaint that line managers could not be expected to take over people management without some help and advice. Other more specialist HR services, which line managers could not be expected to master, are charged out as a service arm.

Finally, all administration tasks requiring large-scale IT services, such as personnel records and payroll, are located in two large operations centres.

Thus NatWest UK has recognised that a number of different purposes are achieved by its HR function:

● It plays a fundamental role in developing corporate business plans and strategy.

- It helps achieve one of the four elements of the balanced business scorecard.
- It ensures that certain values underpin the employment relationship.
- It helps individual businesses formulate and achieve their business objectives.
- It helps line managers with their people management responsibilities.
- It provides essential administrative and technical services.

It is noteworthy that the HR function moved very quickly to service the devolved businesses and to decrease the size of corporate HR. Perhaps the speed of adaptation and the obvious desire to add value to the businesses are two of the reasons why it has actually enhanced its influence at NatWest UK. Certainly, the advantages of an in-house facility have been recognised in the case of all the services just examined. There is little contracting out of HR services, probably because the way NatWest UK maintains its relationship with its staff is now considered by top management to be one of its core competencies that bring it competitive advantage. And you certainly do not contract out your core competencies!

EVALUATION AND PLANNING

The final source of HR's success is to be found in the way in which it is evaluating progress and planning future actions. There is a current fashion for benchmarking against other organisations which discourages careful analysis of one's own organisation. NatWest UK uses its own previous attitude surveys as benchmarks, in order to establish whether there are changes in attitudes over time. Comparisons are primarily internal because NatWest UK is looking to estimate the effects of certain interventions (for example, changes in benefits) on particular attitudes (for example, satisfaction with the package).

More important, however, is the use of the framework of the 'Proposition for Staff' in order to estimate progress. In other words, it has confidence in its own framework to use it as the benchmark. Why benchmark against others when your own framework is an element of your core competence and itself a source of competitive advantage? The HR function established that its own degree of devolution and the management skills of line managers are the key determinants of perceptions of the deal. Given that devolution has preceded any concerted effort to enhance line managers' people management skills, the diagnosis was clear. There would need to be more such training and development of the line before staff attitudes to the deal shifted entirely from 'What's my deal?' to 'My deal'. And the process of devolution itself should pause for the balance to be redressed.

With this diagnosis in mind, it is hardly surprising that one of the three options for going forward appears preferable to the others. If the framework is seen as making certain values explicit in the way in which the employment relationship is conducted, then the third option seems preferable, for it offers the flexibility in the contents of the deal so that the motivation of the different types of staff in the different businesses will be enhanced, while at the same time it maintains the NatWest UK brand of fairness, choice, and flexibility in a two-way deal.

What is important, though, is not which option appears preferable at this point in time. Rather, it is the evident benefit of evaluating one's progress in improving the employment relationship for both parties in terms of the framework which is informing that improvement. For alternative action plans follow from such an evaluation. However, no such implications for action follow from a traditional benchmarking exercise. Or rather, the implications are seen in terms of the need to adopt the processes and practices of the 'superior' performers with whom one's own organisation is compared. Very seldom is this an appropriate response, since processes and practices are set in a specific history and culture of interrelated HR and business activities.

ORGANISATIONAL TRANSITIONS

The NatWest UK experience points to a fundamental issue which any HR function will have to address in the future, if it is not already doing so now. It is this: structural change is now so frequent an event that organisations are permanently in a state of transition. Nicholson and West (1988) take the stages of transition to be preparation, encounter, adjustment, and stabilisation. Our habitual analysis has always assumed that stabilisation was the norm, and that the other three stages simply punctuated periods of stability. Yet there is an argument for saying that the stability stage actually seldom occurs. Rather, organisational life today consists increasingly only of preparation, encounter, and adjustment. Many would assert that there is little or no opportunity to prepare, since many changes are forced on organisations by external events they could not possibly have predicted. And those who allow that preparation is usually possible nevertheless admit that preparation for the next change has to occur while they are still adjusting to the previous one.

This is very difficult for organisations such as NatWest UK to become used to, since the radical structural changes of the last five years followed a long period of stability. Yet already NatWest UK's six devolved businesses have become five in number, and acquisitions, mergers, and flotations are frequent events in the financial sector. New products and services, many of them driven by technological advances, new markets, and changes in regulatory mechanisms are almost daily events. All these developments indicate that structural and process changes will follow, and therefore that organisational transitions will be regular and frequent events.

The necessary conclusion is that HR functions will not in the future need to concern themselves with planning to get to a new, steady and stable state. Rather, they will be busy enabling the organisation to prepare for, encounter and adjust to new structures and processes. And that will in turn require them to help employees make the individual transitions which these organisational transitions imply.

In the finance sector the 'Big Bang' of eleven years ago caught the vast majority of organisations unprepared. HR functions had failed to comprehend the scale of the competition, especially from abroad, and the new skills that would be required to design, market, and sell new products and services. Furthermore, many HR practitioners were slow to see that diversity of products and markets would lead to devolved businesses. Hence, instead of helping in the design of these new organisations, they continued to busy themselves with their corporate level administrative tasks. Moreover, when that other form of restructuring, downsizing, occurred, they had problems in managing the process in a satisfactory way and in helping the survivors adjust to their new situation. In sum, instead of managing the transitions of the last ten years, many HR functions became their victims.

A key test case for HR's fitness to manage organisational transitions in the future is mergers and acquisitions. HR functions are now involved in the planning and management of most downsizings, since the treatment of the redundant and the morale of the survivors are obviously people issues that no one else is keen to tackle. Mergers and acquisitions are another matter. They are the stuff of top management strategy and of media publicity. They involve intrigue, high finance and merchant banks. They can be represented as military campaigns, with all the individual glory or disgrace that victory or defeat can bring the players.

Yet here if anywhere the case for HR to be involved from the very first is irrefutable (Mirvis and Marks, 1992). Time after time the incompatibility of two organisational cultures has been cited as the reason for the failure of a merger. Time after time the combination of two organisational structures into a workable whole has proved impossible. Time after time it has proved impossible to select the best out of two sets of organisational processes so that the new set meets the merger's needs and is internally coherent at the same time. The easy solution – to adopt the culture, structure, and processes of the more powerful partner – has failed repeatedly. Why should it succeed, when the junior partner has usually been acquired because it adds something different to the senior partner's portfolio?

All of these issues are just as important as the financial ones which normally occupy the attention and interest of actors and commentators alike. All of them require the knowledge and skills of HR practitioners if they are to be successfully addressed. Yet how often are they involved in the decision whether to attempt an acquisition or merger? The planning of the campaign? The design of the new structure? The management of culture change? The selection of new systems? Given the evidence about the causes of failure of mergers, the answer seems to be not very often, or, if they were involved, not very effectively, and in a reactive rather than a proactive mode.

So the area of organisational transition is perhaps the most vital for the HR function to annexe. I use the word annexe advisedly, since as Abbott (1988) has pointed out, professions gain or lose power as a consequence of the amount of occupational territory to which they can lay claim. The terrain of that territory is, of course, constantly changing. Technicians now use IT to do much of the routine auditing which used to be the staple of the accountancy profession. Yet that profession has busily acquired new territory as it has annexed, for example, the whole new goldmine of compliance. Organisational transitions are another such area of growth, but the HR profession is in danger of losing out to the ubiquitous accountancy firms and management consultants, not to mention the merchant banks who arrange the finance.

INDIVIDUAL TRANSITIONS

Transitions are constantly occurring at the organisational level, but the same is true at the individual level of analysis (Stephens, 1994). And just as organisational transitions are so truncated that the initial preparation stage is often limited and the final stabilisation stage is omitted entirely, so individual transitions often consist of encounter and adjustment only. And even while adjustment is occurring, preparation for another transition may start.

It is dangerous to assume that the current fashion for devolution in organisations will continue, or that it will be considered appropriate in every national culture. Centralisation may return. Organisations are also likely to teeter between taking a longer and a shorter term perspective, and between growth and contraction. Hence the range of transitions which individuals may need to make is wide and hard to predict. Among them, however, the following (or their opposites) are bound to make an appearance:

- from full-time employment in an organisation to unemployment
- from full-time employment to self-employment
- from full-time employment in one organisation to full-time in another
- from full-time employment to part-time or fixed-term employment
- from one form of career (e.g. upwardly mobile) to another (e.g. sideways)
- from one functional or occupational specialism to another
- from a specialism into general management
- from one industrial sector to another
- from one location to another
- from one role to another
- from one project to another
- from one role to an enlarged version of it.

These individual transitions can be distinguished from one another along several dimensions.

First, their *outcomes for the individual*: a role change may be seen as an opportunity, a cross-functional move as an irrevocable step, redundancy as personal disaster (or as freedom at last). The result may be more time and less money, in which case we may start worrying about survival; or more work and less time, so that lifestyle and health may become a problem.

Second, the *predictability of the transition*: has it been signalled in advance, and do people know when it is going to happen? Uncertainty generates helplessness or anxiety, whereas advance notice permits a degree of preparation and mental practice.

Third, the *optionality of the decision*: has the individual had any say in whether a transition happens to them, and its nature? Imposition usually results in resentment or helplessness, choice in commitment to the transition and motivation to make it succeed.

Fourth, the *clarity of the post-transition role*: has it been described, but not so specifically as to inhibit its adaptation, or so loosely as to raise anxiety?

Finally, the *justification or purpose of the transition*: have the reasons been clarified to the individual? (Konovsky and Brockner, 1993). And are those attributions external (e.g. to the organisation's current business situation) or to the individual (e.g. we think you have reached your ceiling)? External attributions run the risk of resulting in feelings of powerlessness, internal ones can damage self-esteem (or enhance it).

The business importance of individual transitions is obvious. Is there sufficient flexibility in the *supply of labour* to enable labour needs to be met? And is there sufficient flexibility in the *skills of labour* to meet changing skill needs? These two forms of flexibility require different sorts of transitions. Supply flexibility implies moves from or to full-time employment and into or out of the organisation. Skill flexibility implies role transitions, cross-functional moves, and job enlargement. In both cases, the successful management of transitions so that individuals get up to speed in their new roles as fast as possible is crucial to the organisation. Hence this new definition of career management, *viz.* the management of transitions, is a fundamental task for HR in the future.

Successful management of transitions, however, can only be achieved if the *feelings* of individuals about transitions and their interests are taken into account. It can only be achieved, in other words, if the process of psychological contracting is conducted with those whom the organisation wishes to make a transition. Organisations have consistently ignored the strength of the feelings aroused by transitions. There has been some discussion of the benefits of learning how to make transitions better on the basis of previous experience of them and of reflection upon that experience. But, except in the case of compulsory redundancies, few have appreciated that many transitions can enhance or damage fundamental elements of the self (Steele, 1988). Hence they have powerful emotional consequences which will affect organisational performance, through such attitudes as organisational commitment, job satisfaction, and work motivation. They will also profoundly affect individual well-being. For example:

● Redundancy, demotion or the move to part-time employment can damage self-esteem, threaten identity (e.g. as breadwinner), and damage people's sense of agency.
● Cross-functional moves can threaten professional identity, but conversely may add to self-esteem.
● Promotions, role changes and allocation to more prestigious projects may enhance self-esteem.
● Promotions may, however, split work and home identity, since taking on a heavier workload may threaten one's identity as effective parent, spouse, or partner.
● The increased frequency of transitions may threaten the stability of our identity, since our capacity to incorporate the new roles into our notions of who we are may be stretched to the limit.
● Our feeling of being in some sense in control of our lives can only be supported if we have a degree of choice about the whether, when, and what of transitions.

Clearly, then, it is vital for the HR function to manage both organisational and personal transitions, since the knowledge and skills required to do so are more likely to be found in the function than anywhere else in the organisation. Transition management does not sound in itself a hugely glamorous or central area. But in an era of ever more rapid change, it is probably the most important task facing organisations today.

8

New organisational forms, processes, jobs and psychological contracts

Resolving the HRM issues

PAUL SPARROW

Sheffield University Management School

At the millennium there is a sense among managers that the real limits to change are self-imposed. The old structural, regulatory and institutional limits no longer seem to act as strong constraints. For those managers and organisations who wish to be radical, there is more discretion and more variety in terms of what is possible within their HRM practices than ever before. Yet, at the same time, it is easy to understand the temptation to succumb to the economic determinism arguments outlined in Chapter 1, and the perception that there is no alternative but to weather out the current changes and cope with the difficult implementation problems they bring.

Yet another example of the dilemmas that surround HR practitioners. Some dilemmas are as old as the profession, and some are very new, but one way or another they must be addressed. The chapters in Part One highlight the issues, many of which result from rapid changes in what is perhaps best termed *organisational form*. Organisational form refers to the combination of strategy, structure and internal control and co-ordination systems that provides an organisation with its operating logic, its rules of resource allocation and its mechanism of corporate governance (Creed and Miles, 1996; Pfeffer, 1992). Managers are the primary designers of this 'form', through the choices they make about the organisation and job design. There are two main changes taking place in organisational form:

- intra-firm form
- inter-firm form.

Changes in *inter-firm form* are the most visible and obvious to detect and flow from the mergers, joint ventures, strategic alliances, outsourcing, virtual organisation and cross-sector co-operative arrangements. All act to serve as opportunities (whether intentional or not) to break up existing HRM patterns, roles and responsibilities and to reconstitute them against a new set of priorities. The new priorities soon become clear within the joint venture, or the outsourced or privatised unit that is under new ownership, new systems of corporate governance, or the many other changes in *inter-firm* form. However, the greatest challenges for HR practitioners stem from changes in *intra-firm* form. This chapter is devoted mainly to issues involved in this latter change in organisational form, i.e. changes in organisation design and co-ordination systems, downsizing and delayering, the design and co-ordination of jobs, and the consequent level of trust built into the organisation.

BUSINESS PROCESS RE-ENGINEERING

The first major change in intra-firm form involves the *redesign of organisational co-ordinating systems*. A series of wonderfully named prescriptions to improve the design of organisations have entered our vocabulary. These include:

1 'Business process re-engineering', which places a new emphasis on the underlying service or production process from the perspective of customer interactions (Hammer and Champy, 1995).
2 'Fractol and modular factories' in which complex industrial enterprises are broken up into smaller divisionalised production units each with a (different) level of autonomy (Warnecke, 1993; Wildermann, 1994).
3 The 'atomised organisation' (Ryf, 1993).
4 The 'virtual corporation', in which new patterns of co-operation are developed within a company and across different companies, but are no longer limited to sequential timeflows (Davidow and Malone, 1993).

Common elements to new organisation designs

Despite the rich set of concepts, there are some elements common to all these organisation design ideas. For HR practitioners, the most common problems stem from the need to:

● create a radical view of decentralisation (Drumm, 1994)
● increase attention to horizontal business 'processes' (Johansson *et al.*, 1993)
● make changes to the design of jobs, and their associated competencies (Parker and Wall, 1996)
● understand the alterations to the levels of trust that are designed into the new control systems (Creed and Miles, 1996; Pfeffer, 1992).

A major commonality, highlighted by Mike Oram in Chapter 5, is the increased attention to horizontal business processes. Business process re-engineering (BPR), also known as 'work effectiveness' or 'process management', is being used to cut across formal organisational boundaries. As Willmott (1994) notes, the BPR approach has not concocted a novel recipe, but has 'put a name to an emergent trend in business organisation'. 'Process' thinking means that HR practitioners have to consider the management of a set of linked activities that take an input to the organisation and transform it to create an appropriate production or service output. These processes may be physical, may involve paperwork, be undertaken by computer, or may simply be a logical sequence of events. They tend to combine both physical activities with information flows. Most organisations are, it seems, designed de facto around five or six such processes.

There has been considerable critical analysis of BPR, but attention to it in one form or another will not go away (Buchanan, 1997; Willmott, 1994). One reason for such continued attention is that international research in the mid-1990s showed that *work organisation was the main factor in labour productivity* – far more important than the workers' skills or motivation. This has highlighted the need to consider the learning from a comparison of international differences and their implications for HRM, such as the relative performance of the German system, with its high number of job classifications (specialisation) which compartmentalises workers and prevents them from assuming broader roles, in contrast to the Japanese system, which stresses integration, with high levels of teamwork and frontline empowerment, as well as group co-ordination rather than craft-based individual excellence (Sparrow and Hiltrop, 1994; 1997). The McKinsey Global Institute studied nine manufacturing sectors (such as automobile manufacture, car parts, metalworking, steel, computing, consumer electronics, processed food and pharmaceuticals). In most industries German productivity was lower than that in the USA. Japanese productivity was significantly higher than that in the USA in the car, metalworking and consumer electronics sectors (by up to 45 per cent higher in steel), although across all nine sectors Japanese productivity was only 83 per cent that of the USA.

The important finding was that *most of the things that caused differences in productivity were subject to the control of managers* – how the workplace was organised in terms of working practices and the manufacturability of products. In some instances these initiatives have accumulated over a period of time. For example, Ford Motor Company has reduced the number of workers needed to make each car per day from five to two over a period of 15 years. In other cases sweeping productivity improvements have been claimed. Similarly, Lucas Industries' automotive business reduced manufacturing lead times from 55 to 12 days, cut order-to-dispatch lead times from 105 to 32 days and doubled inventory turns, thereby increasing productivity by half and reducing floorspace requirements.

BPR is, then, a business philosophy and a means by which the organisation can potentially achieve a radical change in performance. As a consequence HR practitioners are having to re-educate themselves to understand how these work effectiveness tools and techniques may be applied to jobs. These tools focus on the organisation as a core set of customer-oriented business processes rather than as a set of functions or tasks that have to be carried out. The techniques that HR practitioners have had to master include data modelling and process mapping instruments such as flow diagrams, multiple activity charts, computer process simulation programmes, business modelling, systems engineering and analysis techniques. BPR does differ from previous horizontal management philosophies such as TQM, JIT or MRPII. It takes a zero-based approach, i.e. it first asks if a process should be eliminated. The philosophy is one of wiping the slate clean, starting from scratch in designing a business process, and pretending that there are no systems or procedures in place to constrain the ideal flow of work. The approach, if conducted properly, analyses many of the cultural issues that have previously reduced the level of effectiveness of TQM, JIT and MRPII initiatives, such as reporting relationships, performance measures and rewards.

However, it also can be seen as a retrograde step that reduces the levels of employee commitment. In Chapter 3 David Guest argues that we have seen an evolution in the way in which organisations ensure commitment, characterised by short swings back (with BPR being an example of a recent swing back to low commitment work designs). He questions whether we are on a simple linear path and asks if instead the progress is circular (*see* Fig. 3.1, p. 46). However, such a view requires a fairly even state equilibrium outside the organisation. What happens if the external environment forces very radical changes to the shape, form and business process that a firm adopts, and if the 'work logic' of those who put the new design in place makes commitment, in any reasonable form, very difficult to construct?

HRM implications of new organisation designs

Even though the specification of many of the organisational designs mentioned already (BPR, fractol and modular organisations, the virtual organisation) is still vague, the changes invoked by the various attempts to implement them are considerable and wide-ranging. They are creating an imperative to reform radically HRM systems. Why? Because existing HRM systems are, as noted in Chapter 1, designed largely around the *person–job fit*. The new organisation designs require a very different form of co-ordination and operating culture. For example, business process redesign '(re)constitutes' the human dimension of organising (Willmott, 1994) and has very significant implications for the sorts of HRM practices that are successful. This is because (Sparrow and Hiltrop, 1994):

- employees are exposed to new sources of information and new networks of relationships
- there are changes to the roles that employees are expected to play
- managers think differently about the tasks that need to be done
- required decision-making processes are altered
- the timespans of discretion before the consequence of an inappropriate decision become known are altered
- the criteria for effectiveness, such as the judgement and leadership capabilities needed by employees, are altered
- there are shifts in the actual work content and business process flow
- the choice of performance management criteria and measurement metrics is changed
- there are changes to career aspirations, problems created by the natural inclination of people not to break the habits of their past and present roles, and significant shifts in their power, influence and credibility.

This has created a very large HRM agenda indeed. Many organisations are being driven towards new organisational designs and solutions, but still have to operate within the bounds of what is possible as a consequence of their history and inheritance (Bartlett and Ghoshal, 1992; Humes, 1993; Ulrich and Lake, 1990). However, to the extent that radical changes have been made in the structure of a business process, it entails dramatic changes in all other aspects of the organisation, most notably in the content and definition of jobs. BPR closes the distance between supply points, production, assembly and customers. In relying on decentralisation, work simplification, streamlining of information systems, the eradication of functional barriers and the promotion of involvement it inevitably results in the streamlining, deletion or change in the content of jobs. The roles of lower level managers are especially affected by BPR, but those in higher levels do not remain unaffected. This is because jobs-based flexibility is required in the effort to ensure that the right people talk to one another, only appropriate information is considered, decisions are made at the right level, and technology is used to carry out mundane or basic control steps.

BPR, then, redefines jobs because roles are understood in the broader context of the business process (*see* the discussion concerning 'Inappropriate structures' in Chapter 5 by Mike Oram). It also changes the corporate performance criteria against which jobs are being designed. In a highly uncertain environment organisations are identifying stable business processes in order to help clarify the architecture into which jobs should be fitted, such as the reporting relationships, responsibilities and control systems. BPR often views the present construction of jobs as an obstacle to change and so is not only associated with a fundamental reappraisal of the content of jobs, but also alters the broader context to which flexibility is focused (Grint and Willcocks, 1995). As organisations blur the distinctions and boundaries between functions, people, the organisation, its suppliers and its customers, they are making notable changes to the performance indices against which jobs are measured. Jobs are now being calibrated against a series of new value-based indices, such as:

1 **Quality**: meeting customer requirements, fitness for use, process integrity, elimination of waste, continuous improvement.
2 **Service**: customer support, product service, product support, flexibility to meet customer demands, flexibility to meet market changes.
3 **Cost**: design and engineering costs, conversion, quality assurance, distribution, administration, inventory, materials.
4 **Time**: time to market, response to market forces, lead times, materials, inventory.

CHANGES IN THE CONTENT, FORM AND CO-ORDINATION OF JOBS

What is in a job? Jobs-based flexibility

A second change in *intra-firm form* can therefore be seen in the response made by organisations at the level of the job, in terms of how performance is measured and jobs are designed (Sparrow, 1997b). Initiatives such as BPR impact the design of jobs in two ways:

● The control of work activities is usually put under a single umbrella, which views the work that jobs are designed to process as part of a continuous and simultaneous set of actions, rather than a sequence of elements that flow from one task to another.
● Changes are made either to the formal structure, occupation, or career stream into which the job is based, or to the design of the work or business process into which the various tasks and elements that have been bundled together as jobs may be placed.

In order to understand the impact that such changes are having on the field of HRM, we need to consider the phenomenon of jobs-based flexibility, the impact that downsizing and delayering is having on the nature of jobs, the common changes that are occurring in the content of modern jobs in the organisation, and the level of trust that is being built into the new work designs. Each issue has created its own agenda for HR practitioners.

It was argued in Chapter 1 that changes in the content of jobs, the form in which they are designed, and the way in which they need to be co-ordinated by HRM systems, have all made the construction of existing jobs 'unsafe' and have rendered obsolete much of the armoury and technical education of HR practitioners. Most of the business literature, and the opening chapters of this book point to a series of deep qualitative shifts taking place in the nature of work. Concepts such as 'process re-engineering', 'delayering', 'downsizing', and 'dejobbing' have all entered the HR practitioner's vocabulary. In combination these changes have significant implications for what is now meant when we talk of a 'job'.

Not only are there fewer of the old-style jobs in existence, but in the work situations encouraged by the current economic and technological realities, it is harder to package work into discrete 'jobs' (Davidow and Malone, 1993). Work, it is argued, should be 'dejobbed' and many of the structural and organisation design assumptions that were used to delineate separate jobs should be thrown to one side and treated as a relic of the early industrial age. Regardless of the debate over how many jobs will eventually be lost, what the new balance between internal labour markets or external or peripheral forms of employment will be, or which forms of work will no longer be organised into discrete jobs and which will remain, there is a general trend towards what is best described as 'jobs-based flexibility'. Before I define this, it is important to note that organisations are currently structured around jobs, but the flexibility they seek is far more profound than simply considering new time patterns of work, multiskilling, and new forms of pay. While all these issues have to be considered, this is increasingly just a part of a total package, and a part of a process which is forcing flexibility in the very definition of what a job constitutes.

In coping with these challenges, as noted in Chapter 1, there is another fundamental tension within the field of HRM in modern organisations. The majority of the personnel management systems – such as job and role descriptions, job evaluations, payment systems, and selection and promotion systems – are based on the historical existence of a formal hierarchy of jobs, which have been brought together under a formal organisational structure and design, which has in turn helped to clarify the reporting relationships between one job and another, the number of levels or bands into which jobs are classified, and the spans of control associated with a particular job. The implications of this go beyond the various impacts that changes in organisation design have on HRM policies (*see* Chapter 1). It also influences employment relations systems. Traditionally, much activity to do with industrial relations and the management of the employment relationship has been structured around an exchange or conflict of views between three parties (the organisation, the individual through their trades union, and the state) about three simple issues (Huiskamp, 1995):

1 **Time**: the total duration of the tasks that make up a job, the amount of time to be worked in a day, week or year, recuperation time, availability for work times.
2 **Qualifications**: the knowledge, skills and psychosocial abilities required to perform the various tasks that make up a job, the required qualifications, the available qualifications in the labour market.
3 **Wages and performance**: the 'wage–effort bargain' that results from the valuation given to job activity, time and qualifications.

Bargaining around these issues was conducted on the basis of the existence within organisations of discrete jobs. As we shall see throughout Part Three, issues of flexibility have therefore been seen mainly as processes which require negotiation about job conditions or changes in the various tasks or work elements that are bundled up into 'jobs'.

Manipulating this bundle of tasks is described as 'functional flexibility', which refers to an organisation's ability to deploy employees between activities and tasks to match changing workloads, production-methods or technology. It is loosely connected with the topic of multiskilling, although in practice this has become the preserve of manufacturing operations in highly unionised environments. The chapters in Part One suggest we must take a much broader perspective and understand a new field of what I call jobs-based flexibility (Sparrow, 1997b).

The very term expresses the problem for HR practitioners and academics alike. What is it? Jobs-based flexibility as a concept captures a kaleidoscope of *ad hoc* and opportunistic initiatives that organisations are making, such as multiskilling, job enlargement and upskilling, labour intensification and core–peripheral job strategies. However, experience shows that these initiatives all risk high levels of failure if the job design and work organisation implications are not considered properly. The traditional view of job design argues that in making choices about how best to differentiate, co-ordinate, integrate and allocate tasks to individuals or groups, the challenge for organisations is how to break the task down into parts that are small enough to be within the competence of individual job holders, but also challenging enough to motivate performance (Parker and Wall, 1996). Jobs-based flexibility is a much broader activity and involves the simultaneous manipulation of four elements:

1 The various components that are bundled together into definable 'jobs' (through the tasks, operations, work elements and duties that are still deemed necessary).
2 Redesign of the context into which jobs are placed and the position of the new job in the broader organisation design (through the family of jobs to which it is deemed to belong, the occupation of the job holder, the career stream to which jobs belong, and the work process of which it forms a part).
3 The way in which jobs relate to and interact with one another (through the roles assigned to jobs, the information and control systems, the relative levels of power they possess).
4 The way in which HRM systems integrate the new bundles of jobs into the strategic process (through the way in which employee contributions to the jobs are co-ordinated, controlled and committed to).

In combination, these changes have both made the construction of existing jobs 'unsafe' and rendered obsolete much of the armoury and technical education of HR practitioners. HR practitioners need detailed technical insights into each of the four fields of knowledge just noted, much of which resides with other specialists or line managers. It is by necessity a very broad concept that captures deep and significant changes being made to the structure of organisations and the purpose of individual work. However, there is no clear academic understanding of what is happening to guide practitioners. As a concept, jobs-based flexibility crosses the work of traditional job analysis academics (who consider the partitioning of work into manageable units), organisation design academics (who understand the co-ordination of work across important vertical, horizontal, and external boundaries) and HRM specialists (who ponder over the creation of HRM systems to control and gain commitment to the implementation of the new systems).

HR practitioners have to digest the messages coming from the many disciplines that contribute an understanding of what is going on and then make immediate, but long-lasting decisions about the job and organisation design issues. In applying this knowledge, they have to consider what is now meant by a job. This is because in many cases it makes more sense to see the organisation as a collection and complex pattern of interrelated roles, for which there is a broad blueprint to ensure that the combination of activity is still co-ordinated. The logic underlying the differentiation, co-ordination, integration and allocation of tasks to individuals or groups is rarely clear or analysable.

Jobs-based flexibility is required when organisations choose to repackage significantly the work elements, tasks, duties and positions that are together bundled into definable 'jobs', or when they redesign the relationship between jobs or the context into which jobs are placed. It is usually required in order to deliver improvements to the organisation in terms of price, quality, variety of goods and services, and so is driven by two major aims:

1 To decrease the tension that exists between the organisation's need for versatility in its production or service strategy and the existing outcomes that result from the way that jobs are currently designed and constructed.
2 To seek increased versatility by tapping (and better matching) the skills, capabilities, adaptability and creativity of the workforce through a range of interventions such as communication, multiskilling, team building, and horizontal process redesign.

The impact of downsizing and delayering

Sadly, the main way in which jobs-based flexibility has been pursued has been on the back of tactical responses in the form of *downsizing* and *delayering*. A recent survey of 400 US Conference Board organisations attempted to differentiate those that had merely downsized from those that had downsized but had also made more significant changes to the design of work and the requisite skills training (Mirvis, 1997). There are two significant learning points for HR practitioners that have resulted from these changes in organisational form:

● They have re-established the importance of, and need to understand, key linkage positions or boundary spanning roles.
● The impact is seen most strongly in the need to change HRM systems and in the changed nature of surviving jobs.

We are being forced to reappraise some very basic assumptions about the nature of jobs, the design and operation of organisations, and the psychological underpinnings of organisational behaviour. Downsizing is often equated with the sudden and dramatic changes to the number of jobs associated with a process of restructuring or rationalisation. Changes to, and flexibility in, the content of remaining jobs are not automatic, but generally follow because of alterations to the volume of work or the way in which the downsizing was achieved. Downsizing is also often focused on one part of an organisation more than another. A related process is 'delayering'. This is where a purposeful decision is made to reduce the number of vertical hierarchies in the organisation. However, while it flattens the hierarchy, it does not flatten the lateral barriers to communication and teamworking.

The changes in organisational form outlined throughout the opening chapters of this book suggest a number of hidden threats to organisational effectiveness, about which we still know little. Organisations remain unclear about the relationship between many of the new emergent organisational forms, what then remains as a strategic human asset in each case, and the different configurations of HRM practices and the role these practices play in creating competitive advantage (Daft and Lewin, 1993). One of the paradoxes is that far from increasing flexibility, in many instances changes in form have decreased it. Job holders may become even more inflexible because some key linking roles may have inadvertently been cut out. In many instances organisations have destroyed 'linchpin roles' and the 'organisational memory' that resides within them. An example of such a role in the health service is a ward sister in hospitals. The redesign of internal activities or the externalisation of activities often destroys such 'linchpin' positions, either by removing key decisions that resided within them, or overloading the role with new apparently more important performance management priorities. Often, only local operators have the tacit insights into the business process that justify the maintenance or creation of such roles. The problem is that often neither the centre nor line managers are aware of the importance of them. Nor, indeed, have HR practitioners been aware, but in future defending the contribution of roles (not people) will be a priority.

HR practitioners are having to reconsider the role of hierarchy in organisations (*see* comments by Karen Legge in Chapter 19) from the perspective of value added activities (such as the transmission of information, location of decision-making and extension of accountability) and functional necessity, rather than in the context of the need to preserve existing careers and rewards structures. If turbulent, global markets require organisations to be more flexible and adopt whatever configuration is needed, then HR practitioners will have to rethink some current value judgements which say that hierarchy is bad and inefficient and flattened horizontal organisational forms are good and virtuous. There is no research yet to prove that decentralised and horizontal organisational forms outperform well-run hierarchies (Overholt, 1997). HR practitioners need to ensure that line managers do not naturally assume that one organisational form is better than another in the interests of political correctness. The real issue to be understood is what works best, in what markets, given our existing competencies.

However, whether or not delayering organisations is always appropriate, it is yet another force that has renewed attention to jobs-based flexibility (Sparrow, 1997b). Why is this? Most jobs require the job holder to make decisions and there is a natural timespan during which the consequence of any decision comes to light. Work at the Individual and Organisational Capability Unit (Stamp, 1990) turned attention to Jacques' early concept of hierarchy. The further up the hierarchy, or the more complex the job becomes, the longer the 'timespan of discretion'. First line workers responsible for direct operating tasks tend to operate in an environment where the timespan of discretion is no more than three months. The consequence of decisions made by first line supervisors or managers, technicians and professional specialists tends to be known within a year, whereas general managers may be making decisions that operate to a five-year timespan of discretion, and so forth. Research has shown that there are seven different levels of these timespans of discretion and each level is associated with a particular set of decision-making and judgement skills and competencies. When an organisation designs out a layer of the hierarchy, it has to reallocate decisions that were once made by the previous jobs. Delayering has generally had the effect of increasing the responsibilities and level of complexity of lower-level jobs. These jobs have to become more self-managed as direct supervision becomes physically impossible.

The challenge for HR practitioners, however, is that immediate financial and performance measurements made today cannot assess the implications of correct or incorrect decision-making, as such decisions now tend to operate and be proved effective over a longer timespan. Consequently many employees are formally charged with empowered responsibilities to make decisions that previously belonged to a different job, but are imprecisely or incorrectly measured and rewarded, and in any event need a different set of skills and competencies. The competency issue becomes clear when we consider some of the common changes in the content of jobs.

Common changes in the content of jobs

As organisations are attempting to introduce less rigid structures, extensive decentralisation and delegation of control, they do so through the design of jobs (Legge, 1995). Both industrial relations specialists looking at the bargaining process in relation to functional flexibility (Huiskamp, 1996) and occupational psychologists examining the implications of changes in job design within manufacturing, note that the requirement for the level of qualification and competence within jobs has increased. Parker and Wall (1996) point to five common developments in job content. The first is the increased relevance of *operational knowledge*. Jobs-based flexibility has tended to place employees in a better position to see the interrelationships between their actions and the consequences of them. A broader perspective on the work process is called for so that job holders can catch errors and make corrections that might otherwise have gone undetected. This requires broader and more proactive role orientations as well as the deployment and learning of more specific job knowledge. In order to 'work smarter' employees need to have knowledge of not just one, but several specialist areas of technical knowledge, functional skill or administrative process.

The second change is the need to design HRM systems that can cope with increased *work interdependence*. The extent to which employees are dependent on one another and the need for collaboration in the execution of work creates a more immediate reliance on the performance of others. This change in job content is forcing HR practitioners to place greater emphasis on the performance management systems of the organisation to integrate work and understand the relationships between the internal customers and suppliers that surround resultant jobs.

The third change is the shift in *production/service responsibilities*, where the roles and activities associated with operations that cover the direct internal or external customer interface now form a higher proportion of the job content. Similarly, the increase in responsibilities tends to be associated with increased significance and contribution of individual performance to the resultant output. This change in job content is forcing HR practitioners to attend to the greater costs associated with failure of newly designed work systems and processes, such as the increased costs of damage to technology, downtime and individual error.

Fourth, there has been an increase in the requirement for *cognitive abstract qualifications* such as decision-making, judgement, accuracy, an understanding of the organisation and the ability to analyse and solve problems in unexpected situations. These demands have increased in two ways: attentional demands (the passive monitoring of aspects of work) and problem-solving demands (the requirement for more active problem-solving and fault prevention). In itself this change in job content may have few adverse effects on employees, but in combination with the other factors such as perceived threats to the psychological contract (discussed later in this chapter) research suggests that it does lead to higher levels of stress. The industrial relations implications of this consequence cannot be ignored and are picked up in Part Two of this book.

Finally, more attention is being placed on *social competencies*, which enable job holders to integrate the various tasks they are assigned both on their own or in conjunction with others. These include punctuality, loyalty, creativity, customer orientation, responsibility and co-operation. There are some common issues faced by organisations whatever developments they are making in their organisational form. They are increasingly buying what is tentatively called 'fitability', i.e. the fit of the individual with the team. This stresses the importance of attitudes over functional knowledge. As organisations start to resource according to a 'fit to team' and not the traditional 'fit to job' model, we can expect to see the development of a new selection orthodoxy as a consequence. Again, this raises deep questions for HR practitioners about how to resource, develop and retain such competencies in a period when employees are themselves reappraising the employment relationship.

The important message for HR practitioners is that there is no systematic relationship between the drive for jobs-based flexibility, the design of the resultant jobs and the performance outcomes from job holders (Parker and Wall, 1996). Job design research shows that the amount of autonomy, control and feedback given to job holders are all dependent on the many different choices being made by individual organisations. Many of these flexibility options are considered in Part Three. Therefore, HR practitioners still have the opportunity to influence the impact of jobs-based flexibility in several important ways. Moreover, once the changes in job content that result from initiatives have been resolved, the more traditional activities of negotiating flexibility issues of time, qualifications and the wage–effort bargain discussed in Part Two can be more easily attended to. In the meantime, organisations seem to trust that they are creating work patterns that will deliver effective business processes, but worry later if the work has any motivational potential.

Trust in the new work designs

This brings me to the last specific impact that changes in organisational form will have on HRM, and it occurs through changes in the level of trust implied by the new work designs. In Chapter 5 Mike Oram drew attention to the relationship between trust and the success of BPR initiatives. Trust is a pervasive feature of organisational design (Bradach and Eccles, 1989) and there is 'a clear and compelling link' between the two. Trust is reflected in the control and co-ordination systems, and the use of incentives to direct behaviour. The higher the level of trust, the fewer the controls and therefore the lower the 'transaction costs' that the organisation has to incur. There are two important trust-related judgements that managers make when they redesign the organisational form:

1 Do they believe there is implicit employee 'task reliability', i.e. do they have the capabilities and potential to exercise responsible self-direction and self-control?
2 Is there sufficient 'values congruence' with the purpose of the organisation, i.e. is there a dominant written and spoken philosophy to guide the ultimate way in which employees will act?

There is, however, a conflict between the higher levels of trust that are both implicit in, and a necessary ingredient of, the operating logic of many of the new organisational forms (such as network organisations) and the levels of trust as reflected in the attitudes and psychological contract of employees. In Chapter 6 the NatWest case study shows that the impact of process thinking fundamentally changes the structure, role and purpose of the HR department. Moreover, the decentralisation afforded by recent changes in organisational form also forces HR practitioners to consider the nature of the employer–employee relationship. It is legitimate that HR practitioners raise questions about the relevance and ability of existing corporate HRM systems, business processes, competency and attitudinal sets to deliver effective performance in this environment. The rest of this chapter addresses the issue of psychological contracting in the context of the changes in organisational form outlined so far.

INSIGHTS INTO THE SHIFTING PSYCHOLOGICAL CONTRACT

The new centrality of psychological boundaries

As a result of the changes in organisational form and the pursuit of jobs-based flexibility, there is a mismatch for many employees between the demands of work life and the rewards it offers. HR practitioners are beginning to question the implicit levels of commitment and engagement of employees. The issue for HR practitioners is no longer simply one of managing the job contract. It is one of dealing with the psychological contract (Rousseau, 1995) and the issue of trust (Kramer and Tyler, 1996). Given the developments outlined by Mike Oram in Chapter 5, Steve Bendall, Chris Bottomley and Pat Cleverly in Chapter 6 and Peter Herriot in Chapter 7, practitioners understandably are asking the question 'so what are the psychological boundaries that will persist in organisations as traditional job, functional and hierarchical boundaries erode?'.

It is a good question to ask, because as organisations become more flexible, the boundaries that matter most are in the minds of managers and employees – the so-called psychosocial boundaries of the new 'soft-wired' organisational environment (Hirschhorn and Gilmore, 1992). The opening chapters highlighted how organisations are replacing vertical hierarchies with horizontal networks, linking together traditional functions through interfunctional teams, and forming strategic alliances with suppliers, customers and even competitors. The metaphor that embodies the emerging model of organisation is the 'corporation without boundaries'. Organisations are increasingly experiencing the gradual disappearance of traditional boundaries of hierarchy, function and geography. These historical boundaries represent the 'hard-wired' aspects of organisation. We have learned to rely on them to orientate and co-ordinate individual behaviour. As they become more blurred a new emphasis is placed on the underlying psychological boundaries that still remain (or are needed) to provide co-ordination.

Rather like those environmentalists attempting to argue that climate change is man made, in the search for a pattern among the myriad empirical attitudinal studies, anecdote, and case example, psychologists are wondering if the emerging pattern is one of impending collapse in many of the behaviours that underlie the employment relationship: trust, mutuality and citizenship behaviours, morale, commitment. Is the crisis in HRM merely a reflection of a deeper discomfort among the academic disciplines that have afforded the field its many prescriptions and predictions? Psychologists begin to question their assumptions about the nature, level and dynamics of employee well-being, commitment, trust and citizenship, reciprocity in behaviour, desire for participation and involvement and employment continuance intentions. Sociologists talk of paradigm shifts and post-modernist uncertainty and question age-old links between capitalist systems, production systems, requisite skill levels and specialisation, and bargaining strategies. It is easy to attribute this range of 'unexpected' behaviours to a subtle but deep climate change, i.e. a shift in the perceived 'deal' between employees and employer.

The psychological contract stands alongside other organisation-wide frames of analysis and constructs such as culture, climate and competencies as a tool which, in times of high uncertainty, helps practitioners and researchers capture complex phenomena, discriminate between organisations and serve as a basis for predicting individual behaviour (Sparrow, 1996a). Certainly, discussion of the psychological contract has provided academics and practitioner alike with a useful umbrella concept which captures changes in the nature of work (Herriot, Manning and Kidd, 1997). The language that comes with discussion of the psychological contract – mindsets and schema, implicit deals, disengagement – captures a multitude of concerns about modern organisational life. Academically, it has been used, rightly or wrongly, to capture recent challenges to our understanding of the more traditional organisational behaviour topics of commitment, job satisfaction, socialisation, employee–employer fit, and organisational climate.

Breach of contract

As highlighted at the beginning of the chapter, flexibility is sought in three 'hard' areas of the employment contract. However, those who talk of the 'psychological contract' believe that there is also a 'soft' set of expectations held by the individual employee that have to be organised and managed. The role of HR managers in defining and maintaining employees' psychological contracts has begun to receive attention (Guzzo and Noonan, 1994; Rousseau and Greller, 1994) as have the theoretical processes through which 'contracts' become violated (McLean Parks and Schmedemann, 1994; Morrison and Robinson, 1997; Robinson and Morrison, 1995; and Robinson and Rousseau, 1994).

There always has been an 'implicit' deal in the employment relationship and as Peter Herriot notes in Chapter 7, the concept has been around for almost two decades. However, the problem with the psychological contract is that you only know what it was when it is breached, and the mid-1990s were all about realising that something important had indeed been breached. The experience of post-rationalisation survivors has been studied in the USA (Brockner, 1992; Brockner *et al.*, 1986; Brockner *et al.*, 1993; and Gottlier and Conkling, 1995), in the UK (Doherty and Horsted, 1995; Turnbull and Wass, 1997) and in continental Europe (Kets de Vries and Balazs, 1996; 1997). In all cultures the syndrome is evidenced by stage processes of shock, disbelief, betrayal, animosity, lowered morale, guilt, higher stress and fears over job security. Given the more recent advent of rationalisation in Europe there has as yet been little comparable research, although an analysis by Kets de Vries and Balazs (1996) explores individual reaction patterns to downsizing in 'victims', 'survivors' and 'executioners' in European organisations. Clinical interview methodologies reveal the cognitive and emotional impacts on the individual and the way psychological processes are affected. Interviews with executives showed clearly the negative impacts the process has on them. Protest, despair and detachment were common to those who leave and those who change roles.

There are, however, widespread individual differences in what amounts to a personal transition (Armstrong-Stassen, 1993). Individual reactions range from low drama and adaptation in those with high skill levels and a more cynical contract, to radical career change, or a succumbing to depression and poor well-being adjustment, and angry 'get equal' contract behaviour. The executioners engaged in compulsive/ritualistic behaviour, reducing inner anxieties and guilt, living to self-imposed high standards, and using isolation as a defence. Driven by a need for perfection, with a constant underlying fear of failure, frustration lead to aggression. Others dissociated, taking emergency measures under stress which evoked powerful emotions, psychological conflict and profound detachment. There are major disturbances of affect, diminished ability to feel, extreme reality-based cognitive styles, a paucity of inner emotional experience and tendencies to engage in stereotypical behaviour. Organisational cultures based on control are reinforced. For Kets de Vries and Balazs (1996) the negative results of downsizing therefore stem from the simplistic solutions arrived at by managers once the organisation's memory and crucial HR skills are disrupted.

Limits to the contracting phenomenon

Not everyone should expect to have their psychological contract developed, and some should expect it to be breached more than others. There is a strong link between the degree of challenge perceived in HRM policies and specific groups of employees, such as older workers. For example, a pressure group of recently redundant employees from Intel called FaceIntel (Former and Current Employees of Intel) are taking their employer to court over alleged US labour code violations. The concerns are focused around the use of a 'ranking and rating' form of performance management in which individuals are benchmarked against their peer group. Welch (1997) outlines the following case study. Staff are rated as 'equal to' or 'slower than' colleagues according to a 'success line' set by the company. Successful employees in absolute terms may still be rated relatively as 'slower than' their peers. Two or three consecutive 'slower than' ratings automatically trigger the disciplinary corrective action programme, and if targets are not meet six weeks after this, dismissal is likely. The objections of FaceIntel (publicised on the Internet but access by Intel employees blocked by the company) are on two grounds.

First, social. Employees unable to commit to the 60-plus hour week that has become the norm, such as older or disabled workers, may be targeted as 'slower than' younger employees. Second, legal. FaceIntel alleged that the company was working to a 5–10 per cent termination quota which unduly targeted those over 40 (who could have expected sizeable pensions and stock options towards the ends of their careers). A random telephone survey of 1400 dismissed employees found that 90 per cent were over 40 and 40 per cent had some form of disability. The technique has been adopted by Intel UK but is unlikely to be a welcome import.

Even when HR practitioners talk of the 'new deal' in employment, in most organisations the 'new deal' has not yet been struck, and even where it has, it may not be working.

Recent research by the Institute of Personnel and Development involving telephone interviews with 1000 employees and eight case studies (in Rover, Thames Water, Caledonian Paper, Amersham, Oxfordshire County Council, the London Borough of Brent and two NHS trusts) suggested that employers who felt they had developed a new 'psychological contract' with their employees were deluding themselves. Employees did not believe in the 'new deal', saw it as one sided in terms of the amount of influence they could exert, and wished they could move but felt that they would not have the opportunity to do so.

The evidence on some of the new employment security agreements, touched upon in Part Two, is also far from clear. Firms such as the Co-operative Bank, Rover, Ford Motor Company, Blue Circle Cement, Scottish Power Generation and Tate & Lyle Sugar have guaranteed a degree of security for full-time employees in order to enlist them as partners in the process of change (Income Data Services, 1997b). In many cases, however, such arrangements have served to increase insecurity because they were negotiated in the wake of large-scale redundancies, or in advance of voluntary redundancies, or in tandem with the creation of temporary staff on fixed-term contracts in order to create an employment buffer.

As is clear from Chapter 6, NatWest UK see their initiatives simply as the beginning of a new journey down the route of building a new proposition for staff. If this is done, as Pascale (1995) notes, we should not fall into the trap of assuming that the 'old' contract was automatically 'good' and was based on job security for all. Of the 100 million workers on US payrolls in 1985 only half, at best, regarded job security as part of their psychological contract. Moreover, the pursuit of 'employability' may prove to be incredibly divisive in society. Today only around 10 per cent of the workforce have the necessary traits of entrepreneurship and being self-starters deemed necessary for the new 'free agent' relationship characterised by the new employability-based psychological contract (Pascale, 1995).

The contribution of a contracting approach

In similar vein, in Chapter 7, Peter Herriot warns against the simple adoption of the language of the psychological contract either as a form of rhetoric or as a 'bastardised' academic concept. He considers the role and contribution of a contracting process from a traditional human resource strategy (HRS) perspective. We see many elements from the HRS literature, with contracting acting as a *philosophy* and set of guiding *values* (through the establishment of a set of overarching principles for HRM practice), providing *integration* (through its links to strategic and business planning processes and systems of corporate governance), facilitating *devolution* (through its ability to be fitted into a decentralised management structure), and *assisting change management* (through its ability to act as a monitoring system and be adapted as a phased project-based implementation approach).

Herriot draws attention to a number of contributions that an understanding of the contracting processes brings to HRM. By applying these to this book, we can position discussion of contracting as follows:

1 As a construct, it cuts across some of the problems associated with the 'end of jobs' arguments covered in both Chapter 1 and the early sections of this chapter. It provides those concerned about the implications of the demise of jobs-based HRM systems with

an alternative people-based system. A message to HR practitioners is to manage the phenomenon of mutual relationships and expectations through negotiations with individuals about their 'deal'; do not pursue negotiations about the job.

2 It links to the partnership debate picked up in Part Two of this book by outlining the areas in which equity of formal process, honouring of trust, and formal information exchange become issues.

3 Formalised contracting processes ensure the negotiating mechanism through which 'voice' in the employment relationship is made relevant. If 'partnership' represents the formal and institutional exchange of perspectives about the employment relationship through which employees are given 'voice', then the psychological contract focuses attention on the areas of mutuality about which the exchange should be had.

4 The effective management of the contracting process becomes one of the new sources of core competence available to the organisation, providing the HRM function with both a basis of identity and a new set of internal service benchmarks to achieve. Coff (1997) outlines a number of aspects which make it difficult to manage people as a strategic asset. To strategists, human assets are an imperfect source of competitive advantage because of their freedom to leave, possession of tacit and boundary-spanning knowledge, links to social networks that alter the value of skills in the marketplace, and their ability to become demotivated, shirkers or subversive. Effective management of the psychological contract lessons these imperfections and facilitates strategies that attract, motivate and retain, thereby allowing the firm to keep firm-specific skills and competencies and develop the organisational capability.

Although the attractions of creating a 'psychological contract' or 'new deal' bandwagon are clear and the concept has obvious relevance and power in capturing the phenomenon of perceived breach of trust and transition, there has until recently been little empirical research directly aimed at testing its predictions. Does the contracting process actually deliver what employees want in the employment relationship? Are both the users of the process (organisations and their line managers) and the receivers of the end deal (the employees) content? What are the standards by which success in this new venture should be measured? What knowledge do HRM professionals need to be able to make contracting work? In order to address such questions, we need to clarify what we know and what we do not know about the debate over the contract and discussion of the 'new deal'.

IMPLICATIONS OF CHANGE IN THE PSYCHOLOGICAL CONTRACT

Documenting and mapping change in the psychological contract in western organisations and suggesting matching HRM policies will likely become a hallmark of many HRM studies at the millennium (Sparrow, 1996a). Yet this observation leaves some very important questions unanswered. In what way has the contract really changed, and with what consequence? Despite recent attention to changes in the psychological contract, it is clear that the 'new deal' and the underlying psychological dynamics it implies need deeper analysis because studies of the psychological contract tend to raise as many questions as they answer.

Scenario 1 – A repositioning of HRM on the trust–commitment continuum scale

There are some uncertainties in relation to the psychological contract when we consider the Anglo-American organisational behaviour literature. While there are strong grounds to believe that the psychological contract is changing for many employees, if this is so, then there are potentially three scenarios that we may face (Sparrow, 1996a). Building on Peter Herriot's comments in Chapter 7, each of these scenarios heralds a different set of *transitions*. First, it could be argued that the psychological contract, while clearly perceived as deteriorating for significant sub-groups of the British workforce, is never the less far more positive than it was generations ago. People who worked in organisations in the 1930s may look at present-day complaints about the quality of working life with some derision. To be sure, a small group of mainly baby-boomers who are now the middle-aged generation, and those nearing retirement, feel betrayed by the decline in employment security. They will go through an immediate negative adjustment. Other groups of (mainly younger) employees do not feel the need to make so much of a correction.

For the majority of employees then, what we are dealing with in this scenario is a transition based on a 'self-correcting animal'. People, given time, are quite capable of making the adjustments required for work at the millennium and will do so in a more instrumental way. If employees perceive that a better contract is unavailable elsewhere, all expectations may be lowered. Therefore, HR practitioners have to deal with a shift in the trust/commitment continuum in a generally negative direction whereby employees respond to the increasingly limited offer of employment for life and career development, by themselves withdrawing down the trust–commitment scale. Herriot, Manning and Kidd (1997) found evidence of this withdrawal in a sample of 368 managers and employees. The employment relationship becomes more explicitly transactional and contractual in order to buy-in commitment where it matters, and the organisation experiences a higher proportion of dysfunctional behaviour.

Although the position moves down the trust–commitment continuum on average, this hides the fact that the contract for some of the strategically less important or lower value added groups has deteriorated even more. Therefore we find a wider variety of 'contracts'. Individual differences come to the fore and HR practitioners become fixated with the lifestyle and personal motivation factors and the consequent need to realign and target HRM policies and practices to these new realities of employee behaviour. HR practitioners will have to become, and will need to learn from, the marketing function. In the same way that supermarkets 'sell' a wide and customised product range to different sorts of consumers, the issue with the contract will be to identify the new patterns of 'contractual stance' that shape the internal labour market within the organisation. How do you create brand image not just outside the organisation, but to each individual within the organisation?

The agenda for organisation behaviour theorists therefore becomes one of helping the organisation learn how to cope with a more complex, variable and individualised set of contracts. In Chapter 7 Peter Herriot argues that if we are to moderate the degree of slide down the trust–commitment scale, a key imperative is the provision of process management skills for HR practitioners and line managers, as the fundamental task becomes one of managing the individual transitions that the new world of HRM has created.

Scenario 2 – A temporary transition in psychological dynamics

The second scenario reflects a deeper change and a more serious set of issues for HR practitioners. Rather than being a 'self-correcting animal' people actually have 'limited capacity'. Therefore, in the world of experiment highlighted by David Guest in Chapter 3 whereby new technology affords a combination of tight performance control with the freedom to design how you do your job, we will see a range of adaptations all the way from withdrawal from the deal through to work addiction. Younger employees may be willing to sign up to a new raison d'être in their work life. However, rather than simply moving to a new bargaining point on the trust–commitment continuum, with its consequential implications for motivation, the nature of motivation itself is seen to have changed. The field of organisational behaviour will be forced to go back to basic assumptions and question whether the traditional motivational drivers and their causal effect on organisational behaviour still work, i.e. we may no longer be playing the game to the same rules. In the second scenario, this change is considered to be *temporary*, whereby the presumed links between commitment, participation, satisfaction, motivation and performance have become 'submerged' as part of a temporary culture shock or stress–reaction process. In the transition period, the motivational power of traditional job design characteristics and work incentives becomes dulled. During the transition period (i.e. until people adapt to the new realities and the traditional psychological links return) much of the recommended HRM toolkit (including intrinsic job design factors, lifestyle-directed time patterns such as annualised hours and sabbaticals, incentivising tools such as cafeteria benefits and performance-related pay; and developmental tools such as potential identification workshops and mentoring) is found wanting. In this scenario, for several important years organisations pull what they think are the right strings but nothing seems to move at the other end. What we are witnessing under this scenario is another *syndrome* – similar to those found by researchers who examine reactions to bereavement, mergers or job loss. The agenda for organisational behaviour theorists therefore becomes one of simulating and predicting a new 'breach of contract syndrome' through longitudinal study of the social, emotive and cognitive responses, developing stage theories of recovery, and identifying 'coping strategies' for HR practitioners by identifying which tools within their armoury still produce individual responses.

It also forces us to become much clearer about the management of what are of course quite separate psychological constructs. Employees can be seen to 'input' various attributes to the 'new deal' such as their work values and attitudes, motivational needs, and personal dispositions or competencies. They are then subjected to various contract formation and breach processes, such as socialisation, the perception of mutual exchanges, and signals sent by the HRM environment. On the basis of which, attention is turned to a series of 'outputs' or outcomes, such as commitment, job satisfaction, trust and organisation citizenship behaviours. Technically, these are separate mechanisms or facets of employee behaviour, measured through different tools and techniques. HRM systems marshal each facet and bring them together in different combinations or balances. There is no 'one best way' of combining these. Japanese organisations, for example, have some of the highest levels of commitment together with the lowest levels of job satisfaction. The issue for HR practitioners then is what is the best combination for the HRM system of the future? And do HRM professionals or indeed their academic advisors really understand the differences between values, attitudes, commitment, satisfaction, trust and citizenship? A large educational agenda beckons if the second scenario holds.

Scenario 3 – New rules of the game

The third scenario presents a more perturbing possibility. The change in motivational drivers becomes permanent. In many areas of management, theorists argue that we are witnessing major discontinuities which mean that the rules of the past can no longer guide our interventions in the present. For example, we see breaklines appearing in the basic values (even across nations) between generations. Under this scenario, new work values become solidified and the dynamics of all the psychological processes mentioned in this chapter – employee values, motivational needs, attitudes, satisfaction, commitment and trust – will be altered and 'reset'. In this scenario what we are witnessing at the millennium is not just the redesign of business processes, but also the redesign of the *mechanisms that underpin the psychological contract*. The agenda for organisational behaviour and HRM theorists is then to identify whether there have been demonstrable alterations to the underlying cognitive schema (or, the more understandable term, 'mindsets') which according to theorists such as Rousseau (1995) form the rootbase of the psychological contract. Which mindset changes are associated with alterations to actual values, which value changes lead to a solidification of (more negative) attitudes, and therefore what new linkages arise down the attitude–intention–behaviour–performance path of employee behaviour? In short, the collective wisdom of organisational behaviour, occupational psychology and HRM findings, which is largely based on research on the 'old deal' post-war generation, is brought into fundamental question. Clearly, without much better knowledge about the relative role and contribution of the causative influences on the contract and without better evidence to help us decide which scenario appears to be the case, the dynamics of the contract will be hard to predict and manage and the agenda for the field of HRM hard to specify.

THE EVIDENCE SO FAR

Recent analyses of the psychological contract, while highlighting the relevance of the concept to the field of HRM, also suggest that there are a number of deep questions we have to consider if we are to provide practitioners with a useful tool for organisational analysis. Within the confines of the Anglo-American organisational behaviour literature there are a number of implications from the psychological contracting debate that have yet to be aligned with findings from the occupational psychology literature. The contracting future for HRM raises many questions. In part, the term has become popular because anecdotal observation, if not hard empirical evidence, suggests many of the tenets of 1970s' and 1980s' social psychology and organisational behaviour seem no longer to apply. But have we really got a problem to manage?

A review of recent evidence presents a conflicting picture. Much of it tends to support the first scenario, but it is difficult to make firm suggestions about the relative size of the commitment problem to be faced by HR practitioners, or the best strategy to deal with the issue. First, let us consider whether changed psychological contracts matter. Many employees still claim to be committed to their organisation. According to the IPD research 77 per cent of employees feel a lot or some commitment to their organisation. Even where commitment levels are low (despite the IPD survey there are many employers currently looking at attitude surveys that show the lowest levels of commitment in their employees that they have ever measured) UK employers can argue 'well, commitment has always been low, so what's new?'. David Guest discusses this issue in Chapter 3.

Is there any evidence of an overt employee backlash? From a theoretical perspective some writers argue that benefits, once given, are hard to take away (Lucero and Allen, 1994). The problem for organisations is that the benefits they offer have not kept pace with expectations and consequently a deterioration in the quality of psychological contracts is predicted. Some researchers point to the assumption that good contracts result in more committed, motivated and trusting organisational citizens, which means that strategic change can be delivered without high indirect costs. Although good contracts do not automatically result in superior performance, poor contracts do act as demotivators and are reflected in higher withdrawal behaviours (lower commitment, higher absenteeism and turnover). The contract operates rather like a hygiene factor. However, evidence for any sustained relationship between the state of the contract and performance has been questioned by Guest and his colleagues initially on theoretical grounds and more recently on empirical grounds (Guest, Conway, Briner and Dickman, 1996).

Within the UK, MORI opinion polls show that the proportion of people who feel secure in their jobs fell from 65 per cent to 54 per cent from 1990–95 (Sparrow, 1996a). However, the analysis of the psychological contract in the UK by Guest *et al.* (1996) found evidence of some modest increases in trust and security, with two-thirds of the working population not being worried about redundancy. Deterioration in the contract was restricted to around 20 per cent of employees who were less well-educated employees in peripheral jobs. Eighty-one per cent of people feel fairly treated and 60 per cent expect still to be with their employer in 5 years' time. This latter statistic may reflect extreme naiveté among the respondents – the 'it's a problem for you but it won't happen to me' syndrome that biases much survey research. For example, in the early 1990s social survey data from the British Institute of Management showed that middle managers tended to feel that they personally were not at risk from unemployment, despite the fact that organisations were cutting swathes out of their numbers. The redundancy data of a few years later told a different story. At a meeting of the HR Conference Board in 1997 it was noted that 'managers and employees often seem to go through a period of denial before irreversible trends are acknowledged'. The 1996 analysis by Guest *et al.* does however show that more people feel loyalty towards their fellow employees than their immediate supervisor, more to their supervisor than to their organisation, and more to their organisation than to their union.

Such conflicting data require us to understand the level at which a 'contract' exists within the underlying psychological structure of employee behaviour. Occupational psychologists have known for a long time that there is a gap between people's attitudes and their actual behaviour. Poor job satisfaction does not automatically lead to poor performance and generally only about 10 per cent of performance levels can be attributed to job satisfaction. As we examine the consequences of perceived changes to commitment at the millennium, we may just find that we simply repeat the experience of the 1970s and demonstrate the 'negative job attitude is unpredictive of actual behaviour' problem which came to dominate the job satisfaction–performance field.

There is conflicting evidence in relation to the withdrawal syndrome. Certainly absenteeism rates and job turnover levels also appear to have remained relatively stable, despite psychologists talking about the development of 'recession fatigue' (where employees finally say enough is enough and are no longer afraid of what might happen to their jobs) and the existence of 'turnover timebombs' in many organisations as they emerge from recession. In a study of bank employees, Sparrow (1996a) found that despite an overall negative attitudinal response, there was no employee backlash in terms of turnover rates. Similarly, an analysis by Littlefield (1996) of UK Institute of Personnel and Development figures (based on analysis of data from 300 companies) shows that actual staff turnover rates in 1995 averaged 15 per cent, which is much the same as in previous years. Yet according to the latest social attitudes survey in the UK, interviews with 3500 people about their intentions showed that 27 per cent of people expected to change jobs in 1996, which is the highest figure since trend data were established in 1983. Fifty-three per cent of the sample anticipated leaving their job. Job insecurity is then not just a figment of psychologists' or employees' imagination.

Certainly there is an issue associated with more frequent job change and the consequential loss of organisational memory. Job tenure has not fallen by as much as the business press would have us believe. It was around six years on average in the 1970s and is around 5.5 years now, up from a low of 4.5 years in the early 1990s (Smith, 1997). This however hides significant sex and age differences. Institute of Employment Studies research shows that since 1976 average job tenure for men in the UK has fallen by 25 per cent, the number of people covered by basic employment rights has fallen from 91 per cent to 70 per cent, and unemployed people spend 20 per cent longer out of work. What has happened for men is that they used to change jobs every eight years, but now change jobs every 6.5 years, while women used to change jobs every four years and now change every 4.5 years (Smith, 1997). Improvements in average tenure may also reflect the fact that some women are now reaching more senior (and more secure) parts of the corporate ladder, and a proportion of those who have good jobs hang onto them for dear life. This does not make them secure. In several organisations or occupational sectors (such as banking) turnover intentions are immediately frustrated because the deterioration in conditions is seen as being sector-wide. This is noted in the NatWest case study in Chapter 6. What may be the implications for organisations of 'repressed' withdrawal intentions and will they shatter even the most well-intentioned interventions, such as psychological contracting?

THE FUTURE OF DEALING?

Despite a lack of such insights, organisations are quickly learning how to cope with contracting. When they look to the future and the HRM agenda at the millennium, Steve Bendall, Chris Bottomley and Pat Cleverly raise a number of pertinent issues for organisations such as NatWest. They bring the issue down to two critical considerations: the level of line management competency, capability and desire to deal; and the strategic positioning of the organisation in terms of its level of decentralisation. This latter dimension does not refer to decentralisation in terms of job and work system design, as discussed earlier in this chapter, but to the overall level of centralisation in corporate decision-making and HRM systems design. Critical decisions have to be made about the rate of devolution of HRM policies and the rate of upskilling of line managers. Considering the second of these decisions – managing the intent behind and pace at which systems are decentralised – it becomes clear how much of the 1980s' and 1990s' style of HRM is at risk of being junked. As was noted in Chapter 1, the last decade has been a period of creating coherence between competing HRM systems, and the easiest way of doing this was to create unitary concepts of effectiveness with the associated weapons of strategically co-ordinated performance management systems, competency frameworks and business processes (what Steve Bendall, Chris Bottomley and Pat Cleverly call the 'the deal is' philosophy). An important HRM issue at the millennium is one of balancing these two drives and managing the tensions that any unequal progress towards the 'my deal is' version of HRM might create. The moment we consider a 'my deal is' scenario, we have to become very clear about which HRM policies and practices need to be devolved to line managers, and which aspects of functioning will be open to line management discretion.

Clearly, we still have much to learn about contracting. Organisational responses to the psychological contract tend to operate at two levels (Sparrow, 1996c). The first is to engage in a new dialogue with employees (either individually or through specialised processes such as focus groups, task forces, etc.) and to identify their HRM preferences. This is akin to the cafeteria benefits approach – tell us what you want as part of the new deal and we will offer a new menu which you, as a group, have indicated is more attractive. A number of organisations, especially in the financial services sector, where pressures for rationalisation stand in stark contrast to the need to develop an engaged customer-skilled workforce, has gone down this route.

The second level of response to the need to renew the psychological contract is to move not just towards local dealing, but towards individual dealing. Those employers experimenting with new initiatives to improve the psychological contract are just beginning to consider the implications of this. Rather than offering a more flexible menu, how do you ensure that the meals on offer are individually tasty? How do you set the individual deal? This is more problematical. First, you have to have an honest dialogue in order really to understand the 'deal' the individual wants. Second, you have to have a forum in which 'deals' are discussed and signed off. Where will this take place? The most obvious candidate is the performance appraisal discussion or some parallel process. But the research evidence does not inspire employers with confidence about this. In general, managers have different views as to what should be discussed in appraisals and they also have poor performance management skills and competencies. Expecting line managers to set the deal will place great strain on their abilities. Moreover, not everyone will want to engage in this debate. Research on the uptake of cafeteria benefits shows that only around 35 per cent of employees take up the flexibility, and research on the psychological contract shows that many employees do not want the 'lifestyle' or 'flexibility' contract. There is the option of treating the individual deal-making in the same manner as career development – an additional and voluntary service for those who want it. But this will require yet another HRM process or forum for handling the deal-making, which will smack of bureaucracy to already over-burdened line managers. Clearly, cultural resistance towards fully engaging the psychological contract and its implications for HRM will remain high within British organisations for a while to come, but one of the few certainties in this uncertain world is that deals will have to be made and the current 'unitary' HRM solutions will not survive for too many years more.

The NatWest UK case in Chapter 6 is an example of the first approach. In deciding which decisions must remain central and which can be devolved to the line and individual businesses, it has realised that it has the opportunity to build the proposition of a new psychological contract with its staff. The emphasis on getting flexibility in the hard issues such as pay and benefits is now being replaced by attempts to get flexibility in the soft issues, such as the psychological contract. For NatWest UK the realisation is that they have to be flexible in more than just 'explicit' HRM practices. They need to engineer flexibility in the soft issues of management style, communication, identification and job security. The employment relationship needs to be perceived as fair and reflecting individual needs. In order to build this proposition for staff the bank is marshalling initiatives in flexible working hours, internal job markets, performance-related pay and rewards, benefits, and training and development. The intention is to move towards a situation where there is local dealing in line with business needs across many of these initiatives.

ARE CONTRACTS MANAGEABLE?

Can organisations manage the transition in psychological contracts? There are two arguments that can be raised by those who doubt whether psychological contracts are really manageable in HRM terms. First, we are faced with conflicting evidence because we do not truly understand the dynamics of the psychological contract in relation to HRM behaviour. Second, it can be argued that 'in every mind there is a different world'. Contracts are wholly phenomenological and idiosyncratic and certainly not worth designing HRM systems around.

Consider the first issue – are they manageable through HRM policies and practices? Recent research suggests that contracting may be a manageable process. First, there does appear to be some commonality in the content of psychological contracts. Herriot, Manning and Kidd (1997) examined the perceived mutual obligations of 184 UK managers and 184 UK employees across a range of sectors and found that 18 constructs captured the perception of mutual obligations. Many organisations may then look towards the psychological contract as a management tool, especially where they feel that traditional labour market segmentations (such as part-time versus full-time, skilled versus unskilled, young versus old, male versus female) are no longer predictive of employee behaviour. HR practitioners are looking for new patterns across the many existing contracts that can help them to redesign their HRM systems. While contracts tend to be combined in very diverse patterns, there are some commonalities emerging. A series of distinctive 'contractual stances' towards HRM were identified by Sparrow (1996a), such as the 'frustratedly mobile', 'still ambitious', 'passively flexible', 'guidance seekers', 'buy me outers', 'just pay me more', and 'don't push me too fast'. What might employees actually do given such attitudes? Career research has identified seven different career responses. Managers will try to:

- 'get ahead' by pursuing power and influence and engineering openings and advantage for themselves
- 'get secure' by finding what they hope is an unobtrusive role in the organisation
- 'get balanced' by rebalancing work, life commitments and relationships so that loss of employment is not as damaging

- 'get free' by creating autonomy and marginal organisational membership
- 'get even' by ensuring that the organisation (or certain members of it) pay a price for what they see as the injustices done to them
- 'get high' by moving to the centre of events and becoming totally absorbed in work
- 'get out', deciding that this is no longer the life or organisational culture for them.

The combinations between the seven attitudinal 'contractual stances' and the seven different behavioural 'career responses' mean that HR managers will face a complex task in matching employee expectations.

This is of course simply a descriptor of employee attitudes and likely career behaviours. However, of note from the study was the finding that traditional internal labour markets variables such as grade, tenure, age and sex were poor predictors of the 'contractual stances'. It was argued that a contribution to contract stance must be made by other individual difference predictors drawn from measures of personality, work values, career anchors and competency. Without clear knowledge of the relative role and contribution of these causative influences, the new dynamics of the contract will be hard to predict and manage. The importance of individual differences is signalled by a number of findings.

The second reason why contracts may be unmanageable – the high level of individual differences – is harder to discount. As has been noted, research on individual reaction patterns to downsizing in 'victims', 'survivors' and 'executioners' using clinical interview methodologies demonstrates the extent to which cognitive and emotional impacts affect several deep psychological processes, but also reveals widespread individual differences in what amounts to a personal transition (Armstrong-Stassen, 1993; Kets de Vries and Balazs, 1996). Similarly, research on the breach of psychological contracts demonstrates that coping requires remedial satisfaction of losses to the contract through the substitution of individually meaningful outcomes, and therefore responses to violations reveal widely contrasting individual tendencies towards either a constructive or destructive and an active or passive response (Rousseau, 1995).

Should we therefore expect that individual differences and personality will once more become a major predictor of career behaviour, perhaps breathing new life into the work of the vocational psychologists of the 1970s? What, for example, is the relationship between Holland's career types and the different contractual stances identified by Sparrow (1996a)? When organisational role requirements and managerial policies are incongruent with an individual's core values, employees attempt to modify the role requirements and failing to so, prefer to change jobs rather than values (Holland, 1976). Personality type is linked to the propensity to make such transitions. Reviews of vocational personality theories suggest that there is indeed some small correlation between vocational personality, role congruence within the career environment, and outcomes such as satisfaction (Tracey and Rounds, 1993; Tranberg, Slane and Ekeberg, 1993). The interaction between such individual variables and overall contractual stance may yet clarify the relationship between the various contract elements and stances, and outcomes such as withdrawal or organisational citizenship behaviours.

So does a contracting philosophy really mean the end of HRM? A contracting philosophy is once again forcing HR practitioners to reject a 'unitary' or 'one best way' approach to their field. Early objections to the unitarist HRM philosophy argued that it ignored different perspectives from a range of stakeholders such as unions and various interest groups. It was argued that it understated the level of conflict within organisations about HRM policies and practices. This conflict is now even more inevitable. Under the dual pressures of a wider variety of contractual stances and a wide variety of organisational form experiments, the field of HRM is fragmenting. As David Guest notes in Chapter 3, the fragmentation of HRM into many different variants brings the unitarist issue back onto the agenda, but the objections at the millennium are more practical and driven by the increasing influence that the individual's psychological contract can have on the workability of many core tools and techniques.

Different positions can be taken on the extent to which this fragmentation creates a major issue for HR practitioners. Those who would argue for a more limited impact would point to the review of the evidence on insecurity, that indicates that the phenomenon is more limited in its immediate impact than might theoretically be expected; employee perceptions lagging behind reality, and the reality at the millennium being one of a slight improvement in job conditions; and the election of a new government on a landslide acting as a release mechanism on a pressure cooker. Talk of damage to the psychological contract could soon drift into history as an artefact of the bad old days of the late 1980s and 1990s. Moreover, as Herriot notes, academics are becoming increasingly concerned that the concept in any event has become diluted and applied to too wide a set of phenomena in organisations.

These are all legitimate points, but they mask some of the underlying problems that will persist for many years to come (*see* Chapter 1). Insecurity, as a sense of uncertainty, is of course as much a state of mind as anything else (Smith, 1997). If people feel insecure, then, regardless of logic, they are insecure. Moreover, it is not really the phenomenon of insecurity that presents the problem. It is the issue of trust and all the behaviours that flow from changes to the 'values to expectations to feelings to intentions to behaviour to performance' link that has always underlain the management of human resources. There is every reason to question whether the old assumptions about these linkages are still relevant at the millennium.

CONCLUSION

The HRM role is becoming increasingly complex and now requires the management of a large range of relationships. The distinction between soft contracts (for core employees) and hard contracts (for peripheral employees) is too simplistic. Understanding what the new fragmented contracts are (in all their complexity), how they pattern, how they create new boundaries within the internal labour market of the organisation, and what preferences each group of employees has for particular sets of HR policies and practices has become a major priority for HR practitioners. Because of the developments outlined in this chapter – the need for knowledge of how best to design jobs-based flexibility and the need for more sophisticated understanding of what will be needed to manage a psychological contracting process – there is a range of new technical fields of knowledge that has to be attended to. Currently many of these insights are lacking in the field and it is likely that many decisions concerning the creation of new roles and the design of new HRM policies and practices in organisations are being made based on naive assumptions.

PART 2

Developing partnership and employee voice

9

Towards a new model of industrial partnership

Beyond the 'HRM versus industrial relations' argument

WILLY COUPAR AND BRYAN STEVENS

Involvement and Participation Association

INTRODUCTION

In the last five years, the Involvement and Participation Association (IPA) has developed several partnership agreements, following the principles laid down in *Towards Industrial Partnership*, published in 1992. Partnership in the 1990s is not a return to institutionalised participation, nor a tripartite approach. It is not so much about institutions or methods, as about attitudes and culture. It is a question of building mutual trust, of recognising differences and finding common ground, and of applying key partnership principles such as commitment to organisational success, and respecting the legitimacy of stakeholders in the business.

This chapter briefly reviews the origins of partnership and describes what the new models of partnership now being developed in UK companies look like. Since 1993 the IPA has been carrying out a research programme examining partnership practices in companies throughout the UK. The 1997 publication, *Towards Industrial Partnership: New Ways of Working in UK Companies*, has shown evidence that a new fusion of human resource management and industrial relations built around a greater reciprocity of interests is emerging in some parts of the UK economy.

HISTORY

Founded in 1884 as the Labour Association for Promoting Co-operative Production amongst the Workforce, what is now the Involvement and Participation Association (IPA) was set up as 'a propagandist committee to arouse working men, and public opinion generally, to the importance of the movement for making workers everywhere partners in their workshops'. It then became the Industrial Co-partnership Association and after World

II, the Industrial Participation Association. In 1989, when some thought participation uncomfortably with Thatcherite Britain, it became the Involvement and Participation ïation drawing a distinction between involvement and participation.

The history of partnership in the UK goes back to the tradition of the medieval guilds. As the Industrial Revolution gathered pace a movement grew up which recognised that if members of the workforce were treated as partners, they would respond by working more effectively. This philanthropic approach was closely rooted in the Christian non-conformist tradition. It could be seen at its best in the Quaker families of Cadbury, Rowntree and Fry, and in places such as Bournville and Saltaire.

This approach could also be viewed as paternalistic and patronising, and was not always viewed favourably by either unions or management. Workers resented patronising attitudes and managers saw it as an irrelevance, distracting them from the main object of running a profitable business. It was not seen by the left to offer any long-term solution to the growing social problems of the time. At its best, however, it spawned companies such as ICI and John Lewis which have successfully adapted to present day conditions and replaced paternalism with partnership.

Collective bargaining spread widely in the period between the wars to form the conflict model in employee relations, which characterises the British industrial relations tradition. During World War II, however, many examples of joint regulation of the workplace grew up. The establishment of joint productivity committees laid the foundations for a new approach to partnership in the post-war period. The war led to a desire for some form of consensus, being a reflection of the wider search for reconciliation and reconstruction.

The underlying aim of the consensus approach was for the three parties (government, management and unions) to co-operate nationally to achieve success. The partnership approach was institutionalised through national committees, productivity agreements and the National Economic Development Office. By the mid-1970s many of these institutions had ossified and there was a virtual impasse between weak management and over-powerful unions. Government attempts to regulate the situation, notably Donovan, *In Place of Strife* and Bullock, achieved little. The domination of free collective bargaining ensured that most of the high-level talk of consensus never reached the workplace where adversarial behaviours were the norm.

While the UK was following this route, something very different was going on across the Channel. British trade union leaders helped the German trade unions to build a new movement from the ashes of the war. The reconstruction of post-war Germany was based on creating a system of checks and balances which would ensure that there could never again be an unholy alliance between government and big business. Starting with coal and steel, and thereafter enshrined in company law throughout industry, the Germans built the social partnership model which today dominates the European Union. Despite recent criticism of the German model, much of the success of the post-war German economy, and economic progress in Europe in general, can be attributed to the industrial relations consensus.

The story of Mrs Thatcher's opposition to the consensus which had dominated post-war industrial relations and her efforts to influence this are well documented, culminating in the Miners' Strike (1984) and Wapping (1986). Key to this change was the systematic use of the law to curb the power of the trade unions and the simultaneous encouragement of individualism and denigration of a representative structure. Serious overmanning was tackled in a way which could never have been achieved in the consensus society.

Yet Mrs Thatcher also took Britain into the single market. In the area of employee relations, the UK became involved in a system very different from its own which has been a potent influence on the way we order our affairs. Resistance to European social pressures has grown, although Britain had been opposing these since Vredeling and the Fifth Directive 20 years ago. Many companies have equated a collective approach with the ills of the 1970s. Some go so far as to say that a trade union simply gets in the way of the relationship with individual employees.

American management ideas, including HRM with its emphasis on direct involvement, have produced some remarkable results. One of the most quoted examples has been Unipart, with its commitment to a learning organisation through establishing its own university, its sharing of success through share ownership and its emphasis on world-class internal communications. But there are many more companies that place more emphasis on 'freedom to manage' than on the key role of the workforce.

Against this there has been a recognition among business leaders that something has to be done to regain the confidence of the workforce. This is not paternalism, or altruism. With capital and production readily transferable to anywhere in the world, and with technology that can be copied easily, businesses increasingly recognise that companies with the best-managed and motivated work forces will be the winners.

The implementation of the European Works Council Directive in September 1996 was the first significant breakthrough. Although few British companies are enthusiastic about EWCs, many companies have ignored the UK opt-out and taken action. Equally important is the legislation introduced in 1995, following the European Court of Justice decision on redundancy consultation. This has led many non-union companies to set up some form of consultation on a broad range of subjects, even though consultation is only required by law in cases of redundancy and transfers.

The work begun by the IPA in 1992 with the publication of *Towards Industrial Partnership* has contributed new insights to the debate about governance and stakeholding at the workplace and helped build a more positive climate of employee relations. The project set out both to identify the key principles underlying partnership – trust, legitimacy and commitment to business success – and to try to identify what a partnership approach actually means for the companies who practise it. In a series of case studies over the last three years the IPA has identified two distinctive features of these organisations:

1 They demonstrate a greater commitment to employment stability and security than other companies.
2 They are organisations with a distinctive and clearly recognisable employee voice, giving staff more input into the business both at the workplace and at a more strategic level.

EMPLOYMENT SECURITY AND FLEXIBILITY

As discussed in Chapters 7 and 8, over the last decade the level of insecurity felt by the UK workforce has increased substantially not least because of changes in the global marketplace. However, attitudes towards employment security are changing. In the 1980s and early 1990s many employers regarded employment security or 'jobs for life' as part of the malaise of an uncompetitive, feather-bedded economy. Weaning people off security was

147

seen as part of the necessary change process. Today, however, these certainties are not so clear cut. Employers want a motivated workforce able and willing to work with maximum flexibility. Employees work best if they have a sense of being secure in their job. If they do not feel that sense of security they can withdraw commitment and personal involvement from their employer.

Organisations do exist which have maintained a long-standing commitment to employment stability despite the upheaval of the last decade. The John Lewis Partnership is a well-known example. When the company recognised that two inner London stores were no longer viable they delayed closing the stores until a new project in Kingston was completed, keeping staff on the books even when there was no immediate prospect of relocating them. Nowadays such a stance is highly unusual. Other companies have abandoned such ideas, feeling that this old-fashioned notion is no longer relevant.

> *Whilst it is impossible to argue emotionally against the appeal of employment security as a desirable framework for improving employee involvement, it is simply so out of phase with present reality that I do not believe it is credible.*
>
> (HR director, merchant bank)

Job cuts and redundancies touch the lives of many people. The IPD study, *The New Employment Relationship* (Kessler and Undy, 1996), found that nearly 60 per cent of people at work had experienced job cuts in their workplace either directly or among colleagues. For skilled workers, this figure rose to over 70 per cent and for industrial staff to over 75 per cent. These experiences had a marked and adverse impact on the attitudes of all staff, including those in managerial positions. The survey showed a strong correlation between a history of lay-offs in a company and low levels of trust, especially about the organisation's readiness to keep its promises. It also led to a discernible reduction in enthusiasm or commitment to the business.

There is also evidence of the importance which staff attach to job security. The GMB Trade Union, which regularly surveys its membership about attitudes towards work, consistently finds that employees value employment security ahead of every other attribute of their working life, except for a wish to do an interesting job. Security scores well above pay, career opportunities, use of their skills or working conditions.

If employees cannot expect a job for life, are there any expectations which they can rightly have of their employment relationship? Jobs for life are not attainable, even if there ever was a time when they existed. Stable employment can, at best, mean working within the same organisation in a variety of different jobs throughout one's working life. One must also not forget that employment is crucially linked to business success. The best guarantee of future employment is a healthy and thriving company. That message is now better understood by people at work than in the past. The link was clearly expressed by British Petroleum, which agreed that 'there can be no declaration of security of employment as a key corporate value without an explicit link to performance.'

The bargain is, however, a mutual one. In a mutual relationship the employee knows that his or her greater commitment leads to enhanced performance. One can therefore expect to have a higher expectation of having a job in the future. At the same time, the employer should reciprocate the staff's commitment to business success by meeting, as far as it can, their desire for maximum sense of security at work. Unfortunately, this reciprocity has not always been evident in the last decade.

One approach has been to limit the mutual relationship and emphasise that the employers' responsibility stops with ensuring that, on exit, the employee is equipped for the job market. There has been much discussion in recent years about the concept of *employability*. This moves the debate away from a concern about how the individual and the organisation relate in work and focuses instead on the responsibility of individuals to foster those skills needed to give themselves the greatest chance of getting a job on the open market. The company too has a greater responsibility to ensure that the skill levels of its staff, particularly those whose longer term prospects in the company are not good, are kept up and enhanced. Employability is a useful addition to the security debate but the central issue remains.

SECURITY IN EXCHANGE FOR FLEXIBILITY

There is evidence that there is a greater readiness for companies to give assurances of employment security in order to achieve maximum workforce flexibility. This trade-off has typically been found in unionised environments such as the automobile industry or utilities. In particular, Japanese companies setting up in the UK regard stable employment as a basic building block of high-quality employee performance.

A 1990 IRS survey of Japanese plants in the UK found that 20 out of 25 companies surveyed offered a guarantee of some form of lifetime employment. These commitments have been part of the organisational ethos for many years. It has not been wrung out of them by trade unions. It stems from a belief that to achieve world-class performance the company should offer each individual stable employment and growth opportunities.

Other car companies such as Rover and Vauxhall have given employment guarantees because they are regarded as essential if the business is to develop the flexible and motivated workforce needed to achieve world-class standards of output and quality. Achieving these standards depends on far greater flexibility and commitment to the success of the company on the part of the individual. A company committed to stable employment communicates that commitment to its staff and ensures that the other signals which it transmits are consistent with its stated objectives, recognising how much the sense of security is influenced by these signals.

This can conflict with the need to send signals to other stakeholders, such as the City, that robust actions are being taken to maintain profitability. Announcing large job cuts is often used to achieve these ends. Such messages run directly counter to the signals which a company seeks to send its staff. A recent example was the pressure placed on ICI in 1996 to deliver 5000 job cuts in response to a profit downturn. The banking sector has also developed a reputation for talking up redundancies for external consumption with very damaging effects on internal morale.

At BT the employee representatives addressed the shareholders directly on this issue, illustrated by a passage from the NCU publication, *Undervalued Assets*.

> *The departure of 100 000 employees has led to an atmosphere of deep insecurity.*
> *The company seems to have reached a position where cuts have become an end in*
> *themselves with no regard to the impact on the workforce or the wider social costs.*
> *That's why job security remains a major cause of concern for BT employees. BT*

> *shareholders should share this concern because BT will only succeed in the long term if its own employees are committed, dedicated and loyal.*

It is also important that the company monitors employees' views and expectations about job security and develops policies to manage those expectations both in the short and the long term. In the short term, a management which wants to minimise insecurity sits down with its staff and works towards a mutually agreed understanding of expectations and likely outcomes. They will also work together to put in place a robust set of processes to deal with the job cuts which do arise.

Company credibility is forged on a track record of consistently applying the company's core values to situations of job cuts and plant closures. Many businesses have actually done this. The strongest form of such a commitment has been a no compulsory redundancy guarantee. The Rover example is best known. Other companies such as Dwr Cymru/ Welsh Water (analysed in the next chapter) have reached similar compacts with staff regarding commitments to employment security.

> *Partnership gives employment security. In these days of rapid change it is impossible to give a guarantee of job security, that is doing the same job at the same location doing the same things. But it does mean that permanent staff who want to continue working for the company can continue to do so providing they understand their obligations as clearly set out in the agreement.*

At Blue Circle, the original 'Integrated Working' agreement did not offer a guarantee of job security and indeed introduced selective compulsory redundancies. The 'Way Ahead' deal in March 1997 offered all of the company's 2000 workers employment security. Security takes away the fear which prevents total commitment to the organisation. In the company's words the aim is 'to get the company's staff to go the extra mile to deliver world class standards of motivation and flexibility'.

As well as policies which manage expectations through consistent messages and behaviours, a robust set of mutually agreed proposals about how job cuts will be handled is also needed. BAXI, for instance, sets out a detailed nine-step process which, in the event of job cuts, will be considered after full consultation with the appropriate groups. The IPA's Rhône Poulenc study tells a similar story of a redundancy policy which was carefully worked through.

The employment security debate rests upon the crucial question of how much value the company places on stability of employment within its overall philosophy. Does the company really believe that stability gives the business competitive advantage, or is it paying lip service to the idea only to abandon any commitments it has made in the face of difficulties?

There has been a change in this debate over the last few years. In 1992 one company chief executive described security of employment as a worthy aim but doubted its value as a foundation for a partnership company. He foresaw a great danger in giving employees any idea that security could in fact be delivered lest the whole edifice of employee expectations came down. This concern has led many companies to feel that the appropriate approach was to talk tough on the subject.

Currently, the shortcomings are more readily recognised and evidence, for example in the banking sector, confirms that mishandling of the security issue has damaged companies more than they expected. At the same time the expectations of staff have changed. Gone is any idea that security of employment can exist without a large contribution from staff themselves, particularly in the areas of training and development, maximum workplace flexibility, and making the organisation successful by continually improving standards of performance. Personal development and training cease to be optional extras but are an integral part of the contract between the individual and the company. This has been well expressed in the IPA study of Elida Gibbs:

> *Elida Gibbs wants people who take responsibility for their job and are ready to be accountable for it, who demonstrate job competency through qualifications and other measures and commit to development of themselves as well as the business.*

When employees make this commitment and employers take security on board as a core corporate value, a virtuous circle begins to be built which provides a substantial foundation stone for business success. The Japanese philosophy which sees stability as the cornerstone of flexibility and motivation has been copied by UK companies as well. Companies such as Toyota have stood the classic UK assertion on its head, and emphasised the essentially mutual nature of the employment relationship:

> *Highly competent motivated people will show great commitment to the fulfilment of the company objectives. Fundamental to the people philosophy is a determination to provide to the individual both growth opportunity and stable employment.*

INFORMATION, CONSULTATION AND EMPLOYEE VOICE

There is a good deal of confusion about what people mean by the terms communication, consultation, information, involvement, direct and indirect participation. They are frequently used with overlapping meanings. In looking at what characterised a partnership company, the IPA has examined the mix of communication and consultative arrangements found in different organisations. Each of the elements of the employee involvement mix is linked. It is not always clear where communication ends and consultation begins. Companies typically use a very wide range of differing activities to develop the mix needed to gain staff commitment and achieve success in the marketplace.

Good communication is only partly about structures and systems. It is also about the philosophy and style of the company. The Nissan company offers a good example of an open communications culture, a basic building block of effective employee involvement in the business. Its '*Communications Philosophy*' states that:

> *Within the bounds of commercial confidentiality we will encourage open channels of communication. We would like everyone to know what is happening in our company, how we are performing and what we plan. Our aim is to build a company with which people can identify and to which we all feel commitment. We want information and views to flow freely upward, downward and across the company.*

This statement sets the benchmark by which Nissan assesses the effectiveness of communication within the organisation. Daily briefings take place to meet the company standard for communication with all staff, *'Every Day Face to Face'*. Information is only valuable if it is believed. The IPD study, *The New Employment Relationship*, by Kessler and Undy, showed that much of what is communicated in companies is not trusted by the staff. Despite large-scale investment in communications initiatives they have a chequered record. The Department of Employment study by Marchington *et al.* (1992) found that only one-third of staff felt that briefing systems added to their understanding of management decisions. Only 25 per cent of staff felt that it increased their commitment to the company.

Although these initiatives are an essential starting point, they do not of themselves build partnership in the workplace. Conflicting signals between what is said and what is done leads to scepticism. In turn this leads to failure in delivering the culture change which is being sought through the initiative. Building a successful partnership means going beyond mere internal communication and addressing a larger agenda around greater consultation and staff involvement. There needs to be clarity about the elements of consultation and communication which are necessary to make the partnership company work. In business, decisions need to be made and acted on quickly. Yet decisions which require staff commitment in order to be effective should have the approval of those who are affected by them. Ideally those people should also be part of the decision-making process.

> *There will be difficulties in reaching appropriate mechanisms which must retain for management the ability to take fast business decisions without consulting ad nauseam.*
> (Major UK retailer)

The challenge is to develop machinery which both maximises staff input into decisions yet ensures that a focus on the business goals is maintained and decisions are not endlessly delayed. Direct methods of consultation at the workplace are concerned mainly with views about, and input into, day-to-day matters at the individual's workplace. Closely related to direct methods of consultation are various processes for delegating responsibility for organising the workplace into individuals or teams.

DIRECT PARTICIPATION

There has been considerable growth in direct employee participation in the workplace, designed to listen more effectively to what employees say and contribute at the workplace. Cellnet has applied a powerful direct involvement philosophy to help build a highly successful business. Its statement of values (EThOS) sets out this approach clearly:

1 Good people management is the key to effective task management. It can only be achieved by a frank and open exchange of ideas, information and knowledge.
2 Open and clear communication with colleagues across the organisation is the responsibility of everyone and is the key to business success.
3 People can make their greatest contribution to the company by taking ownership of issues and problems, making commitments and delivering against those commitments.

This takes as its foundation a commitment to good communication processes and builds a highly delegated participatory approach to running the business on that basis. A closely integrated cycle of empowerment, teamworking, quality initiatives and personal training and development is now commonplace. At Elida Gibbs the company set out three goals – world-class products, world-class service, world-class speed. The company uses all the elements of the cycle – teamworking, a learning culture, and considerable emphasis on the skills needed to meet the world-class goals.

Effective consultation is not just about delegation, it is also about structures through which the company listens to its staff. Employee attitude surveys are widely used as a means of getting regular and systematic feedback from employees. To be credible, employee surveys must be followed up and acted on, or they quickly fall into disrepute and response rates start falling. Employee surveys confirm that people value face-to-face communication with colleagues and their line manager. Not only is this the way people want to receive information, it is also the channel through which they want to be able to feed back their ideas and opinions to the company.

There are other feedback mechanisms which do not rely on surveys. At the John Lewis Partnership each branch has a committee for communication which operates as a two-way forum for communication and feedback. These committees act as a weathervane of the state of opinion among staff with the added requirement that all complaints and suggestions are published and followed up by the relevant manager.

The emerging pattern of best practice in direct consultation is of a participative culture where problems are shared, where loyalty is valued, where one's contribution is recognised and praised and where mistakes are dealt with constructively. The individual is therefore better able than in the past to have some direct involvement in the decisions made at the workplace and greater control over aspects of their daily activities themselves. Staff want to give greater prominence at their workplace forum to subjects like forthcoming projects and plans of their division or business. There is a growing desire to debate issues of a longer term and more strategic nature.

The presence of good participative relationships at the workplace does not resolve the question about influence. When staff are asked in surveys if they want greater involvement the answer is generally very positive. The FI group, for example, has found this among their staff members who are already some of the UK's most involved employees. Employees cannot easily voice their general views and concerns on a one-to-one basis. It needs a system of consultation through representatives.

REPRESENTATIVE CONSULTATION

Indirect or representative methods of consultation include systems of joint consultation such as works councils and joint consultative committees. Representative consultation enables the employee voice to be heard at a higher level putting forward employee views into the company strategic decision-making processes. When the IPD surveyed employees for the *New Employment Relationship*, they found a clear mismatch between the influence staff wanted and what actual influence they felt they had in all areas of work other than the immediate task in hand. According to its authors, Kessler and Undy (1996):

> *This general lack of influence is not through the employees' lack of desire for any influence. Empowerment of employees has not yet reached many of those parts of work which employees wish to influence.*

There is a sense that influence over the big issues is missing. Kessler and Undy found in the IPD study that the influence gap was significant in areas such as training and development, goal-setting and even over such non-controversial matters as health and safety standards.

Input at company level cannot be achieved on an individualistic basis but relies on representative consultation, which gives employees a more effective channel to the senior executives within their companies. The purpose of such a representative system is spelt out in the statement of common understanding which introduces ICI's joint consultation policy.

> *It is mutually agreed that in order for all businesses to have the best chance of attaining and sustaining the highest levels of competitiveness it is essential that all employees co-operate with each other to understand as fully as possible the business, economic and social context in which they are asked to work and have appropriate forums to influence decision makers at all relevant management levels so that there is the best chance of a well judged and full hearted contribution to business success from every employee.*

Interest in representative consultation has recently grown because of the legislative requirements to consult in fields such as pensions, redundancies, transfers of staff and the introduction in several UK companies of European works councils. The IPA's work points to many examples of representative systems operating successfully in the UK. This covers a wide spectrum from manufacturing to retail, from non-union to unionised, modern Japanese incomers to old established native companies. In some organisations the forum for consultation is directly elected, in others it is partly elected directly and partly nominated from existing staff representatives. This is particularly the case in organisations where some sectors have unions and others do not.

At their best, employee consultation forums have transformed trivial agendas into those which offer an effective employee contribution to the success and direction of the business. This is very different from the stereotype in the 1970s and 1980s of ineffectual, bureaucratic 'tea and toilets' talk shops which contributed little of value to the business. The unions regarded these as the poor relations of the more powerful collective bargaining arrangements which they then enjoyed in most larger companies. The evidence from WIRS3 (Millward, 1994) is that these old-style joint consultative councils have been in decline in the last decade.

The Partnership Council at Scottish Power set out their philosophy of representative consultation:

> *The Partnership Council exists to provide an effective vehicle for the representatives of management and the trade union representatives to deliver the joint commitment to the continued growth and future success of Generation Wholesale division.*

> *The Partnership Council shall develop effective two way relationships between the management of the division and employees and their trade unions with the objective of achieving a business recognised as world class by all stakeholders.*

> *To this end the Partnership Council shall promote best in class practices which create success both for the business and those employed in it.*

Well-established systems of consultation exist in leading UK companies. The example of ICI has already been quoted. The John Lewis Partnership has a structure which combines a central council with direct access to, and indeed seats on the company board. Branch councils carry out a similar function at each individual store. All of these positions are directly elected by partners giving a cross section of the Partnership which not only represents all ranks and occupations but embraces a wide range of ages, knowledge and experience. The chairman and a number of the principal directors give an annual account of their stewardship to the council and can be directly questioned by its members.

In practice, the distinction between union and non-union representation is becoming increasingly blurred, reflecting the diverse nature of the UK workforce. At the Rhône Poulenc Staveley Chemicals unit, the directly elected consultative council operates alongside a unionised negotiating structure. At companies such as Boots and HP Bulmers, employee councils were set up in the late 1970s at the time of the Bullock Report. At Bulmers, the council has grown out of a desire by the company to extend and develop the involvement of employees in decisions and policies which affect their future. Reflecting the composition of their workforce, the council has both nominated union participants as well as directly elected staff. The council has an oversight of such matters as redundancy policy, internal cultural change programmes, and has undertaken the company's employee attitude survey.

REPRESENTATION

Towards Industrial Partnership recognised both the importance of representative arrangements and the shortcomings of the single-channel, union-only, model. It excludes over 60 per cent of the UK workforce and there are still examples where the mismatch is evident between the views of activists and the workforce in general.

Companies which favour the unitarist HRM model argue that representative channels simply get in the way of the relationship that counts, namely that between the company and the individual. Describing the approach at Sheerness Steel the company's personnel director described the company's philosophy as HRP (human resource performance).

> *HRP is a business philosophy in which employees create and sustain compliant behaviour aimed at satisfaction in the workplace and success for the business. This leans towards a unitary perspective of industrial relations which emphasises the individual and either marginalises or eliminates the trade union.*

Others, such as Sir Bob Reid, ex-Chairman of British Rail, have argued that representation is essential as a way for the company to relate meaningfully to its workforce. In a business of that size it is simply not feasible to organise workplace relations in a coherent way without a representative structure. Employee voice does not necessarily rely on a union to be effective. In companies where the employees are also shareholders with a substantial holding, as was the case at the FI Group before listing in 1996, the employee voice is powerfully heard both at the AGM and through the shareholder trust. The Group is also a good example of how the employee voice at company level can alter a major decision. Arrangements for profit-sharing in the company were amended to give the same entitlement to all regardless of salary instead of a salary-related schema as was proposed at the outset.

The John Lewis Partnership has staff councils both at company and at branch level. JLP has a culture which lays greater emphasis than any other company on the importance of enabling the voice of the partners to be effectively heard through representatives.

Representation through trade unions has been the model in companies such as Blue Circle, Scottish Power and Royal Mail. In a company such as Cellnet the union involvement has been small. Many organisations are grappling with highly complex cultures with a mix of unionised and non-unionised sections, where the business needs of different parts of the organisation vary, and where a stark contrast exists between militant unionism in some parts and a culture of individualised relationships elsewhere in the business. This experience underlines the fact that many organisations need to make their direct and representative processes work together.

An employee voice implies a pluralist view of consultation which gives both weight and legitimacy to the views of the workforce. The 'inclusive company' described in the RSA *Tomorrow's Company* report does not recognise that employees have their own interests separate from those of the business. To achieve alignment of the interests of the firm and the employee stakeholder means first recognising that fact. For the concept of inclusion to have genuine meaning, employee stakeholders must be able to express that interest, either individually or as a group. The agenda of any employee forum must be strategic and business focused. It must also meet employee needs and adequately cover the legal requirements to consult. To be successful it must work within a framework of mutuality, i.e. a respect for the interests and aspirations of all the stakeholders in the company. The challenge for the company is how to combine business focus with a commitment to mutuality. Unions must move away from a bargaining mindset to a participative style which emphasises a joint approach to solving problems. At Dwr Cymru/Welsh Water, the unions were quite candid about this issue:

> *Partnership does mean a different and sometimes a more challenging role for the trade unions. It is easy to confront and say NO. It is far more difficult to create a new role working with employees and the company to develop a better future not only for ourselves but more importantly for our customers.*

The ACAS approach to joint problem-solving has helped many organisations move away from slow and cumbersome processes which treat every step in the dynamic of change as a trade-off to be haggled over. A consultative, problem-sharing approach leads, in time, to a much enhanced understanding of the issues involved, better resolution of points of difficulty, tangible benefits to the organisation and identifiable improvements in trust within the company. This has enabled companies to take their staff with them when resolving such potentially difficult issues as the introduction of performance management, workforce flexibility, redundancy programmes or productivity improvements.

Every organisation needs to improve employees' understanding of the business issues which it faces. Debates about company performance, awareness of investment and divestment decisions, the state of the marketplace, training and personal development policies, redundancies and cut backs all help to build awareness. The input of the employee's voice to the decision-making procedures makes for better decisions.

Decisions which have been reached after consultation with the workforce have a degree of legitimacy in the eyes of the employees affected by them which cannot be achieved when that process has not taken place. When difficult decisions are being made in areas like redundancies, this legitimisation requirement is recognised in law.

Direct involvement of employees at the workplace and representative consultation do not always exist in harmony. In some sectors, there is a suspicion of direct methods – which has only recently begun to wane – stemming from a view that direct consultation exists mainly to circumvent union channels. There is a marked difference between the public and private sector as far as this issue is concerned. In the public sector there is often a tension. In studies at a major local authority and a health trust, there was mistrust and hostility between the union and the employers about the introduction of direct communication and consultation machinery. Steps were being taken at the local authority to bridge the gap but the evidence was of two parallel activities with differing agendas and fundamentally different views of what the objectives for good employee involvement processes should be. The IPA research confirms the view expressed by Millward (1994) that much of the best private sector practice in direct employee involvement exists in tandem with good consultation systems at company level.

CONCLUSION

There are differing views about where the partnership debate now stands. Partnership is not about clinging onto the status quo. Every organisation studied by the IPA is going through change which is often deep rooted and swift. There is evidence of different organisations dealing with change in new ways which do not always fit a HRM or an adversarial model.

One view of partnership held by a number of advocates of the HRM school argues that it is simply a way of managing the workforce through the process of change which is particularly appropriate to a highly unionised workplace. The cultural change will be driven through anyway, and partnership merely offers a place at the table for employee representatives. Alternatively, there is also a view from the left that partnership is essentially a fudge through which the workforce loses its ability to defend its interests against those of capital. This argument has underpinned the view about partnership which is heard in some unions.

The IPA sees partnership as a unique combination of employee involvement processes which has the potential to maximise the benefits to the company and to the employees in the process of change. There are three behavioural aspects which distinguish the partnership approach:

1 a commitment to working together to make the business more successful
2 understanding the employee security conundrum and trying to do something about it
3 building relationships at the workplace which maximise employee influence through total communication and a robust and effective employee voice.

In both Welsh Water and Blue Circle, partnership evolved gradually out of a series of changes which began in the mid-1980s and which have been built on since then. The partnership journey has involved a series of steps and some false turnings, but there are certain common elements:

● a vision of the goal
● a cultural change programme which began with managers
● a systematic revision of reward, status and conditions

- the development of new business-focused consultative arrangements from the workplace to the boardroom
- a carefully thought-out and agreed policy to manage employment security
- a major commitment to employee development and training.

In both cases there have been heavy job cuts: a 36 per cent reduction at Blue Circle Cement plants over five years, and a 16 per cent reduction at Welsh Water over the three years from 1992–94. Yet these have been achieved in such a way that the sense of security remains more intact than in many other companies where job cuts have been much less. Many of the companies which demonstrate partnership structures or behaviours have shown a commitment to the practices of employee involvement for a long time. Companies such as ICI, Unilever subsidiaries such as Elida Fabergé, Boots, Rover, Blue Circle and the John Lewis Partnership demonstrate many of these qualities.

For others the trigger has been a change in the status of the organisation. Some of the most interesting examples of new approaches following the partnership model have been utilities like TRANSCO, Scottish Power, Thames Water and Dwr Cymru/ Welsh Water. In each case privatisation has created an opportunity for company and workforce to sit down together and put in place new structures to change the culture of the organisation. A partnership approach has not been inevitable in these privatised utilities, and there are well-known cases where an altogether more hard-line approach has been taken by the employer enforcing terms on staff, derecognising employee representatives and driving through change with minimal consultation.

For many organisations the changing marketplace acts as the catalyst. This was the case at Blue Circle, Elida Fabergé, Cellnet, and Rhône Poulenc among the companies examined. Paradoxically, it was also a major driver at Royal Mail London, where the major overhaul of sorting offices provides a good example of the joint problem-solving approach involving a highly unionised and militant workforce. Both sides implicitly recognised that the opening-up of the mail service to competition was only a matter of time. The study also highlighted a problem which unions encounter when they are more actively involved as partners in the strategic process. They are short of the resources which enable them speedily and expertly to engage in a detailed debate about strategic options.

Over recent years one can see a shift in the position of trade unions towards the partnership model. The most significant breakthrough occurred in 1994 when the Towards Industrial Partnership (TIP) principles were used as the basis of a report on *Human Resource Management* by the TUC. This report fully endorsed the TIP approach as the foundation on which a full engagement by the unions with new management practices should take place. The TUC also incorporated the IPA's views into its 1996 report on stakeholding and confirmed its support for the work the IPA is doing in its 1997 policy statement on *Partnership for Progress*.

There is less evidence of the rebuilding of a national consensus in business and union relationships. There is little enthusiasm for the establishment of structures which are seen as characterising the corporate state. The concept of social partners as understood in continental Europe sits uneasily with prevailing opinions in the UK. Such an approach is limited to quite specific areas such as training and development. The CBI emphasises that any approach must be voluntarily agreed and based on the workplace rather than at national level.

There has also emerged a clear attempt to construct a business case for partnership. One of the most powerful expositions of this in recent times has been from Pfeffer (1995) addressing the *Basis for Competitive Success*. Arguing for a central focus on people and organisational culture he quoted Toyota, John Lewis Partnership, Land Rover and FI Group as organisations which had either outperformed rivals or achieved a turnround in performance through a commitment to involvement or partnership. Work by Fernie and Metcalf (1995) at the Centre for Economic Performance, based on a sample of over 1200 companies in WIRS, has also shown a positive relationship between the existence of consultative councils and economic performance as measured by productivity growth. Looking at the car industry, Sako (1996) has shown that the combination of direct consultative mechanisms for problem resolution – for example, quality circles with employee voice mechanism such as a joint consultative council – gives positive business outcomes in terms of training, quality and stockholding.

There is now a need to build on the evidence so far accumulated and examine systematically the characteristics of partnership companies across different business sectors. This will enable many more companies which are developing the concepts to be surveyed and a critical mass built up. A major research project on the partnership company commenced in 1997, involving David Guest of Birkbeck College and Riccardo Peccei of LSE to address these issues. This will enable the IPA to benchmark partnership across the business community, defining the values and behaviours which can better deliver long-term business success as well as an enhanced experience for people at work.

10

Dwr Cymru/Welsh Water

A case study in partnership

COLIN THOMAS AND BRIAN WALLIS
Welsh Water and Unison

INTRODUCTION

Dwr Cymru/Welsh Water is a subsidiary of the Hyder plc – a group of nearly 9000 employees. It provides utility services, primarily within Wales, and is involved in the development of infrastructure investment in 30 countries worldwide.

Dwr Cymru/Welsh Water formed the original part of the group when the organisation was privatised in 1989 and still remains a key part of its activities. It employs just over 2100 employees. The company supplies 3 million customers with water and deals with sewerage treatment and disposal. It employs a range of staff from people who repair mains and services, operators in process plants, network controllers who operate the distribution network, customer service staff, and professional support staff and managers.

This case study is the story of the development of employee relations following privatisation and the end of national pay arrangements. The story starts with a brief history of industrial relations in Welsh Water set against a background of fairly traditional national bargaining arrangements. It then outlines the reasons why the company and its unions decided to adopt a partnership approach. The major features and development of partnership are set out together with the formula used to govern annual pay awards. The benefits and the implications for each of the parties are then assessed. Finally, the future development of partnership is assessed in the context of the expansion of the group following the acquisition of SWALEC (the regional electricity company for South Wales) and the creation of a common services company, Hyder Services.

THE HISTORY AND TRADITIONS OF INDUSTRIAL RELATIONS IN WELSH WATER

The company's roots lie in local government in the water boards which were set up by local authorities and the sewage works which were an integral part of local council activities. In 1974 the regional water authorities were established, with Welsh Water Authority being created to manage these functions as one entity for most of Wales and Herefordshire.

Terms and conditions were agreed through national bargaining arrangements for the three main negotiating groups – staff, manual and craft. The approach reflected typical national pay bargaining practice, with annual pay claims being submitted by national trade union officers/committees to a central negotiating group on the employers' side (usually chairpeople or chief executives). The links with the local workplace were remote with minimal input from operational managers and local trade union representatives.

Within the new Welsh Water Authority, consultative and negotiating arrangements were established for each negotiating group both at authority level and in operating divisions. While bringing the various boards and ex-local authority departments into the new body was a detailed and sometimes difficult process, the industrial relations 'machinery' continued to reflect the local authority origins of the new organisation. There was an over-emphasis on procedure and bureaucracy which appeared remote from the local needs of operational managers and staff at workplace level. The personnel function in particular was perceived as semi-detached from the mainstream management of the business, and its role in the industrial relations machinery was largely that of 'honest broker'; through this, it helped to resolve local disputes in formal panels where the advocacy skills of the trade union officers and management representatives played a major role in determining outcomes.

The autonomy of the three bargaining groups was strongly defended by the respective trade unions. This was also reflected in the nature of local work organisation, with demarcations between manual and craft occupations being particularly strong, such that white collar staff were generally excluded from 'hands-on' working on plant and equipment.

While relationships, particularly between full-time officers and senior management, were generally sound, there was an underlying mutual suspicion. A lack of openness on the part of management led to feelings among local trade union representatives and staff that there were 'hidden' plans for change, with management being given credit for a level of strategic planning which was not reflected in reality. Trade unions were perceived by management as 'conservative' – unwilling to accept change. Indeed the trade unions played a superb defensive game – delaying and minimising change on the ground.

This remained the position until the mid-1980s when, under the influence of a new board, chairman, chief executive and personnel director, the organisation culture began to change. The appointment of a former full-time trade union officer, initially to the board and later as personnel director, brought a fresh approach to people management in general and employee relations in particular. In this position, Noel Hufton and his reformed personnel team started, with strong support from senior management, the process of change which was eventually to lead to the development of partnership after privatisation and the end of national bargaining.

In the period before privatisation, two key foundations were put in place. A joint project under the bland title 'Measures to Improve Operational Efficiency' set out to involve the unions in updating working practices and improving flexibility. While this was carried out within the national terms and conditions, it did build up confidence among the senior managers and full-time officers involved, not only in one another but also in their ability to deliver a 'package' which was more in tune with local needs.

The second vital element was a heavy commitment by Welsh Water to management development and training. All senior and middle managers attended programmes designed to highlight the importance of management style, and this also reinforced the development of a clear set of principles and values which were eventually to help form the basis of the partnership approach. This was accompanied by more rigorous selection of operational managers to ensure that their style and behaviours reflected the emerging organisational culture. This new culture was based upon promoting involvement, recognising the importance of contributions from frontline staff, seeing the need for openness, and the desire to build long-lasting relationships based on trust and co-operation. This process was greatly helped by having a senior management team in place which shared these values. This ensured that gradually a critical mass of senior and middle managers who shared these values was put in place.

THE DEVELOPMENT OF PARTNERSHIP

Preparation – shared thoughts

Well before privatisation in 1989 both senior trade union officers and the senior personnel team – which had been delegated the task of introducing local arrangements following the demise of national bargaining – shared ideas about how future arrangements would work. Interestingly, both sides had independently consulted Templeton College, Oxford, on possible options, with both concluding that 'a sophisticated consultative model' was most appropriate for Welsh Water. This combined the benefits of sound collective arrangements with a recognition of the importance of individual employees.

Another shared view was that the national collective bargaining process had produced a series of settlements that were within 1 per cent of the annual rate of inflation. More importantly, both sides recognised that the 'ritualistic dancing' of collective bargaining in the context of the water industry produced only a negative result. The company was seen to be only giving a reasonable increase each year under pressure from the trade union. For their part, the unions themselves portrayed any deal as the best that they could force the employers to concede. As a result, staff usually felt let down, even though their relative position remained healthy compared with many other organisations in the local labour market.

There was also a consensus that if the challenges of privatisation were to be met, it was to the mutual advantage of all parties to work together, recognising that the company, trade unions and staff had many shared objectives, even though their priorities might differ. There was also a shared understanding that there must be a better way forward; this proved to be the foundation of the three partnership agreements of 1991, 1993 and 1995.

Partnership 1

A one-year 'holding deal' was concluded in 1990, which harmonised pay review dates on 1 April, where previously the staff review date was July. It also set down a number of objectives for further consideration, such as harmonisation of conditions.

The key breakthrough, however, was the partnership agreement of March 1991, which set out clearly the foundations of the approach, namely:

1 The development of a mutually acceptable pay formula.
2 The establishment of single-status conditions for all employees.
3 The required co-operation defined as an obligation within partnership.

The replacement of the traditional annual pay negotiation by an agreed objective formula was a key change. This was based on three factors: first, using the November Retail Price Index percentage, the same figure as the company was allowed to use to review its prices to customers each year. Second, a market safeguard was introduced which linked the value of this award to the Welsh labour market. This was measured independently by staff at Cardiff Business School who surveyed over 70 of the largest public and private sector organisations in Wales, in order to determine not only the total value of their annual pay award but also relative pay levels. This was done by making comparisons of more than 30 benchmark jobs from Welsh Water with their counterparts in these other organisations. Third, there was a link to the profitability of the organisation through a profit-related pay scheme. This utilised the (then relatively new) government legislation which encouraged the linking of pay to profit through the provision of tax relief on this element of pay.

In addition, this agreement identified seven action areas, all of which were implemented on time over the next two years. These were:

1 The establishment of a single-table representative council with specific work being delegated to 'issue groups'. These comprised mainly lay representatives, operational managers and personnel staff.
2 Changing working patterns, including a reduction in the working week to 37 hours for manual and craft staff. This involved moving away from the traditional fixed working week pattern of Monday to Friday – with an early finish on Friday – to a flexible pattern more suited to the needs of customers. This also led to the introduction of the Welsh Water version of annualised hours called 'planned working time'.
3 The harmonisation of other working conditions, policies and procedures.
4 The introduction of monthly pay through credit transfer for all employees.
5 A commitment to introduce a new unified pay structure.
6 Various measures to improve productivity through greater flexibility between work groups, skill enhancements, and acceptance of new responsibilities previously carried out by supervisors.
7 A no compulsory redundancy policy.

In many ways, this agreement was a breakthrough. It moved the company – and more importantly the trade unions – away from the traditional adversarial stances embodied in the annual pay negotiation. The introduction of a 'no compulsory redundancy' policy also started to build the trust necessary for the organisation to introduce many of the changes required to face the new challenges of privatisation. For manual and craft employees, hitherto the 'second-class citizens' of the industry, this was recognition that they were equally important to the success of the organisation as other staff. A further key aspect of the agreement was the method of 'internally marketing' its contents. It was agreed that this should be a joint responsibility of management and the trade unions through joint presentations. The result was a two-to-one majority in favour of the proposals.

Partnership 2 – 1993

The 1993 agreement completed the commitments of Partnership 1 with the introduction of a unified pay structure for all staff. All the preparation for this new structure was carried out on a joint basis with the trade unions, based upon the foundation of Hay job evaluation. This agreement also introduced performance appraisal for all staff together with new understandings on performance management and focused in particular on the management of absenteeism and how to deal with poor performers.

A particularly innovative aspect of the agreement was a document entitled 'Planning Our Future'. This set out possible future developments over the course of the next few years and the response needed from the company, staff and trade unions. In this context, the necessity to achieve manpower reductions was recognised by all parties – a difficult step for the trade unions traditionally committed to defending jobs. The provisions in this document concentrated on the means rather than the ends; for example, on the importance of staff who were leaving being treated fairly and properly, and being given the opportunity to agree to leave at a mutually acceptable date in the future. It also recognised that there was a need to consult and involve those who were remaining with the company in how jobs would be managed in the future.

The pay formula was further refined and the employment security provisions were renewed. To promote local ownership of the new agreement, local representatives and managers explained its contents to their colleagues using an agreed script plus video – the result was a majority of three-to-one in favour of the deal.

Partnership 3 – 1995

Both management and the trade unions share a strong belief that the output from their joint deliberations must have relevance – relevance both to the needs of the company and to the views and needs of staff. In order to ensure that future developments matched everyone's needs, the unique feature of the third agreement was its preparation. Senior personnel staff and the full-time trade union officers undertook a series of joint roadshows, meeting small groups of staff. Starting with a review of progress to date, the sessions then split into four or five small groups to identify priority issues for the future and staff concerns about existing agreements. Through this medium, the views of over 75 per cent of the staff were heard and more importantly listened to.

The Partnership 3 Agreement reacted in a number of ways to the views expressed by staff. The continued uncertainty about the nature of 'partnership' was met with a restatement of its basic principles. The new agreement spelt out that partnership was two-way:

> *What you give – sharing responsibility for continued improvements in performance. Dwr Cymru can be assured that everyone shares the responsibility in meeting our business objectives and in providing the highest levels of customer service. What you get – the benefits of Partnership are that our people have continuing employment and pay security with good conditions of employment.*

Concerns that the employment security provisions were held as a threat each time the agreement came up for renewal were countered by placing the new agreement on an ongoing basis – not just for two years at a time – with appropriate review clauses.

Complaints over the complexity of the pay review process were answered by changes to the market safeguard and an agreement to transfer a fixed proportion of the pay review to the profit-related pay scheme. The position of temporary staff was also addressed through a new review procedure. The value of adopting this thorough preparation was borne out by the ballot result which saw the majority in favour increase yet again to five-to-one in favour.

THE BENEFITS OF PARTNERSHIP

Partnership works on the very simple principle of a virtuous circle with four key elements. First, it starts with the idea that the success of any service organisation – the basic service nature of water companies is often masked by the word 'utility' – rests heavily on the commitment and enthusiasm of its workforce. Second, if employees feel that they are well treated and involved in their work, they will feel more motivated. Consequently, their reactions to customers will be more positive. This is reflected in a variety of ways: the response on the telephone or on the doorstep; the emergency teams that repair bursts in the middle of the night; the process teams that deliver a 'food product' directly to the home; or the impact on the environment of the teams that run sewerage treatment works. If this response is effective and customers are well satisfied, our collective image will be much improved. The ability of Dwr Cymru to continue to provide drinking water without restrictions during the 1995 drought achieved a major step forward in the public's perception of the company. But its ability to do this rested heavily on the ability, ingenuity and enthusiasm of its workforce. Connected with this is the third point, that employees who feel involved are more willing to co-operate in and contribute to making the organisation more effective, both from a service and a financial perspective. Finally, if the company is financially successful its ability to continue providing employment and pay security is enhanced and the circle is complete.

Partnership has therefore produced a range of benefits to Welsh Water and its customers. Some major examples of this are:

1 Flexible working arrangements allowing customer contact to be carried out at a time to suit the customer rather than a time to suit the company. This has been achieved through the establishment of a 24-hour call centre and through flexible working patterns for customer representatives who call on the customer if there is a problem.
2 Improved quality, in that the teams that run the water and sewerage treatment plants are now formally qualified through extensive NVQ training programmes. More important, they have been 'empowered' to run their works within an agreed framework of quality standards with managers changing their role to one of supporters rather than controllers. The net result has been that quality standards are at an all-time high.
3 Significant reductions in costs have been achieved, partly as a result of savings in staffing which have been passed onto customers in the form of reduced prices. Prior to this, water charges had risen continuously for 17 years.
4 Customer service standards as measured by the director general have continued to hit the 'very good' or 'good' category.
5 Organisational change has continued apace. Again, the two-way nature of the approach

is demonstrated by staff showing a willingness to accept and contribute to required changes, and the company being flexible with out-posting of work to some locations where the need for employment had disappeared.

6 A willingness to work with other forms of labour, such as contractors, agency and temporary staff. Utilising contractors had led to major industrial relations problems in the early 1980s.

IMPLICATIONS OF PARTNERSHIP

As with any partnership, all parties need to see mutual benefits to offset real and perceived changes which arise from the creation of the arrangement in the first place. In the Welsh Water case, these can be seen from the perspective of the three main parties – the staff, the trade unions and the company.

Implications for staff

There have been a number of tangible benefits for *staff* arising from the partnership agreements:

1 Employment security under the no compulsory redundancy policy has provided staff with additional assurances in relation to their future, certainly compared with the majority of employees, even in the utility sector. Commencing with the preparations for Partnership 3 and more recent work with Hyder Services, the desire to have a job remains the number one priority for the vast majority of employees.

2 The pay formula has also produced a degree of security in an uncertain world. Profit-related pay has produced additional benefits above RPI pay awards, together with the tax-free benefits of such schemes.

3 Harmonisation of conditions has ensured that all employees are treated equitably as far as major conditions are concerned, particularly former manual and craft employees whose conditions were previously inferior to their white collar colleagues.

4 The agreements have facilitated an acceptance of significant organisational and technological changes. New technology, whether in the form of new IT systems or new automated plant and equipment, has been introduced rapidly over the last few years; generally this has been welcomed by employees.

5 For employees, the greater empowerment and control given to frontline staff and to their teams has meant a greater degree of freedom than ever before in controlling their own working lives. For the most part, this has been welcomed by staff although recently there are signs that staff are beginning to expect specific recognition for these new responsibilities, in a way which places new demands on the existing payband structure.

Implications for trade unions

Arguably, the *trade unions* have had to make the biggest and most difficult adjustment. This change has not been easy, as it requires strong leadership and a firm belief that partnership is a better way of operating. It also demands the tenacity to argue with more traditional colleagues who view such co-operation as 'getting into bed with the employer'. There are a number of implications of this:

1 The fundamental role of trade unions is to protect the interests of their members and to advance their cause through the negotiating process. The ability of the full-time officer to act as an 'advocate' either on the part of individuals or the collective, is seen as the opportunity for the union to prove its value to the members. In simple terms, to achieve something which the employer would not have conceded without union intervention. Under the traditional process, the officer or lay representative displays his or her negotiating skills in public, to reinforce the value of belonging to a trade union. The consensual nature of partnership restricts the number of opportunities for union officials to demonstrate publicly their value to the membership. It does not eliminate the need for unions because there are still problems and issues where they have a vital role, but set-pieces such as the annual pay negotiation are eliminated under this type of arrangement.

2 The trade union has therefore to move its position from 'outside' to 'inside the tent'. It has to accept that some well established rituals are exactly that, and has to adapt its role to one of working with the employer for the benefit of its members – and just as importantly the success of the business. Clearly if the union is to demand key assurances like employment and pay security, it must recognise that the business has to be successful and profitable if these assurances are to be maintained on an ongoing basis. To be successful, any business has to change and adapt, and this includes staff and their representatives. Therefore, clinging to well-established principles much vaunted by the trade unions – such as opposition to privatisation and opposing job cuts – is just not possible if partnership is to mean anything. There has to be a willing acceptance that the long-term interests of their members is best served by helping the company to be successful.

3 The role of trade unions therefore needs to move into new territory by helping the organisation to become more effective and dealing with the problems of achieving significant manpower reductions. This latter issue particularly requires a significant change of stance on the part of union officials. They need not to be over-concerned with the ends – the reduction in numbers employed – but with the means – the methods of achieving the job reduction and the impact that has on members who continue in employment. Partnership 2 ('Planning Our Future') set out exactly these issues. It described the likely changes in open terms, setting out how by working together the changes can be effected to everyone's mutual benefit.

4 For full-time officers and senior lay representatives, the emphasis within partnership of local consultation and agreement, mainly at the depot or local office level, inevitably required them to let go of the reins of control to some extent. At the other end of the spectrum, local representatives were required to take responsibility for agreements made and in co-operating with management. As with managers, this was very difficult for some individuals to take; some relinquished their responsibilities with the union, and some even took advantage of 'exit' arrangements and left. For others, the change took time but adjustment was eventually achieved. Some welcomed the new ways of working and relished the involvement and responsibility for real issues, rather than being a passive member of a trade union delegation.

5 For the full-time officers who had to lead the way, a number of brickbats were hurled

at them. They were sometimes regarded as being in management's pocket, as they seemed to get on well with managers – sharing a joke or participating in corporate events. While these might all be quite appropriate actions for 'partners' in an enterprise, they were seen by others as close to collaborating with the enemy.

6 Another critical change for the trade unions, and to a lesser extent for management, has been an acceptance that communicating the contents of proposals is a joint responsibility. Information is power, and historically management had left it largely to the union to communicate with their members. Partnership brought with it joint responsibility for communication and a willingness on both sides to give ground on who would be responsible for communicating the message.

7 On the positive side, involvement in partnership has enabled the trade unions to demonstrate how co-operation can work successfully to the mutual benefit of all. Numerous companies and organisations have visited Welsh Water to learn of the advantages and pitfalls and many have gone on to develop versions of partnership to suit their own business needs.

Implications for management

Just as for trade union representatives, the company and its managers have to reconsider their traditional stance. With hindsight perhaps it was easier for managers because of the unwavering support for this approach from senior management before and since privatisation. There were a number of implications, however, for *management*.

1 Clearly, there has been a healthy interest in the costs of partnership. However, the shift in style required an intrinsic belief that the values and approaches expressed under partnership were right if the organisation was to change from a moribund public sector bureaucracy into a modern customer-oriented business. This required faith in the abilities of frontline staff and a trust in the trade unions that both parties could deliver a changed approach.

2 There was clear recognition early on that management style had to change. Managers had to recognise that the days of autocracy and control were gone – that now they could only successfully manage an increasingly qualified and intelligent workforce if they worked *with* people. This has required a fundamental adjustment in their roles – away from the all-powerful decision-maker towards being a supporter of frontline teams. Just as with the changing role and style of trade union officials it requires a different approach. Leadership qualities are still required but of a more subtle kind. Many supervisors and managers were brought up to believe that managers were there because they were generally more experienced, and more capable than the people they supervised. Like the trade union officer, they had to prove their worth, telling people what to do, planning, organising, controlling and monitoring – in short being seen to be in charge. The shift to a facilitator role has been a difficult transition for some, while others have learnt new tricks. The new environment has seen some managers blossom as strong advocates of empowerment.

3 Relationships between managers and trade union officials/representatives also had to change. Partnership does not work if every issue becomes a negotiating item, so both sides had to recognise that their role was to solve problems not put obstacles in the way of progress.

4 Above all, partnership has enabled managers to act with openness, honesty and integrity. Trust is difficult to build and easy to destroy. This process of adjustment has to start with managers as they essentially have the power to make or break such arrangements. In the early days, there were still examples of managers acting autocratically. This provoked a response from local trade union representatives that the fine words and principles of senior managers were one thing, whereas in the real world managers were still acting as they always did. To a degree this was true, but time has led to the promotion of managers with an appropriate style, and the frequency of disputes/incidents has dropped dramatically.

5 For the company, the pay formula has been valuable because it has produced some certainty with regard to a critical element of cost. Employment security has removed an easy and convenient method of eliminating poor performers through the redundancy route. It has put an extra strain on performance systems to identify and deal with poor performers – an area which all sides admit could be handled more proactively.

THE FUTURE

The acquisition of the local regional electricity company, SWALEC, in February 1996 by Welsh Water (later to be renamed Hyder Group) brought with it significant implications for employee relations in the company. Unlike previous acquisitions which were largely non-unionised consultancies, SWALEC was another utility with a very similar background and style to Welsh Water. With one exception the unions were the same, and in the majority of cases the same officials dealt with both companies. To make matters more complex, however, a new company was formed – Hyder Services – which took over responsibility for common activities such as customer services and billing, information technology, transport, and financial services. This meant bringing together employees from SWALEC and Dwr Cymru into the new business to work alongside one another, with the inevitable harmonisation issues that this move brought.

While employee relations in SWALEC were reasonably sound, the approach was more traditional. There had been a difficult set of negotiations leading to a new company agreement following the end of national bargaining in the electricity industry, and this protracted negotiation had left its mark in terms of mutual suspicion. Management style in SWALEC had been more autocratic and formal than in Welsh Water. In broad terms, the organisation was less empowered and subject to a 'plan, organise, control and monitor' philosophy.

The new situation represented a significant challenge to the partnership approach, helping a well-developed and mature relationship come to terms with a completely new scenario. Given the fact that these were three separate companies, there were concerns about how relationships would develop. Would there, for example, be three sets of terms and conditions, three sets of pay negotiating arrangements, with the obvious danger that SWALEC or Hyder Services might secure a higher settlement than that produced by the pay formula in Welsh Water? Such an outcome would seriously undermine partnership.

Initially, both sides saw this as an issue for Hyder Services, although the trade union saw the obvious dangers for partnership from an early stage. To build trust both the unions and management conducted a series of roadshows with staff in Hyder Services to elicit their views on future priorities. While employment security came top of the list, not surprisingly as Hyder Services had announced job cuts of 25 per cent of its 1700 workforce, a major factor which worried staff was the future relationship with SWALEC and Dwr Cymru. From the viewpoint of employees, the three organisations were not as distinct as they were from the vantage point of senior management. Increasingly, staff felt that the three organisations would develop closer working relationships, and therefore felt that there was merit in promoting a degree of harmonisation between all three, not just in Hyder Services.

The outcome is a new stage of partnership, 'Working Together'. This is a two-level agreement with some major issues – such as pay review, including a profit related pay scheme, and employment security provisions for permanent staff – in common across all three businesses. The agreement foresees some further harmonisation, where all parties agree that this makes sense, but still gives businesses the freedom to respond to their own problems and work out their own responses.

The ballot on the 'Working Together' Agreement held in early March 1997 produced an excellent result. With a response rate of over 70 per cent the vote in favour of partnership across the three businesses was seven-to-one, so continuing the series of successful partnership results.

CONCLUSION

The Hyder Group faces many challenges – increased competition, for example in the electricity supply market, tougher regulation, increasing customer demands for better service at lower prices, the imposition of a 'windfall tax'. The new agreement, 'Working Together' is a sign that the Group believes its future success depends largely on the people who serve the customer. In the final analysis, the partnership approach is based on the simple belief that by treating people reasonably and involving them and their representatives in the business, they are more likely to feel good about themselves and their work, and thereby give good customer service. Satisfied customers lead to a successful business, thus completing the virtuous circle of potential business and individual success. As a fiscal note, SWALEC, Welsh Water and Hydro Services have just (at the time of writing) merged into a single utility business and this has given added reason and impetus to the Working Together philosophy.

11

Trade unions, enterprise and the future

JOHN MONKS

General Secretary, TUC

INTRODUCTION

There are three main arguments to make in this chapter. First, I would argue that the present system, and also the culture, of corporate governance in Britain has led to too many companies concentrating on short-term shareholder interests, to the detriment of their other stakeholders, and also at the expense of long-term company success.

Second – and making this argument is central to my mission as General Secretary of the TUC – partnerships between employers and trade unions can make a real contribution to company success. The tide is turning on union–employer relations and new opportunities for co-operation between unions and companies are opening up which neither side can afford to ignore.

Third, I will outline what partnership means in practice, and what sort of involvement I would seek for employees in the companies where they work. To be classed as a 'partnership organisation', I would anticipate that four main prongs should be in place:

- employment security
- employee voice
- fair financial rewards
- investment in training.

THE NEED FOR CHANGE IN CORPORATE GOVERNANCE

There are some world-class companies in Britain whose success is built upon a tradition of investing for the future. These are companies which combine long-term, committed relationships with their stakeholders, and in particular their staff, with long-term business success. I will return to some of these companies later. But too many firms are not like this. As Michael Heseltine's 1996 Competitiveness White Paper pointed out, there is a 'long tail' of poor and mediocre companies which are lagging behind in terms of competitiveness. Many of these companies also lag behind in the way in which they treat their stakeholders.

The problem of the dragging tail also featured as one of the issues identified by the Commission on Public Policy and British Business, of which I was a member alongside David Sainsbury of the Sainsbury supermarket group, George Simpson of GEC, Bob Bauman of British Aerospace, and a number of other equally distinguished businessmen and academics.

There is one area in which consensus crosses party divides and unites the representatives of employees and employers: we are all agreed that, as a nation, we can do much to improve our competitiveness simply by learning from current best practices. Bringing the rest up to the standard of the best is a simple goal, but one whose achievement rests on an analysis of what works best and how good practice can be transferred from one enterprise to another.

There is also an increasing public consensus that the world of work has shifted too far in favour of the employer, leaving employees increasingly out in the cold. The 1997 election result had some impact on this. Consensus might not stretch as far as Michael Heseltine and many of his Conservative Party colleagues – though there are some in the Conservative ranks who do recognise that prising apart the so-called 'fat cats' from the rest of the workforce is not a way to build success, and in their post-election reflection, there could be some movement in Conservative thinking.

The problem at the heart of all this can be summed up in the phrase 'security at work'. By early 1997 claimant unemployment was well down from its peak in 1992–3. But, as the opinion pollsters found throughout 1996, it takes more than a reduction in unemployment figures to make people feel secure in their workplace.

What has become increasingly apparent is that poor workplace relationships, where trust, respect and commitment are lacking, are a major contributory factor towards more general feelings of insecurity. It is not just those who have experienced unemployment themselves who feel less secure as a consequence. The feelings spread as rapidly as a winter 'flu epidemic. You do not need to be a direct victim of downsizing, re-engineering or any of the other fashionable euphemisms for dismissal in order to feel insecure. If it happens to a workmate, a neighbour or relative, the 'there-but-for-fortune' or 'me-next-time' feelings come into play and insecurity sets in. Even pressures to work ever harder, the ill-digested theories of maximum output and constant improvement, can do as much to demotivate as they are intended to spur on.

The UK system of corporate governance has played a significant part in creating this climate. Short-termism in British boardrooms is encouraged by incentives linked to shareholder value for top executives, fear of hostile takeover and pressure from financial institutions. These have combined to create a situation where companies jostle to pay higher dividends today even if it means slashing staff and investment. A situation has arisen where the shareholder is king, while other stakeholders come a poor second. This was perhaps seen most vividly late in 1996 when one retail chain's shares soared on the news that it was to cut back on staff, while another's plummeted as it announced an expansion to the business – the former was taken by the market as a sign of higher dividends to follow, the latter as a sign that money which might have come back to the shareholders was to go into the long-term future.

According to the Bank of England, the share of profits allocated to dividends roughly doubled in the 1980s, and continued to rise even during the recession of the early 1990s. It increased by over a fifth between 1990 and 1992, despite stagnant profits, while unemployment soared to hit the historic 3 million mark. Figures produced in 1996 showed that the profits/dividend divide was widening still further. While profit growth was slowing to 6 per cent in 1995, dividend payments rose by a third.

High and inflexible dividend payments reduce the funds available for investment, and have had a particularly damaging impact upon long-term research and development (R&D). The ratio of dividends to R&D spending in the UK is 3.5 times higher than in the USA, 10 times higher than in Germany and 13 times higher than in Japan. Under-investment has long been recognised as a historic problem for Britain. What these figures show is that the case for remedial action is as strong now as it has ever been.

Business investment was much weaker in the recovery of the mid-1990s than in those of the 1970s and 1980s. By 1996 manufacturing investment, which had followed a faltering path since the recovery began, was 22 per cent below the pre-recession level.

Short-termism is bad for all groups with a stake in the firm and, indeed, for the country as a whole. Successful companies are at the heart of a successful economy that can generate jobs and prosperity for the future.

So who is to blame? There have been several forums where financial institutions and corporate executives have traded insults about which party is responsible for short-termism. What this seems to illustrate to me as an outsider is that the nature of the relationship between many companies and their shareholders is flawed.

In part it is institutional. Pension funds are obliged to produce the best returns each year. There is pressure to be among the top performers. Yet often that can only be achieved by flitting from shareholding to shareholding, movements dictated by takeovers, the logic of the casino and the stability of a house of cards, rather than the strength of solid and regular financial growth alongside the stability of a business built to last, with a vision that stretches beyond the next balance sheet.

I believe it is crucial that long-term partnerships between shareholders and companies are fostered, and that shareholders look for long-term, organic growth rather than short-term gains. I also believe that with ownership goes responsibility: institutional shareholders, which now own the majority of shares in British companies, should be obliged to vote their shares at company AGMs.

But partnerships with shareholders should complement, not exclude, partnerships with other stakeholders. In the vast majority of situations the long-term interests of shareholders and a company's other stakeholders – customers, suppliers, employees and the local community – converge. And indeed, the country as a whole has an interest in the long-term success of Britain's corporate sector.

In our report, *Your Stake at Work – TUC Proposals for a Stakeholding Economy*, we set out proposals for the way in which we would seek to boost a long-term perspective among investors. Reforms to encourage long-term and responsible shareholding will help, such as raising the current 30 per cent threshold on owning shares in a company after which a shareholder is required to bid for all shares. Measures that make hostile takeovers more difficult would also help. These could include giving employment and competitiveness more weight in merger criteria, requiring consultation with employees affected and extending European requirements on transfer of undertakings: protection of employment (TUPE) to takeovers that occur through share purchase.

But, in itself, this is not enough. The concept of stakeholding which I would like to see put into practice challenges fundamentally the way British companies are run. It says they should be run in the interests of *all* the groups that have a stake in the firm. It is through developing long-term, committed relationships with their stakeholders that companies will equip themselves for the competitive challenges of the global marketplace.

For a start, I would argue that directors' legal duties should be changed to require them to consider employees, suppliers and customers as well as shareholders in decision-making. This would be a simple, but fundamental change. The more thought which is given to the present position, the more ludicrous it appears. Isolating one interest for legal purposes is not an approach which you see applied in other areas of the law. Road users, for instance, are required to have due regard for all other road users. It is not a matter of simply looking out for lorry drivers and paying no attention to the needs of car drivers, pedestrians and cyclists – though it might sometimes appear that way in practice. Disclosure is the second element of our proposals. I would like to see an obligation on companies to report regularly on their key stakeholder relationships and on their environmental impact.

So what would a stakeholding company do differently?

First, relations with suppliers would change. There would be greater involvement in quality and efficiency drives. Partnership sourcing would be developed. And we would look for an end to late payments.

Second, with customers, we would be looking for the setting of quality standards. We would seek commitments to produce and publicise clear product information. There should be clear lines of communication between the company and its customers.

Third, stakeholding could also benefit the local community in the areas where a company committed to the stakeholding principles operated. Recruitment would reflect the diversity of the local community. Links would be built with schools and local organisations. There would be more consultation over planning decisions. And there would be wider benefits too: company strategy would be based on long-term investment and planning; and responsible environmental procedures would safeguard the future for all.

Finally, there are many changes we believe are appropriate as far as employees are concerned. We would seek agreements guaranteeing job security in exchange for positive work flexibility. The 1996 agreement at Blue Circle is one example frequently quoted, in which employees received guarantees of employment security provided they were prepared to undertake a range of jobs. Social plans should be drawn up by employers in cases where there is no alternative to redundancy. And, in that context, consultation rights for employees and trade unions in the event of a proposed redundancy should be improved. More generally on consultation and information, we would want to see all workers and trade unions having the right to information and consultation on a wide range of strategic issues. Procedures for consultation should be agreed jointly between workers and their representatives and employers. And consultation should be with a view to agreement on both sides.

THE STAKEHOLDING COMPANY

Fair financial rewards are of course an important feature of the stakeholding company. Pay awards at the top must reflect those at the bottom, and particular effort should be given to stamping out low pay. Financial participation schemes must be open to *all* workers and should be introduced in consultation with the workforce and trade unions – there can be no place for generous share schemes for those at the top while the rest have no opportunity to benefit from their own contribution to company success. Share ownership schemes should also provide for effective involvement of employee representatives in decision-making.

As far as my prescription for the creation of a genuine stakeholder company is concerned, the importance of investment in skills cannot be stressed too much. Employers should commit themselves to developing the skills of their workforce through quality off-the-job and on-the-job training. Furthermore, training and development should be introduced with the full involvement of employees and trade unions. Workers in a stakeholder company will expect high standards and would want to be treated as partners in company success.

These then are the concepts which would contribute towards the creation of a stakeholding company. As I indicated earlier, these are no Utopian dream ideas. Most can be seen in some form or other in the best of British companies. We are talking about some important changes in the law, but at least as crucial is the spread of best practice.

The reality of life in those poor and mediocre companies that are dragging so far behind the best of British, as identified by the Competitiveness White Paper and the IPPR study, is very different from the world of the stakeholder company. It is forecast that by the year 2000, half of all jobs in the UK will be temporary, part-time or sub-contracted. Although it may be too soon to write the obituary of the steady job, we ignore its demise at our peril. Casualisation looms for many. Its virtues are preached by those who say that you will have to have six jobs in your lifetime while some of them have six jobs at the same time.

Yet without hard-working, skilled and committed workers, no company can succeed. This is more true today than ever – one of the greatest challenges facing firms all over the world is the development of new information technologies, the implementation of which puts a new premium on the knowledge and skills of workers, and facilitates changes in work organisation. The only basis on which companies can compete in today's global markets is on the basis of technological innovation and skills. The key to combining these elements successfully is people.

I believe the strongest foundation a company can have for success is to put its trust in the development of a working partnership with its employees, and that the most effective way of creating such a partnership is through the collective voice of trade unionism. A partnership approach is one that puts centre stage the concerns of both employers and employees, so that representatives of each can work together on issues of importance to each group and to both. It is a matter of recognising the issues that matter to others involved in the enterprise and developing what is referred to as a 'win–win' situation, maximising the benefits to each group.

It involves both sides acknowledging the other's role and legitimacy, and seeking new ways of working to solve differences. Often the most effective way of solving difficulties is through building on areas of agreement and common concern, some of which have in the past been obscured by the adversarial nature of industrial relations. Class war rhetoric will not do. It cannot be a matter of defeating the other side of the class divide, but of uniting the undoubted strengths of employers and employees working together towards a common, shared goal. The charge has been made that trade unions are prone to rigidity, and that working closely with trade unions will prevent flexibility at work. The term dinosaur is one that springs all too easily to mind. It is a glib term too often used by writers who have rarely seen a workplace other than their own computer terminal.

What has struck me, as I have visited workplaces across the country, is the diversity between the different examples of partnership in practice. No two are alike and indeed should not be, because no two companies are alike and no two workforces are alike. The whole point about partnership is that it gives both sides the opportunity to be truly creative in their approach to one another and to negotiations.

THE PARTNERSHIP APPROACH IN PRACTICE

As I indicated when referring to our proposals on stakeholding, there are four main prongs of a partnership approach:

- employment security and new working practices
- giving employees a voice in how the company is run
- fair financial rewards
- investment in training.

Let me deal with each in more detail.

There is no doubt that for workers, employment security is the main priority. Too often in debates about the future of work, security is painted as an old-fashioned concept desired only by people who lack the initiative or the skills to go it alone in the brave new labour market of the 1990s. Common sense and experience tells us that in fact security is the one thing that practically everybody desires, and that the security of knowing where the money to pay the bills is coming from is bound to be important to the peace of mind of any rational person. It is also important for the economy as a whole. If people lack the confidence to make major purchases, demand and growth will suffer – and that was precisely what we saw in 1996 as the 'feelgood factor' proved to be so elusive.

Worse still, security is often assumed to detract from flexibility, which is perhaps the most abused buzz word in employment jargon today. But true flexibility is not the 'freedom' to hire and fire. Companies that follow this path will find to their cost that if they are not committed to their workforce, the workforce will not be committed to them. True flexibility is achieved by companies whose workers have the skills and motivation to respond positively to changing requirements.

Key to this is employment security, so that workers can co-operate with developments in either technology or work organisation without the fear that any increases in efficiency may cost them or their colleagues their jobs. You do not need to be a Luddite to see the disadvantages of working yourself out of a job.

The competitive advantages of long-term employment relationships are illustrated by OECD research showing that employment tenure is strongly linked to the willingness of both employers and employees to invest in training. In January 1996, a meeting of the OECD's education ministers called upon governments to work with the social partners as well as the learning providers to set the policy framework for developing action for lifelong learning. In the UK, unions are working with employers, training and enterprise councils, local enterprise councils, colleges and local authorities on the design and delivery of training.

Security in exchange for positive work flexibility is at the heart of the partnership approach. Fortunately, this is starting to happen. Increasing numbers of companies are developing partnership agreements, many of which recognise the potential of the security-for-flexibility bargain. For example, Toyota has made a commitment to its employees that productivity improvements will not be used to shed jobs. Rover has a job security agreement in exchange for flexibility and skill enhancement. Jaguar has negotiated an agreement that there will be no compulsory redundancies as a result of any improvements in efficiency. The partnership agreement at Scottish Power contains commitments to multiskilling on the one hand and a commitment to doing everything possible to avoid compulsory redundancies on the other. The partnership agreement at Welsh Water, discussed in detail in Chapter 10, also contains a commitment to job security. And of course there is the example of Blue Circle mentioned earlier.

The TUC would also like to see legal constraints to the hire and fire culture that has developed in Britain – an obligation to consult with employees and trade unions as early as possible in advance of proposed redundancies and an obligation to develop social plans including training options for any staff who are made redundant.

The second prong in a partnership approach is giving employees a voice in their companies. Information and consultation are a vital part of treating employees as partners and enabling them to act as partners too. There are two aspects to this. In the partnership agreements that I have come across, an important element has been a substantial increase in information made available by management to the trade union to enable the union to play its part in discussions on an equal footing with management. Some of this information has been confidential to the union representatives, under the phraseology of 'commercial and in confidence'.

But there should be no commercial reasons why *all* employees should not have a right to basic information about the company they work for: information on strategic direction, future plans, finance, and so on. Such information should be provided regularly by companies for all their staff. Central to the concept of partnership is a recognition that employees are a vital constituent of any company. There are very few decisions that a company takes that have no impact upon its workforce, and it is very important that companies are able to have access to the views of their staff when taking decisions. This requires consultation procedures to give employees a voice in their companies.

Appropriate mechanisms for consultation can be worked out in each case between the company and trade union concerned. Three elements are required to make consultation meaningful. First, employees must be able to express collective views: consultation with individuals would be highly impractical in all but the smallest companies, and it is not democratic, as individuals will invariably feel inhibited about expressing controversial views if they know that they will be identified with that view. Partnership in theory and in practice cannot remove the fact that in the end the boss is the one with the hire and fire power, and the relationship between the individual employee and the employer can never really be one of true equality. That is the historic argument for trade unionism: 'If we all stick together, they will have to listen' is one way of putting it. Or as recent advertisements by our largest affiliate UNISON graphically put it: 'A bear doesn't have to listen to an ant. But an army of ants – that is something different.' Clearly, where they are recognised, trade unions are the natural mechanism for representing the employee voice in consultations. And to my mind, partnership and recognition go hand in hand. The law can and, in the TUC's view, should provide more of an encouragement to recognition than it does in the unbalanced employment laws which have resulted from 18 years of Conservative erosion of employment rights – not that the pre-1979 position was ideal. There is a need for fresh and clear legislation on this matter, as promised by Labour in its 1997 manifesto. But that is to raise an issue beyond the immediate scope of my theme in this chapter.

Second, consultation should be undertaken with a view to agreement on *both* sides. There are bound to be times that the employee view does not prevail, but it should always be carefully considered in good faith. And third, the scope of the consultations should include major issues such as mergers and takeovers, and naturally any issues that directly affect the workforce, although these would normally be the subject of negotiations.

The third prong of partnership is fair financial rewards for work. Employees, who are after all the main creators of the cake, must be given a fair slice of its profits. While we would argue this case on the grounds of fairness, it was Adair Turner of the CBI who pointed out that the share of wages in national profits is declining, and that this is not good for the economy in the longer term – lower wages mean lower demand and reduced future growth.

So, what constitutes 'fairness' in financial rewards? A bottom line here is that workers should be free to choose to come together and bargain collectively over their wages. Clearly, very low rates of pay are unacceptable, and without actually putting a figure on this, it is only reasonable that workers are entitled to take home a living wage for an honest day's work. Hence Labour's proposals for a national minimum wage are welcome. High rates of differentials also concern me: our research has shown that in a number of companies, the chief executive is paid more than 100 times the amount ordinary workers are being paid – and that's just basic salary and bonuses, and does not include share options and so on. 'One rule for me and one rule for you' is not the basis of a partnership. We believe that pay increases at the top should reflect those at the bottom, and where they differ this should be clearly stated and the reasons for it explained.

Financial participation schemes can play an important role in cementing a partnership agenda. In my experience, such schemes add most value to workplace relationships when they are introduced after thorough consultation and where employees are involved in both the design and implementation of schemes. I am particularly interested in ESOP (Employee Share Option Plan) schemes because they provide for collective share ownership and because the trust structure in many instances provides a mechanism for employees to feed into decision-making. This, it seems to me, reflects the central tenet of partnership – you get something out and you put something in. Financial participation is not an alternative to the other elements of involvement and commitment. However, it can complement them, and it is a useful way of recognising the work that employees have done in creating a profitable and successful company.

Finally, but definitely not least, investing in training is essential to create a situation where workers are able to play a fully developed partnership role. Training raises skills levels and enables employees to work more flexibly and efficiently. It also strengthens the ability of the workforce to deal with change. Investing in training is a sign of commitment to staff and thus it can help to create the conditions in which social partnership can flourish. Training is also an area which benefits from partnership and the involvement of trade unions. An influential study for the Department of Employment by Winterton and Winterton (1994) concluded that 'those managements that have shared decision-making over training have been the most successful in transforming workplace attitudes to training and change'.

CONCLUSION

It was heartening to hear the director of the Institute of Personnel and Development, at their 1996 Harrogate Conference, call on employers to respond to a new willingness to co-operate among trade unions. I would like to second that call.

I believe that we could be about to enter a new era of industrial relations in which unions and employers work together to find the best solutions to their common and individual problems. Building long-term relationships based on mutual commitment and trust with their employees is the best insurance for future success that companies can have. The obstacles are, as I have indicated, part cultural, part legislative, part a matter of attitude. The legislative obstacles are severe – the obligation on companies to make shareholders not just the most important stakeholders but the *only* stakeholders is perhaps the single most important factor preventing the growth of a stakeholding and partnership approach. Yet legislative obstacles can be overcome, by looking to the longer term – by looking beyond this week's balance sheet, beyond the next dividend, to the long term.

It is perhaps harder to change attitudes. While companies are content to stick with the mediocre, to remain part of the long tail, then they will not change. Unions can act as agents of change. Yet it is difficult to do so if management remains entrenched, and will not provide either encouragement or information.

The fact is that the partnership approach feeds on itself. You need a commitment to partnership to introduce the partnership approach. Making the change is the hardest thing. Government, employers organisations and trade unions at national level can help. Even academics can play their part in pointing objectively, as they must, to the benefits of such an approach.

But, worryingly perhaps, the greatest incentive is the pressure of competition and globalisation. The only alternative to the development of good practice is to go to the wall. The choice for those in that long tail is to catch up or get lopped off, as competitive pressures play the role of the heavily armed farmer's wife in the nursery rhyme about the three blind mice.

12

Problematising partnership

The prospects for a co-operative bargaining agenda

TIM CLAYDON

Department of Human Resource Management,
De Montfort University, Leicester

INTRODUCTION

The concept of partnership has emerged as an important theme in the debate over the future of trade unionism in Britain. As expressed by leading figures within some national unions and the Trades Union Congress, it represents an attempt to define a role for trade unionism which balances its central concern to represent employees' interests with a productivist appeal to employers and government. In mounting this attempt, trade unionists who advocate partnership appear to be addressing two main issues. The first is how can employees obtain secure, rewarding employment in an increasingly competitive and volatile economic environment? The second is how can trade unions arrest their decline and maintain and develop a significant organisational presence which allows them to act effectively in support of employees on the first issue?

These concerns have developed in response to declining union membership and influence which has been encouraged by policies of union exclusion pursued by government and employers since the early 1980s (Smith and Morton, 1993). At the organisational level, union exclusion can take a number of forms, with derecognition and deunionisation as extremes. Other more limited forms include narrowing the scope and depth of bargaining, by-passing unions in communication with employees and seeking to win 'hearts and minds' away from traditional union loyalties through human resource management (HRM). These developments are widely seen as posing a challenge to trade unionism; some analysts suggest that unions should embrace HRM and use it to develop new forms and channels of influence if they are not to be sidelined by it (Storey, 1992; Guest, 1995). Others such as Smith and Morton (1993) and Kelly (1996) see it as fundamentally hostile to trade unionism, a possibility also raised by Millward (1994).

Against this backdrop, advocates of partnership appear to be arguing that in a post-Fordist world characterised by intensifying international competition, increased mobility of capital and rapid technological change, employers and trade unions must recognise the importance of management–worker co-operation as a condition for business survival and success. They must also recognise that it is the most effective way of addressing the interests and concerns of employees; indeed that business success is the overriding common interest of both parties (Monks, this volume). In these circumstances, they argue, there is a need to move away from a so-called 'adversarial' approach to industrial relations towards a more problem-solving approach to issues of common concern. This is not only more likely to be acceptable to employers and management; it is also more likely to win the approval of employees. Yet there still appears to be a recognition that in certain areas at least, employee interests will remain distinct from those of management; for example, the TUC continues to argue for the right of workers to bargain collectively over pay and for enhanced legal rights for employees (Monks, this volume).

The concept of partnership has received support from some employers and from some recent academic literature (e.g. Guest, 1995; Marchington, this volume; Metcalf, 1991). However, it has also been contested, not only by those committed to 'free' labour markets and the individualisation of the employment relationship who see partnership as another union Trojan horse, but also by trade unionists and academics who remain sceptical of the possibility of genuine partnership on a broad scale and/or who question the desirability of partnership on the grounds that it will render unions less rather than more able to defend and advance workers' interests (e.g. Kelly, 1996; *see also* views cited in Bacon and Storey, 1996).

In seeking to contribute to the partnership debate, the discussion in this chapter is organised in three main sections. The first shows how current ideas of partnership as expressed by the major unions and the TUC have developed from the 'New Bargaining Agenda' of the late 1980s and early 1990s. It is argued that the limited take-up of the new bargaining agenda by employers, together with evidence of growing resistance to trade unionism and collective bargaining among British employers and managers, gives grounds for scepticism about the future of current proposals for partnership. The second section looks at partnership from the perspective of theories of union power and argues that it represents an attempt by trade unions to reconstitute their power by 'enrolling' management and workers to a reconstituted conception of their interests and the relations between them. This discussion draws on an approach to the sociology of power developed by Callon (1986) and Clegg (1989). The third section locates partnership as a strategy of union power in relation to strategies of 'militancy' and 'incorporation' and goes on to examine the problematic nature of partnership and how this casts doubt on the possibility that partnership could develop more strongly in the near future than it has done in the recent past.

PARTNERSHIP: FUTURE PROSPECTS IN THE LIGHT OF RECENT EXPERIENCE

The Trades Union Congress views partnership in industrial relations as being based on four main elements at enterprise or organisation level:

- employment security in return for acceptance of new working practices
- collective employee voice in organisational decision-making through wider consultation

- fair financial rewards
- investment in training (Monks, Chapter 11 of this volume).

In the political arena, the TUC has argued the need to minimise industrial action, strengthen the legal rights of employees and introduce a national minimum wage. Some of these elements echo the principles currently advocated by the Involvement and Participation Association: commitment to co-operation in the interests of the business, a recognition of employees' concerns for security of employment, and the importance of communication and effective employee voice mechanisms (Coupar and Stevens, Chapter 9 of this volume).

The TUC's social partnership concept has its recent origins in the 'New Bargaining Agenda' of the late 1980s and early 1990s (Trades Union Congress, 1991). At that time, with the possibility of a Labour government following the 1992 General Election, the TUC made a point of arguing for a move away from 'the traditional, often adversarial approach' to industrial relations towards a more 'constructive' and 'developmental' emphasis, centring on 'job security, job creation and the elimination of under-employment, providing satisfying, fulfilling and . . . rewarding jobs . . . emphasising the "fair pay" aspect of these policies' (Trades Union Congress, 1991).

Then as now, a strong productivist slant was apparent within the new agenda:

> *real terms and conditions cannot be improved towards the best European levels without improvements in underlying economic performance towards the best European levels.* (Trades Union Congress, 1991)

At the same time, the 'new bargaining agenda' was presented as a means of extending union influence in decision-making:

> *The more trade unions start to talk about employee development and the devolution of management responsibilities, the more they will find themselves questioning existing managerial prerogatives and the financial advantages management have appropriated to themselves on this basis, disproportionate to any efficient ordering powers and responsibilities.* (Trades Union Congress, 1991)

This is also a theme which has been echoed in recent statements on partnership, although so far its expression has been noticeably less assertive; reference has been made to substantial increases in information made available to trade unions where firms and unions have adopted a partnership approach, and concern has been expressed about unwarranted differentials between executive pay and that of the rest of the workforce (Marchington; Monks, both in this volume).

It is clear that there are strong similarities with the early 1990s in the increasingly emphatic rejection of 'adversarial' industrial relations contained within recent statements by some trade unionists (*see*, for example, Edmonds in Storey *et al.*, 1993; Monks, quoted in *Financial Times*, 26 February 1997). In the light of this, it is worth examining the impact of the new bargaining agenda during the first half of the 1990s. First, it must be said that key supporting elements of the New Bargaining Agenda, such as a national economic assessment to guide wage bargaining, and the extension of legal rights for employees, advanced in the hope of a Labour election victory, were ruled out with the return of the Conservatives for a fourth term of government. Attempts by individual unions such as the General, Municipal and Boilermakers (GMB) Union and the Manufacturing, Science and Finance (MSF) Union to develop co-operative bargaining over issues of 'common concern' through voluntary agreements with employers made minimal progress during the late 1980s. Thus, the findings of the third Workplace Industrial Relations Survey of 1990 were that:

> *Issues that trade unions have aimed to raise as bargaining issues in recent years – such as equal opportunities and training – had clearly been conceded as a bargaining issue by very few managements in recent years.*   (Millward *et al.*, 1992)

Little further progress was made in getting these issues onto the bargaining agenda in subsequent years. To take training as one example, an analysis of the details of collective agreements reported in *Incomes Data Services Report* between January 1991 and June 1993 found minimal evidence of bargaining over training, which was a key element of the 'new agenda' and an issue which major unions such as GMB, Transport and General Workers Union (TGWU) and MSF had been pursuing since 1987. Details of 944 agreements in the public and private sectors contained only 40 references to training, of which a mere eleven could be seen as approximating to the kind of substantive and procedural arrangements regulating training provision that were envisaged in the New Bargaining Agenda (Claydon and Green, 1994).

Meanwhile, there was strong evidence that employers' 'antipathy' towards trade unions and collective bargaining, noted in the third Workplace Industrial Relations Survey (Millward *et al.*, 1992), was continuing to spread. Thus the director of employment affairs at the Confederation of British Industry wrote that 'collective bargaining no longer presents itself as the only, or even the most obvious, method of handling relations at work; and fewer employees – and employers – feel the need of union mediation in their dealings' (Gilbert, 1993). Kelly, drawing on material published by the TUC and Storey's research in 'mainstream' organisations has also commented on the growing readiness of employers to by-pass or marginalise trade unions, using HRM to implement redundancies, intensify work and reduce the range of issues over which trade unions have influence (Kelly, 1996).

This hardening of attitude has been reflected in an acceleration in the pace of union derecognition since 1988 and its spread across a wider range of employment. Thus on the basis of Claydon's findings, the incidence of derecognition during 1989–93 was double that during 1984–88 (Claydon, 1996). A more comprehensive survey which also used a broader measure to include derecognitions occasioned by moves to single union deals, carried out by Gall and McKay, found an even sharper increase, from 71 cases during 1984–88 to 391 during 1989–94. While the number of cases of derecognition recorded by Gall and McKay was exceeded by the number of new recognition agreements, almost twice as many workers were subject to union derecognition as were covered by new recognition (Gall and McKay, 1994).

The increased incidence of derecognition was accompanied by its extension to a wider range of industries and occupational groups, notably in public utilities such as water, gas and electricity; and in health and education, metal, engineering and vehicles, wholesale and retail distribution, and banking and insurance. These developments meant that derecognition became increasingly common among manual workers (Claydon, 1996; Gall and McKay, 1994). At the same time, earlier trends towards derecognition in publishing and broadcasting and petrochemicals continued. There are signs that this has taken a purposive and strategic form in these sectors. In the oil industry in particular, the TGWU has stated that employers have collaborated with one another in developing and implementing a long-term strategic approach to derecognition (Higgs, 1994).

In the light of this and other developments in industrial relations during the late 1980s and 1990s, including the spread of unilateral impositions of new pay arrangements and working practices in unionised workplaces in the public and private sectors and a narrowing of the scope and depth of collective bargaining, the prospects for widespread partnership seem to be unpromising. In the following section theoretical arguments concerning the problematic nature of partnership as a strategy for the reconstitution of union power are presented in conjunction with the results of recently published work by a number of researchers. This casts doubt on the possibility of unions being able to achieve a break with the recent past, and promote and sustain the wider acceptance of partnership.

PARTNERSHIP AND THE QUESTION OF UNION POWER

In many fundamental respects, the partnership debate is about the nature of, and limits to, trade union power and the possibility of reconstituting union power, primarily through a redefinition of relationships with management. Conventional analyses of union power use the terms 'manifest' and 'latent' power to categorise the concept. Manifest power, the ability of the union to exercise control over the employment relationship, is seen as the key measure of union strength. Manifest power is revealed in unions' procedural status at organisational and national level and their ability to achieve goals in economic and political arenas which compete or conflict with those of employers and management. However, manifest power is dependent upon the availability of the latent power resources at the disposal of unions; in particular, organisational power based on membership density, positional power of the membership and the membership's willingness to act in support of union demands; political power resources such as support from government and public opinion; and managerial sources of power such as recognition, union membership agreements, facility time, etc. (Poole, 1986). A weakening of the latent power resources available to unions undermines their manifest power and this in turn may lead to a further weakening of latent power if employees and/or managers perceive trade unions to be increasingly ineffective and reduce their support for them.

In terms of this model, partnership can be seen as a response to the general weakening of the latent power resources available to unions since the early 1980s. However, this response cannot be described simply in terms of a growing reliance on managerial support as the ability of unions to generate and mobilise organisational and political power resources has diminished. Managerial support has also been reduced, as is clear from recent research on trends towards union exclusion and individualisation of the employment relationship (Bacon and Storey, 1993; 1996; Smith and Morton, 1993; 1994). Therefore partnership has to be seen as a proposal for reconstituting the basis of employee, managerial and political support for trade unions and, hence, the nature of trade union power.

Supporters of partnership argue that the intensification of competitive, political and financial pressures to achieve higher productivity in the workplace generates opportunities for unions to exercise influence on behalf of employees by giving up traditional job controls in exchange for improved employment security, training, better pay and improved conditions. This approach is exemplified by the recent pay and conditions agreement between UNISON, GMB, the TGWU, and local government employers for manual workers. The agreement, which came into force on 1 April 1997, provides for the removal of all existing demarcation lines between manual occupations in local government services. Management is free to allocate work on the basis of ability to perform the job. In return, all staff have been put onto a single pay spine, a programme of job evaluation incorporating equal pay for work of equal value is to be implemented, and manual workers' standard hours are to be reduced to 37 a week by 1999 (Clement, 1997; Taylor, 1997). A related line of argument, which can be traced to the work of Walton and McKersie (1965) and Fox (1974), argues for the possibility of positive sum outcomes from an integrative or co-operative approach to collective bargaining which focuses on ways of achieving mutual gains rather than on distributive shares.

The discourse of partnership, therefore, favours a facilitative conception of power, that is, 'power to' in preference to a coercive conception, 'power over', which is associated with 'adversarial' industrial relations. Yet both aspects of power are implicit in any industrial relations system which includes independent employee organisations. The possibility that order and control in production can be enhanced by management sharing control of the employment relationship with unions – the possibility of generating facilitative power – is predicated on the possibility of collective employee resistance to the unilateral exercise of managerial prerogatives. At the same time, the long-term ability of unions to constrain and extract concessions from management on the basis of coercive power is dependent on a degree of acceptance by, and support from, management and the state. This makes the rhetoric concerning the need to 'replace' adversarialism with co-operation problematic, since industrial relations were never wholly 'adversarial', and co-operation, to be meaningful, has to encompass the possibility of non-co-operation or resistance. This raises questions concerning the scope and meaning of the concept of partnership.

In his study of the sociology of power, Stuart Clegg (1989), using work by Callon (1986), analyses the simultaneous processes by which relationships of power are constituted among various agencies. The first of these is 'problematisation'. Problematisation refers to an agency's attempt to 'enrol others to their agency by positing the indispensability of their "solutions" for (their definition of) the other's problems'. If successful, the agency's definition of the problems and its solutions to them become 'obligatory passage points of practice' fixed by the enrolling agency (Clegg, 1989). In other words, the agency succeeds in fixing the discursive and practical parameters within which relationships are conducted.

Problematisation is linked to the second process, 'interessement', by which an agency enrols other agencies to its own by coming between them and a third agency in such a way as to encourage them to categorise themselves in terms of meanings and membership so that they provide the enrolling agency with resources of power and control. Together, problematisation and interessement are aimed at persuading agencies or agents that their interests in relation to a third party are best defined and most effectively pursued through, or in alliance with, the enrolling agency. This constitutes the third element of the process; 'enrolment' itself, i.e. the agency's attempt to 'construct alliances and coalitions between the memberships and meaning which they have sought to fix'. The fourth element is 'mobilisation', i.e. the means by which the enrolling agency tries to ensure that the enrolled agencies 'do not, as it were, betray or undercut their representatives and representations' (Clegg, 1989). The importance of this analysis is that it emphasises the role of agencies in constituting interests, as opposed to simply representing assumed prior interests of other agents.

Trade union behaviour can clearly be represented in these terms. Trade unions are agencies which seek to enrol other agencies – that is, employees, management and government – by problematising situations in such a way as to promote the indispensability of 'their' solutions to these problems. In this way they seek to translate social phenomena into resources of power and control. From this it follows that trade unions are not simply representatives of employee interests, since they seek to enrol other agencies besides employees in order to effect their own agency. In doing so, they are to some extent themselves enrolled by these other agencies. This is in line with the recognition that trade unions occupy a contradictory position in relation to capitalism, being capitalist institutions which embody oppositional elements within it. At the same time, trade unions, like other agencies, are not simply representing interests; they are also in part constituting those interests. Militant versus moderate unionism, for example, is as much about how interests of employees and management should be constituted as it is about how they should be represented.

STRATEGIES FOR UNION POWER: 'MILITANCY', 'INCORPORATION' AND 'PARTNERSHIP'

From the perspective outlined so far, we can identify a range of practices through which unions attempt to enrol workers, managers and governments to their own agency and thus establish and maintain relations of power. Different practices will have consequences for the conception of interests and the relations of power which are thus constituted. Three ideal types of enrolment strategy are postulated here. The first, which we can call 'militant' (*see* Kelly, 1996) is associated with the 'adversarial' tradition in British industrial relations, being based on a primary appeal to workers which represents management–worker relations in terms of a conflict of opposed interests in which the relative powerlessness of individual workers renders them open to exploitation. The 'solution' lies in the exercise of collective power by organised workers as a countervailing force to managerial and/or state power. Managers and the state are enrolled to the unions' agency on the basis of the unions' organisational power – their membership and its willingness to act in support of collective demands. The unions' ability to mobilise these as resources of coercive power means that the possibility of generating facilitative power is made conditional on acceptance of union claims to joint control over aspects of the employment relationship.

The second strategy, that of 'incorporation', is based on a primary appeal to management. 'New style' agreements, such as that at Nissan UK, exemplify this approach. Such an appeal emphasises the contribution that the union can make to profitability in return for management support for its organisation in the enterprise. The 'problem' as defined by the union is how to make most effective use of the energies and resources of all members of the enterprise. The 'solution' is represented in terms of the union's ability to ensure a supply of suitably skilled labour, and its ability to 'deliver' its membership to management by ensuring disciplined performance and observance of agreements which concede control of the labour process to management and formally preclude industrial action. Here, interests are represented in terms of the mutual benefits accruing from business success. Union power is derived largely from managerial support and legitimacy.

The third strategy, which might be called 'partnership', involves a simultaneous appeal to workers and management in which the union seeks to identify areas in which management and workers have common concerns. On this basis the union seeks to enrol workers and management to its agency by defining and problematising these concerns in such a way as to make its own proffered solutions appear to be necessary to both parties. Recent attempts by trade unions to develop a co-operative bargaining agenda based on issues of equal opportunities, health and safety and training are examples of this. Unions have sought to enrol workers by representing these issues as being increasingly central to their interests. They have also appealed to employers on the basis of the problems which they may face as a result of the increasing complexity of the law relating to equal opportunities and health and safety issues, offering their own expertise as a source of advice and support to management. In the field of training, unions have taken up concerns over the adequacy of vocational training and skill formation in the UK and argued that they are in a position to advise and help managers in analysing training needs, devising training programmes and co-operating over working practices to ensure full utilisation of employees' skills (Manufacturing, Science and Finance Union, 1989; Transport and General Workers Union, 1989; General, Municipal and Boilermakers Union, 1990; Trades Union Congress, 1990; 1991).

The effectiveness of any of these strategies, however, is contingent on a variety of factors. Militancy is dependant on members' willingness to act in support of union demands. As well as being contingent on material factors affecting the likelihood of a militant strategy being successful, willingness to act may be undermined if members come to feel that they are being mobilised as objects in struggles between union activists and management which they see as being of little relevance to their own concerns.

Strategies of incorporation on the other hand, may secure managerial or state support but their effectiveness in constituting sustainable relations of power within which trade unions can exercise agency will also be affected by their capacity to generate and sustain employee support. As with militancy, if workers feel that they are simply objects of an accommodation between union and management which has denied them a role in the constitution of their interests, and that consequently they are not being met, the relations of power which the union has sought to establish are likely to be undermined (*see* Grant, 1994; 1996).

Furthermore, in terms of the theory of enrolment, incorporationist 'strategies' involving new style agreements raise the question of whether, rather than the union enrolling management to its agency, the reverse is not the case. This is because it is the management of the organisation which is engaged in the process of 'interessement', putting itself between the union and a potential membership. It is also the case that it is management which is defining the 'obligatory passage points of practice' by making union recognition conditional on the union's acceptance of a role within the organisation which has been defined by management. This is clearly illustrated by the contents of new-style agreements. Thus, Oliver and Wilkinson (1992) have presented details of the way in which such agreements define the union's role in terms which emphasise working to ensure harmony, mutual benefit and commitment to commercial success and downplay its function in constituting and

187

representing distinctive group interests within the company. This is not to say that unions are inevitably rendered impotent by new-style agreements. However, recent case study research has suggested that managers' commitment to involving unions in genuine partnership under such agreements is questionable, that employees tend to retain traditional expectations of unions under new-style agreements, and that where new-style agreements prevent the union from meeting these expectations they may contribute to a decline in union membership (Grant, 1994; 1996). Moreover, the ability of trade unions to continue to act as representatives of collective employee interests under such agreements may well depend on 'workers' ability to *overcome* restrictive trade union agreements and develop active and effective opposition from within their own workplaces' (Stephenson, 1996, my emphasis).

Partnership strategies based on a simultaneous appeal to shared concerns of employees and management raise a number of issues. Is partnership to be seen as a new principle governing all aspects of employment regulation? Some recent statements advocating a rejection of 'adversarialism' have given this impression. If so, does this not raise a danger that trade unions might succumb to pressures similar to those generated by new-style agreements, thus running the risk of weakening employee support for trade unionism and so, in turn, reducing still further the unions' ability to exercise agency on behalf of employees? This possibility was envisaged by Fox (1974) in his typology of management styles in industrial relations, subsequently modified by Purcell and Sisson (1983). In discussing the consultationist variant of the sophisticated modern approach, Fox argued that there was a danger that union co-operation could come to be demanded by management as a pre-condition for entering into bargaining, so that management came to dominate the bargaining process, controlling the bargaining agenda and determining the principles upon which bargaining was conducted. He also suggested that a consultationist approach could provide a basis for the emergence of unitarist perspectives among managers, particularly at times of difficulty, which could in turn lead to the role of the union being questioned. This judgement appears to have been borne out by recent developments in the oil industry (Higgs, 1994). Clearly, much depends on the terms of partnership agreements and, just as importantly, on the willingness of management to act in the spirit of such agreements. Recent research into managerial attitudes and behaviour in employee relations suggests that confidence in this is probably misplaced (Waddington and Whitston, 1996).

Alternatively, partnership might be seen as a more limited attempt to redefine union–management relations in specific areas of the employment relationship, while maintaining more traditional collective bargaining arrangements in others. This interpretation is one which seems to find expression in more developed statements on partnership coming from the TUC (Monks, this volume). Yet it remains problematic for a number of reasons.

As we have seen, 'interests', whether they be common or competing, have to be constituted. This raises the question of whether unions can actually come between managers and workers and problematise issues in such a way as to constitute a set of common interests – in the sense not only of identifying substantive issues but doing so in such a way as to define a common approach to them. There are two aspects to this. The first relates to the capacity of unions to enrol management to their agency on the basis of a problematisation of productivity and flexibility goals which generates a 'solution' consisting of co-operative bargaining over an extended range of issues and involving greater union involvement in higher level decision-making. Thus, are the areas identified by union leaderships as the focus for partnership arrangements likely to generate co-operation rather than conflict? Kelly (1996) has questioned this, pointing to 'serious conflicts of interest' over issues of training, health and safety and equal opportunities. This argument gets some empirical support from a recent large-scale survey of trade union activists by Waddington and Whitston (1996) which shows that health and safety issues were the second most common set of grievances (after 'management attitudes') reported by individual workers to their union representatives.

Furthermore, there are problems in redefining interests in terms of a co-operative approach to the issues which are represented by unions as being of 'common concern' in order to enrol employers. The problematic nature of the concept of co-operative bargaining has been identified in the (mainly American) literature on bargaining behaviour. In their discussion of the possibility of developing 'integrative' or co-operative bargaining behaviour so as to generate 'positive sum' outcomes, Walton and McKersie (1965) make it clear that the concept has to be extended to encompass situations:

> *in which the total payoff is varying sum in a significant way even though both parties may not share equally in the joint gain and indeed one may suffer minor inconveniences in order to provide a substantial gain for the other.*

This raises the question of how relative shares are to be determined and reintroduces distributive or adversarial bargaining behaviour into the relationship. Walton and McKersie attempt to deal with this by defining a hybrid situation of 'mixed' bargaining strategies in which each side may decide to give greater priority to increasing the total sum of gains available than to maximising their own share of gains. However, they recognise that mixed bargaining creates dilemmas for negotiators which may pre-dispose them towards a distributive approach to bargaining.

One possible solution to this problem is to have separate procedures for dealing with 'integrative' and 'distributive' issues. This was the approach favoured by the TGWU in its efforts to get training onto the bargaining agenda during the late 1980s. It argued that while there might be benefits from including training within existing bargaining structures, for example better integration of training and other issues, the danger was that this might prevent the development of co-operative discussions of training matters. Hence it advocated the establishment of separate joint training committees (Transport and General Workers Union, 1989). However, minimal progress has been made in this direction. This reflects longer standing managerial opposition to entering into specific agreements on the basis of co-operative bargaining. The new technology agreements during the late 1970s and early 1980s were a case in point. The TUC favoured new technology agreements as a means by which trade unions could co-operate in the technical modernisation of industry while safeguarding workers' interests in terms of employment security, job content, working conditions and pay. However, managements in general resisted entering into new technology agreements, preferring to include issues relating to new technology within existing arrangements. According to Dodgson and Martin (1987), this was because it enabled them to confine negotiation to employment – rather than control – issues and because it gave them a better chance of dealing with new technology on the basis of informal consultation rather than formal negotiation. This does not provide encouraging news for advocates of partnership, since employers have become less 'unionised' in their thinking than they were in the 1970s (Dunn, 1993). The deep-seated obstacles to developing co-operative bargaining behaviour have been commented on in the negotiation literature. According to American research, even after training interventions, negotiators tend not to adopt new approaches to bargaining and low trust seems to be a feature of bargaining encounters in the western world (Hunter and McKersie, 1992; Susskind and Landry, 1991).

The second aspect of the problem of how to reconstitute interests in terms of partnership concerns the processes of 'interessement' and 'mobilisation' in respect of the union's membership and potential membership: that is, the ability of union officers to gain and maintain workers' acceptance of a conception of the union and its relations with management which is defined in terms of partnership. This may depend in part on the degree of membership involvement in union affairs. Where this is low, there is a likelihood that, in their desire to consolidate relationships with management, unions will try to 'deliver' employees to management on issues such as flexibility, and justify this to workers as the price to be paid for greater employment security. Yet this may not command employees' support if their experience of flexibility is primarily one of work intensification. Partnership in these circumstances might prove difficult to sustain, either because workers begin to put pressure on the union to adopt a more adversarial stance in defence of their interests, or alternatively if they leave the union as a result of disillusionment, since declining membership may undermine the union's credibility with management. Studies of companies operating new-style agreements show that both of these outcomes can occur (Grant, 1994).

However, while a high degree of employee involvement would strengthen partnership arrangements, it could lead to priority being given to traditional, 'adversarial' issues, thus inhibiting or preventing moves towards partnership. This possibility is supported by recent research which has indicated the continued importance of 'us and them' attitudes among employees and the traditional nature of employees' grievances and their expectations of trade unions (Grant, 1994; Heery, 1996; Kelly and Kelly, 1991; Waddington and Whitston, 1996). This highlights the critical role of shop stewards and local officials in the process of enrolment since members may have to be persuaded of the advantages of partnership. Shop stewards' attitudes to partnership appear to be mixed (Marchington, this volume) and shaped by management style and action as well as by pressures from the membership and full-time officials. Kelly and Heery's study of local full-time officials in the mid-1980s found them to be 'a bulwark of traditional, adversarial industrial relations' (Kelly and Heery, 1994). We do not know how much these values have changed over ten years.

This in turn raises questions about the desirability of strategies of incorporation and partnership as well as their practicability. Clearly, employees' and unions' attitudes and actions will be influenced in specific cases by various situational factors such as management style, workforce characteristics and workers' sense of vulnerability to job loss (Edwards, this volume). However, there is a case for arguing that unions should retain an adversarial conception of industrial relations, even if current conditions require that they have to engage in some form of concession bargaining. Kelly (1996) has argued that moderate unionism, i.e. strategies of incorporation and partnership, yield little that is concrete in the way of concessions by management, render trade union organisations dependent on management and therefore vulnerable to attack should the employer decide to deunionise. This argument is supported by the recent history of the petroleum industry, where supposedly co-operative industrial relations and concessions by unions over workforce reductions and changes to working practices have been the prelude to union derecognition rather than the defence against it (*see*, for example, Ahlstrand, 1990). Members' willingness to act in defence of collective bargaining may be the best way of maintaining an independent role for trade unions, given that it is generally accepted that it has been the strength of trade unionism in Britain that has slowed down and moderated the development of the employers' counter-attack on trade unionism (Gall and McKay, 1994; Purcell, 1991).

If we accept that unions are able to achieve certain gains as a result of partnership, there are still good reasons for maintaining an ideology based on the distinctiveness of workers' and managers' interests. Wright (1996) has shown how the presence of strong collective identification among workers, a sense of separateness from management, and possibly an ideological commitment to trade unionism based on distrust of management, has been important in sustaining informal union membership agreements and independent trade union organisation. Given that survey and case study evidence indicates strongly that low trust, 'them and us' views of management, is held by many employees and the majority of trade union members, that employees retain traditional views of the role that unions should play, and that these views are based on employees' experiences at work, these phenomena constitute potential resources of organisational power for trade unions which they would do well to cultivate rather than ignore or minimise.

CONCLUSION

On the basis of the experience of the first half of the 1990s there are strong grounds for remaining sceptical about the likelihood of union–management partnerships developing as a major force in British industrial relations. Recent attempts to develop a new bargaining agenda based on a co-operative approach to issues of 'common concern' have had little impact and the trend towards union exclusion continues. As this chapter argues, this reflects the inherently problematic nature of current approaches to partnership as a strategy for reconstituting trade union power in response to long-term decline. It is doubtful whether trade unions can problematise employment issues in such a way as to reconstitute the interests of managements and workers on the basis of a definition of common interests and, in this way, reconstitute their own power as agencies. Not only is it uncertain whether substantive issues which can form the basis for genuinely co-operative bargaining actually exist, unions' ability to generate support for a common approach to these issues, from both management and workforce, is problematic. This is so for reasons deriving from the contradictory nature of the employment relationship – the simultaneous presence of co-operation and conflict, resistance and 'consent' – which makes co-operative bargaining behaviour extremely difficult to accomplish.

In addition, the ability of trade unions to reconstitute interests on the basis of partnership has to be seen in the context of wider factors relating to British economic development. Britain's comparative advantage lies in low technology, low value added sectors of production. Also, British financial institutions have a historical predisposition to emphasise short-term financial performance over longer term performance indicators, and this has led to British firms holding back on long-term investments on the grounds that they detract from annual profit and loss accounts and depress the share price. Consequently, the attempted regeneration of the economy since the end of the 1970s has been based on work intensification rather than increased investment in physical capital. This, together with continued inadequacies in the provision of vocational training, has maintained a deep-rooted bias in the economy in favour of 'defensive' labour flexibility in the form of work intensification and a relative lack of formal commitments to employment security. In these circumstances, while there will be notable exceptions, managers in general are unlikely to place a high value on generating partnership relations based on high co-operation and high trust because of the perceived costs involved and the relatively low perceived additional benefits in terms of performance. At the same time, employees subjected to a regime of defensive labour flexibility are unlikely to be convinced of managers' commitment to partnership should it be espoused.

These problems are compounded by the absence of institutionalised political support for collective representation of employee interests which has resulted from a decade and a half of industrial relations law reform. While the partnership strategy understandably seeks to change those features of British economic life referred to above, those features themselves reduce the possibility of realising a partnership strategy which is of real benefit to workers. It seems relevant that the renewed public expressions of interest in partnership took off with the approach of the 1997 General Election which the Labour Party was fully expected to win. It is possible that the Labour government will provide a policy environment more supportive of partnership, but there are grounds for scepticism. In its economic policy, the Labour Party appears to have become imbued with liberal individualistic principles. This means that political support for partnership is likely to take a rhetorical form which emphasises the need for wider consultation within enterprises, possibly linked to support for 'European-style' works councils. However, whether this will make a practical contribution to improving the position of the unions seems doubtful in the absence of a policy framework which not only supports consultation rights but also collective bargaining. There appears to be a tendency to forget that in the European Social Partnership model, the distinctiveness of employer and employee interests is recognised, as is the necessity for political, institutional frameworks to encourage 'conflictual co-operation' (Streeck, 1989). Consultative machinery at workplace level is supported by and integrated with positive rights to collective bargaining at company and/or regional/national industry level. In the absence of institutionalised political support for social partnership at national and sectoral level, it is highly questionable whether partnership, as opposed to incorporation, will be realised in the workplace.

Note

I am grateful to Trevor Colling, John Kelly and Mick Marchington for helpful comments on an earlier version of this chapter. Any errors and misjudgements are entirely the responsibility of the author.

13

Bridging the gap?
Employee voice, representation and HRM

IAN BEARDWELL

De Montfort University, Leicester

Much workplace change is presented as though it cuts through old relations of conflict to promote total unity. Yet any unity has to be actively created, and it cannot be total because of the structural conditions in which employees and workers find themselves. (Edwards, 1995)

INTRODUCTION

The structural conditions to which Edwards refers are bound up with the issues of control and commitment which have been as critical to the discussion of HRM over the past decade as they have been to the analysis of the employment relationship over the past century. Within that debate a range of themes has been employed to express various means of moderating that relationship, including 'partnership', 'participation' and 'mutuality'. In Chapter 3 the emphasis on the analysis of HRM and the link of certain types of HRM ('bundles' of practice) to outcomes in terms of performance ('competitive advantage') was noted. In Chapter 4 the explicit theme of the 'resource-based' view of HRM was discussed. It argues that mutual gains for managers and employees may be achieved where 'best practice' HRM leads to superior economic performance, enhancing profits, pay and long-term employment security. The implicit assumption underlying this analysis is that there is a win–win situation that benefits such a joint partnership, and in which employee interests are subsumed within the general economic well-being of the organisation. In such circumstances it would almost be perversity on the part of employees to stand apart from this economic gain and assert a different range of interests and concerns. To this extent, therefore, questions of *employee voice* and representation have tended to take a relatively low profile in recent years. The purpose of this chapter is to examine the issues of employee voice, representation and the management of these processes in terms of 'mutuality' and 'unity' as they affect the employment relationship. Choosing these two terms indicates that they pose analytically distinct categories of explanation for industrial relations processes and outcomes, particularly in the contemporary world of HRM, a point that will be explored at a later stage in the argument.

EMPLOYEE VOICE AND REPRESENTATION: PUBLIC POLICY PRESCRIPTIONS 1968–79

Throughout the decade 1958–68, marked by the London Transport strike at its inception and the report of the Donovan Commission at its close, there was little explicit discussion of the problems of employee voice and representation. Much the greater amount of attention was given on the one hand to the supposed 'abuses' of union 'power' (*Rookes* v *Barnard* [1964] AC 1129) or on the other, to the potentialities for indigenous industrial relations reform (Flanders 1964; 1967). Explicit questions of direct representation by means of union recognition, and the means by which this could be achieved, had to await the full examination of the Donovan Commission. Thus a thorough-going examination of the purpose of expanding employee voice was, almost automatically, bound up with other questions of industrial relations reform, principal among them the 1960s concerns with shopfloor order, inefficient labour practices, and wage inflation. The public policy stance of the Donovan Commission was expressed in these terms:

> *There is now a dilemma for public policy. Collective bargaining is recognised as the best way of conducting industrial relations and as depending on strong trade union organisation. The proportion of employees who are organised has however been declining. Employment is increasing in areas which have proved difficult to organise, so that the effect of obstacles to the development and recognition of unions in these areas is assuming a greater importance for the future of collective bargaining.*   (Donovan Commission 1968, para. 224)

So the problem for Donovan was not so much that of providing a framework for further expansion of union recognition as of providing a protective framework in order to secure collective bargaining and prevent its gradual erosion, at the expense of what, today, would be termed non-unionism. In retrospect, what is lacking in the Donovan description of this issue is any sense of the basis on which recognition might be viewed either as a policy objective or as a process. While there was what Dickens and Hall (1995) later described as a general 'expressed preference' for union recognition across much of this period, the Donovan report confined itself in this area to the second of the two underlying principles which set its agenda, that of the extension of 'the coverage of collective bargaining and the organisation of workers on which it depends' (para. 212). For the decade that followed Donovan, the public policy stance on union recognition governed this approach to dealing with the voice/representation issue. However, it is possible to view the principles of recognition as requiring a more detailed framework for analysis in order to assess how far such policy successfully addressed the question of representation.

FOUR APPROACHES TO RECOGNITION

Recognition may be conceived of in four different ways. Each starts from a different premise and seeks to achieve different goals, some complementary and some contradictory.

The 'floor of rights' approach

First, recognition as a *'floor of rights'*. A general assumption in the Donovan analysis, drawing strongly from the prevailing ethos of the time, was that union recognition provided individuals with key protections and freedoms that enhanced and widened their 'space' in the employment relationship. If the employment contract per se remained narrow, and the collective agreement failed to develop beyond certain important but constrained elements (c.f. Hepple, 1983), then issues such as procedures for recognition could be seen as building in additional elements that would substantially improve the relative strength of the employee in the employment relationship. As Donovan argued:

> *Collective bargaining is the most effective means of giving workers the right to representation in decisions affecting their working lives, a right which is or should be the prerogative of every worker in a democratic society.* (para. 212)

This was especially the case if one accepted the line of argument, advanced by Kahn-Freund (1954), that British industrial relations had largely been characterised by the absence of the legal concepts of disputes of 'rights'. A means to provide 'rights' over and above either individual or collective labour law could be seen as achieving the expansion of the individual's prerogative referred to by Donovan. The problem for this definition of recognition was that it required some means of achieving it; in other words a way had to be found of permitting its implementation that provided the desired policy outcome but did not go against the grain of the voluntaristic philosophy that was elsewhere employed in the Report. The device which emerged was a masterpiece of legerdemain that instilled a heavily prescriptive element but with the semblance of voluntarism. This required employers to act as the principal suspects, arguing against their 'conviction' for having not conceded recognition – even in circumstances where the employee voice had not been heard or expressed:

> *If a company does not recognise trade unions, it will have no agreements to register, and this will have to be reported to the Department of Employment and Productivity with reasons. In this event the company will be failing in its public duty unless it can show that its employees are unwilling to join trade unions and be represented by them (para. 196) . . . Failure on the part of a company to register its agreements, or to report that it has no agreements and why, will render it liable to a monetary penalty.* (para. 204)

Considered in terms of the 1990s' experience this reads as a world apart, with companies required to argue why it was that they were now required to register agreements without any recognition procedures having taken place. Even where suggested means of testing for union support were outlined, for example the principles that underlay recognition and both substantive and procedural agreements (para. 203), the exact mechanisms were vague and were suggested for a future Commission on Industrial Relations to determine. It was clear that this did not rely upon a simple plebiscite:

> *the test in dealing with any dispute over recognition – other than a dispute between unions over recognition – should be whether the union or unions in question can reasonably be expected to develop and sustain adequate representation for the purpose of collective bargaining . . . A ballot may be useful in applying the test, but could rarely determine the issue by itself.* (para. 203(2))

Rights, therefore, were to be acquired via the construction of various types and levels of agreement; there was no indication that it might be a 'right' enshrined in statute law. Indeed, the Appeal Court ruled in both the Grunwick (1978) and W.H. Allen cases (1980) that ACAS (the successor to the commission suggested by Donovan) had exceeded both its discretionary power, as envisaged by the Royal Commission, and its statutory powers and duty as laid down in the prevailing legislation of 1975 (Lewis, 1983).

The 'buying in' approach

The second conception of recognition is as *'buying in'*. This involves building trade union commitment and attachment to industrial relations processes by means of beneficial outcomes (such as increased membership via recognition procedures) that would otherwise have to be achieved by voluntary action. Although draft legislation was sponsored by the Labour Government after the Donovan Report, the practical impact of recognition procedures could only be tested in the 1971 Industrial Relations Act after the Conservatives won the 1970 General Election. An important plank was the direct link between legislation and industrial relations practice, with the Department of Employment's Code of Practice in Industrial Relations viewing the law as the principal instrument in achieving desired reforms (1970). In order to convince (or coerce) trade unions into using the new provisions the government included comprehensive statutory recognition (I.R. Act 1971; Sections 45: 50: 51) which was given legal backing by recourse to the National Industrial Relations Court which could both initiate a reference to the Commission on Industrial Relations for subsequent investigation, and apply sanctions in the case of refusal of recognition where the CIR had reported favourably. In order to participate in these procedures, trade unions had to register with a newly-created Registrar of Trade Unions; failure to do so invalidated any attempt to approach the NIRC for a statutory investigation. The thinking behind this proposal was that union opposition to the overall legislative package would be overcome by the 'buying in' of union interests to the positive factors associated with union growth, among them recognition and statutory powers to enforce recalcitrant employers to accede to formal recognition recommendations. In the event no such 'buying in' occurred; unions were too confident in the labour market of the first half of the 1970s to require comprehensive statutory recognition procedures. For many unions it was more a question of responding to 'natural growth' as Beaumont (1985) noted; drawing on Jenkins and Sherman (1979, quoted by Beaumont), the usual position was 'to take a more reactive approach and wait for potential members to come before setting a campaign in operation'. As greater numbers moved towards unions throughout the 1970s Donovan's concerns of the late 1960s began to look dated:

> *a continued shift from relatively well-organised manual employment to relatively ill-organised white collar employment will, other things being equal, lead to a decline in trade unionism . . . With all these factors working against trade union-ism, it is not surprising that the proportion of British employees has gently declined from a peak of about 45 per cent in 1948 to about 42 per cent today (1968).*

> (para. 220)

This gentle decline was to be reversed quite dramatically in the succeeding decade so that the 1948 figure was overtaken within two years of the Report's publication, and it was exceeded by 10 per cent within a decade.

The formal policy approach

Third is recognition as *'completing the picture'*. If the necessity of 'rewarding' unions with recognition proved unsuccessful, the retention of such provisions in the 1975 Employment Protection Act implied that there was at least a public policy stance that favoured extend-ing employee voice in a formal sense. The experience of the 1971 legislation was that widescale recognition via statutory means had failed but that it had been used (often covertly) by unions where there were difficult pockets of recognition that required help over and above the normal tactics available to trade unions. In the case of Immingham Bulk Terminal (CIR Report No. 41, 1973) a group of coal-loading operatives employed by the NCB at a former (pre-1947 nationalisation) railway port on the Humber sought to remove the rail union as their recognised negotiator in favour of the transport union who organised dockers at the adjacent Immingham Docks. The transport union took a close interest in all stages of the case while still maintaining the formal TUC position of non-involvement. A number of other white collar cases involving the former ASTMS union were progressed in this way. However, these were largely cases that filled in the detail of existing collective bargaining coverage; what was conspicuously lacking was a major impact on the large, and potentially growing, area of non-unionism that Donovan had alluded to and came to characterise British industrial relations 30 years later.

The in-fill of unionisation accounted for very little of the total growth of union mem-bership across the 1970s. Beaumont's (1985) estimate is that in the period 1976–80 some 9.4 per cent of growth was accounted for by formal recognition arrangements. Even accepting Beaumont's proviso that this figure is on the low side, and using a rounded figure of 10 per cent, the IPD study (Wood, 1997) has established that between 1976 and 1980 (within which operative dates 'policy on' recognition procedures applied) the statutorily derived increase in employees covered by collective bargaining was 64 000. In the equiv-alent 'policy on' period under the 1971 Act (March 1972–February 1974) a maximum figure of only some 6000 might be estimated, but this is almost certainly an over-estimate because of the lack of widespread trade union acceptance of the procedures. Allowing for this bias in the earlier period, the net effect of statutory recognition procedures might be estimated as some 70 000 against a general increase in union membership of 1 588 000 across the eight-year period 1972–80. A deflator affecting the union membership compo-nent of recognition, as opposed to general coverage of a bargaining unit for collective bargaining purposes, would suggest that even this aggregate is unreliable. Beaumont (1985) estimates a 19 per cent deflator for the period 1973–78; on this basis the figure of

70 000 would reduce to no greater than a 56 000 increase in actual union membership.

The concept of 'completing the picture' is not merely a historical phenomenon however. The most recent TUC policy statement on membership notes that membership is set to fall by a further 500 000 to 6.8 million in 2001 and recommends that unions launch recruitment offensives among specific groups: 'these include professional employees such as teachers, engineers and lawyers as well as associate professionals such as nurses, social workers and technicians' (*Financial Times*, 24 Feb 1997) as well as non-union members in otherwise unionised workplaces.

The 'partnership' approach

Finally there is the concept of recognition as *'partnership'*. This approach to recognition conceives of the process as 'adding to the fairness of the industrial relations system' (Wood, 1997). The primary intention of the Donovan Commission had been to 'bring greater order into collective bargaining' (para. 212) and an important part of that process was to create conditions of 'mutuality', in which the respective parties to the agreement undertook not only to recognise and deal with each other but to accept their joint responsibilities and obligations under those agreements. To a degree this approach to recognition accords with the concept of pluralism that underpinned a great deal of the work of Flanders, Fox and Clegg, but it may also serve to describe a pattern of industrial relations that saw unions, union members, collective bargaining and 'voluntarism' as the means by which a volatile but established employment relationship could be sustained over time. The mutuality that arose from this mix has been described aptly by Dunn (1990) as 'live and let live', using the analogy of trenchlife in World War I; such mutuality need not be based on an acceptance of the values of the other party, or indeed any sense of approbation as to the ideological position that either party to the employment relationship might espouse. Rather, the mutuality that grew out of the post-World War II industrial relations experience was based on the nervous obsession with what 'the other side' is up to (Fussell, quoted by Dunn, 1990) rather than the jointly developed sense of shared ownership of procedures, processes and outcomes.

It was this lack of mutuality that lay behind a great deal of the failure of the statutory procedures across the 1970s, whether derived from the 1971 or 1975 legislation. As James (1977) has pointed out, many of the recommendations made by the CIR were simply ignored by employers while unions, ostensibly more favourable towards the 1975 Employment Protection Act, found the procedures lengthy and cumbersome. In some instances there were legal challenges to ACAS proceedings which elongated recognition cases to almost unbearable length (note: the W.H. Allen case which began as a recognition case in 1973 with the CIR, reappeared as a case with ACAS and was the subject of a Court of Appeal and a House of Lords hearing in 1980). Thus both management and unions failed to find the mutuality in recognition that Donovan had sought to foster.

Taken together, these four approaches to recognition reflect the complex pattern of public policy, rule-making and procedural reform that have impacted on the recognition debate over the past 30 years. All of these arguments for recognition have been articulated; sometimes one as a predominant rationale, sometimes others in a combination. What is increasingly obvious is that the circumstances in which any further developments in recognition policy may develop are greatly changed from those that fuelled the Donovan analysis and prompted the legal interventions of the 1970s. In order to examine these changed circumstances, it is necessary to examine the issue in the context of HRM and the prescriptions of the 1990s.

BRIDGING THE GAP? PUBLIC POLICY REPRESENTATION AND VOICE

I am not a fan of the adversarial system of industrial relations. We have a common interest – a common interest in the success of our enterprises, in wealth creation and in a country whose products and services can compete with the best in the marketplaces of the world.   (John Monks at the CBI Conference 1996)

Donovan spoke of order and unrest, of demarcation, restrictive practices and the under-utilisation of labour. There is no mention of product markets, competitiveness and international trading. In these circumstances what are the issues now arising from the question of representation? How far do reversals in public policy on the one hand or developments within HRM on the other offer viable routes forward?

The public policy route to representation: 'mutuality' 1990s' style

The question of recognition has assumed a greater degree of attention more recently as the 1997 General Election focused attention on the possibility of political change. In the aftermath of the Labour victory, there was no immediate legislation on recognition, although clearly the policy context has changed. In 1995 the TUC published the report of its task force on representation at work, entitled *Your Voice at Work*. This adopted the 'recognition as a floor of rights' approach, discussed in the preceding section, by arguing for a statutory right to representation for all employees on certain basic employment issues (discipline and grievances, for example) coupled with a statutory right for trade unionists to be represented by an independent trade union. The report argued further for a representation agency which would be able to award general consultation rights under the EC directives on redundancy and transfers of undertakings, and take on powers over trade union recognition with a requirement for employers to bargain and so avoid the problems of rejection experienced by both the CIR and ACAS.

The Institute of Personnel and Development (IPD) report, prepared by Wood (1997), is a response to the broad pre-Election indications of the Labour Party that it would bring in legislation to require employers to bargain if more than 50 per cent of employees in a workplace were in favour of union representation, although none is envisaged in the first tranche of Government legislation. The IPD itself argued against statutory recognition as reflecting a pattern of industrial relations which had passed, while Wood argued that there had to be some 'significant appreciation of the value of union-based industrial relations' for a statutory policy to work.

The merits of the 'floor of rights' approach are open to debate, as are the other three approaches. A particular public policy dilemma, whichever of the four approaches is taken (either singly or in combination), is that considerable practical difficulties arise in constructing a formula for recognition that would be robust enough to meet all the objections to its introduction and all the requirements for its success. Among the most pressing issues would be the necessity to have procedures open to all legally independent and certificated trade unions, as indeed the Labour Party outline proposals suggest. However, a general disposition to encourage bargaining where 50 per cent employee support has been achieved (or an automatic right where that figure has been achieved in the TUC's proposals) does not address the question of disputed territory either between TUC unions or between TUC unions on the one hand and non-TUC unions on the other. In order to clarify the current legal situation it would be necessary for any legislative initiative on recognition to be linked to a repeal of at least that part of the Trade Union Reform and Employment Rights Act 1993 which gives a right to join any union organising an appropriate class of employee, regardless of the TUC's Bridlington procedures. This could lead to a complex and potentially fragmented pattern of representation in many sectors, particularly where unions were using such a procedure as a 'completing the picture' as envisaged in the TUC's policy statement on recruitment of February 1997, discussed earlier.

The issue of compliance is also problematic. In the quasi-legal world of post-1980s' industrial relations is it enough to leave this issue to voluntary action and resolution? The experience of the 1970s suggests not. Enabling legislation without the ultimate sanction of legally binding recognition would be no legislation at all. Thus new procedures would have to address the question of coping with the recalcitrant employer as well as whether employers will have the equal right to seek derecognition. As Wood (1997) points out, 'Assuming that the legislation permits employers to use the procedure to derecognise . . . it is even conceivable that it might actually reduce union density.' This point is particularly important when one considers that it may well have been the lack of explicit recognition/derecognition procedures that prevented derecognition becoming so widespread a phenomenon in the UK (Claydon, 1989; 1996) as it has in the USA.

A final point on this group of issues resides in the difficulties experienced with legal challenge and review and the prolongation of the process of resolving representation. The W.H. Allen case was, perhaps, extreme, but in circumstances where individuals and organisations are now open to far greater judicial review and consideration than hitherto, it must be assumed that cases will be disputed by disappointed parties. The situation envisaged by Flanders in evidence to Donovan 30 years ago no longer obtains:

> *a body dealing with disputes of this character would not be acting as an arbitrator but more like a permanent Court of Inquiry. It could not possibly rely, for example, only on the parties' submissions for evidence . . . It would certainly be empowered to arrange a secret ballot, if that was thought to be desirable, although equally it should not be compelled to do so . . . It would in fact have gradually to evolve a set of working principles.*   (Donovan, para. 255)

Thus a 1960s' construction of recognition as a voluntary process in a voluntary system has given way to a 1990s' statutory 'right' in a legal procedure.

Managing the employment relationship at the millenium

A further set of issues resides in the management of the employment relationship in the circumstances of the late 1990s. The question of union recognition is closely tied in with the wider issue of union membership; in situations where there has been widespread de-unionisation, on a variety of grounds, there can be no automatic presumption either that recognition can be achieved against a low numerical membership base or that, if achieved, it will assist in the rebuilding of membership numbers. It has been customarily argued that the 'virtuous circle' effect will operate where recognition is achieved (Bain and Price, 1983, for example) but this case is set in the context of labour market conditions of 20 years ago; more recent circumstances have presented us with a different range of complex issues.

In turning to examine some of them, perhaps the biggest shift to note is the context of extreme deregulation in which any debate about recognition has to be located. A particularity of the British HRM scenario is the legislative and public policy environment which has encouraged decollectivisation and decentralisation in industrial relations; the difference between 'then' and 'now' – the 1970s and the 1990s – is profound. The operation of a public policy commitment to recognition took place against a background of almost constant bi-party governmental intervention in the operation of the labour market; far from achieving the relatively loose 'indicative practice' envisaged in Donovan and derived from the tradition of voluntarism, recognition took place in a world of 'directive intervention' and legalism which overtook the work of ACAS in this area and led the ACAS Council to decide in June 1979 that it was no longer possible to operate statutory recognition procedures (Kessler, 1995). Running alongside these specific industrial relations factors were government concerns and intervention in pay bargaining and the effect of pay settlements upon incomes policy. A recreation of that environment would appear to be unlikely in the short term. The Labour Party's position on a general right to representation requires far more detailed work before being brought forward for legislation and still leaves open the question of how far a legal element will secure its successful operation.

Beyond the questions of public policy lie the difficult waters of industrial relations at the level of the establishment and the argument that management have found ways to handle the employment relationship that are different from former practice. Donovan saw the establishment as being the cockpit of industrial relations; it was in this circumscribed environment that managers, stewards and workgroups performed the quadrille of collective bargaining. In order to put a framework around disorganised collective bargaining practice, greater emphasis was to be placed on procedural reform. The basis of this reform was on the mutuality that these groups recognised and tolerated within this relationship. But the contemporary establishment has become the cockpit of a different kind of relationship. So far from being characterised as the fulcrum of *mutuality*, it has become the location of the managerial agenda in regaining control over industrial relations. The mutuality of the workplace has come under severe pressure from the unity of the workplace, an environment that has seen much change – not least of which is that management may conceive of the relationship as essentially being composed of managers and individuals with a common purpose, rather than of groups with mutual interests. By an irony of history, the establishment emphasis of Donovan has provided subsequently rich grounds for managerial initiative, and the 'voluntarism' that would carry forward procedural reform has been eroded in favour of the freedom of action of managements in reshaping their industrial relations.

This shift in industrial relations policy is partly explained by the exogenous factors of government deregulation and hostile trade union legislation; but another explanation for the change has to be a consideration of the weakness of industrial relations mechanisms themselves which could have played a stronger role in this process. Nolan (1996) has argued that:

> *the system of industrial relations and employment regulation which came to dom-*
> *inate key sectors of the economy after 1945 was not conducive to industrial*
> *modernisation: not, it should be stressed, for the reasons cited by proponents of the*
> *conventional wisdom, but because trade unions and other regulatory mechanisms*
> *were too weak to force firms to abandon progressively outmoded business*
> *practices.*

Nolan's purpose was to demonstrate that the weaknesses of British industrial relations mechanisms both influenced, and were in turn affected by, the relatively poor post-war record of the economy. In these circumstances the independent efforts of unions to max-imise membership and extend recognition on a secure basis rested on a long tradition of *ad hoc* adaptions to immediate pressures. For 'mutuality' to have become deeply rooted in British industrial relations practice, there would have been a requirement for it to have developed from a more profound grounding in the long-standing ethos of 'voluntarism'. This institutional weakness was also noted in Dunn's (1985) analysis of the expansion of the closed shop, which indicated that the developments of the 1970s had left a legacy of 'robust' and 'fragile' arrangements which were increasingly under pressure throughout the 1980s from politico-legal reform on the one hand and managerial-technological initiatives on the other. Thus, while the introduction of a regulatory framework encouraged the belief that the expansion of collective bargaining could be achieved, the fragilities and weak-nesses noted by Dunn and Nolan indicated that important parts of the infrastructure of industrial relations were open to a combination of threats from public policy and internal structural faults.

The reworking of unitarism and pluralism throughout the past decade and a half, exem-plified by the move from 'mutuality' to 'unity', has had a major bearing on employee voice and recognition. It puts a different complexion on the notion of 'partnership' as one that is constructed around the internal relationship within the firm and without an external rep-resentative agency. The deeply rooted articulation of the employee voice through formal union membership and recognition lay at the heart of the thinking and practice of policy for some 15 years, until 1980; is that approach now relevant over 15 years later? Indeed, the very thoroughness of the discussion of recognition in Donovan is focused on a partic-ular institutional format of the content of agreements, while the seeming completeness of the criteria set out in the report for judging the adequacy of agreements does not engage with major areas of the employment relationship that have come to play a significant role. Over the past 15 years, questions about employee commitment to collectivism and collec-tively determined pay and the individual's commitment and assent to the organisation, all set within a managerial framework for the management of the relationship, have assumed a critical importance. It is to the relationship between HRM and representation that the argument now turns.

THE HRM ROUTE TO EMPLOYEE VOICE: FROM 'MUTUALITY' TO 'UNITY'

The discussion of employee voice is one of the less well-developed areas in the wider considerations of the HRM debate. Whether one conceives of HRM as operating within the framework of mainstream institutional industrial relations (Sisson, 1993) or as a phenomenon whose influence is powerfully felt in newly emerging workplaces (Guest and Hoque, 1996), there is little that addresses the nature of the topic under discussion. Recent HRM examination has developed away from 'input characteristics' to look at the 'output outcomes' that might arise from a mix of HRM strategies and policies; among these approaches are the 'resource-based' HRM models of Prahalad and Hamel (1990) and Pfeffer (1994) in the USA; the 'bundles of best practice' analysis of Huselid (1995) in the USA and Guest and Hoque (1996) in the UK; and the 'high mutuality/high commitment' models of Kochan (1995) and Wood (1995) in the USA and UK. Implicit in these approaches is the notion of employees occupying a 'win–win' situation, where high levels of managerial commitment ensure both employment security and superior terms and conditions as a result of the stronger economic performance of the firm; the economic performance of the firm, in turn, validates management's willingness to retain and underscore high commitment. However, there is little by way of a fully worked through position on employee voice, and that which there is makes some heroic assumptions. In many respects Kochan's work presents the fullest reading of the shift from traditional 'New Deal' labour relations to the HRM-based approach of 'mutual commitment' in the USA, with an examinable model of which components of employee voice operate in the context of 'commitment'. For Kochan (1995), the critically important element in the discussion of commitment is the necessity to achieve national competitiveness. In order to achieve commitment a set of 'generic principles' is outlined (drawn from Kochan's earlier work (Kochan *et al.*, 1986)). These operate at the strategic level, the functional (human resource policy) level and the workplace level.

At the strategic level, business policy should be built around quality, innovation, flexibility, speed to market and customer service. At this level, top management offer a 'value commitment' and an 'effective voice for HR' in strategy making: 'at the strategy and policy-making level it is necessary that there be one or more mechanisms for giving voice to employee and human resource interests' (pp. 335 *et seq.*). To achieve this Kochan suggests that: 'one possibility is the use of planning mechanisms to ensure that human resource issues receive their just due (sic)'. Two further possibilities are that 'informal labour–management information-sharing and consultation might be used', and 'more formal methods of worker representation in corporate governance structures (e.g. labour leaders on the board of directors, works councils)' might be considered. At the functional level, the explicit discussion of employee voice disappears, just as a river might burrow underground in the course of its flow, and is replaced by some of the behavioural expectations of both firm and employee. Firms must make the necessary investment to have appropriate skills and training: 'That is, they – and their employees – must be prepared to adopt the concept of lifelong learning' in order to promote what Kochan sees as the trinity of commitment, flexibility and loyalty of employees toward the organisation.

At workplace level, employees must have the ability to learn and 'the willingness to learn' throughout a career as an 'extremely important personal attribute'. Further, this suggests job and career structures which 'eschew narrow, Tayloristic job assignments in favour of flexible work organisation that features expanded jobs and the free-flowing movement of employees across tasks and functional boundaries'. Employee voice is addressed in two ways:

- by providing opportunities for employees or their representatives to be engaged in decisions affecting their jobs and terms and conditions
- by actively resolving disputes of interest.

Kochan concedes that conflicting interests exist with the employment relationship, but that there is an overriding imperative that these are resolved: 'they must be resolved efficiently and in a fashion that maintains the parties' commitment and capacities for pursuing joint gains'. As the underground water course re-emerges at the workplace level, we may observe the 'win–win' model successfully riding the flow.

How far does this exposition satisfactorily address the issue of employee voice in the HRM-based model of 'high commitment' management? It is worth noting that Kochan chooses to use the term 'mutual commitment', implying that there is a shared ownership of the commitment process, but a closer examination of his model shows it to be built of many different materials. The strategic level principles engage with a series of prescriptions about HRM in general and employee voice in particular. Thus, within the same set of generic principles at this level we find an organisational culture that views employees as stakeholders, a corporate view on the advisability of giving voice to 'employee and human resource interests' as if the two were synonymous, and a constitutionalist approach to senior level involvement which runs informal information-sharing and consultation together (despite the real differences between them noted by Marchington, 1995), and – alongside both of these – board level representation and works councils. The elision of five varied components – stakeholding, employee interests, corporate HRM interests, information and consultation, and formal representation – suggests, at best, a complex agenda of priorities and prescriptions and, at worst, an ill-fitting mix of competing and contradictory interests. The absence of discussion over voice at the functional policy level merely serves to demonstrate the latter proposition more forcefully. Simply to chant the litany of 'commitment, flexibility and loyalty' overlooks the rich diversity of perspective and assumption which is bound up in each of those terms, while the compensation model is a masterpiece of managerial discretion: 'Over and above the competitive basic compensation levels and structures, would be variable, or contingent, compensation schemes (e.g. bonus plans) designed to reinforce desired forms of quality, flexibility and the like.' Whether or not this is 'mutual commitment' must remain a moot point for the moment.

The argument over employee voice re-emerges at the workplace level and, once again, demonstrates a mix of thinking over its operation and effectiveness. Employees must bring key personal attributes to the job and, while there can be little argument with that, contribute to a new world of job content and job design. Gone are the certitudes of Taylorism and defined job descriptions; in their place comes 'free-flowing movement of employees across tasks and functional boundaries' and although competing interests are nodded to, the conflict arising from them cannot stand in the way of 'globally competitive business results', for these will provide 'globally competitive standards of living' – also known as the 'win–win' situation. In this context employee voice seems to fulfil a functionalist role, so long as the function is to maintain a set of rather widely conceived but loosely expressed corporate goals, for, as Kochan argues, 'they do not translate into a universal set of "best practices", but rather stand as broad guidelines to be implemented in ways that conform to particular cultural or organisational realities'. Distilled from the rhetoric we may reasonably infer that the 'realities' are those defined by the organisation and to which it wishes to direct the efforts of its employees. Thus 'mutuality' in 'mutual commitment' firms turns out to be 'unity', or, put another way, 'pluralism' turns out to be operating within a framework of 'unitarism' which is where we got to with Fox (1974) nearly a quarter of a century ago.

CONCLUSION: GAPS, BLACK HOLES, ACCOMPLICES AND VICTIMS

What then of employee voice in the light of public policy reform and HRM? Is there an unbridgeable gap between our traditional response to representation on the one hand and new forms of employee attachment on the other? And is 'mutuality' the victim of 'unity' in the workplace? The research data currently available certainly suggest that a gap has opened up in arrangements for formal representation (WIRS3, 1992) and one might reasonably suppose that the forthcoming WIRS4 will demonstrate the extent to which some of these key trends have established themselves further. In terms of a public policy response, the reintroduction of enabling legislation for a basic form of representation leaves open the question of which of the four rationales for recognition (either singly or in combination) will provide the impetus to genuine extension of employee voice. In terms of a disaggregated 'high commitment' approach, how far will the internal contradictions of 'mutuality' and 'unity' prevent employee voice from establishing itself in the HRM agenda?

To an important degree the argument depends upon the perspective which is brought to bear on the issue. The public policy stance has, historically, been concerned to express the necessity of 'levelling up' the employment relationship so that Kochan's elision of 'employee and human resource issues' discussed earlier is separated out and afforded the proper attention that the two different sets of interests warrant. To this extent, therefore, public policy has conceived of the employee as a 'victim' requiring protection and rights which ensure a mutually recognised and agreed space within the employment relationship. The HRM stance, particularly in its high commitment mode, sees the employee as an 'accomplice' who is willing to go along with the 'win–win' model of the employment relationship, indeed the economic imperative of global competition would suggest a mutant form of 'false consciousness' on the part of the employee in not so doing. Who, in their 'right mind' would want to argue against such a proposition? Marchington (1995) has noted the dilemma that faces those who are involved in commitment and workplace performance:

> the role of workplace trade unionism will also be adjusted so that employee representatives and union members acquiesce with management plans and policies, or indeed are further marginalised or removed altogether.

But perhaps it is a dilemma that, in the newly constructed workplace of the late 1990s, many employees are willing to contemplate? While one cannot discount the rejection or lack of take-up of unionisation across the last decade and a half as being composed of at least some elements of fear, powerlessness or lack of opportunity, one has to admit the possibility of personal choice in the matter. For many employees the question of being a 'victim' in their employment relationship is as unrecognisable a concept as becoming a lottery jackpot winner in any given week. 'It Could Be You', but not this time and, anyway the odds are 15 million to one against. So the high-commitment 'accomplice' sits more easily with a pattern of employment that has become more contingent. Paradoxically, in a world in which flexibility and insecurity affect a wide range of jobs, high commitment offers the kind of fixity which 'career' and 'occupation' once promised. If you are on the inside, in a high commitment firm, the role of the 'accomplice' is to hope for sufficiently regular smaller payouts to make the investment required by the employer worthwhile.

In this respect we are entering uncharted territory. For some (Beardwell, 1997; Guest, 1995) this is where the 'Black Hole' resides. In Guest's model the 'Black Hole' represents no HRM and no industrial relations:

> *All the evidence suggests that when confronted with a decision about whether or not to recognise a trade union, companies are increasingly deciding not to do so. It is possible to conclude that this is now the dominant pattern in new establishments; indeed, it raises the question of why unions are recognised at all.*

Millward *et al.* (1992) set out some of the key findings in non-union firms, and note that managers felt relatively unconstrained in organising work, deployed greater numerical flexibility of labour, set pay more in relation to performance and used wider differentials. In a quarter of workplaces, employee relations were so informal that there was no grievance procedure for employees. As far as Kochan's functional human resource policy level is concerned, Beardwell (1997) notes that personnel practice in 'Black Hole' firms is likely to be carried out by a non-qualified generalist operating a non-formally organised function in which pay is highly likely to be set by very wide managerial discretion and where employee communication and involvement is minimalist. As Millward *et al.* (1992) note:

> *All this suggests that employee relations in non-union industrial and commercial workplaces had relatively few formal mechanisms through which employees could contribute to the operation of their workplace in a broader context than that of their specific job. Nor were they as likely to have opportunities to air grievances or to resolve problems in ways that were systematic and designed to ensure fairness of treatment.*

So we may observe the notion of the 'victim' in the 'Black Hole' firm, but it is operating against the wider context of high commitment and its 'accomplices' which may appear doubly attractive by comparison.

The concept of a 'Black Hole' has become a popular image, and it has particular attractions in connection with industrial relations, for it permits a number of related images to be subsumed under its influence. One strand of the 'Black Hole' connotes something akin to the Black Hole of Calcutta, with appalling conditions and maltreatment and so, by association, the unregulated world of marginalised workers in low-paid and low-skilled jobs with little security, little upward advancement either financially or occupationally and highly dependent upon arbitrary managerial discretion. Another strand draws upon the image of the 'Black Hole' as a fathomless pit with little hope for any who fall into it. Both of these have found a ready acceptance as a metaphor for the uncertainties of late

20th-century employment. However, it is instructive to return to the original meaning of the term, coined in the 1960s to describe an astronomical construct; for the astronomer, a black hole is a highly gravitational forcefield with so strong a magnetic pull that no form of matter or anti-matter can resist being drawn towards it. It is not so much a construct about which we know little, rather it is a construct about which we have little firm information which yet has the capacity to exert a profound influence on the environment about it. If one accepts this concept of the 'Black Hole' as having as great a relevance to the employee relationship as the two earlier versions, then it offers up an insidious and troubling image. This may be the compelling image of HRM, with its ability to reconfigure the employment relationship in ways that can be attractive to both employers and employees. Indeed, within this imagery, it is HRM which is the vibrant influence in this relationship, not our former reliance on public policy and procedural reform. We have moved a long way in the debate over employee voice from the liberal/interventionist stance of the Donovan Commission to the internalised world of the high-commitment organisation. So, far from exhausting itself as in the imagery of the comet, HRM is demonstrating a capacity to present new challenges to conventional wisdom and the issue of employee voice may not be rectifiable by the usual policy/prescription mix.

Note

I am grateful to Trevor Colling, David Guest and Mick Marchington who commented on the earlier workshop version of this paper.

14

Partnership in context: towards a European model?

MICK MARCHINGTON

Manchester School of Management, UMIST

INTRODUCTION

The terminology of 'partnership' has gained much wider currency over the last few years, partly due to the continuing efforts of bodies such as the Involvement and Participation Association (IPA) in promoting its usage. In tandem with this semantic shift, there is evidence that some employers and professional bodies (e.g. the Institute of Personnel and Development) have taken a more positive stance to the idea of 'jointism' (Storey, 1992) and a partnership approach for managing employee relations (*see*, for example, *People Make the Difference* (IPD, 1995)). The trade unions have also shifted ground during the last decade, as the 1997 TUC publication (*Partners for Progress: Next Steps for the New Unionism*) illustrates clearly. The social partnership model outlined in that report suggests a link between a consultative management approach (informing, consulting and listening to employees and their trade union representatives, providing decent conditions, and job security) and a reduced likelihood of industrial disputes. Greater awareness of European models of consultation and representation, and a realisation that European regulations are likely to affect British employment practice irrespective of which political party is in power, has also encouraged some employers to consider the potential *benefits* as well as the costs of works councils. In short, a number of issues have helped to propel the partnership concept into the mainstream of human resource management in Britain.

However, as Willy Coupar and Bryan Stevens make abundantly clear in Chapter 9, it would be incorrect to argue that partnership is a new idea. Its roots have a long and well-established pedigree in this country, especially in firms which have always prided themselves on adopting an 'enlightened' approach to people management. Although some may scoff at the paternalist model adopted in firms which saw value in consulting with staff in the late 19th and early 20th centuries, these employers were extremely progressive compared with the majority who saw little need to consider workers as anything more than economic objects to be exploited. By way of contrast, the model of partnership which has emerged towards the end of the millennium is built rather more on mutual obligation than on one-way paternalism. In its European variant, it acknowledges the fact that employees have rights at work and can reasonably expect commitments from employers to employment security, information, consultation and representation. In other organisations, which have entered into voluntary arrangements with employees, shades of paternalism undoubtedly remain as managements recognise some moral imperative (albeit implicit) for employee involvement.

Increased interest in various forms of 'partnership' has not been accompanied by any consensus about what it means in practice, a problem compounded by the fact that there is as yet no commonly-accepted definition of its key components. The elastic nature of many partnership ideas may lessen its organisational impact, so it is important to provide some definitions. Using IPA documents (e.g. *Towards Industrial Partnership*, and case studies of Royal Mail and Rhône Poulenc) as a starting point, it is possible to draw out several key themes which might be included in such a definition:

- communication (direct information and communication, evaluating employees' views about the organisation, representative communication processes, recognition of independent employee representation, managing change in the company, influence)
- training (employability, training and development)
- terms and conditions of employment (commitment to employment security, processes for handling redundancies, employee financial participation, single status)
- corporate values/ethics (durability of processes and company culture, influence, values, minimum standards).

The philosophy underpinning this literature acknowledges and emphasises multiple perspectives on the employment relationship with employers, trade unions, employees and shareholders all given a voice.

Relevant though each of these themes is, there is a danger that partnership comes to be seen as a catch-all term for employee involvement or 'best practice' human resource management. Indeed, many of the cases identified by the IPA as partnership organisations practise much of what Pfeffer (1994a), Wood (1995) or Marchington and Wilkinson (1996) would regard as best practice. Clearly, in order to foster further analysis, to explore practice and, in particular, to construct benchmarks against which organisations can compare themselves, the distinctive elements of partnership need to be identified.

Partnership can be viewed at three levels:

1 It can be seen as a set of operational practices and processes which can be used to define the term more precisely, and provide some benchmarks for evaluating partnership in practice. This includes direct communication (e.g. active team briefing), upward problem-solving (e.g. employee attitude surveys), financial involvement (e.g. profit-sharing) and representative participation (e.g. joint consultative committees or works councils).
2 Partnership can be considered as a set of values and behaviours which are held and displayed by people within the partnership organisation, and which characterise attitudes to other stakeholders. This would include a recognition on the part of management that employees should be accepted as having a legitimate voice and right to influence (some) decisions. For their part, employee representatives would accept the right of management to expect certain levels of performance and the need for flexibility to achieve

higher levels of competitiveness. Both management and employees acknowledge, however, the essential value of mutual obligation, trust and openness, and the need for a durable and consistent perspective on employment relations.

3 There is a set of complementary HRM features which are not in themselves characteristics of partnership, but which are crucial to its successful operation; these include single status and harmonisation, a commitment to employment security, and a willingness to invest in employee development and lifelong learning.

Running through each of these levels is the notion that partnership is rather more than merely a set of structures, but comprises key processes which govern the way in which organisations are managed.

The partnership idea certainly does not find universal support, however, and representatives of both employers and trade unions urge caution in its application. While some employers are keen to proclaim the virtues of partnership, others are equally hostile to the concept that more can be gained by working with trade unions rather than trying to marginalise their activities through exclusion or derecognition (Smith and Morton, 1993). Yet others question whether the time spent consulting with trade union representatives provides benefits in terms of improved organisational performance. The partnership principles do not find total support from trade unionists either, with some arguing that working with managements to find joint solutions to issues confronting the employing organisation is akin to 'sleeping with the enemy' (Marchington, 1994a). Far from leading to improvements in conditions of employment and long-term security, it is argued that partnerships merely help to legitimise decisions which managements would have made anyway, in the process rendering them less susceptible to challenge through collective bargaining.

These introductory comments set the scene for the remainder of this chapter, which aims to do three things. First, it considers the attitudes of managers and shop stewards towards partnership, by drawing upon research conducted by the author and colleagues at UMIST (Godfrey, 1994; Godfrey and Marchington, 1996; Marchington, 1994a) as well as reports from the IPA. Second, it explores the European dimension to partnership, focusing in particular on the recent Directive on European Works Councils and reviewing the experiences of organisations which have implemented new initiatives in this area; this illustrates well some of the contested issues inherent in the partnership debate. Finally, the chapter re-examines the notion of partnership, placing this in the context of key human resource management concepts such as trust and commitment, power and control, and performance.

PARTNERSHIP: MANAGEMENT VIEWS

Employers which engage in partnership deals with their staff believe that a number of gains are made through these, as was apparent from the Welsh Water case analysed in Chapter 10. Among these were the following: streamlined bargaining arrangements through a single-table deal, greater workforce flexibility, increased employee commitment, and easing the process of change. In addition, Welsh Water introduced a new pay formula which is linked to the retail price index with a market safeguard, along with the development of a profit-related payment system. This goes some way beyond the majority of PRP schemes, as employees decide by ballot the percentage of pay to be placed in a pool, to which the employer also contributes.

There appear to be three general advantages for employers from partnership arrangements. First, it is felt that employees show greater commitment to the business and are prepared to think more carefully about the delivery of high-quality service and products if employers willingly enter into partnerships with their staff. Improved performance might be achieved if managements are prepared to promise employment security, as Coupar and Stevens reported in the case of Toyota in Chapter 9 of this book. Here, management recognised that it was unrealistic to expect employee commitment to improved company performance without any explicit link with individuals' needs for employment security. Similarly, Nissan's Communication Philosophy specifically relates employee commitment to the company's upward, downward and lateral communication channels through which employees gain an understanding of organisation-wide developments and performance levels. Many of the employers in Marchington and colleagues' (1992) study for the Employment Department also identified the contribution which an open management style made to greater levels of employee commitment, and the extent to which employees trusted managements who made efforts to involve them, either in a personal capacity or through their shop stewards. It should be remembered, of course, that 'commitment' is not a simple notion, but operates at a number of levels and in different directions. As Guest (1992) argues, employees may demonstrate commitment to their work group, trade union or occupation, as well as to their employing organisation.

Second, managements can gain contributions from shop stewards which can also lead to the achievement of better quality solutions, on the grounds that a broader range of ideas are considered in decision-making. Gaining inputs from groups with a diverse variety of 'mindsets' can encourage a more creative approach to problem-solving, and allow for the incorporation of alternative ideas in the framing of management decisions. Managements which take the view that employees are 'resourceful humans', a source of competitive advantage, can apply the same sort of reasoning to their relations with workplace union representatives.

Third, partnerships provide the basis for more orderly and stable relationships with trade union representatives. There are two aspects to this: first, the introduction of a partnership approach is frequently allied with a shift to single-table bargaining – as happened at Welsh Water. This requires trade unions to co-operate with each other, rationalising arrangements for representation and pay bargaining, and working together to establish a common agenda for employee interests. Since one of the 'problems' identified at the time of Donovan in the late 1960s and throughout much of the next decade was inter-union conflict, the opportunity to reduce or remove this can be a source of great attraction to managements. Incidentally, at a time when unions are also short of resources, it makes little sense for them to expend energy in battles with one another instead of establishing common objectives. The idea of a unified workplace trade union organisation may be of benefit to both the unions and management (Purcell, 1979). The second strand of this argument is that agreements which are made following extensive discussion with shop stewards have a greater legitimacy than those which are imposed. Even if this method of decision-making is more time consuming in its early stages, less time is spent in trying to correct mistakes or persuade employees after the event of the logic of management ideas (Marchington and Loveridge, 1979). Similarly, operating jointly devised and monitored committees and training sessions can also increase the likelihood that unionised employees will adopt a more positive stance towards these initiatives. This argument rests upon the assumption that management will have greater success in achieving its objectives by working with trade unions, in particular by encouraging union membership and participation in union affairs, as well as assisting unions to work together through support for joint shop steward committees.

But not all employers see the value of partnership deals. Reservations relate to operational issues, about the time devoted to running union–management committees or with the impact of their discussions on performance. The direct and indirect costs (e.g. travel and subsistence, management time) of spending time dealing with union representatives is frequently cited as a major problem, especially in multinational companies which bring together employees from various countries and when there is seen to be little direct impact either on shopfloor or office staff or on organisational performance. Language difficulties represent another problem: at Unilever, for example, deliberations about the setting-up of a European works council required nine booths of interpreters offering simultaneous translation to participants and anyone who wished to speak had to press a button and await their chance. Stirk (1996) felt that this 'prevented any spontaneous discussion and led to a series of prepared statements'. As in the debate about worker directors in Britain approximately 20 years ago (Brannen, 1983), many employers are concerned that shop stewards lack the knowledge and expertise to make a meaningful contribution to high-level discussions, especially those which require an understanding of financial and product market data. At root, employers have doubts that partnership schemes – as with any other industrial relations process – do improve organisational performance. Given the difficulties of measuring the impact of human resource management and employee relations processes, it is relatively easy for the critics to argue that partnership fails to make a directly quantifiable contribution.

Other employers are opposed to partnerships not so much for operational concerns, but at a more deep-rooted philosophical and strategic level. Some would prefer to see unions marginalised or derecognised, forced to withdraw from any meaningful role in the management of human resources. This argument rests upon the assumption that unions make no contribution to organisational performance, and that employers would be better rid of them while the opportunity exists, that is at a time when their power and influence is much reduced. While derecognitions have been on the agenda for a number of years (Claydon, 1989), it is also apparent that they have been more talked about than implemented. In cases where derecognitions have taken place however, employers have either sought to recast employment relations by a process of individualisation and an enhancement of employees' conditions, or they have removed trade unions and left nothing in their place (Gall and McKay, 1994).

PARTNERSHIP: SHOP STEWARD VIEWS

As with managements, shop stewards also have divergent views on the value of partnership, with some firmly and implacably opposed to the existence of such arrangements while others believe that this form of collaboration with management is the most effective way to protect and improve their members' employment conditions. Indeed, those who support the notion of partnership are generally aware of the potential hazards of working with management, and of the degree to which this may make it more difficult to oppose agreements which have been reached with union involvement; we return to this issue in the final section of the chapter.

The lure of partnership deals for shop stewards can be categorised under three headings. First, they welcome the provision of more extensive and timely information than was previously available, and the fact that there has been a shift to more open management styles. Many of the stewards in the Godfrey survey (1994) noted an increased frequency of meetings with management in recent years, especially of an informal nature which provided them with an opportunity to address issues in a more constructive manner. Shop stewards at a large manufacturing plant felt that 'meetings with management are now a lot less abrasive, and occur more often. Topics tend to be more about achieving a common goal rather than confrontational.' They also noted that the subject matter discussed at these meetings had also changed, with a clearer focus on business issues and rather less about conflict resolution and grievance handling. Being privy to commercially sensitive information had also helped them to understand better the position of the company, as well as helping them make a more constructive contribution. The stewards acknowledged that managements appeared at least to be trying to consult and adopt a more open and integrative approach, even though there were times when this was difficult. Among many of the public sector stewards, managers were still considered reasonable, even though they were having to implement decisions which it was felt were not of their making. The perception that management appeared genuine seemed to carry a lot of weight, as did the view that they were doing their best in difficult circumstances. One person involved summed up this feeling in the following way: 'At the moment, management is very supportive. They have acknowledged the importance of our role in writing, and we are moving towards a new climate by working together.'

The second advantage of partnerships, according to the stewards, is that it allows them to have greater influence over management decisions. The stewards at the companies in the Godfrey survey which had a 'genuine' partnership deal were quite convinced that their influence over management was substantial, and that it had increased since old adversarial relationships had been replaced by more open employee relations styles. There was a feeling that management had become more open thanks to the partnership programme, and that facilities had improved to provide stewards with a higher profile and the opportunity to play a bigger part in the company. One of the stewards made a clear comparison with the previous regime:

> *After three years when collective bargaining broke down, we have broadened our outlook and gained in credibility with management. Trade union representatives are now involved in joint decision-making rather than conflict resolution. We have joint identification of problems, the setting-up of joint problem-solving groups and joint team-building training with management.*

The third advantage relates to the maintenance of shop steward organisation. Partnership may act as a catalyst for closer inter-union relations or it may help to cement a more unified shop steward organisation which takes a broader establishment-wide perspective on new management initiatives. Rather than dissipating their energies by fighting among one another, there is an incentive for unions to work together and to promote co-operative relations. On defensive grounds as well, there may also be advantages to be gained from closer working relations. Without inter-union co-operation, managements may decide that derecognition or marginalisation offer more appealing prospects than partnership. Conversely, co-operation may represent to shop stewards 'an optimum strategy for maintaining strong workplace organisation' in the face of difficult circumstances (Batstone and Gourlay, 1986). In a number of the cases reported by the IPA, including Welsh Water, partnership had encouraged the unions to find ways of working together and presenting a common front to management in the event of shared problems.

This is not to say that shop stewards fail to recognise the potential pitfalls of entering into partnership arrangements. Their concerns are varied, but two seem particularly important. First, there are worries that the terms of the partnership are defined solely by management, and that the offer to become a partner is on strictly limited terms, falling some way short of envisaging equality of contribution and decision-making powers. Since it is typically managements which make the offer to unions to enter into a partnership, this is inevitably conceived in terms of business goals and objectives rather than based upon arguments of equality and democracy. Despite being stakeholders in the enterprise, it is unlikely (apart from exceptional cases) that employees will find that they or their representatives have been accorded that much influence. While employee views will be taken into account, some would argue that unless they are given equal weighting to that of shareholders, the whole exercise is little more than a sham. In such a situation, for shop stewards to enter into partnerships with management is merely to participate in the ultimate demise of the unions and the removal of the right to veto management decisions. One of the stewards in the Godfrey study summed it up thus: 'Management is very supportive of us and our role . . . provided our suggestions are to the company's benefit.' Another felt that, while having some influence at his plant, management 'tolerated' the unions rather than assisted them.

The second major concern about partnerships was the disparity between the espoused (intended) policy of senior management and the reality of workplace employee relations (Brewster *et al.*, 1983). There are of course many reasons for this: a lack of commitment on the part of managers to new programmes; covert opposition from managers in different functions or at different levels in the organisational hierarchy; production or customer pressures which take precedence over matters of employment relations; a lack of training or development for managers charged with the task of implementing new programmes. Whatever the cause, the result is the same: a distinction between what senior management publicise is happening and what really happens. This gap between rhetoric and reality can do much to undermine the success of partnership, or for that matter any other change programme. As Wilkinson *et al.* (1993) found in their longitudinal study of a chemical firm shop stewards felt that, despite being accorded more influence in the formal institutions, they were often by-passed by management keen to establish direct links with the workforce; as a consequence, their influence was reduced rather than enhanced.

Stewards from the 'partnership' organisations in the Godfrey survey often reported contradictions and discontinuities such as this, and indeed in one of the manufacturing companies not one respondent mentioned the programme while being questioned. Their concerns took two forms:

● Some stewards were sceptical about the depth of management's real commitment to partnership, accusing them of paying lip service to the idea while trying to undermine unions behind the scene.

● Many stewards referred to differences in practice due to contrasting attitudes among management members, and especially to the fact that junior managers adopted styles which flatly contradicted the broad principles of 'open management'.

The following quotes illustrate this well:

Superficially they are supportive, but there is a traditional underlying distrust of unions amongst many managers here.

On the whole, they prefer to gain our consent for things, but senior management can be very secretive and devious when they want to be. They will attempt to undermine the unions wherever possible.

We have tried to change the nature of the meetings, but the company's intentions are clear . . . they are meant to be an 'information sharing' session, in other words, management tell us what they will do.

EUROPEAN WORKS COUNCILS: PARTNERSHIP IN PROGRESS?

The most important public policy instrument in the partnership area is the European Works Council (EWC) Directive, which came into effect in September 1996. The centralist philosophy which underpins this initiative is in sharp contrast with the voluntarist approach promulgated by successive Conservative governments since the early 1980s, in which employers have been encouraged to adopt measures which suit their own circumstances and predilections, with an absolute minimum of statutory enforcement (Department of Employment, 1989). As the British election campaign of April 1997 illustrated well, the EWC issue (as part of the social framework) highlights continuing tensions between voluntarism and regulation both within the field of employment relations and indeed across the entire spectrum of management. When the Labour government was elected, with a massive majority, it soon became clear that the European social partnership model, through institutions such as works councils, would receive strong support from Westminster.

Since Britain entered the EU in the early 1970s, there have been a number of attempts to create a more coherent and uniform 'social' framework for the Community/Union by harmonising certain standards of employment and company law across the member states. Commencing with the Fifth Directive in 1972 (which proposed a two-tier board structure for all companies employing 500 or more, with at least one-third of the supervisory board drawn from employees), the idea of high-level representative participation has re-emerged in various guises since that time. More recently, in the latter part of the 1980s and early 1990s, further attempts have been made to harmonise policies in the areas of information, consultation and participation.

Seventeen countries in the European Economic Area are covered by the EWC Directive – that is, all EU states (except the UK which opted out of the Social Chapter at Maastricht in 1991), plus Iceland, Liechtenstein and Norway. The countries had two years from 1994 to put in place national legislation to implement the Directive, but by the September

1996 deadline only six had measures in place: Belgium, Denmark, Finland, Ireland, Norway, and Sweden. A further seven countries (including France, the Netherlands and Germany) were expected to finalise arrangements by the end of 1996, but the remainder were still some way off implementing legislation (*European Industrial Relations Review*, October 1996). The Directive applies to 'community-scale undertakings' and 'community-scale groups of undertakings' with at least 1000 employees in the member states and at least 150 in at least two member states. These numbers are the average employed over the previous two years, including part-timers. It is estimated that approximately 1200 multi-nationals are covered by the Directive, a third of which are German- or French-owned, with a further quarter being US- or UK-owned (Rivest, 1996).

Under the terms of the Directive, three options have been proposed (Carley, 1995):

1 set up voluntarily by September 1996 a transnational information and consultation forum with representatives of all employees, often referred to as Article 13 agreements
2 set up a negotiating committee (SNB) under the terms of the Directive to agree its own version of an EWC or other information and consultation procedure by September 1999
3 implement the minimum terms of the Directive by the same date.

There is scope for the negotiation of a customised agreement, but in the event of a failure to agree, a standard package will apply. In broad terms, this provides a template for the composition of the EWC and its remit, as well as a stipulation that an annual meeting should take place. At this meeting, the EWC meets with central management to be informed and consulted about the enterprise's progress and prospects in a number of areas, including the broad economic, financial and employment situation, as well as trends in employment and substantial changes in working methods. Obviously, a key point here is future employment projections, in particular closures, cutbacks and redundancies. The Commission is to review the operation of the directive in 2001. More detailed information on the options and the outcomes which are likely to emerge from deliberations of the SNB are available in Hall *et al.* (1995).

The Directive does not, as yet, have statutory force in relation to employees of multinational companies employed in Britain. Equally, although the provisions do apply to British companies which employ people elsewhere in the EU, managements are not yet required to include workers employed in Britain in an EWC. Both of these create the potential for internal divisions, even more so because of the large number of British companies covered by the provisions.

Of course, there has never been anything to prevent UK or other employers deciding of their own volition to set up EWCs, so as to keep up with 'good' practice and be seen as model employers (Hall, 1992; Ramsay, 1991). By the middle of 1992, for example, approximately 20 EU-owned companies had already taken this opportunity (Gold and Hall, 1992), a figure which had doubled by the end of 1994 (Hall *et al.*, 1995), nearly two years before the deadline date. By the end of 1995, about 80 multinationals had entered into voluntary agreements (Schulten, 1996), a figure which rose to between 200 and 250 by September 1996. While impressive at one level, this represents only about 20 per cent of those companies affected by the provisions (*European Industrial Relations Review*, October 1996). Voluntary agreements have been most popular in France and Germany, and in four industries (metalworking, chemicals, food, and construction) according to analysis by Rivest (1996), but even in these cases it still represents only a tiny minority of the companies covered by the EWC Directive. Many well-known names are among the companies with voluntary company-wide information and consultation arrangements: Bull, Rhône Poulenc, and Thomson (whose first EWC was set up in 1985) from France; Bayer, Siemens, and Volkswagen from Germany; Electrolux, Norsk Hydro, and Volvo from Scandinavia; and BP Oil, Coats Viyella, ICI, Marks and Spencer, and United Biscuits from the UK (Schulten, 1996). There was a rush to sign Article 13 agreements during the summer of 1996, with 46 separate companies making announcements about new or impending arrangements (*People Management*, 26 September 1996). Many of these are not known as EWCs, and the list of titles includes Employee Forum, European Group Committee, European Trades Union Committee, and European Information and Consultation Forum.

There has been a great deal of interest in these voluntary agreements, especially those which have been introduced into British-owned multinationals, given that they are not under any legal obligation to implement the EWC provisions. The United Biscuits European Consultative Council (UBECC) is particularly interesting given that it was one of the first to be agreed in Britain. The Council comprises 20 representatives from around the company's operations in Europe, of which 13 are drawn from UK sites. Members are nominated by the unions or works councils, and up to four full-time union officials are eligible to attend in addition to the worker representatives. Hall *et al.* (1995) note that the company has placed limitations on membership of UBECC, most importantly in being able to object to nominees if they are deemed 'inappropriate'. UBECC is chaired by the group human resources director, attended by the group chief executive and other divisional managers, and it is scheduled to take place annually. The Council focuses on the performance of the United Biscuits Group, its overall strategic direction, on jobs and employment policy, and on the broad commercial factors which affect the operations of the company. UBECC is precluded from dealing with employee relations issues which remain the preserve of national or local negotiating or consultative processes, operating rather like the 'adjunct' consultative committees described in Marchington (1994b). In an article in *People Management* in 1994, the company's group human resources director felt that the long history of consultation at United Biscuits and the company's single product market focus had both helped to ease the implementation of the works council. In a later assessment, following the first meeting of UBECC, it was described as 'the icing on the cake' of the company's communications policy, a forum which could begin the process of deepening understanding and allowing trust to build up. For its part, the GMB felt that UBECC provided staff with an opportunity to suggest alternative solutions to management and contribute to enhanced organisational performance, as well as being useful for the European unions to meet with each other (*People Management*, 13 July 1995).

Not all of the recently established Article 13 EWCs have escaped criticism however. At Bull, the French computer multinational, problems arose during 1995 between the management and the French unions whose members occupy about one-third of the employee places on the committee. The company's HR vice-president for Europe felt that the French unions were aggressive and hoped that the union representatives from other European countries would encourage them to adopt a less adversarial stance. At one stage, the French union representatives walked out of an EWC meeting, only to re-enter discussions after meeting with their colleagues from other countries (*People Management*, 13 July 1995). The employee representatives at Coats Viyella more recently accused the company of failing to consult over proposed job losses even though this is the kind of issue which might be expected to form an agenda item at an EWC. For its part, the company insisted that redundancies were 'hinted at' at a meeting earlier in the year without giving specific figures or the intended locations of cutbacks (*People Management*, 2 May 1996). PepsiCo ran into problems right at the outset in its attempt to set up a European employee forum to cover employees in 14 countries. The company chose Ireland as the country in which to register its arrangements, but there were claims of strong-arm tactics and blackmail, and a commitment has been made by the Irish government to amend its legislation to ensure that agreements have to be made with the workers who are to be covered by them (*People Management*, 12 September 1996).

Concerns such as these have led some commentators to argue that striving to beat the September 1996 deadline for Article 13 agreements was likely to be counter-productive, largely because these were 'extremely trade union friendly' in allowing for union experts to be present at the EWC (*People Management*, 30 May 1996). Wild (1996), who has advised a number of companies and employers' organisations in this area, has drawn up a nine-step plan which employers need to observe in setting up an EWC. In particular, managements are urged to ensure that they know and understand the legal position and the terms of the Directive, to have sufficient data on existing communications and consultation practices already operating in the company, and to engineer a good 'fit' between the new representative arrangements and the company's organisational and financial structures. Wild is concerned that some employers have been rushed into signing agreements without sufficient knowledge of the Directive, resulting in EWCs which are likely to be inefficient, costly and confusing. He estimates that £35 000 would be needed for a two-day meeting for 25 people from around a multinational company, with a Swedish firm reporting that its first works council negotiations cost £100 000 (Wild, 1996).

Many of the companies which have recently implemented new EWCs have a long history of partnership with trade unions at corporate level. In the case of ICI, for example, consultation has been in existence throughout the company for more than 50 years, structured to provide joint consultative committees (JCCs) from plant level to an annual central committee where trade union representatives met with directors. In circumstances such as these, converting a long-standing joint consultative committee structure into a European works council should prove relatively easy, even though employee representation now has to be at a transnational rather than nation state level. Managers within the organisation should be accustomed to dealing with employee representatives at all levels, sharing confidential information with little fear that it will be leaked, and working in a climate where mutual trust is already established. In short, in circumstances such as these, the implementation of an EWC is more a matter of fine-tuning rather than radical upheaval and substantial change.

Within this context, the decision by J. Sainsbury to introduce a new Group Staff Council in late 1996 is particularly interesting (*IRS Employment Trends*, December 1996). The company has operated with JCCs for over a decade, both at head office and in the areas where the unions recognised by the company (Union of Shop Distributive and Allied Workers (USDAW) and TGWU) were able to claim that their membership exceeded 500 staff. Even though these committees were attended by a senior personnel manager, there was no formal provision for centralised consultation in the company. Triggered partly by the EWC Directive, but also to a large extent by the results of an employee attitude survey, the company decided to introduce a new consultative structure. Although J. Sainsbury does not currently employ staff in other EEA countries, senior management felt that it would be better to gain experience of high-level consultative arrangements in advance of any expansion into Europe. A key forum in this new consultative structure are the local councils, most of which are at the stores, but there is also provision for each head office department, depot and other parts of the company as appropriate. The Group Council comprises 30 members from the company's 140 000 staff: 18 delegates are from the regions, one each from the depots and head office, four from Homebase, two from Savacentre, and two specifically from the unions. The Group Council is chaired by David Sainsbury and also attended by the group personnel director. The delegates were chosen by a voting process overseen by the Electoral Reform Society. The Group Council, which meets twice a year, is seen as the pinnacle of the system, as a supplement to local consultative arrangements. The delegates were given a training and induction programme designed to increase awareness of the business as a whole and help develop communications skills. The Sainsbury EWC-equivalent is one of the few to have been established in a company with very low levels of unionisation and without – at the time it was introduced – a presence in mainland Europe.

A key question which needs to be addressed is whether or not EWCs are likely to act as a spur to further partnerships or as a brake on their development. On the one hand, it might be anticipated that as senior managers and employee representatives become more used to working with one another and with corporate-level consultative arrangements, patterns of trust will be consolidated and further joint initiatives will emerge. Social partnership might then make a greater contribution to organisational success. On the other hand, if both parties enter the EWC with narrow and distributive bargaining agendas, the councils will not develop into co-operative and non-adversarial bodies which characterise the partnership organisations which have worked with the IPA. A lack of mutual trust would probably also prevent the emergence of partnerships at establishment level which are necessary for employees to make a meaningful contribution to performance improvements.

As yet, there is little research on the *practice* of EWCs as opposed to studies which focus on formal agreements (Schulten, 1996), although this is hardly surprising given that so many of these are new arrangements. As with partnerships in general, opinion is divided. Some employer bodies, such as UNICE (the European employers' confederation) regard the EWC Directive as inflexible and inappropriate, likely to cause problems as it would cut across decentralised management structures and local consultative arrangements (Gold and Hall, 1994). Others (for example, Hugh Stirk of Unilever) are concerned that the impact of EWCs will be minimal on shopfloor or office workers, even more so if trade unions end up filling all or most of the places on committees when they represent no more than 50 per cent of the workforce (*People Management*, 24 October 1996). Some employers clearly fear that EWCs will be a platform for the establishment of European-wide collective bargaining, resulting in delays to business decision-making (Hall *et al.*, 1995). At the other end of the spectrum, other employers see advantages to be gained from 'working with' rather than against employee representatives on an EWC, viewing this largely as a long-term development in the company to extend trust and generate a shared vision among employee representatives of future trends, as well as comply with current or projected legislation. Among those organisations which have established EWCs, the tendency has been to involve British employees in any arrangements even though there is no explicit need for this. Although equally divided in their opinion of EWCs in the early 1990s, British trade unions leaders are now rather more positive about this form of regulation, viewing it as an opportunity to make an input into corporate decisions at an earlier stage than in the past: as John Monks notes in Chapter 11, the right to information and consultation is a key part of the stakeholder society. Welch (1994) certainly feels that trade unions might be able to gain significantly from their participation in EWCs. As ever, though, given the range and diversity of employee relations in the UK, as well as substantial variations in employer and employee attitudes towards each other, ultimately the *formal arrangements* for EWCs may matter considerably less than the *processes* which accompany them.

PARTNERSHIP IN PERSPECTIVE

Each of the chapters in Part Two of the book refers in differing degrees of detail to the concepts underpinning the partnership debate, and indeed all of the topics which have been addressed in the book as a whole. Three of these are taken up again here:

- trust and commitment
- power and control
- performance.

First, there has been regular reference to the role of trust in the forging of partnerships between managers and employee representatives, and the impact which partnerships are expected to have on employee commitment to the organisation. For a number of years, commentators have focused on the role of trust as a major contributor to the achievement of effective human resource management and industrial relations (Purcell, 1981). On their own, it is argued, structures are unlikely to provide a sound and sustainable basis for the management of people, and the ways in which the parties interact is seen as crucial to the climate and culture of an organisation. Trust can be seen both as a prerequisite for the establishment of the partnership initially, and one of the outcomes of an ongoing relationship. It can be seen through the actions of the parties; a willingness to adopt an 'open' approach, to share information with the other party, to admit that much can be learned from other people (especially non-experts), and to value the importance of establishing long-term relationships. As Brown (1973) noted in relation to workplace collective bargaining many years ago, 'without trust, you are like a conger eel on ice'. It is also acknowledged that trust takes rather less time to lose than it does to establish in the first place, and that strong trust relations are required in order to cope with the setbacks which occur in employee relations.

The whole notion of trust is summed up well by the words of a personnel manager responsible for the operation of what could be described as a 'partnership' JCC long before the terminology became fashionable: 'The committee is important because it gives us a chance to develop a mutual trust and understanding of each other (which) means that discussions can take place in a much better frame of mind' (Marchington and Armstrong, 1981). Several of the chapters in this book note the positive impact which a partnership culture can have on employee commitment, as workers come to believe that management is making a genuine attempt to improve employee relations and reach agreements on employment security. A recent analysis of ACAS assistance to employing organisations by Kessler and Purcell (1996) also suggested a clear link between partnership and trust. They found that 'when employee representatives were actively involved in establishing the terms of reference and in implementing the agreed programme of change . . . trust levels increased by the greatest amount.' Moreover, '*real* participation at the critical stages is associated with the highest trust improvement scores' (Kessler and Purcell, 1996, my emphasis).

The second issue, that of power and control, remained implicit in most of the chapters in this section, although it figured more prominently in Claydon's analysis in Chapter 12 which treated partnership as a problematic and contested concept. This draws upon a tradition which regards management as conspiratorial, overwhelmingly preoccupied with finding ways to marginalise trade unions, and making use of opportunities to achieve closer working relations with shop stewards principally as a device to reduce employee solidarity and resistance to change. Some of the early labour process writers (such as Braverman, 1974) saw the employment relationship solely in terms of conflict and a struggle for control. According to this viewpoint, the interests of workers automatically collide with those of employers, since what is good for employers (capital) is inevitably bad for workers (labour) because surplus value – which is required in order to finance and reward capital – can only be achieved through the exploitation of workers. Workers who co-operate with employers, who take part in participation and involvement schemes by offering their advice and ideas to management, are effectively doing themselves out of jobs by helping organisations to become more efficient. In addition, by sharing their expertise with management, workers also make it more likely that their jobs in the future will become deskilled (or disappear altogether) as employers replace labour with new technology. Others (e.g. Smith and Morton, 1993) have assumed that employers have been engaged in a conspiracy to weaken and exclude trade unions since the early 1980s, and that all their initiatives have been promulgated with this as its principal objective. Some authors have applied this message to a critique of joint consultation, arguing that a closer involvement of union representatives has the effect of convincing them of the 'logic and inescapability' of management plans and solutions (Terry, 1983).

Others (for example, Marchington and Parker, 1990) disagree with this perspective, suggesting that shop stewards, especially those with experience, are usually able to determine which data they receive from management should be accepted and which should be treated with caution. It seems somewhat patronising to assume that employee representatives will be unable to disentangle fact from opinion, and also rather perverse to assume that managements will automatically and continually adopt anti-labour stances.

At the same time, however, opinions about whether partnerships increase or decrease employee control remain contested precisely because the employment contract is built upon both conflict *and* co-operation. Paul Edwards (1995) reminds us that employees have shared interests with employers (e.g. in the development of new skills and the greater employment security which may come from a more successful business), as well as potential conflicts (e.g. in new demands upon them and disputes about levels of reward for taking on new responsibilities). He regards the employer–employee relationship as characterised by 'structured antagonism' which is created by the *indeterminacy* of the employment contract. The contract can never be constructed precisely enough to specify every aspect of an individual's work, and it relies upon both employer and employee showing some degree of trust and discretion for it to be discharged effectively. The contract is both contradictory and antagonistic: contradictory because managers not only have to exercise control but also learn how to tap and release creativity, yet antagonistic because workers offer the only opportunity for employers to realise surplus value.

The issue of performance is equally problematic at an empirical level. Some observers argue that partnerships, and especially EWCs and other 'imposed' arrangements, are inefficient for a number of reasons: they cost money and time to implement and administer; they make no explicit contribution to productivity and quality improvements; they give implicit support for a system which focuses on processes rather than outcomes; and they provide trade unions with an opportunity to establish contact with each other and the potential for cohesive resistance to management. One of the problems with measures of human resource practices, however, are that they are extremely hard to quantify. For example, a company with a long-standing partnership arrangement may point to the absence of industrial action and a positive approach to change on the part of its staff as evidence of success. But it is difficult to quantify the 'absence' of industrial action, and impossible to determine whether or not the partnership arrangement actually contributed to this. Moreover, it is a matter of conjecture whether a more aggressive stance may have produced higher levels of productivity, at least in the short term, in any single organisation. Much depends upon managements and trade unions accepting partnerships as an act of faith.

There are some data at an aggregate level which appear to suggest that partnership and co-operative labour relations are associated with higher levels of performance. It is difficult to determine directions of causality however, and it is just as feasible that successful organisations are prone to implement partnership deals as it is that partnerships contribute to organisational success. Notwithstanding this, the data come from a number of studies and several different countries. For example, using US data, both Cooke (1989) and Cutcher-Gershenfeld (1991) found links between collaborative union–management activities, productivity and product quality. Data from the Australian Workplace Industrial Relations Survey also show a correlation between representative participation arrangements – such as JCCs – and the quality of management–employee relations, co-operation in the management of change, productivity, and product/service quality (Lansbury and Marchington, 1993). More recently, Fernie and Metcalf (1995) argue that 1990 WIRS data – which show that JCCs 'improve the climate of industrial relations and productivity growth, and have no malign effects' – should cause us to question why the previous British government and some employers' organisations were so opposed to European-wide initiatives. It would appear that the concerns are not so much with employee involvement per se, but with the methods used by the Commission in trying to achieve greater harmonisation.

CONCLUSION

This section of the book has been concerned with partnerships between employers and employees, typically though not exclusively through trade union representation. It comprises a range of views about partnership, from the more enthusiastic proponents such as Willy Coupar and Bryan Stevens of the Involvement and Participation Association to the more sceptical academic critique advanced by Tim Claydon in Chapter 12. Chapter 10 by

Colin Thomas and Brian Wallis described the practical implementation of partnership at Welsh Water, while in Chapter 11 John Monks outlined some of the policy and institutional impediments to its extension across the country as a whole. Ian Beardwell analysed the relationship between human resource management and employee voice in the partnership organisation in Chapter 13, while in this chapter I have tried to place the whole issue in a European, attitudinal and theoretical context. In sum, therefore, Part Two of the book represents a detailed and focused review of the partnership concept.

There are now many examples of partnership in practice but, as Coupar and Stevens remind us, the practice itself is hardly novel. Some organisations – such as ICI and the John Lewis Partnership – have a long history of this form of co-operative relations. Others have developed arrangements over the course of the last decade, with Welsh Water being a case in point. There, partnership first emerged during the late 1980s as part of a shift from the traditional industrial relations environment which existed prior to privatisation. An important aspect of the Welsh Water experience has been the series of agreements since 1991, each of which has been put to a ballot of the workforce. Support for the various partnership deals has grown from a ratio of 2:1 in favour in 1991 through to 7:1 in the most recent ballot in 1997. A lot of work has been done at Welsh Water jointly by the unions and management, and this has undoubtedly helped to secure such a large majority in favour of partnership, despite the fact that it has also been associated with job cuts at the company.

The growth in the number of organisations claiming to practise partnership has not been accompanied by any clearer definition of what it actually constitutes; indeed, as we mentioned earlier in this chapter, there is a danger that the terminology has become more confusing, acting as a catch-all for employee involvement or 'best practice' human resource management. Case studies describing partnership deals typically include some or all of the following: employment security, flexibility, information and consultation, employee voice and representation, 'fair' levels of pay and reward systems, and a commitment to training. It is clear that a tighter definition is required, one which seeks to differentiate between the *components* of partnership – as a set of operational practices and processes and a system of values and behaviours – and the human resource management features which are a *complement* to partnership, such as single status, employment security, and lifelong learning. Each of the latter features may well be found in the partnership organisation, but they are not exclusive to this type of workplace nor are they central to the partnership concept. A more rigorous definition of partnership is therefore long overdue, the bare bones of which have been articulated earlier in this chapter.

It is also evident that partnership has significant implications for the way in which organisations are managed, as well as for employees and trade unions. It is clear that managers in this type of organisation need to be able to adopt a much more open stance, both in relation to individual employees and to trade union representatives. On several occasions in this section, there has been reference to the notion of trust: the importance of building new relations, the role of managers in sharing ideas and information, and in recognising that employees have much to contribute to successful organisational performance. The pressures on trade union representatives are even more intense in many respects, largely because an involvement in partnership requires them to adopt integrative rather than distributive approaches to bargaining, and in being able to justify their actions to members who regard them as collaborating with the enemy. In the Welsh Water case, it was argued that employees need to understand that convivial relations between union representatives and managers should not be taken as a sign that the former have been 'incorporated' into management.

There is little doubt that the proponents of partnership tend to employ a win–win conception of power, one in which managers and employees are both able to gain from more open systems. Other commentators are less inclined to see employment relationships in such a positive and harmonious manner, and prefer to analyse power as a zero-sum or at least more complex concept. Drawing upon Clegg's work, Claydon examines partnership using notions such as problematisation to suggest that union representatives might seek to 'enrol' managers and members by persuading them of the indispensability of their solutions for other parties' problems. However, he argues that union officials have to exercise care in ensuring that it is *they* who are 'enrolling' managers and employees into their interpretation of events, and not the reverse. Moreover, he also calls into question whether a term such as flexibility is value-free, and how this might be reinterpreted as consonant with work intensification and management control. His treatment of partnership as just one of the strategies which can be adopted by unions, the others being militancy and incorporation, might help us to evaluate which approach yields the better results for employees/union members, and in which circumstances.

For John Monks, partnership and stakeholding represent a practical step forward for unions and their members, as well as for employing organisations which have to compete in world markets. Yet he is concerned that there are fundamental barriers to the extension of partnership in modern Britain, principally due to factors beyond the control of personnel managers and trade union representatives. His argument is that structures of corporate governance encourage a short-term perspective on financial returns, which ultimately undermine the development of long-term and stable relationships between employers and employees based on partnership principles. Beardwell has similar anxieties, based at the level of the organisation, about the potential incompatibility between employee voice as a component of partnership and the unitarist assumptions which underpin some versions of human resource management. There is a danger that mutuality and unity are seen as synonymous, and that the notion of 'employee voice' is equated solely with contributions which lead to improvements in performance – to the neglect of expressions of concern by employees which challenge current priorities. If partnership is to be seen as an example of mutuality, employees must be allowed to articulate concerns about work organisation and management behaviour (say, in relation to excessive workloads and aggressive supervisory styles) just as much as they are encouraged to offer ideas for enhancing the quality and quantity of their work.

The contributions in this section of the book clearly demonstrate that partnership is still a relatively undefined concept, with differing views about how it operates in practice, about its relationship with human resource management, and about prospects for its extension to more organisations. Nevertheless, the election of a Labour government which is committed to a European model of social partnership and the implementation of the Social Chapter ensures that it will remain at the centre of political, practical and academic debate at the millennium.

Note

I am grateful to Adrian Wilkinson and Irena Grugulis, colleagues at the Manchester School of Management, UMIST, and to Graham Godfrey of Coventry University, for comments on an earlier draft of this chapter, and for their contribution to the development of ideas about the nature of partnership.

PART 3

The pursuit of multiple and parallel flexibilities

15

Employment flexibility: threat or promise?

MIKE EMMOTT

Institute of Personnel and Development

SUE HUTCHINSON

Bath University School of Management

INTRODUCTION

In Part One changes to the overall form of organisations, trust and the psychological contract in general were discussed. In Part Two issues of employee voice were considered in the context of developments in involvement, participation and partnership. Part Three considers broader questions concerned with the changing and more flexible nature of work. In this opening chapter to Part Three, we present an audit of the current state of affairs in the UK in the areas of working time, part-time work, temporary work, self-employment and sub-contracting. After considering the benefits and disadvantages for employers, we review the evidence on employee attitudes. Finally, we consider the managerial issues of casualisation, control, commitment, career development, consultation and communication.

If there is a single word that encapsulates our perception of many of the changes that are currently taking place in the labour market, it is 'flexibility'. Its impact can be seen, for example, in employees' changing attitudes to their work (as monitored through the 'psychological contract'), in employers' often misguided enthusiasm for 'downsizing', and in the decay of institutions and processes that have helped to define the employment relationship in the past.

As the UK economy has emerged from the recession of the early 1990s, and unemployment has continued to fall, the realisation has dawned that there will be no return to the labour market of the 1960s and 1970s. For example, a declining proportion of the workforce is in full-time, permanent employment; more women are employed, while 30 per cent of men between the ages of 50 and 65 are economically inactive; the demand for low-skilled workers is falling, while that for managerial and professional staff has increased. The longer term significance of these changes is however not clear. Major studies, for example by the Royal Society of Arts (1995), have focused on 'the future of work', with the implication that work as we know it may be disappearing. As noted in Chapter 1, many of these issues cannot be separated from changes in the nature of work in society.

Where does the word 'flexibility' come from? The concept of labour market flexibility is a familiar one to economists, meaning the speed with which employers or employees respond to changes in circumstances and market failure is remedied or avoided. In a flexible labour market, for example, reduced demand for unskilled labour means that pay rates for such occupations will fall; and unemployed people will have an incentive to apply for jobs which they are capable of doing. A major policy aim of governments in the UK in the 1980s and 1990s has been to see that the 'supply side' of the economy is functioning smoothly so as to increase levels of education and training, reduce long-term unemployment and increase national competitiveness. A key component of supply side economics is labour market flexibility.

Since the mid-1980s the commitment to flexibility has had an important influence on the UK's employment policies. In 1991, for example, the Employment Department's overall aim was stated as being 'To support economic growth by promoting a competitive, efficient and flexible labour market' (Employment Department Group, 1991). In the opinion of successive Conservative governments, other European countries had imposed an unacceptable level of regulation on their labour markets. The Labour government elected in 1997 maintains this stance. A majority of members of the European Union has high non-wage labour costs and employment legislation in those countries places constraints on employers' ability to hire and fire. This has produced relatively low increases in employment and continuing high levels of unemployment. In the UK, the government has adopted a deregulatory agenda which, while leaving intact the bulk of employment protection legislation passed in the 1970s (or even expanding it at the margins), has weakened trade unions' ability to take industrial action, repealed the legislation on wages councils and increased the length of time employees have to work for an employer before they can bring a claim for unfair dismissal. Although the direct effect of these policies is unclear, they have underlined the degree of flexibility characterising the current employment relationship.

This chapter tries to make sense of the idea of employment flexibility. First what *is* flexibility, and how do we know it when we see it? What is changing in respect of those elements of flexibility that can most readily be measured because they are reflected in the nature of the employment contract itself: are we facing a fundamental shift in the employment relationship, as was argued in Part One? And what are the implications for employers and employees: does flexibility herald an era of casualisation and insecurity?

WHAT IS EMPLOYMENT FLEXIBILITY?

Employment flexibility is not an easy term to define and has been categorised in many different ways (*see* the discussion on the range of 'battles' associated with seven forms of flexibility in Chapter 1). In practice however the most commonly used terms are as follows:

- **Functional flexibility** relates to the employer's ability to deploy labour on different tasks: for example, it may mean a reduction in demarcation lines between occupations, or in the boundaries between individual jobs. There are fewer jobs reserved for employees with specific occupational backgrounds: in the NHS, for example, nurses are increasingly taking on functions formerly reserved for medical staff. Job definitions become increasingly unhelpful in many workplaces, particularly where teamworking or multiskilling is introduced.

- **Financial or wages flexibility** is the ability of pay and payment systems to respond to changes in the demand for and supply of labour, and to reward and encourage good performance. From 'payment by results' for production workers and bonuses for high performance, e.g. by sales staff, performance- (or profit-)related pay has spread to other groups throughout the workforce. This element of flexibility is important to employers as a means of linking costs to output and reducing the importance of the link between pay and prices.
- **Labour mobility**, or the movement of people to different jobs, occupations and geographical areas according to economic conditions.
- **Flexibility in the pattern and organisation of work** which describes a wide range of practices including:
  - numerical flexibility, or the ability of firms to adjust the number of employees or the number of hours worked to reflect business needs. Many more employees are now on short-term or temporary contracts, or are employed on a part-time basis, or are self-employed. This issue is discussed more fully later. We note here simply that the changes are driven primarily by changes in the nature of employers' business. For example, supermarkets employ part-time labour so as to better match the hours when customers prefer to shop; temporary contracts for nurses may be used to match peak demand for hospital services;
  - working time, or temporal flexibility, which relates to variations in the number and timing of hours worked. Examples include flexitime, annual hours contracts and overtime;
  - locational flexibility, or flexibility for employees to work away from the office base, e.g. homeworking and teleworking.

How can we measure flexibility and progress towards the flexible firm? Chris Brewster discusses models of flexibility from a theoretical perspective in the next chapter. At this point it is important to note that in the 1980s the 'flexible firm' model was developed on the hypothesis that firms were achieving numerical flexibility by employing a 'core peripheral' labour strategy. The model assumes that firms use an internal market for core jobs and the external labour market for other jobs. The core consists of full-time permanent employees who perform key tasks, and the peripheral workforce of part-time, temporary and self-employed labour. By adjusting the 'peripheral' workforce the firm can meet changes in product/customer demand, thereby offering a high degree of security to the core workforce. This model has attracted much discussion, the critical issue being whether increases in the use of part-time, temporary and self-employed labour reflect a deliberate management strategy to create a flexible workforce. Most of the evidence suggests, however, that employers' decisions about the type of employment to offer tend to be made in an *ad hoc* manner, and casts doubts over whether employers have adopted clearly defined strategies.

Much of the debate in the UK about the flexible labour market has been concerned with the trends in non-standard forms of employment such as more part-time work, self-employment and greater use by employers of contracting out work. The impacts of tenure, turnover and absenteeism were covered in Chapter 8. Over the last few years numerous surveys report that people feel more insecure in their jobs and that employees are suffering from increased stress. There are many reasons for this, including longer working hours and increased workloads, but a number of commentators have also pointed to the growth in these 'non-standard' forms of employment. A recent research report by Gregg and Wadsworth (1995), for example, found that between 1975 and 1995 the proportion of the working population in full-time tenured (or permanent) employment fell from 55.5 per cent to 35.9 per cent. Others however, such as David Guest and Kate MacKenzie Davey of Birkbeck College (1996) report that the extent of the 'flexibility revolution' has been much exaggerated and suggest that 'the traditional organisation . . . is alive and well' (Wilsher, 1996).

Nonetheless, there are many types of non-standard forms of employment and their implications for employees and employers are diverse. Before considering the consequences of a more flexible labour market we present some factual information about trends and characteristics of major forms of non-standard working.

TRENDS IN WORKING TIME FLEXIBILITY

According to official figures (Labour Force Survey (LFS), 1993) almost 40 per cent of those in employment are part of the so called 'flexible' workforce (defined as all those working who were *not in full-time permanent employment*) representing an increase of 1.25 million since 1986. These figures are, however, likely to underestimate the size of the flexible workforce since the more traditional workforce of full-time permanent employees can also be flexible by, for example, varying the number and timing of hours worked on a weekly or daily basis or the place of work.

Most studies suggest that flexible working is set to increase. A recent survey by the Institute of Management and Manpower (1995) found that over the next four years 80 per cent of employers predict an increase in flexible working and 70 per cent in the incidence of contracting out. A survey on local government (an area with a high incidence of flexible working) predicts that '. . . if current trends continue, annual hours, career break schemes and working from home are likely to become a standard part of local government employment in future years' (New Ways to Work, 1995).

Part-time working

Almost a quarter of the workforce, or 6.4 million people, now work part time (LFS Spring 1996) and the incidence of part-time working in the UK is one of the highest in the European Union. Over the period spring 1984 to spring 1996 the number of part-time workers rose by 31 per cent, compared to a rise of just 3.2 per cent in the number of full-time workers. According to most reports, this growth is likely to continue. For example, the Institute of Employment Research at Warwick University forecasts that the number working part time could rise to 7.3 million – 32 per cent of the working population – by the millennium.

The growth in part-time working, however, is not just a phenomenon of the 1980s and 1990s. In fact, growth was greatest during the 1960s to early 1970s when the proportion working part time increased from 9 to 16 per cent of the workforce. In the last 25 years the growth in part-time jobs has been fairly steady, averaging around 2.5–3 per cent a year. According to a recent report on the flexible labour market (Beatson, 1995) changes in the industrial composition of employment account for a good deal of the growth in part-time work between 1971 and 1991. Analysis shows that although less than half of the growth in part-time employees between 1971 and 1981 was due to changes in industrial composition, between 1981 and 1991 nearly three-quarters of the growth in part-time employment could be accounted for by shifts in industrial structure. This suggests that the extent of the shift towards part-time work within individual industries may not be as significant as the overall growth in part-time jobs would imply.

What are the main characteristics of part-time employment? Part-time jobs are predominantly held by women. In summer 1995 almost 82 per cent of part-time jobs were held by women, representing almost 45 per cent of all women in employment. In contrast only 8 per cent of all men in employment work part time. However, the proportion of women in the part-time workforce has been falling – in 1984 the corresponding percentage of part-time jobs held by women was 89 per cent, so male part-time employment has increased faster. In fact the number of male part-timers has more than doubled over this period (albeit from a relatively small base) compared to a 20 per cent increase for women. Much of the growth in male part-timers came in 1991–92 reflecting the effects of the recession on men's ability to obtain full-time employment. Half of all part-time employees are women aged 25–49 and the percentage of employees who work part time is highest for those above retirement age and for young people aged 16–19.

Over 90 per cent of all part-timers work in the growing service sector such as public education and the health service. The banking, finance and insurance sector have shown the most dramatic recent increases: part-time working in this sector increased by over 66 per cent between spring 1984 and spring 1995 (LFS). This is followed by public education and health services (37 per cent) and distribution, hotels and restaurants (21.1 per cent). Only two sectors show a decrease over this period – manufacturing and energy and water. Part-time jobs still remain principally in unskilled work (such as secretarial or clerical work) or lower grades in skilled and professional jobs, although there is a gradual shift towards more part-time openings at senior levels. Part-timers may be critical to the quality of customer service, for example in retailing, where they can provide cover at busy times or outside normal hours. Pressure is likely to continue to improve the pay and conditions of (often female) part-time employees and this will tend to reinforce the integration of part-timers into the mainstream workforce.

Nearly 90 per cent of part-time jobs are permanent. Part-time jobs are typically of shorter duration than full-time jobs partly because of the characteristics of those who work part time, such as students or women returners to work. There are, however, some strong gender differences. On the whole part-time working appears to offer women stable and relatively secure employment. Some 41 per cent of women working part time had more than five years' service in autumn 1993 compared to 48 per cent of women working full-time; around 21 per cent had more than ten years and 25 per cent between two and five years' service. For male part-timers however the proportion with over five years' service is much lower – 19 per cent (compared to 57 per cent of men working full-time) suggesting a higher turnover of jobs for men than women.

According to a recent CBI survey (1994) a typical firm employs very few part-timers, on average only 5 per cent of staff. Only in the very largest of firms – those employing

50 000 or more employees – did part-time employment rise dramatically to an average of 18 per cent. This is consistent with the findings of another recent survey by Reed Personnel Services and the Home Office Partnership (1995), which showed that the incidence of use of flexible working increased with the size of the organisation.

Temporary workers

A slightly different picture of the labour market emerges, however, when we look at another form of 'non-standard employment' – temporary work. Since 1984, temporary jobs have increased by almost 31 per cent, compared to a 0.5 per cent increase in permanent jobs. Between 1984 and 1991 the proportion of temporary workers in the labour force changed little, remaining at around 5 per cent. Since 1992, however, there has been a significant increase in the incidence of temporary working – in the order of 30 per cent between spring 1992 and spring 1996. By spring 1996 there were around 1.6 million workers in Britain representing over 7 per cent of the workforce. In absolute terms most of this increase has come from the more widespread use of fixed-term contracts. In percentage terms, however, agency temping shows the most dramatic increases – rising by 148 per cent over this period, followed by fixed-term contracts which rose by 39 per cent.

What are the characteristics of temporary working? LFS figures (spring 1996) show that over half of all temporary employees (51 percent) are on fixed-term contracts. This is followed by casual work (20 per cent), agency temping (13 per cent), 'other' (10 per cent), and seasonal work (5 per cent). Women are more likely to hold temporary jobs than men. Women made up just under 53 per cent of the temporary workforce in summer 1995. Part-time temporary workers represent 46 per cent of the temporary workforce and of part-time temporary employees the largest category (covering 37 per cent of such employment) was fixed-term contract work.

The significance of temporary jobs on the labour market is rather more than their 7 per cent share might at first suggest. According to the LFS, temporary jobs account for almost a third of all engagements since 1984 – so a significant proportion of the jobs taken by the unemployed and by new entrants to the labour market will be temporary. This is supported by the claimant unemployed figures which show that nearly half of the people leaving the count return within a year, i.e. their jobs are short term. Temporary jobs are also disproportionately filled by relatively new entrants to the labour market: for example, people under 25 account for 15 per cent of those in employment but 29 per cent of temporary employees.

Temporary jobs however do appear to be lasting longer. In 1995, 42 per cent of people in temporary jobs had been in that job for over a year compared to 37 per cent in 1990. (In fact 12 per cent of all temporary workers have been with their employer for five years or more). This is undoubtedly due to the growth in fixed-term contracts which are typically of longer duration than other forms of temporary working, often extending to a number of years. Some employers may misguidedly believe that the use of fixed-term contracts for less than two years will relieve them of their obligations under employment protection legislation; if so they may be disappointed.

The growth in temporary working since 1992 is primarily attributed to the slow climb out of the recession (with many employers cautious to take on permanent employees) and the relatively weak labour market. Other factors include improvements in maternity rights which has led to an increasing number of women taking maternity leave and means that there is an increasing demand for temporaries to cover absence. The employment agencies themselves have also had a part to play by trying to lift the quality of the services they offer to clients; for example, by becoming involved in longer term supply contracts and in supplying whole teams of people to work on sites. In some arrangements, for example, the agency takes responsibility for the management of an entire department or function in the client organisation, including recruitment, training, performance contribution, allocation of work and administration of benefits.

Recent reports also suggest that many of these new jobs are being taken by students working to supplement their grants and loans. In fact there are now almost twice as many temporary as permanent workers in the 16–24 age group (LFS) although it is not clear how many are students.

Care should be taken not to exaggerate the significance of temporary work, though the fact that its share of total employment has been rising in the 1990s could indicate an emerging trend. A recent report by Business Strategies Ltd (1996) forecast an increased rate of growth of temporary jobs – with most of the growth coming from the public sector due to contracting out – and this view appears to be shared by other analysts. Only time will tell, however, if this is the case; a sustained economic recovery could see a return to more permanent jobs.

Self-employment

There are currently around 3.25 million self-employed people in Britain or around 13 per cent of the workforce, compared to only 7.3 per cent in 1979. Self-employment fell during the 1970s before growing rapidly (by 96 per cent) between spring 1979 and spring 1990. Between spring 1990 and spring 1993 the number and proportion of the workforce in self-employment fell slightly, only to rise again between spring 1993 and spring 1994. In the year to spring 1995 the number continued to rise, although the proportion of the workforce in self-employment fell slightly. Self-employment is more common amongst men than women. In spring 1995, 17.5 per cent of the male workforce in employment was self-employed, compared to only 7 per cent of women. The proportion of the self-employed who are women, however, has risen from 19 per cent in spring 1979 to 24.3 per cent by spring 1995.

The construction industry and hotels and restaurants account for the highest numbers of self-employed people, although the highest proportion who are self-employed compared to all people in employment are to be found in the agriculture and fishing sector. Recent growth in self-employment (between 1984 and 1995) has been concentrated in manufacturing (32.3 per cent), construction (32.7 per cent), banking, finance and insurance (81.1 per cent, probably due to deregulation) and public administration and education (25.4 per cent).

Figures for autumn 1995 show the number of self-employed has fallen in non-manual occupations by 0.4 per cent and in manual occupations by 1 per cent. There were rises in four out of the nine occupational groupings – the largest being in personnel and protective services (minus 7.5 per cent) and in selling (minus 11.7 per cent). On a sectoral basis there were rises in four out of the nine sectors, the largest being 'other services' (3.5 per cent), while the largest fall was in distribution and hotels (minus 6.5 per cent). It is likely that self-employment is cyclical – growing in recessionary times and falling when the economy and permanent employment prospects improve.

Sub-contracting

Sub-contracting, as defined by ACAS (ACAS, 1988) involves 'workers who carry out work at the establishment who are either self-employed or employed by an outside organisation'. Unlike most other forms of flexible working, sub-contracting might not necessarily involve 'non-standard' forms of employment – an employee may be a full-time permanent employee in the contractor firm.

Sub-contracting allows employers to vary the size of their workforce according to fluctuations in demand, and buy in services from specialist organisations. There are disadvantages, however, such as the costs involved in monitoring sub-contractors' performance and ensuring that agreed standards are adhered to. These costs can exceed the costs of direct employment. Furthermore, once a contract is entered into it is difficult to change and therefore may be inflexible. It is often reported that sub-contractors 'lack commitment' although the survey evidence is thin. The nature of sub-contract working may also mean that training is neglected.

Evidence of the extent of sub-contracting in the UK is limited (one reason being measurement difficulties) and not particularly recent. A report by ACAS (ACAS, 1988) found that 77 per cent of all respondents used outside contractors and as many as 90 per cent of manufacturers sub-contract. According to data from the Price Waterhouse/Cranfield survey (Brewster *et al.*, 1993) by 1992 the number of organisations not using any form of sub-contracting was 20 per cent. The 1987 Employers Labour Use strategies survey found that a quarter of establishments surveyed did not use any sub-contractors. Of the remainder, the services most frequently contracted out were maintenance, cleaning and transportation. Comparing 1983 with 1987 there was an increase in the percentage of employers using sub-contractors for each of the types of work specified. A more recent survey by the Institute of Management and Manpower (1995) showed 70 per cent of organisations contracting out non-core operations. The ACAS survey also reveals a significant correlation between size of organisation and the use of sub-contracting; the larger the organisation the more frequently sub-contracting was used.

On the basis of these surveys it would appear that between 70 and 80 per cent of firms use outside contractors and that sub-contracting increased during the 1980s. With the widespread adoption of compulsory competitive tendering in the public sector this is likely to continue well into the 1990s.

Other forms of flexible working

According to LFS (1993) the most common types of other flexible arrangements are shift-working (19 per cent of the workforce), flexitime (12 per cent of the workforce), annual hours working (9 per cent of the workforce), job sharing (3.6 per cent of the workforce). Of recent interest has been the growth in zero-hours contracts although little is known of the extent of their use. With the possible exception of flexitime, most of these working arrangements appear to be on the increase as employers seek greater flexibility.

WHY EMPLOYERS ADOPT FLEXIBLE WORKING PRACTICES

The most common factors driving organisations to adopt more flexible working practices are well known:

- increased competitiveness both nationally and globally
- new technology
- changes in labour demand and supply (that is, changes in the types of employment available and changes in the composition of labour supply such as increased participation by women)
- government policies (*see* Beatson, 1995).

Employers benefit from flexibility since it increases their freedom of action. It enables them to redirect their efforts, refocus resources and consider new approaches. In many ways, employment flexibility is more important for what it gets away from than for its positive content. In fact, it was argued in Chapters 4 and 8 that managers have been slow to take advantage of the freedoms they now have, for example, to change working practices. At the same time, many are beginning to recognise that using the flexibility to reduce the size of their labour force can have negative effects on efficiency and profitability.

With regard to flexibility in the pattern and organisation of work the main benefits for employers are that it:

1 enables employers to match work provisions more closely with customer/product demand
2 reduces fixed costs, e.g. homeworkers do not require office space
3 aids recruitment and retention of employees
4 increases productivity – those working for a reduced period of time are likely to be less tired and less stressed
5 reduces absence and labour turnover.

For example, in the case of part-time working the main benefits are seen to be that it provides flexibility of cover and allows employers to match part-time hours to specific business needs. Before the European Court of Justice ruling in *R* v *Secretary of State for Employment ex parte Equal Opportunities Commission* in 1994, there were also differences in levels of employment protection which might have encouraged employers to use part-time workers; however these legislative differences have now been removed. There may be further cost advantages if there is differential access to non-wage benefits such as occupational pensions or sick pay. The system of NI contributions encourages employers to use certain forms of part-time work, because employers do not have to pay NI contributions for employees with weekly earnings below the lower earnings limit.

A further possible motive for employing part-timers is to avoid making redundancies. For example, the National Westminster Bank recently announced proposals to introduce worksharing in the form of a four-day week in order to cope with cuts in employment estimated to mean the equivalent of 15 000 jobs.

In the case of temporary working, most of the evidence (such as the *Employers' Labour Use Strategies*, McGregor and Sproull, 1991) suggests that the demand for temporary staff is primarily on an *ad hoc* and emergency supply basis to cover, for example, seasonal surges in demand, absence, to carry out one-off projects or to provide specialist skills.

There is also recent evidence to suggest that temporary work could be a stepping stone into permanent employment – a study by the Institute of Employment Studies (Atkinson and Rick, 1996) showed that a fifth or more of employers used temporary jobs as trials for permanent ones.

The main disadvantages for employers associated with flexible working patterns are:

1 increased training costs
2 higher direct costs – for example, part-timers who receive pro rata benefit
3 more complex administration
4 communication difficulties
5 management of the 'flexible' workforce.

These issues are discussed in more detail later in this chapter.

EMPLOYEE ATTITUDES TO FLEXIBLE WORKING

Survey evidence of employees' reactions to flexible working arrangements is thin, but generally they are perceived as a 'good thing', offering employees:

1 the ability to combine work with outside interests, e.g. as caring responsibilities or hobbies
2 greater job satisfaction
3 improved motivation
4 less tiredness.

There are negative implications however for the employee, including:

1 unequal treatment in terms of pay and benefits
2 reduced career development opportunities
3 limited training opportunities
4 the 'pyschological contract' is threatened
5 increased job insecurity
6 increased stress.

The main benefit is undoubtedly that flexible working patterns can help individual employees in balancing the demands of earning a living and looking after a family. Many people prefer to work part time rather than full time. Evidence from the LFS (spring 1996), for example, shows that 72 per cent of part-time employees work part time because they do not want a full-time job (compared to 62 per cent in 1984) and only 13 per cent do so because they cannot find a full-time job. As women form a larger part of the workforce, many employers have developed family-friendly policies which can effectively 'customise' working patterns to suit employees' individual circumstances. There are, however, clear gender differences – men are more likely to say that they could not find a full-time job (25 per cent) although the proportion who say they could not find a full-time job is still less than the proportion who do not want a full-time job. Women are more likely to say they do not want a full-time job (80 per cent).

This evidence, that men appear less happy to work on a part-time basis, is supported by the labour turnover figures quoted earlier. Some commentators have claimed that men are becoming increasingly disadvantaged at work because employers prefer to create part-time jobs which more women than men apply for and obtain. Evidence shows that men are not willing to apply for jobs in the expanding service sector because they perceive them to be 'women's jobs' (this is in contrast to southern Europe where more women want to work but their unemployment is increasing because, the report claims, men are willing to do these jobs). The changing nature of work is therefore reducing job opportunities for men. The report concludes that employers will either have to reverse the trend to part-time work or men will have to accept jobs traditionally seen as women's work.

In contrast to part-time employment, however, many temporary workers do not take this type of work out of choice but do so because there is no permanent work available. In spring 1996, according to the LFS, about 42 per cent of temporary workers gave this as a reason, compared to 24 per cent (of a much smaller number) in 1990. The proportion who could not find a permanent job varies considerably across the workforce. For example 49 per cent of men, compared to 36 per cent of women, said they could not find a permanent job; older workers and students are more likely to say they do not want a permanent job than full-time prime-age workers.

The distinction between contracts of service and contracts for services is notoriously uncertain but there is no doubt that most self-employed people have voluntarily opted for this status and perceive real benefits in doing so. Recent research at the University of Huddersfield noted that workers on zero-hours contracts – who have no guarantee of regular work but are required to work any number of hours on demand – are generally not provided with the same level of benefits of permanent workers, though the issue of their entitlement to such benefits remains to be tested. There seems to be little evidence, however, of the attitudes of the workers concerned.

Recent studies undertaken on behalf of the Institute of Personnel and Development (IPD) do throw some light on employee responses to flexibility. A report by the Universities of Bath and Warwick on the people management implications of leaner ways of working described lean production as 'founded on the principle that by instilling a philosophy of continuous improvement (*kaizen*) and flexible working practices throughout the organisation, firms will be better able to win, retain and meet the needs of their customers'. The link with flexibility is underlined by the comment that leanness has involved overturning the old Taylorist maxim that efficiency is best achieved through the continuous division and separation of tasks by senior management. The report found that, although only limited research has been conducted in this area, there are both pluses and minuses for individuals. Thus a lean system can have positive benefits by involving employees in decision making and giving them more freedom and power over the performance of their work. At the same time it can also lead to greater stress and work pressure, unrealistic workloads and spans of control and feelings of blame and isolation.

A major study of employee attitudes undertaken on behalf of the IPD by Birkbeck College also registered conflicting responses, as noted by Paul Sparrow in Chapter 8. On the one hand, it found that the traditional psychological contract built around job security and a career is alive and surprisingly well. It also found that the biggest factor associated with a positive psychological contract is the use of enlightened people management practices including job design and policies of avoiding compulsory redundancies. On the other hand, the study confirmed that many workers are being stretched to their limits, with a third saying they are putting in so much effort they could not imagine working any harder, and a further third claiming to be working 'very hard'. Only one in four respondents claims to be more committed to life outside work than to work. One in four employees had little or no trust in their organisation to keep its promises or commitments. Interestingly, the attitudes of temporary employees and those on fixed-term contracts were generally at least as positive as those of other employees, suggesting that such employees do not feel themselves to be a particularly disadvantaged group.

MANAGING THE FLEXIBLE WORKFORCE

So what are the main issues for employers? What are the problems they face in managing flexible employees? The issues can conveniently be addressed under the following broad headings:

- casualisation
- control
- commitment
- continuity/career development
- consultation
- communication.

Casualisation

This is a key issue, both for employers and for employees. The relationships between employers and people employed by sub-contractors raises legal and financial issues which go well beyond issues of motivation and control. However, managers can face a challenge to ensure that people employed by sub-contractors fully understand the nature of the work they are required to do and establish effective working relationships with people employed directly by the main contracting organisation. Where sub-contract staff are working alongside direct employees, the use of project teams that meet frequently and address key issues may be critical to delivering an acceptable product and getting value for money.

By comparison, managing part-timers is – or should be – considerably less of a challenge. Following the 1997 judgment by the European Court of Justice, employment legislation in the UK has been amended to give part-time employees the same employment protection as full-timers and there is pressure on employers to remove unnecessary differences in treatment. Research at Roffey Park suggests that, unsurprisingly, part-timers want to be treated in the same way as other employees. Basically, they want to feel part of the organisation, they want to see their contribution recognised and they seek opportunities for training and development. In other words, the challenge for managers is not to treat this particular group of flexible employees differently from others, but to treat them the same. It should be emphasised that many part-timers are employed on precisely the same permanent or indefinite basis as full-timers and are in no sense 'casual' employees.

The paradigm case for casual employment is, of course, that of temporary employees or those on fixed-term contracts. As shown earlier, although their numbers have increased in absolute terms the number of temporary workers in the UK remains much lower than the number of part-time employees or self-employed people. Most of the growth in temporary work has been in areas which have long relied on this form of support, for example secretarial, clerical and nursing. The evidence that the UK is moving towards a more casual pattern of employment is at best inconclusive.

Control

Traditional employment structures relied on bureaucracy and management direction to ensure that employees did what they should. Within more flexible employment structures, employees have more opportunity to define their own job; this is the basis of 'empowerment'. So how do managers manage empowered employees? The answer is generally by some form of performance management: by establishing clear goals and targets, monitoring their achievement, and designing pay systems so as to provide employees with incentives to achieve targets.

This is a fairly dramatic shift away from traditional ideas about how managers secure high performance. The decline of agreed procedures and the substitution of targets, which may in themselves be no more than proxies for what the organisation is aiming to achieve, introduce an element of uncertainty which parallels the need to track and match changing product and customer requirements. The manager is no longer so confident about telling employees how to do their jobs, but must place more emphasis on employees' own understanding of, and ability to deliver what is needed. This is likely to have clear implications for training and development: not, it should again be noted, in relation solely to employees on flexible contracts but for all employees.

Commitment

There is conflicting evidence on the commitment and motivation of flexible workers. However, data from the *Employment in Britain* survey carried out by the PSI (Gallie and White, 1993) found that flexible workers were underperforming and when employees were asked to measure their own performance in terms of output and quality, it was found that part-time and temporary employees were much less likely than full-timers to rate themselves above average. One reason for this is likely to be lack of training. The evidence suggests that employers are less likely to train such employees, largely because they calculate that the return on their investment would be less attractive.

If employees have more freedom to determine their own job content and how they achieve agreed targets, employers will naturally look for means of maintaining and reinforcing their commitment to the organisation. Hence the increased reliance by large organisations on mission statements, core values and team building. For such employers commitment may be more important than motivation as a lever for securing high performance, contrasting sharply with the traditional model based on 'command and control'.

If employees are to show commitment, then employers must necessarily also be committed to their employees. This is the model of mutual trust, where each side understands what is expected of them and seeks to deliver their side of the bargain. Recent IPD surveys of employee attitudes have explored the extent to which this trust exists in UK organisations. The findings from the 1996 survey showed that some 72 per cent of employees have some trust in their organisation to keep its promises and commitments: a significant improvement on the responses a year earlier. However comparative statistical surveys of employee attitudes in a number of European countries tend to suggest lower levels of trust among employees in the UK than among those in other countries. Unless managers are more effective in maintaining the confidence of their workforce, there must be some doubt about their ability to manage flexible employment contracts.

Continuity/career development

The evidence from attitude surveys suggests that employees continue to attach considerable importance to career development and security of employment. The concept of 'employ-ability', implying that employers will offer necessary training and outplacement support to ensure that employees are capable of finding alternative work, does not have the same resonance. Some major employers such as Rover and Blue Circle have explicitly offered employees a deal based on using redundancies only as a last resort and committing themselves to long term employment relationships.

There are also sound financial reasons why employers may choose to retain existing employees. The enthusiasm for delayering and downsizing has been criticised not only by academics but by practitioners on the grounds that it has squandered scarce talent and experience and reduced rather than enhanced companies' competitiveness. Managers' ability to deploy their workforce flexibly is often essential to business performance; reducing the number of employees may have damaging effects on the business. Flexibility cannot be a mantra to be repeated in all circumstances: trust and commitment are increasingly seen as key business drivers and they are unlikely to flourish within short-term or precarious employment relationships.

Consultation

If employers wish to develop employee trust and confidence, they need to take seriously the whole issue of communication. In large organisations, this generally involves some form of consultation with employee representatives, allowing managers to share information about business strategy and its implications for employees. Many companies of all sizes are placing increased emphasis on employee involvement, which can take a wide number of forms including job redesign, initiatives aimed at increasing quality or customer service, and team building. There is, of course, no necessary link between flexible employment and consultation or involvement, but loosening up systems of managerial control needs to be balanced by a greater emphasis on employees' contribution in the interests of improving business performance.

Communication

Employers may find it significantly easier to change working practices if they do not have to negotiate the changes in detail. Increasing competitiveness pressures have in most cases persuaded trade unions and employees of the futility of resisting change. Employers are increasingly required to 'involve' employees in the process of change, however, not least since employees' contribution to improving quality or simplifying processes among other things may be critical.

The contractual relationship between the employer and employee has also become more variable. This is partly due to the increased reliance on performance-linked pay, and the importance which this places on performance assessment. The significance of collective agreements, applying 'standard' terms and conditions to large groups of employees, has also been substantially reduced. This might be expected to increase employees' identification with the employer, and reduce the perceived benefits of trade union membership. In any case it has highlighted the importance for employers of direct communication with employees.

CONCLUSIONS

The discussion in this chapter suggests a number of important messages for managers. Flexibility does not offer any shortcuts to securing efficiency. In order to manage the flexible workforce, managers need to establish a positive psychological contract, as discussed in Part One. This means, for example:

1 recognising the need to build employee commitment and loyalty through involvement, consultation and communication
2 providing training and career development opportunities for all employees
3 implementing personnel policies that ensure fair and equal treatment, including not creating 'ghettos' of employees on less favourable terms and conditions of employment or using short-term contracts in order to limit the application of employment protection legislation.

The IPD research referred to earlier shows that simply reducing the size of the workforce in order to reduce costs is fraught with risk. Managers may need to make difficult judgements about balancing skills, employment costs and product or service quality. Genuine 'lean systems' depend on maintaining a high level of trust between managers and employees: the necessary changes in behaviour cannot simply be imposed. Research into the psychological contract shows that 'a history of redundancy or lay-offs in the workplace is by far the most important negative influence on relations in employing organisations'.

In these circumstances it is not entirely surprising that some of the people who originally took the lead in urging managers to downsize have subsequently concluded that 'if all you do is cut then you will eventually be left with nothing'; or that in one study almost as many companies reported negative as reported positive effects on productivity. Corporate anorexia or amnesia are just two of the possible consequences. The pressure on managers to reduce costs will undoubtedly continue. Unfortunately there is little case study evidence available at this stage showing how organisations have successfully managed the process of downsizing.

There is clearly a continuing trend towards employers seeking greater flexibility in the pattern and organisation of work. Part-time and temporary working continues to grow and to some extent this is at the expense of full-time permanent jobs, although there is also evidence that temporary work is being used as a 'stepping stone' into permanent employment. Other forms of flexible working, such as annual hours and job sharing, are also increasing. These arrangements are being adopted to meet employers' business needs. However, it is less clear that other forms of flexibility including downsizing and contracting out are being managed in employers' own long-term interests.

For employees the benefits of flexibility are mixed. There appear to be clear gender differences, For men, for example, some types of flexible working, particularly temporary work, are less a matter of choice than an alternative to full-time permanent work. Part-time work may also be disadvantaging men by reducing their job opportunities. For women, however, the advantages of flexible working are more apparent – greater choice and improved opportunities to work, in what in most cases is relatively stable and secure employment.

A clear distinction needs to be drawn between flexibility, casualisation and insecurity. There is some evidence that employees feel insecure though the extent of this has almost certainly been exaggerated and is not matched by detectable labour market trends. However, this feeling of insecurity no doubt reflects an awareness that even large organisations may be powerless to protect employment in the face of adverse trading conditions, and has little to do with the nature of the employment contract itself. A reduction in the high unemployment levels of recent years or changes in public sector funding arrangements may reverse the recent growth in temporary employment.

An article in the *International Labour Review* (1996, No. 1) remarks that Taylorist work organisation assumes that workers are gathered together in one establishment, for a fixed number of hours, performing given tasks. The contract is of indefinite duration, fixed wages are based on time worked and skills, and the employees have complete independence from their employer outside working hours. The article goes on to comment that 'in the past few years, each of these components has been whittled away by the spread of new forms of employment. Is the model about to collapse? No but it will gradually lose ground to an expanding grey area.'

Flexible employment contracts have always been used for commercial reasons; as competitive pressures have increased, employers have been less willing to carry employees through periods of low demand. The 'job for life' – never a reality for most employees – is likely to be increasingly hard to find, whether for managers or others. Nevertheless, employers may be unable to secure employee commitment and maintain their competitiveness unless they can offer employees a degree of commitment of their own. Provided flexible employment practices are adopted and managed as part of a considered strategy, they can bring practical benefits to both employers and employees.

16

Flexible working in Europe

Extent, growth and the challenge for HRM

CHRIS BREWSTER

Centre for European HRM, Cranfield School of Management

INTRODUCTION

Flexible working is a concept bedevilled with terminological problems. This chapter adopts the terminology most commonly used in Europe, even though it has certain linguistic connotations which may be inaccurate. Even in Europe some commentators prefer the term the 'peripheral' workforce adopted by Atkinson (1984) following the American analyst Morse (1969), or the (equally inaccurate) expression 'atypical working'. Some trade unionists talk about 'vulnerable work'. In the USA the most common terminology, which largely overlaps what is referred to in Europe as flexible working patterns, is 'contingent work' (*see*, for example, Freedman, 1986) while some consultants have tried to foster the term 'complementary working'. Others have referred to the 'just-in-time workforce' (Plewes, 1990) or the 'disposable workforce' (Pollack and Bernstein, 1986). Karen Legge has great fun working out the implications of such terminology in Chapter 19. The extent of such practices, and the implications for practitioners and policy-makers in the area, have been much discussed, as evidenced in the references for this chapter and in the bibliography of *Working Time and Contract Flexibility in Europe* by Brewster *et al.* (1996a).

Whatever the terminology, these are critical issues for employers, trade unions and governments. Recent opinions from the European Court of Justice have raised the political profile of the subject and the European Commission is committed to further action on this issue. There are important implications here for the concept of HRM and the ways it is considered and managed within organisations.

This chapter addresses these issues in a comparative European context. It presents evidence on developments in flexible working from organisations across Europe. Flexible working here covers only working time and contractual variations (temporary contracts, outsourcing, etc.). The chapter summarises briefly the debates on the topic, and equally briefly outlines the research undertaken, and then shows the extent and growth of flexibility. This is followed by an examination of the implications of the findings, particularly for certain approaches to the topic of HRM and for the HRM function.

THEORIES OF LABOUR FLEXIBILITY

The concept of 'labour flexibility' remains, both in theoretical and practical terms, highly problematic. Despite the huge volume of literature devoted to the so-called 'flexibility debate' relatively little progress has been made in resolving many of the problems associated with the concept.

In the literature, the term 'flexibility' is applied to a series of quite distinct (if related) theories: 'post-Fordist' (a group of writers focused on production systems rather than employment); 'neo-Marxist' or 'neo-Fordist' (a group of writers also concerned with flexible production, though taking a less positive view of its likely effect on individuals and including discussion of the impact on labour markets); a rather different conception of flexibility provided by researchers in the operational management area; and an important set of literature labelled by some as 'managerialist' or 'neo-managerialist' (*see* Brewster *et al.*, 1997). This latter category is typified by the work of Atkinson and colleagues (Atkinson, 1984; 1985; 1986; 1987; Atkinson and Gregory, 1986; Atkinson and Meager, 1986). His work has been subjected to critiques which have attempted to demonstrate the limited utility and lack of theoretical robustness of his work or even, in the early debates, to deny that the labour market had changed substantially (Pollert, 1988a and b). Nonetheless, Atkinson's work has been extremely influential. His vision of flexibility has influenced policy debates internationally (OECD 1986; 1989).

It has been argued by a variety of different commentators that three main factors have contributed to these moves to greater flexibility:

- economic factors
- uncertainty
- technology (Brewster *et al.*, 1997).

The labour that an organisation employs is, in nearly all cases, the most expensive item of its operating costs. There is increasing pressure on operating costs. In the private sector, competition, particularly internationally, is getting tougher. In the public sector, ever-tightening public sector financial constraints mean that organisations here too are having to use their most expensive resource in ever more cost-effective ways.

These changes and the development of a more flexible labour market have been controversial. There are those who see the development of the flexible workforce as a long-overdue move away from an insistence on standard forms of employment towards forms which can be more responsive to the needs of employees, or can be 'family friendly'. There are many parents who would argue that part-time, shift or homeworking allows them to spend more time with their children; there are other carers, perhaps of children or elderly or disabled people, who are unable to work in a 'typical' pattern and therefore can only work if non-standard hours are available (Bevan, 1996). And there will certainly be some examples at the top end of the market, or among certain individuals, who themselves choose not to make a full-time, long-term commitment to an employing organisation (Social Europe, 1991; Wareing, 1992). While this has undoubtedly been a factor, the growth of flexible working at a time of mass unemployment cannot be explained to any great extent by pull factors. The growth in flexibility in the 1980s and 1990s has been driven by employer demands.

THE EVIDENCE: THE EXTENT AND GROWTH OF FLEXIBILITY IN EUROPE

What then is the extent of flexibility across Europe, and what are the trends? This chapter is based upon data collected by the Cranfield Network on European Human Resource Management (Cranet-E). In 18 European countries identical questionnaires (subject to local 'translation') were distributed to senior HR or personnel specialists in organisations of over 200 employees over four rounds of data collection, starting in 1989 with five countries; increasing in each round of collection since then. The data cover all sections of the economy and are in broad terms representative. Well over 20 000 questionnaires have been collected including nearly 6000 collected in 1995. This chapter draws mainly on the first eight countries to report in the 1995 survey round, but uses the trend data where appropriate. Data collection procedures and sample distributions for the years 1990 to 1992 are discussed in detail in Brewster and Hegewisch (1994) and for 1995–96 in Brewster *et al.* (1996b). In 1995–96 a total of 6289 questionnaires were returned from the first 15 countries, giving a 21 per cent response rate, which is high for population-based postal surveys. There was, as in past years, some variation in response rates across countries (*see* Fig. 16.1). This may in part be due to differences in attitudes to surveys and the disclosure of organisational details across countries.

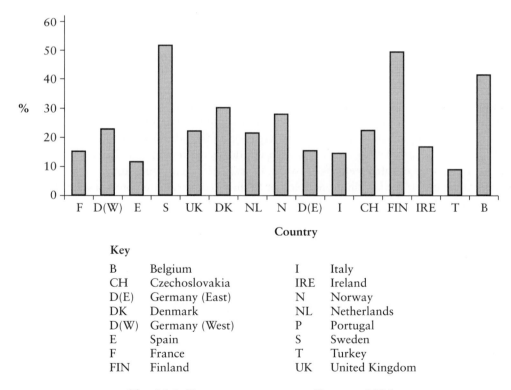

Key

B	Belgium	I	Italy
CH	Czechoslovakia	IRE	Ireland
D(E)	Germany (East)	N	Norway
DK	Denmark	NL	Netherlands
D(W)	Germany (West)	P	Portugal
E	Spain	S	Sweden
F	France	T	Turkey
FIN	Finland	UK	United Kingdom

Fig. 16.1 Response rates across Europe, 1995

Source: Cranet-E, 1997

The survey covers, *inter alia*, various forms of flexibility in working time, contracts, place of work, task or job, and in the financial package. The data presented here are those for time and contractual flexibility.

The most important finding of this research is that it reinforces with organisational-level data evidence from national statistics showing that flexibility affects a substantial number of organisations and individuals, and is growing significantly, across Europe. Space limitations mean that here only a few examples of extent and trends will be presented: the most commonly used forms of working time flexibility (part-time and shiftworking) and contractual flexibility (short-term contracts and sub-contracting). Evidence on other forms of time and contract flexibility is available in Brewster *et al.* (1996a).

Part-time working

Part-time working is the most widely used form of flexibility. The degree of flexibility in part-time work has been debated: the argument is that if someone is doing regular part-time work, and has other commitments which cannot be moved, then they are not themselves very flexible. However, from the viewpoint of the management, part-time employment, which in some cases can in practice be readily reduced, extended or moved to a different place in the day, is more flexible then standard full-time work. It enables managers to match the labour available to peaks and troughs during the working day.

Part-time employment is playing an increasingly important role in Europe. One in seven people in the European Community is working part time, and part-time employment has been the major area of employment growth during the last decade. However, definitions of part-time work and, taking that into account, the levels of part-time work, vary greatly between different European countries. There are also variations in the treatment of part-time workers in legal and social security systems (Brewster *et al.*, 1993). Given that a substantial majority of part-time workers in the EU are female, it is no surprise to find that there is also a correlation with female participation in the labour force (Rubery and Fagin, 1993; Rubery *et al.*, 1996) and even with childcare arrangements (Rees and Brewster, 1995). Part-time employment is now highest in the Scandinavian countries, in the Netherlands and in the UK, and much lower in the Mediterranean countries. In the former case, part-time accounts for over 20 per cent of all waged work, with more than four out of ten women working part time. At the other end of the spectrum Greece, Portugal, Spain and Italy have well below 10 per cent of all employment as part time.

Across Europe, employers are making more and more use of part-time work (*see* Fig. 16.2). In many countries more than half the organisations had increased the use of part-time work with hardly any reducing it. Sweden, which has high levels of part-time working and where part-timers bore the brunt of the redundancies in the early 1990s, was the only country to have more organisations decreasing the use of part-time working than increasing it.

Shiftworking

Shiftworking is not new. In some industries equipment, services and production processes operate on a 24-hour cycle. Examples as diverse as newspaper production, public transport

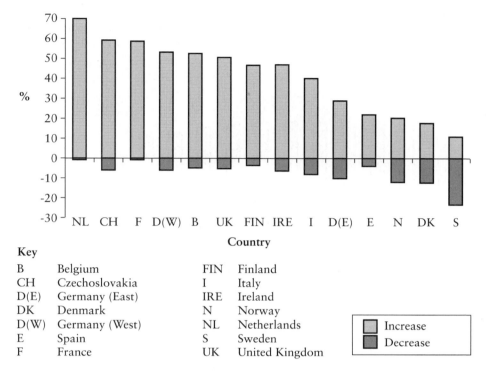

Key

B	Belgium	FIN	Finland
CH	Czechoslovakia	I	Italy
D(E)	Germany (East)	IRE	Ireland
DK	Denmark	N	Norway
D(W)	Germany (West)	NL	Netherlands
E	Spain	S	Sweden
F	France	UK	United Kingdom

Fig. 16.2 Change in the use of part-time work across Europe, 1995
Source: Cranet-E, 1997

and utilities, food production and delivery, and hospital and emergency services have always used shiftworking. New technology, as well as debates over work sharing and working time reductions, have put shiftworking into the limelight during the 1980s. Ever more expensive technology has increased competitive pressures on employers to extend operating hours and increase productivity; working time reductions for the individual employee were simultaneously facilitated by introducing new shift patterns which extended plant utilisation and gave management greater flexibility in working time arrangements (Bielenski *et al.*, 1993; Blyton, 1992). A key development in recent years has been the spread of shiftworking to industries, such as telephone sales and banking, where it has not been used previously.

Concern with the impact on employees' health and social welfare of changing working patterns, new shift arrangements and work during unsocial hours led the European Commission to introduce the 1996 Directive on Working Time. Limits on night work and requirements for periods of rest once a week have obvious implications for many shiftworking patterns, particularly some of the newer and more varied patterns now operating. The implementation of the Directive will require some legislative adjustments in most EU member states, particularly in the UK which currently has no working time legislation.

It is not easy to get comparable national statistics on the incidence of shiftworking among employees in Europe. Our research at the organisational level shows that across

Europe shiftworking is a widespread practice and only in Denmark, Norway and Sweden are there fewer than 80 percent of organisations using shiftworking (Brewster *et al.*, 1994). Once again the picture of widespread increases is clear (*see* Fig. 16.3).

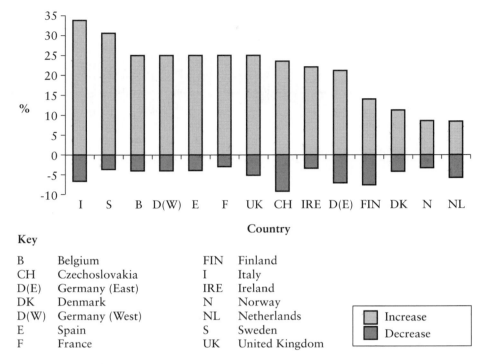

Key

B	Belgium	FIN	Finland
CH	Czechoslovakia	I	Italy
D(E)	Germany (East)	IRE	Ireland
DK	Denmark	N	Norway
D(W)	Germany (West)	NL	Netherlands
E	Spain	S	Sweden
F	France	UK	United Kingdom

Fig. 16.3 Change in the use of shiftwork across Europe, 1995

Source: Cranet-E, 1997

These increases in flexibility are not restricted to working time. They apply in the same way to contractual flexibility. There are a range of methods by which organisations can get work done. In some cases these involve contracts of employment which are quite distinct from 'typical' contracts in more significant ways than just a change to the time at which the employee works – they may involve short-term or even casual employment, for example. Or they may involve getting the work done through a non-employment option: as examples this chapter presents evidence on 'non-permanent' (short-term) employment and sub-contracting.

Non-permanent employment

'Non-permanent' employment is a phrase used to cover any form of employment other than permanent open-ended contracts. To some extent 'temporary' and 'fixed-term' contracts are substitutes, and which is used most heavily in a country depends largely on legal and quasi legal regulations and national expectations; therefore the two forms are considered jointly in this section.

Temporary work in Europe plays a lesser role in the overall labour market than part-time employment and its growth during the 1980s is less dramatic; however, as with part-time employment, levels and growth rates of non-permanent employment vary substantially across Europe. In general it is the poorer countries of the European Union which have the highest levels of employees on such contracts. Non-permanent employment is highest in southern countries such as Greece and, particularly, Spain where such contracts apply to one-third of the total working population, and lowest in Luxembourg, Belgium, the UK and Italy where less than 7.5 percent of the workforce is on such contracts.

Our research shows that at organisational level the use of non-permanent employment is widespread: used by eight or nine out of every ten employers in all countries. However, the 'wealth divide' is clear if the proportion of organisations in each country which are high temporary/casual or fixed-term users (those where at least 10 per cent of the workforce are on such contracts) is examined; in Spain, Portugal, Turkey and Ireland more than one fifth of organisations are 'high users'.

Growth rates for non-permanent employment varied substantially during the 1980s, increasing rapidly in some countries while remaining at a low level or declining in others (OECD, 1991). The largest increases occurred in France, where the proportion of non-permanent employment for both men and women more than doubled between 1983 and 1989 (to 9.4 per cent of the female and 7.8 per cent of the male workforce); Ireland, Greece and the Netherlands also show positive increases (Commission of the EC, 1992). In all countries included in our survey, except Norway, the growth in the number of organisations using short-term contracts far outweighed the numbers reducing their use (*see* Fig. 16.4).

The evidence is that, in contrast to part-time working, most employees with a temporary or fixed-term contract would prefer a permanent one. The drive to increase their use has

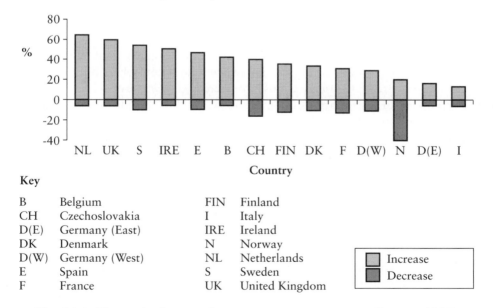

Key

B	Belgium	FIN	Finland
CH	Czechoslovakia	I	Italy
D(E)	Germany (East)	IRE	Ireland
DK	Denmark	N	Norway
D(W)	Germany (West)	NL	Netherlands
E	Spain	S	Sweden
F	France	UK	United Kingdom

Fig. 16.4 Change in the use of temporary contracts across Europe, 1995 (percentage employers)

Source: Cranet-E, 1997

come from managers. They see five main advantages in short-term contracts. First, managers frequently have little idea how long demand for certain goods or services will last or whether further work will accrue. Second, they know that some jobs only involve a short period of time (seasonal work, housebuilding, etc.). Third, in many cases the costs of short-term recruitment will be less since less care may be needed in selection, temporary employees will require less, and sometimes zero, administration for sickness or pension schemes, etc. Fourth, short-term appointments may be an answer to an immediate problem where skills are otherwise unavailable. In these, and a number of less important ways, short-term employment is extremely flexible. In most cases, crucially, the complications involved in terminating long-term contracts are absent: it is easy to dispense with the services of these employees. A final major advantage for many managers is that short-term employment is the ideal way to assess whether a particular employee would 'fit in' if taken on as a permanent staff member. It has clear advantages over even the best selection or probation system.

Sub-contracting

Sub-contracting is 'the displacement of an employment contract by a commercial one as a means of getting a job done' (Atkinson and Meager, 1986). For some employees this will make little difference in terms of flexibility: they might well be a permanent full-time employee in the contractor firm. In many other cases, however, this system – which has always been common in industries such as construction – will mean the displacement of more traditional contracts of employment with individuals by contracts for services with other organisations. The employment relationship will have been superseded by a commercial relationship and the organisation giving out the contract will have no further concern with employment issues since these are passed on to the contractor.

There is an increase in sub-contracting in all major West European countries (*see* Fig. 16.5). In West Germany and the Netherlands, half of all organisations surveyed indicate that subcontracting has increased. In Spain, Switzerland, France, Finland, Ireland and the UK one-third or more of all organisations have increased their use of sub-contracting; very small percentages of organisations in any country say that they have decreased use of it (other than Norway, where slightly more organisations decreased their use of sub-contracting than increased it, largely as a response to new legislation in the run-up to the vote on EU membership). There appears to be generally less uptake of sub-contracting in the Nordic countries than in other parts of Europe with Denmark, Finland and Norway having a quarter or more of their organisations not using sub-contracting. Sub-contracting is used by fewest organisations in Ireland and the former East Germany, both having more than a third of organisations not using it.

There is, of course, a wide variety of other flexible employment patterns available – some of them very new and imaginative. A number of organisations has taken up particular forms of flexible working time in a major way, but in general they are less widespread. They include such approaches as annual hours contracts, weekend working and term-time working; networking, consultants or government sponsored trainees and teleworking. All are much smaller in extent, but all are growing.

Taken overall, the evidence is incontrovertible: there has been a substantial change in Europe's labour markets. Employers now have open to them, and are using more

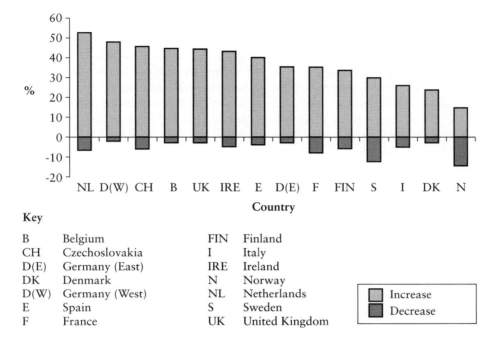

Key

B	Belgium	FIN	Finland
CH	Czechoslovakia	I	Italy
D(E)	Germany (East)	IRE	Ireland
DK	Denmark	N	Norway
D(W)	Germany (West)	NL	Netherlands
E	Spain	S	Sweden
F	France	UK	United Kingdom

**Fig. 16.5 Change in the use of sub-contracting across Europe, 1995
(percentage employers)**

Source: Cranet-E, 1997

extensively, a wider range of means of getting work done. In every EU country in the research a clear majority of employers in our sample report that the range, extent and use of nearly all forms of flexible working hours and contractual arrangements is increasing. There is no obvious sign that these changes have 'peaked' or are likely to reduce.

THE IMPLICATIONS

Implications for those involved

It is instructive to note that despite the assumptions of many commentators and the (perhaps self-serving) arguments of many politicians, the extent and the growth of flexible working bears no correlation to the labour legislation in force in the various countries. Thus, the UK is the most deregulated country, the country with the least social protection for workers – and British Conservative speakers argued that this meant that the UK has the greatest flexibility. The evidence shows, however, that the UK has a varying position depending upon which form of flexibility is examined. There is only one form of flexible work where the UK has the highest proportion in Europe of organisations using it, and that is the expensive and inefficient practice of overtime working (the evidence is less conclusive, but the UK may also lead in organisational use of shiftworking). On the other forms of flexibility the UK's position varies from being among the leaders to being well back in the pack.

What is happening is that working patterns and contracts are established according to a complex of factors – employers' needs, competition, the sales market, the availability of particular skills, the bargaining power of employees (a factor that must have been obvious to the Post Office in 1996, for example), managerial understanding, tradition and employment legislation. The law is only one strand in many and it may not be the first thought in the minds of employers and workers when they come to organise the way in which work is conducted.

The evidence shows that there has been a drive to develop different forms of working practice, including some that may not even involve employment, right across Europe. This drive is created by the requirement to use the most expensive item of operating costs – the labour that an organisation uses – in the most cost-effective manner. It is not determined by legislation although the national circumstances (including such factors as history, culture, trade unions, markets and legislation) do have a profound effect and one that militates against convergence.

Going beyond the evidence adduced here, there are some important implications of these developments, which are different for employers, individuals and the state. Figure 16.6 indicates the relationships involved.

Organisations need flexible use of labour, and in particular time and contractual

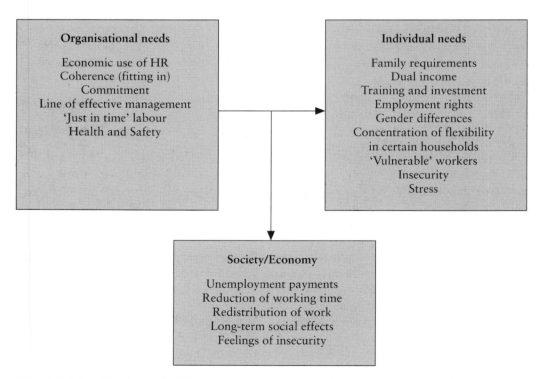

Fig. 16.6 Implications of different working practices for organisations, individuals and society, and the relationships between them

flexibility, in order to ensure the most economic use of labour. But in HRM every solution comes with built-in problems. Employers are less ready to invest their resources in the training of employees who will not be in a position to provide a long-time, long-term pay-back of that investment. The implications of these developments for skill levels in the EU, widely acknowledged as being an important component of competitiveness, are negative. Other problems centre around the difficulties in establishing rational policies and administering the system. The most significant problems come in terms of communication and commitment. It may be harder to communicate with workers who are not on the premises when the manager is, or who are employed by another organisation. And there are obvious problems of commitment. If the organisation makes a limited commitment to the workers, why should they invest their energy, enthusiasm and innovative ideas in the organisation; why should they worry about the organisation's customers or respect its confidential information?

There are obviously benefits for employers in better matching the work they pay for and the work they get done. Arguably, however, the major benefit of the use of flexibility for organisations lies in the transfer of cost and risk from the organisation to individuals and to the state, or to society as a whole.

For the *individuals* flexible working patterns can provide additional opportunities to work, can enable family incomes to be supplemented and can allow work to be fitted in with family responsibilities. However, the transfer of the costs means that flexible work is often low paid. It often leads to racial and sexual discrimination. The individual and the family bear the cost of not working on standard hours and contractual arrangements. In addition, these workers may well be expected to arrange and to pay for their own training and skill updating. The transfer of risks means that many individuals and the families that they support cannot be sure of employment much beyond the near future. This becomes more than just an immediate financial problem for the families involved; it has a major issue on the rest of their lives, because so much of our society is built on the assumption that most people have standard employment. Thus, the ability to purchase goods on credit, to have bank loans, to arrange housing and to provide pension arrangements are all dependent, to some degree in every European country, on having a full-time long-term job.

For the *trade unions*, the organisations representing workers, it has been argued that the growth of flexibility has been directly linked to the fall in trade union membership. Internationally the argument fails: the Nordic countries are among the most frequent users of flexibility and also retain the highest levels of trade union membership in the developed world.

Even in those countries, however, the growth of flexibility puts additional strains onto already overworked union structures. By definition, temporary workers may need recruiting again for each employment, part-time and shiftworkers will be more difficult to communicate with, homeworkers will be more difficult, and more costly, to help than groups of workers. At the same time many of these workers are more likely to be making demands for the union's assistance as their working conditions become increasingly fragmented.

The Nordic comparison tells us is that it is the failure of the British and Irish trade unions to respond adequately to the growth in flexibility that accounts for much of their difficulty. In countries such as Finland or Denmark, where the unions in effect 'manage' the unemployment benefit system, high levels of unemployment (recently over 20 per cent in

Finland) have almost no impact on union membership or indeed on union subscriptions. Even in the UK a union like the Transport and General Workers Union (TGWU) has a long history of representing self-employed taxi drivers, casually employed dock workers and part-time health service workers. The problem for the unions is not flexibility but their failure to develop and implement coherent strategies to cope with the effects of flexibility. Thus, the focus on workplace-based organisation and large-scale bargaining that typifies most British unions may need rethinking as the labour market changes in the ways that we have highlighted in this chapter.

Governments will be affected by these changes in the labour markets. One important implication concerns the effect on government finances. The problem of 'dependency ratios' has been exercising many analysts throughout Europe. As people stay on longer in full-time education and join the workforce later, and as people retire earlier and live longer, so the proportion of those contributing to government finances shrinks compared to those making demands on them. Some governments, notably the British in the 1980s and early 1990s, saw the greater efficiency of flexible working as one way of alleviating this problem. However, even if it reduces unemployment, flexible working tends to increase the number of those in employment who because they do not work enough hours per week, or enough weeks in the year, end up paying no taxes and indeed may still, in much of Europe, be drawing benefit from the state even though they are in work.

For *society* in general the costs have been transferred directly, because the state will supplement low earnings and provide support for the unemployed. The costs have also been transferred indirectly in that the requirements for training, for health and safety and for the provision of other relevant benefits will have to be borne by the state. The transfer of risk means that during periods of unemployment, between short-term contracts, for example, the state will again be expected to provide support. And there are arguably many indirect aspects of this transfer in terms of the effects of insecurity and stress on health levels, in terms of pension arrangements and in terms of housing support. It appears, for example, that part-time jobs are likely to be replacing full-time jobs on a one-for-one basis, rather than that full-time jobs are being replaced by two part-time jobs to cover the same number of hours. Even if two people were getting work rather than one, however, the overall benefit may be extremely limited if one or both remain on income support, do not pay tax (or even in many cases National Insurance) and have little extra money to spend in the economy. The increased flexibility in Europe means that risks and costs have been transferred from employers to individuals and to the state. This may make the employing organisations more efficient, but not necessarily make the country more competitive.

There are also wider societal implications of these changes in working practices – there are the implications of flexible working on the social security system, on housing and on pensions, to take just some instances. Since the markets in the UK currently depend on the assumption that most people have full-time permanent jobs the decline of that form of employment may have far-reaching effects.

Implications for HRM analysts

Flexibility is one aspect of HRM where practice is ahead of theory. We are used to theory being ahead of practice: having extensive commentaries on topics like quality circles, 360 degree appraisal, assessment centres and the like, only to find that very few organisations use them. Here, the reverse is the case: only now is our awareness beginning to catch up with what has happened

One advantage of the concept of HRM over, for example, 'personnel management' is that by focusing on the human resources that the organisation uses it is able to include the full range of flexible working practices. Thus, for example, even the use of non-employment options, like consultants, freelancers or agency workers can be encompassed by the term. Personnel management is focused on the (declining) percentage of 'employees'. In practice this advantage is rarely exploited. Like the texts on personnel management the literature on HRM tends to continue being written as if all or most of an organisation's human resources are found among employees on standard (long-term, full-time) employment contracts. As long as that remains the focus, the literature, like the profession, will be doomed to discussing an ever-smaller proportion of the way work is done. More attention needs to be paid in the literature to the notion, and the practice, of work as opposed to employment; and for many (though obviously not for all) theorists, researchers and teachers of HRM a recognition of the fact that standard employment packages are now cover a minority of the ways in which work is performed is long overdue.

In some versions of HRM, particularly those that deal with the soft, friendly face of HRM, concentrating on 'high commitment', 'high performance', 'competence' and 'human resource development', this chapter is particularly challenging. How are organisations to develop highly committed, energised and enthusiastic contributors to managerial objectives when the organisation's commitment to the employees is severely limited? Why should organisations train and develop people when the costs of doing so are the same as the costs for the long-term full-time employees, but the pay-off is obviously limited to the proportion of time the employee is at work or the length of their association with that organisation? It is no surprise to find that, in practice, employers simply do not train or develop the atypical employees or their workers who are not employees (Brewster *et al.*, 1996).

The notion of flexibility also challenges a number of other current prescriptions in HRM. In the first place, it is likely that some elements of flexibility are 'complementary, substitutional or partly mutually exclusive' (Tüsselmann, 1996). For example, performance-related pay (PRP) will encourage employees to become good at, and therefore to stick with, a limited set of tasks. Financial flexibility militates against functional flexibility. And so, almost by definition, does contractual flexibility.

Flexibility may, in addition, be exclusive: it may exclude other popular prescriptions. As an instance, the idea that an organisation's employees are its most important resource and should be cherished, developed and improved, sits oddly with the notion that the organisation is not prepared to offer the individual any security of employment.

Implications for the HRM department

One implication of this analysis is that the HRM department is under some threat. If its raison d'être is dealing with employment issues, then increasingly it is going to become less and less relevant to the overall costs and the overall output of the organisation. These are going to be linked more and more to options outside employment or at least to options outside the standard employment package.

So will the profession accept a reduced function or will it seek to create a wider role?

There are, certainly, opportunities. From personal experience and from anecdotal evidence there is more than a suspicion that the contracting of consultants, to take one example, is often, and occasionally spectacularly, out of control. Consultants and managers will (in the right circumstances) tell stories of one consultancy working for two different parts of the same organisation, charging very different rates and subject to very different performance standards and controls. If the HRM department is prepared to shift its focus from employment to managing the work done for the organisation, this opens up substantial opportunities to contribute to the bottom line of the organisation.

Of course, this is going to mean a new positioning of the HRM function and the HRM practitioner. It may mean the development of different knowledge, different attitudes and different skills. Unless the function and the people in it are prepared to change to meet the circumstances and requirements of the new labour market, HRM will indeed be in crisis.

17

The French experience of flexibility

Lessons for British HRM

DR. ALAN JENKINS

Ecole Supérieure des Sciences Economiques et Commerciales, France

INTRODUCTION

In present-day France there is no issue more urgent or more controversial than that of flexibility in work. The country seems gripped in a severe crisis of confidence which, while rooted principally in a seeming incapacity to tackle the progression of unemployment (up in mid-1997 to 12.8 per cent) is also nourished by increasing doubts about the indigenous 'model' of employment relations. French labour law, with its battery of employer and works council obligations, although accepted as effective in defending workers' rights, is more and more suspected as a source of rigidity. Furthermore, as the German system continues to suffer under mounting redundancies the French are questioning this traditional 'social democratic' employment benchmark; many employers are now looking to neo-liberal British and American methods of labour management. Furthermore, the crisis seems society wide. As more and more aspects of the traditional welfare state and of public sector work also come under the microscope, the French ability to contain poverty, social exclusion and injustice while offsetting the worst negative impacts of market relationships has become questioned. Despite the strength of republican commitments to national unity and equal citizenship – reiterated at changes of government and president – increasing inequality, the rise of the extreme right and the recrudescence of social conflict all reveal fissures in the structure of social solidarity and cohesion. In this context the French seem deeply perplexed and divided over the meaning, the costs and the benefits of flexibility in work.

My purpose in this chapter will be to give a dispassionate account of its progression in France while generally stressing that understanding national interpretations of the phenomenon is vital for a more penetrating look behind European statistics on employment relations. In the latter part of the chapter, I pose the question of what the French and the British can learn from one another's experiences of flexibility in work, but to begin with I will tackle two aspects of French flexibility – on the one hand functional or job flexibility, and on the other contractual and time flexibility. I need not stress here that these are in fact only two dimensions of a very complex phenomenon (*see* Sparrow and Hiltrop, 1994).

FUNCTIONAL FLEXIBILITY: THE EXAMPLE OF 'LEAN PRODUCTION' IN INDUSTRY

Some of the most important manifestations of increased job flexibility in French industry in recent years have been rooted in the diffusion of new methods of work organisation referred to internationally as 'lean production' (Krafjic, 1988). This diffusion has substantially modified 'Fordist' modes of work organisation. In lean production two sets of practices are combined – 'total quality management' (TQM) and 'just in time' (JIT) – which are actually different in scope; while TQM entails a revision of management thinking on a number of qualitatively different levels, JIT concerns essentially the logistics of component and product flows on the factory floor. However as Miyake *et al.* (1995) have explained in their conceptual review, the two policies share the following common 'logic' which makes their *combined* implementation in appropriate industrial conditions strategically compelling:

1 continuous incremental improvement of processes and products
2 promotion of functional flexibility and teamwork
3 use of worker participation for knowledge exploitation
4 extensive skill development through tailored HR policies on training and rewards.

Taking JIT alone, we are dealing with a complex phenomenon, covering a variety of practices overlapping TQM:

1 Streamlining or smoothing of process flow by rearranging the physical layout of production.
2 Reducing work set-up times to reduce batch sizes.
3 Reducing inventory/buffer stock levels to render more visible process and quality defects.
4 *Kanban* – a simple information system triggering the movements of materials from one operation to another.
5 Quality improvement techniques such as statistical process control, and work team quality management and maintenance are crucial.
6 Simplification of products to ease material flows and work preparation.
7 Flexibility and multiskilling of the workforce in order to match production levels to order demand at all times.
8 Autonomous teams, with wide responsibilities, working in production cells.
9 Creation and sustaining of a 'learning culture' throughout the workforce.
10 Supplier co-operation and/or control; the right quality and quantities of supplies to be provided at precise times and places.

The combination of these ten processes and techniques varies from one industry, organisation and technical production process to another, as of course do many aspects of the 'embedding' process and of subsequent social impacts.

While detailed evidence about the effects of JIT and TQM use in French firms is scarce, we do have some solid recent evidence as regards their implementation across industry alongside other innovations. In the first place there are the overall industry indicators published by INSEE (Institut Nationale de la Statistique et des Etudes Economiques) which register the movements of stock levels in industrial firms. In comparing these indicators across the period 1989–1995 INSEE gives a clear statistical signal of the across-the-board diminution in stock levels in French industrial firms since 1991. Thus in the *Notes de Conjoncture* for March 1995, INSEE note that the *déstockage* of the previous year:

> *faisait suite à plusieurs années de limitation de l'accumulation des stocks au sein des entreprises (contraintes de trésorerie, adaptation aux méthodes de production aux flux tendus . . .).*

Second, there is the particularly important evidence of the survey 'Réponse' conducted for the DARES (Ministère du travail) and INSEE in a comprehensive sample of 3000 plants (in all sectors) during 1993 (Coutrot, 1995). Here companies were questioned on the *presence* of practices – without, it should be noticed, being asked to clarify their degree of development or 'maturity'. We can see both the considerable extent of workplace innovation in recent years, and the strong specific position of JIT, in the results shown in Table 17.1.

Table 17.1 Types of innovation in work organisation, by broad sector, 1995 (percentage)

Work organisation	JIT	Quality circles	ISO 9000 certified	Autonomous teams	Cross-functional teams	Flattened hierarchy
Food industry	35.7	36	14	11.8	31.2	19.3
Energy and materials	49	49.2	27.6	20.7	48	36.9
Machinery and equipment	43	53.3	36.2	15.4	50	47.2
Consumer goods	55.8	26.1	12.3	11.7	26.5	30.3
Construction	26.8	39.1	17.4	15.9	26	31.8
Commerce	19.6	22	7.5	8.8	21.9	23.7
Transport and telecommunications	20.4	36.5	7	6	24.7	21.3
Services	16.8	32.7	11.5	11.7	42	23.3
Health	8.6	18.4	0	4.7	48.8	16.6
Financial	2.9	41.3	0	9.8	30.8	29.8
All sectors	23.6	34.3	10.6	11.4	33.9	27.3

Although the breakdown of sectors in this table is crude, we can see that the 45–50 per cent figures for configurations of JIT and quality management, added to the fairly high investment in autonomous and cross-functional teams (around 20 per cent for the former and 50 per cent for the latter), plus a diminution in hierarchical levels represents strong evidence for a substantial spread of the major elements of 'lean production' in 'energy and materials' and 'machinery and equipment'. 'Consumer goods', with the highest proportion of JIT firms, is also noteworthy. Strong across-the-board use of quality circles indicated in the table also contradicts the popular, and invariably pessimistic, wisdom in France that they died out in firms after 'peaking' at the end of the 1980s.

As well as giving reliable data about the take-up of innovations, the study also provides correlations between the use by organisations of five broad innovations (JIT, quality circles, ISO certification, flattened hierarchy and cross-functional teams) and a number of organisational and HR variables.

Functional *flexibility* is at its highest in firms certified by the ISO, those using JIT and those combining three or more of the innovations in their internal operations. As regards management *control*, we find that employee autonomy increases but with this the constraints over the individual performance of work itself change in nature and, sometimes, intensity. More responsibility is pushed down the hierarchy but with it the specification and control of a number of parameters of worker performance increases – a mix of control through socialisation into an 'ideology' of employee responsibility and through peer, hierarchical and technical performance control is often in evidence. HR practices play an extremely important role in both elements of the mix; they define aspects of employee selection and socialisation, and also of performance appraisal and evaluation procedures. Greater attention to individual employees' potential, skills and results is a central element here – this '*individualisation*' is the complement of functional flexibilty.

However, studies critical of the implications of lean production for employees and working conditions tend to stress a variety of problems (Charpentier, 1991; Dawson and Webb, 1989; Klein, 1989; Oliver, 1991; Sewell and Wilkinson 1992; Turnbull, 1988; Zipkin, 1991):

1 The rationalisation and simplification of production flows increases the visibility of defective work and thus the need for greater worker vigilance and responsibility. Peer control of work quality, such as is required by TQM, is a corollary of this (*see* point 4).
2 Buffer stock and inventory reductions reduce slack time and thus workers' pauses and their control over the pacing of work. This entails an increase in work intensity.
3 Workers are themselves given some responsibility for finding the optimum standardised task performance. They are expected to internalise industrial engineering techniques.
4 Grouping tasks and technologies in 'cells' to facilitate better materials flow and flexibility in manning entails multiskilling and teamwork. Peer group worker assessment is instituted.
5 The rationalisation of labour use entails job rotation between teams to eliminate any 'idle time' caused by lower demand and the policy of no stock accumulation. This also intensifies work.

What is the evidence of these effects in France? It seems clear that in certain sectors use of the elements of lean production *has* led organisations to implement a work system placing relatively extreme demands on employees. The *automotive industry* is one well-researched example, an interesting one because of its high degree of simultaneous development of JIT and TQM. This industry has often been in the forefront of organisational experimentation. Up to the early 1980s for example, automotive firms were early adopters of job enrichment and autonomous work groups (Volvo's influence on Renault was important here (Freyssenet, 1995)). These changes prepared the ground for others which were to come in the later decade and which were in fact structurally similar (e.g. job redesign and work-teams feature, albeit in a rather different way, in the two 'waves of innovation' (Jenkins, 1994)).

Since that period, massive rationalisations by the car producers of the supply chain have taken place, and with this the constitution of a number of '*greenfield*' sub-contractor plants close to the operations of Peugeot, Citroën and Renault, working with them 'synchronically'. This is a group of plants where continual improvement in work organisation and methods takes place through TQM and JIT (Gorgeu and Mathieu, 1995). Their hierarchies are flat (three or four levels only) and substantial flexibility in production working a norm. Employees are predominantly young and recruited mainly from within high unemployment areas by a demanding process which insists on technical and behavioural qualities seldom demanded in 'traditional' industrial production. Those forming the core of semi-permanent production employees (performing 'strategic' work) are supported by substantial numbers on temporary and short-term contracts. The career perspectives of the former are limited and, despite performance and competence-based 'individualised' pay systems, their remuneration levels are really relatively poor, not much above the SMIC, the national minimum wage. Working conditions in these lean plants are dominated by the demands of time, productivity and quality control – passed on by Renault, Peugeot and Citroën – and this produces an experience of job flexibility for these workers of some severity; the constraints of such conditions seem poorly balanced by the reward and promotion possibilities these firms are prepared to offer. Furthermore, union avoidance, or emasculation, seems to be current and this (helped by the youth of core workers) renders stable negotiated improvements all the more problematic. An explosive social climate developing as a result cannot be ruled out, a number of French commentators are detecting this already in some of the greenfield plants in Alsace (Collomp, 1995).

Despite this example however, generalisations about lean production in French industry based on data from the automotive group, and in particular the greenfield 'high performance' plants, would be rash, especially as regards the employment 'deal' on offer to core workers. In other sectors – and even within the automobile constructors themselves – that deal is modified by work organisation, HR and industrial relations differences, and is often less severe. It would thus be rash to suggest that other sectors can see in the employment relations of the automotive suppliers an image of their own unfolding 'flexible future'. This is reinforced by other case study evidence of the embedding of JIT and TQM down at the level of the workshop. It shows that the way new work constraints due to these two systems are experienced by employees is strongly conditioned by the way new working norms on quality and delays (e.g. those related to the certification in ISO 9000) are collectively elaborated. As Blain (1994) has shown in her study of five workshops in a chemical processing firm, when this is a participative, negotiated process the likelihood of developed understanding and shopfloor 'ownership' of the changes emerging is increased substantially. The potential for 'different readings' of constraints between first-line managers, engineers and operators is diminished when mechanisms for knowledge sharing, consultation and negotiation between these groups are actively developed during the development of TQM. Other work on French 'high performance' plants (often called *organisations qualifiantes*) confirms this view (Amadieu and Cadin, 1995).

The conclusion has to be a nuanced one. While the spread of the elements of lean production and of accompanying 'individualised' HRM methods has substantially modified French industrial work in recent years, there is no really conclusive evidence that the workplace flexibilities they have brought add up to a new 'régime' of employee subordination. On the other hand, employment stability and security have been major casualties of the 'rationalisations' that transition to 'lean' techniques have involved.

FLEXIBILITIES IN WORKING TIME AND CONTRACTS

Turning now to the second type of flexibility, to begin with we need to stress the way the recent long and difficult French recession, generating widespread company restructuring, has made time and contract flexibility a focus of national attention. During this period of rising unemployment, governments, alarmed by the implications of widespread 'downsizing' have not hesitated to strengthen the law to try to *push* firms towards more proactive HR and use of better methods of redundancy *avoidance*. Since 1989 formulation of a *plan social* (a programme of redundancy avoidance measures including practices of redeployment, retraining and working time adjustment) has been compulsory for firms with more than 50 employees, and since 1993 the courts have had powers to annul programmes considered lacking in detail and substance, forcing employers to provide better measures (for example, the company Möet et Chandon, in a famous 1996 case). Modifications of working time have more and more become central to such downsizing programmes. Over time, company experimentation and state pressure have come to reinforce one another (Bosch, 1992).

Before elaborating, some general tendencies in French employment in the last ten years need to be recalled: the growing proportion of part-time, temporary and fixed-term jobs offered in the labour market, and thus the general increase in *contractual flexibility*. This is made clear in a recent study by the Conseil Supérieur de l'Emploi des Revenus et des Côuts' (CSERC).

Whereas France may have, compared to some other European partners, a relatively low overall use of such labour contracts (Brewster *et al.*, 1993a) there has been, in the past six or seven years, an *acceleration* in their use, as the statistics show. An increase in recourse to part-time contracts from 2.3 million jobs in 1991 to 3.5 million in 1995 is a steep rise (Fig. 17.1), as is that registered between the same two dates for the percentage of fixed-term jobs (*Contrats à durés determinés* (CDD) in France) being offered to both the under 25 (from 77 per cent to 83 per cent) and the 25–49 (from 54 per cent to 64 per cent) age groups (shown in Fig. 17.2). As for the recourse to temporary workers (Fig. 17.3) a dip in numbers between 1991 and 1993 was more than compensated for by a sharp rise up to the peak of 1995 (275 000). When the ever-rising national unemployment levels are added to this picture (up to a high of one person in every eight of the active population) it can be easily hypothesised that job *insecurity* has been on the increase throughout the 1990s, a factor which almost certainly conditions both the internal employment climate in firms and the wider industrial relations climate. However, this depends, among other things, on how

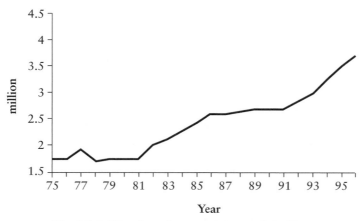

Fig. 17.1 Numbers in part-time work in France
Source: Cabanes, 1996

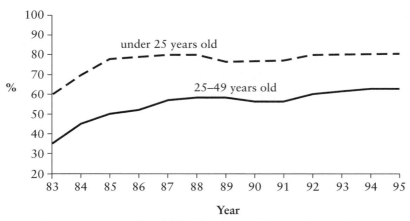

Fig. 17.2 Proportion of fixed contracts in recruitment in France
Source: Cabanes, 1996

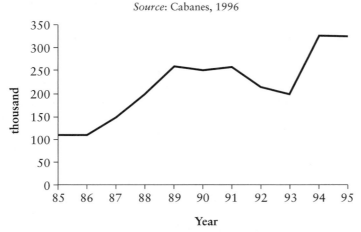

Fig. 17.3 Numbers of temporary workers in France
Source: Cabanes, 1996

the newer forms of job contract have been *perceived* by the French themselves – an important issue to which we will return later.

Governments have for some time sought to encourage the more flexible use of working time and contracts accompanying these trends. The important 1993 law, the *Loi quinquennale*, promoted two mechanisms for flexibility. First, there is the *Temps réduit indemnisé de longue durée* (TRILD) which allows firms to place groups of employees in temporary or partial unemployment (without an imposed break in their employment contracts) in order to manage periods of financial difficulty (poor seasons, deficits, etc.). By waiving social charges and providing financial help to companies to pay part of the 50 per cent of salaries to the employees involved, the state commits itself to help firms over problem periods (*see* Example F that follows). Second, there is the annualisation of, and conversion to, part-time work. The law stimulated firms to *convert* the jobs of redundancy threatened employees into part-time status. A company has to sign a convention with the state (maximum two years) in order to receive financial aid, from the *Fonds national pour l'emploi* (FNE), which can then be transferred to the part-time employee in the form of a salary complement. In principle, redundancy is avoided (the firm must prove its imminence) while the employee, although becoming part time, loses only a minimum of pay (thanks to the FNE). Example G that follows gives a case of this.

WORKING TIME AND REDUNDANCY AVOIDANCE METHODS

Company working time adaptation (and redundancy avoidance) methods which have developed in recent years are difficult to summarise, but we can cite some recent striking cases. Firstly, we can *take varied modifications to the duration and organisation of full-time working* (Boisard, 1996; Dumoulin and Lombard, 1995).

Varied modifications to the duration and organisation of full-time working

Two examples of employer-led changes to working time in which there was consultation with the work's council (the *comité d'entreprise*) can be used to demonstrate modifications to the duration and organisation of full-time working. In Example A, the company Amphenol Socapex avoided 14 redundancies by reducing normal working time from 39 hours (over 5 days) to 38 (over 4.5 days) along with a 1.86 per cent reduction in wages. In Example B, Sercel reduced weekly working time from 39 to 35 hours (over 4 days) without salary reductions. However, a wage freeze was accepted and workers (80 per cent of those polled) favoured the 4 day week when the economic upturn came. The next example highlights state-aided union–management signed agreements on working time in which hours were envisaged and salaries reduced. In Example C, Iveco France in 1994 signed such an agreement and obtained state financing for a project of reduction of working time from 38.5 hours to 36. This replaced short-time working and temporary unemployment. The last example demonstrates the flexible use of overtime hours. In Example D, Kodak-Pathé (Chalon-sur-Saône) signed an agreement with unions to reduce *yearly* working time and to plan it better to tackle seasonal demands. Here job *creation* took place. As many as 11 100 overtime hours worked in 1993 were 'converted' into ten new full-time posts. This reduced an individual employee's annual overtime hours from 130 to 90 and a compensation bonus of Fr 4000 (approximately £480) was paid by the firm.

Experimentation with new forms of part-time work and job sharing

Second, there is *the experimentation with new forms of part-time work and job sharing*, strongly stimulated, as we have seen, by the *Loi quinquennale* of 1993. Some preliminary points must be recalled here. First of all a part-time job in France is considered as being one whose weekly or monthly hours are *at least one-fifth less* than the weekly or monthly legal limits (32 or 169 hours respectively, or less depending on the written 'convention collective' of the sector). Above the maxima, the worker is considered in law as full time, with the appropriate rights. Second, the part-time worker must be given a written contract bearing a number of elements, such as the legal standing of the part-time worker in relation to those working full time (specifically that articles L212-4-2 al 9 and L212-4-5 al 1 of labour law are recognised, meaning that the part-time worker will, theoretically, enjoy the same rights as a full-timer within the firm) and a specification of the hours to be worked. The latter can be changed freely by the employer, so long as the employee is given at least seven days' formal notice.

Two examples demonstrate state-aided creation of part-time jobs or conversion from full-time to part-time work. In Example E, Tefal signed an agreement with the main unions on part-time working. One of its main features was the provision of part-time contracts for young parents up to the fifth year of their child. In Example F, the UAP insurance group similarly provided flexible part-time contracts for mothers which allowed them to stay at home during the school holidays and on Wednesdays (children are off school on that day).

Another example demonstrates innovations in the context of the FNE 'conventions' signed between the employer and the state. In Example G, the BRED (Banking) formulated a *plan social* in 1993, concerning 3000 employees, to avoid redundancies. Rigorous job analyses were conducted and they opened up the possibility of splitting one job between two employees. A supple formula was used with sharing on either a daily, weekly or monthly basis. Wages and salaries for the 'new' part-time jobs were increased by lump sums payable by the state in the first two years (thanks to the BRED's successful application for the FNE funds), and by the bank itself in the third.

The last example, Example H, is one of TRILD and partial unemployment. Usinor-Sacilor, in order to deal with a prolonged drop in economic activity, obtained state FNE aid to reduce working time up to 1200 hours over a period of 18 months (more than in usual partial unemployment agreements) while at the same time keeping open all departments and workshops and maintaining salaries at 85 per cent (minimum) of their usual levels.

A STRATEGIC HR RESPONSE OR NOT?

While most of these experiments seem uncontroversial (even highly positive) uses of flexibility, other far more contested practices have appeared, contributing to insecurity and conflict in a number of firms. Most abuses have been found in sectors such as mass retailing and in textiles and clothing, with cases of split part-time shifts leading to very unsocial hours, annualisation leading to long lay-off periods and pay levels well under legal minima (Lemaître, 1996b). The growth in these phenomena has fuelled the debate over the limits of flexibility and the quality of part-time work, as we shall see later.

Over and above such developments, it is necessary to explain the real surge in company interest in time flexibilities which came after the 'Robien' law of 11 June 1996. This measure pushed the encouragement to adaptation much further than that of 1993 by offering extremely generous reductions in social charges to firms in return for either redundancy avoidance pledges or new recruitments. More precisely the 'deal' proposed to companies was as follows: if they establish a collectively bargained agreement to reduce collective working time by at least 10 per cent, and they at the same time formally agree to avoid redundancies for at least two years, or to recruit new employees, then the state would lower social charges on the employer by 40 per cent in the first year and by 30 per cent in subsequent years (up to a maximum of seven).

Redundancy avoidance corresponds to a '*defensive*' use of the law – here firms must sign collective agreements stipulating the number of jobs saved, the period of commitment to maintain a given level of employment, and how lower pay for those in the firm (should this be instituted) will be compensated. A pledge to recruit new employees – the '*offensive*' use – by the same token must be formalised in a signed agreement with the state (a *convention FNE*) which allows a period of one year for recruitments to take place. Firms must also so commit themselves to maintaining the new headcount attained, subsequent to the recruitments, for at least two years (*Liaisons sociales*, 1996(a)). The attraction of this measure to firms became immediately clear in the second half of 1996. By mid-October 40 agreements had been signed with another 100 in the pipeline (*Liaisons sociales*, 1996(b)). Those reached in the companies Villages, vacances et familles (VVF), Yves Rocher and Giat Industries were given considerable publicity, the first two creating jobs (38 and 240 respectively) and the latter saving 700. The bank, Crédit Lyonnais, also signed a much discussed 'defensive' accord, this time as part of a much larger 'social plan' envisaging 5000 redundancies before the end of 1998. It was calculated that by reducing working time to 33 hours a week 1100 of these redundancies could be avoided. Agreements recently signed at EDF-GDF and at France Télécom covering huge numbers of employees move in a similar direction.

However, despite these seemingly very positive developments in adapting working time and job saving, the Robien measures have become highly *controversial* in France, mainly because of a series of doubts about their range of application, cost effectiveness and effects on collective bargaining. Indeed in the first half of 1997 the law was being described as a 'victim of its own success' as the government was criticised from its own camp on the use of the measures, with many commentators fearing the potentially colossal costs to the state implied by, on the one hand, extending the measures to areas of the *public* sector employing hundreds of thousands of workers, and on the other, maintaining the long-term (seven years) reductions in social charges granted to companies through its measures (Lécluse, 1997(b)). Other criticisms highlighted the possible negative effects of the law on company behaviour – as in forms of fraud and state aid manipulation – and on the important but delicate ongoing processes of conventional working time negotiation with the unions at sector level.

More generally it is very difficult to determine the extent of a 'strategic HR mentality' lying behind the recent French innovations in the use of working time. Lemaître (1996(a)) considers that most approaches remain, on the whole, essentially 'defensive', the product of rapid union–management negotiations and often short-term thinking. Furthermore, as Bertrand and Azoulay (1996) point out in their empirical study, in many companies reductions to working time fail to attain their objective because strong organisational consensus over their logic and impact is lacking. Without this consensus the measures are undermined, either by unions, management or workers. Significantly, this seems to point the finger at the failure of many French companies to develop effective negotiation processes in the relatively 'new' areas of working time modification and downsizing. Innovations often reach their limits when the industrial relations ground in which they are embedded proves to be infertile.

FLEXIBILITY AND EMPLOYMENT INSECURITY

Functional, working time and contractual flexibility have together produced the modernisation of vital areas of the French economy but, along with restructuring and high unemployment, they have also disrupted often long-standing employment equilibria, increased job insecurity for many, and raised new question marks over the ambitions of French HR policies to 'integrate' firms socially while at the same time effectively serving business strategies.

It would be naive to believe that the innovations in the adaptation of working time mentioned earlier– which have often, it is true, permitted some redundancy avoidance – have diminished the general sentiment of insecurity in employment. Survey data and the recent rise in the level of industrial conflicts prove otherwise (Beuve-Méry, 1997; Lécluse, 1997(c)). Although the protection of workers' rights in French employment law has remained relatively strong and has withstood both increased union weakness and governmental change, unlike in the UK, increased use of fixed-term, temporary and part-time workers has reinforced the feelings of instability engendered both by waves of downsizing and by functional flexibilities (Rojot, 1992).

This is nourished by the fundamentally *negative* overall French perception of the newer forms of contract. While many employers – and this is clear in the recent declarations of both the CNPF and the CGPME (the latter representing smaller firms) – want more and more contractual flexibility, French employees and the jobless, according to most data, view its rise with concern. While a majority of those in part-time work themselves experience it as a poor and hopefully only temporary substitute for 'proper' work (Guéganou, 1996), the young coming onto the labour market still have high expectations of work – stimulated by the relatively advanced levels of educational attainment obtained through the French educational system – and remain firmly attached to the traditional notion of a career. At the moment 'non-standard' contracts seem a long way from being legitimised in French working culture in the way that they have in the Netherlands, or in the UK for that matter. Meanwhile, national *debate* over flexibility is often polarised by evocation of the vices of employment insecurity and low pay in the British system on the one hand, and of the virtues of the Dutch use of flexible contracts on the other.

Furthermore the spread of 'individualised' techniques of performance management, formalised appraisal and remuneration associated with job flexibility has undoubtedly had the effect of splitting employees along new lines. A number of groups, dependent for their work identity and stability on the older collectivistic traditions of employee management (rule of thumb appraisal, across-the-board wage increases, fixed job gradings, etc.) have become particularly disoriented and 'fragile' (Eustache, 1996).

On the management side, this phenomenon of insecurity has become complemented by the sentiment of many HR managers that the gulf between optimistic and neutral company discourses on 'HR and social strategy' and their own daily work (invariably and repeatedly of redundancy containment and 'picking up the pieces') has become *unbridgeable*. The 1980s was a decade of optimism about full participation of HR in company strategy formation (Rioux, 1989) but the constant and widespread preparation of redundancy plans has inexorably had its withering effects on the confidence and the self-identity of the function (Lewandowski, 1996). French HR is suffering its own particular crisis.

THE LIMITS TO FLEXIBILTY: LEARNING FROM FRANCE?

Consideration of how the British might learn from French flexibilities (and vice versa) is confronted by the inevitable issue of the radical differences in legal and institutional structures which condition employment relations in different countries. What is considered 'best practice' in one country may clearly be meaningless outside its cultural and socio-legal setting. Nonetheless the contrasts and similarities between French and British experiences of flexibility provide food for thought.

The similarities are greater than some commentators have suggested (Lane, 1989) and this applies particularly to the diffusion of *functional* flexibilities. Work and organisation redesign has progressed rapidly in France in recent years without generating substantial conflict and this is no doubt due substantially to two factors: on the one hand, the absence of effective opposition to change at plant level, and on the other, management and HR expertise in using participative and consultative means (quality circles, joint socio-technical analysis, works councils, etc.) already quite well developed in the 1980s. There are some echoes of British experience here, but it seems to me that the French have been particularly adept and dynamic in propagating ideas on best practice in work redesign and, on a number of occasions, in finding collaborative methods of change. State funded agencies offering consultancy and expertise like *l'Agence Nationale pour l'Amélioration des Conditions de Travail* (ANACT) and industry leaders (like Renault, Danone and Rhône Poulenc) have had a real influence on a French rapprochement between industrial engineering, ergonomics/human factors and HR practices which has sought to follow German and Scandinavian innovations. Ministers of labour, of both right and left persuasions, have not hesitated to take the lead in endorsing 'human-centred' production and employee involvement in socio-technical change; indeed this has been seen as a legitimate part of any policy on industrial 'modernisation' (Aubry, 1991). Unions such as the CFDT have developed some real expertise in the area through projects jointly initiated by managements and works councils, as Gadbois *et al.* (1995) show in their analysis of organisational changes in the healthcare sector. There may well be a lesson here for 'New Labour' in Britain – learn from company innovations and invest in the guidance, influence and development of HR in order to improve the *human* stewardship of functional flexibility.

Contrasts come more to the fore when we consider *time and contract* flexibilities, and this is because of the weight of differences in both the provisions of law and in national perceptions of the employment relationship (for example, the long-term legitimacy of non-standard contracts). French labour law is of daunting scope and complexity; as company size increases the range of employer obligations does so, with important thresholds at 10, 50 and 300 employees. French firms are more and more calling for a simplification (as are, incidentally, external institutional critics like the OECD), but this is very controversial because it could erode the very employee protections that some commentators see as woefully lacking in 'neo-liberal' systems of employment relations. Turnbull and Wass' (1997) damning criticism of redundancy management in the UK steel, mining and port transportation industries, and their recommendation that 'a statutory solution' constraining employers be adopted in Britain, suggests that a lot could be learned from an examination of the French use of legally required redundancy programmes (*plans sociaux*). It is true that laws do not change company behaviour straightaway and they are not – as the French would be the first to ruefully admit – the 'answer' to downsizing and spiralling unemployment, but they can stimulate HRM innovations and begin the process of their diffusion, thus progressively changing the principles and practice of personnel management (as Cole (1989) has shown in his study of teamwork in the USA, Sweden and Japan). Furthermore, legal control of 'worst practices' in companies is important both in terms of sparing human distress and in progressively 'raising the bar' for national HRM standards. However, it seems clear that both stern resolve in confrontation with recalcitrant business groups and long-term continuity of thinking at the level of government on the acceptable and unacceptable faces of flexibility are necessary for effective implementation and use of such legislation – political and ideological conditions not easily attainable.

The French insistence that flexibility and the cohesion of society as a whole really need to be thought through *together* strikes me as fundamentally positive; French debate over how to render part-time work a real alternative to the traditional 'standard' job while guaranteeing protection from abuses continues to highlight the issue. Amid all the uncertainties about the future of the French 'model', one heartening sign in France is that many participants in the analysis refuse to dissociate the question of contract flexibility from that of social inequality and 'exclusion'. It is understood that allowing an uncontrolled expansion of *poor quality* part-time contracts may well only generate low pay and further insecurity in work, which will have their own social costs. Perhaps the strength of this conviction is linked to the traditional French wariness of *petits boulots* – low value, low status work – and the importance attached to the notion of a *métier* – a craft, profession or set of competences which carries with it social status, recognition and a stable working identity. The technical problems (of redefining part-time employment rights and obligations) remain to be resolved, as do those on the level of the popular image of non-standard jobs; a major difficulty for the French lies in the slowness of adaptation of culture and opinion compared to the rapidity of contemporary economic and business changes.

18

HRM and commitment

A *case study of teamworking*

PAUL EDWARDS AND MARTYN WRIGHT

Industrial Relations Research Unit, University of Warwick

TEAMWORK AND COMMITMENT

In Chapter 3 David Guest noted that human resource management (HRM) is widely seen as promoting employee commitment to the organisation (Guest, 1987; Legge, 1995). Commitment can be pursued in many ways, but it seems to be equally widely accepted that teamworking is a particularly developed means of doing so. Marchington (1992) describes it as the 'most extensive form of job redesign' that he considers, for it embraces the extension of jobs both horizontally (workers do more tasks at the same level, as in job enlargement) and vertically (workers take on more tasks that were formerly in the hands of management). This idea is captured in Marchington's definition of teamworking as 'a form of work organisation in which tasks are assigned to the group as a whole rather than to specific individuals' and the group itself assumes responsibility for the allocation of work tasks. Thus teamwork involves not only the delegation of tasks but also the willingness of management to cede a degree of control of the task to the work group (*see* the discussion of changes in organisation design and trust in Chapter 8).

High commitment 'means that behaviour is largely self-regulated rather than controlled by sanctions and pressures external to the individual' (Walton, 1985; Wood and Albanese 1995). This implies high trust management–worker relations and the absence of 'them and us' attitudes. Teamworking, with its concentration on self-regulated groups, is thus an ideal test case in which to explore the generation of commitment.

There are, however, various forms of teamwork. In their survey of Japanese-owned companies in the USA, Cutcher-Gershenfeld *et al.* (1994) identified three types of team:

- socio-technical systems, involving worker autonomy and job rotation
- lean production
- off-line teams.

Arguably, it is only the first which has any genuine team empowerment over day-to-day decisions. Lean production often involves very tight supervision while off-line teams such as quality circles may be useful in resolving problems but do not directly give the group the responsibility for the allocation of work tasks (Berggren, 1993).

These contrasting forms of teamwork may explain some of the conflicting evidence on teams. Some writers are clear that 'teamworking works'. Reviewing the American evidence, Appelbaum and Batt (1994) conclude that 'performance gains reported by companies that have transformed their production processes appear to be impressive'. A study of the Digital plant at Ayr, where teams operated without supervisors and were responsible for a range of tasks, found favourable employee responses and business performance outcomes (Buchanan and McCalman, 1989).

Geary (1993) studied semi-autonomous work groups (SAWGs) at a US-owned electronics plant in Ireland and argues that worker autonomy often has discrete limits, with direct supervision replaced by close, computer-monitored surveillance. Control is reorganised, rather than devolved to workgroups, within a structure of continuing management dominance. Pollert (1996) reports a teamwork experiment in a chocolate factory and concludes that it had failed, with the ideology of co-operation contradicting the reality of fragmented and tightly controlled work. Scott's (1994) case of a frozen food works showed that SAWGs were undermined by a lack of management commitment to worker self-discipline. Where managers disagreed with the outcomes of self-governance, they frequently imposed their own rules about discipline and time-keeping. In Buchanan and Preston's (1992) study, cell manufacturing was undermined by inappropriate human resource policies, such as an inflexible pay system that cut across the need for cross-functional working within cells.

These differences may reflect the extent to which truly advanced forms of teamwork had been introduced. As Marchington (1992, emphasis added) notes, many studies, *'especially on car assembly lines*, [find that teamwork] does induce higher levels of stress among employees'. Teamwork in such assembly line technologies may well involve more intense working, a point which would also apply to the mass production instances studied by Pollert and by Scott.

By contrast, Cutcher-Gershenfeld *et al.* (1994) found that elaborated teams were promoted by the existence of continuous process technology. Marchington (1992) agrees that teamwork may be particularly appropriate to another continuous process sector, chemicals, because of 'technological, product and labour market' factors. He does not, however, elaborate on why these factors may be important.

LIMITS TO THE DEVELOPMENT OF FLEXIBILITY THROUGH TEAMWORKING

This chapter focuses on advanced forms of teamwork, and thus does not address the extensive debate on the team concept in sectors such as cars. One task is to provide elaboration of Marchington's point: explaining why it is that teamworking fits in certain sectors. The obverse of this point is that it may not fit so well elsewhere, and hence that it is not a generic part of the agenda of HRM and commitment. To the extent that teamwork is context dependent, it cannot be offered as a general solution to problems of low trust. A second key delimitation concerns the reasons for the adoption of teamwork. It is well established that many Swedish firms moved away from assembly lines and experimented with advanced teamwork systems because of concerns about absenteeism and labour turnover (Pontusson, 1992). In so far as firms adopt teamwork, not because of HRM issues such as a desire to promote commitment, but because they are induced to do so by market pressures, general endorsements of it may fall on deaf ears.

A second role of the chapter is to explain how teamworking fits within a firm's wider competitive circumstances. A subsidiary feature of this theme concerns the extent to which teamwork is a company-wide strategically driven choice and how far it is, by contrast, a local response to specific conditions. We can thus throw some light on debates about strategic HRM. It is also possible to consider the roles of HRM practitioners and line managers in the introduction of teamworking.

A third feature is a detailed focus on employee responses. Several studies of involvement initiatives have rather limited information on workforce reactions (e.g. Hill, 1995; Marchington and Parker, 1990). We set out to explore such reaction in some detail, and in particular to see what effect teamworking had had on the overall amount of trust between management and worker. We will show that it led to a sense of increased *involvement* in workplace decision-making but that it did not increase *commitment* in the wider sense of a high-trust system. In this chapter, we set our results in the context of existing debates on high commitment. Detailed data on the training and payments systems, and on the process of implementing teamwork, may be found elsewhere (Wright and Edwards, 1996).

CASE STUDY SITE AND THE STRUCTURE OF TEAMWORK

The study was conducted at the Lynemouth aluminium smelter in Northumberland owned by the Canadian multinational, Alcan. It was built in 1970, recruiting many of its workers from the nearby mines. It has always been fully unionised. The plant operates around the clock, with most workers doing 12-hour shifts. At the time of the study in 1995, the site employed about 350 workers. This represented a sharp fall from a figure of 694 in 1991, a decline which was due to the closure of one of the plant's two main production lines. The site had three main plants: the carbon plant produced anodes (blocks of carbon); these were then used in the 'pot rooms', where molten aluminium was produced; the aluminium was then taken to the casting centre to be turned into ingots.

A combination of qualitative and quantitative data was collected. Fieldwork was carried out in August and September 1995, approximately one year after a move to full teamworking, with additional follow-up interviews in July 1996. Complete access to all plant personnel was granted. Interviews were conducted with all levels and specialisations of management; with union officers and shop stewards; and with team leaders and some workers on each of the four main shifts. The plant was also visited at night. In addition to these qualitative methods, we used a structured questionnaire which was returned by 31 workers from all parts of the plant. We also drew in interviews with senior personnel management at Rogerstone, the plant immediately downstream, and with senior management at Alcan head office, Montreal, Canada, conducted in May 1996.

The site is pertinent to these themes in several ways. First, smelting is a classic continuous process industry, so that we can explore how this technology promotes teamwork. Second, an advanced form of teamworking was introduced, which involved the eventual elimination of supervisors and the delegation of responsibility to teams, which were organised by team leaders (TLs) who remained essentially part of the work group. TLs had to apply for the position, and they were chosen by managers according to formal criteria. They were paid £18 a week more than regular operators (about 6 per cent more), and had no role in the key managerial functions of discipline or attendance control.

The selection of, and duties undertaken by, team leaders are critical aspects of teamworking. The Alcan case falls mid-way on a continuum of team autonomy. At one extreme, TLs are chosen from existing managers, as appears to have been the case in Salaman's (1996) study of a food company, or are clearly seen as having managerial functions. The critical studies of teamwork regularly stress tensions between workers and TLs. At the other extreme, there are cases where TLs are elected by work groups (Murakami, 1995). At Lynemouth, groups certainly had no say in the choice of the TL, but the fact that workers had worked together for many years and that many of them had a sense of group loyalty carried over from the mines meant that no one would apply for the TL position without the confidence of the group. We persistently asked whether there were tensions and whether TLs had had to be replaced. With a few small exceptions, we found acceptance of the role by TLs and team members. The system may not have been as democratic as one based on election, but in practice TLs had more acceptance from members than seems to have been the case in the studies discussed earlier. Our follow-up interviews revealed no tendency for team leaders to become more autocratic.

Since 1994 there has been a flat management structure. Above the TLs there were nine group leaders (GLs), who replaced the previous 31 supervisors in production areas. A further 18 supervisors remained in place in craft and maintenance areas. GLs covered a whole area of the plant, and at weekends and on nights a GL could be the sole management representative on site. Above GLs were the managers of the three plants and the site manager.

The third feature is that the study was conducted four years after the first move to teamwork, which involved the introduction of the TL position and team briefing. (Supervision remained in a reduced role, until 1994 when various supervisory grades in production functions were removed). The critical period for the plant was the closure of one pot line in 1990; five years later, the shock of this may well have worn off. We can thus deal with the point, made frequently in relation to studies of change and specifically by Storey and Sisson (1993) on the Digital study, that soon after implementation studies pick up early enthusiasm which soon wanes. There was plenty of time for cynicism to creep in. This opportunity was heightened by the tradition of the plant. All the shopfloor workers were men, and the macho atmosphere was enhanced by the dirty and sometimes heavy work and the operation of continuous shiftworking. From its opening to the late 1980s, it was agreed by managers and unions to have had a fairly confrontational climate. All these conditions could well have promoted scepticism about teamwork on the part of the workers.

INTRODUCTION OF TEAM WORK

Product markets and company policy

In much of British manufacturing, the major employment shake-out occurred during the early 1980s, with new forms of work organisation appearing thereafter. At Alcan, perhaps because of the distinctive product market for aluminium, this process commenced in earnest only in 1991. Through much of the 1980s there was a decline in the real price of the metal and an erosion of the market dominance enjoyed by the 'big six' producers (of which Alcan, along with the US producer Alcoa, was one of the two largest). But this was a relatively slow trend. Then in the late 1980s the market was flooded with metal from the former Soviet Union. The price of aluminium fell from US$2705/tonne in 1988, to US$1055 in 1993 (Bélanger, 1996: Appendix 1). Firms cut capacity, and one of Lynemouth's two pot lines was shut in 1990.

Product market pressures provided a climate of crisis, previously absent, within which HR practices and work organisation could be reappraised. But teamworking was not a top-down initiative, as in the food MNCs described by Coller (1996) and Salaman (1996) where, in both cases, the head office saw teamwork as a standard company approach and expected local operations to follow the model. Alcan's overall philosophy was certainly consistent with a team model. Our head office interviewees stressed the context of growing competition and the need for flexibility of response. The firm's Annual Report for 1993 contains numerous examples of team experiments. Yet these were not seen as top-down impositions. There was no head office template. A weaker possibility, observed in some other MNCs (*see* Edwards *et al.*, 1996), is to have a standard model which plants can vary if they can demonstrate the reasons. A UK engineering firm, for example, used cell manufacturing as its central recommendation but was willing to entertain local variation. Alcan was not even this standardised. There was no direct mechanism suggesting specific HR initiatives. For example, at Rogerstone, the rolling mill which Lynemouth supplied with much of its output, there had been no change in management philosophy. Teamworking was absent and management claimed to have secured only minor alterations to manning levels and technology. Yet it is true that, in Canadian and other sites, teamwork emerged from the late 1980s (Bélanger *et al.*, 1995). The explanation is twofold:

- there was the pressure from the common market environment
- Alcan's corporate environment was open to teamwork experiments without necessarily requiring them.

The differences from food are likely to stem from differences in production technologies. Food manufacture is labour intensive and the costs of building plants are relatively low. It thus makes sense to monitor labour costs closely and to use the results to shape investment decisions. Head offices can lay down requirements for plants. Aluminium is more capital intensive and long term (Alcan's new smelter at Laterrière in Quebec cost C$800 million), and investment switching is less feasible. There is less of a directive approach from the centre. Plants are, as our head office respondents put it, 'autonomous but not independent'.

Plant-level conditions

Product market pressures and the company approach to teams thus provided a key part of the context for change at Lynemouth. Some internal conditions were also favourable. The closure of Line 1 was a major shock which brought home the vulnerability of the plant. In an area of high unemployment, workers were aware of the pressure for change. The trade union structure was also capable of assisting change. Given the common view that strong unions impede change and that HRM is incompatible with unionism, this point merits careful consideration. Strong unions can certainly challenge managerial wishes, but they also have the discipline to co-operate in change. Numerous studies have shown that effective union–management relationships can ease the introduction of change (Batstone *et al.*, 1987; Smith, 1994).

These facilitating conditions required, however, a change agent. The top management team at Lynemouth was changed in 1990. A new personnel manager was recruited with a mandate to improve industrial relations at Lynemouth, which UK headquarters considered to be poor. The plant personnel manager devised the teamworking programme, and secured its adoption, against resistance from some plant managers. Indeed, it was middle management rather than employees who had to be convinced of the practicality of the initiative.

Certain factors assisted the establishment of teamworking at Lynemouth. First, the personnel manager was recruited from outside Lynemouth and other senior managers were at first unsure about his brief from head office and the extent of his influence. Second, teamworking was introduced incrementally, with a two-year lag between the implementation of team briefing and job rotation and the subsequent elimination of supervisors in production areas. This enabled the plant manager to demonstrate, through output statistics and climate surveys, the positive impact of the new work regime.

Third, the personnel manager worked closely with the unions. Other studies have shown that where there is a strong collectivist culture, the quickest way to undermine change initiatives is to use them alongside efforts to marginalise unions (Collinson *et al.*, 1997; Rees, 1996). Working through the union was an essential element in the change process. The continued role of the union is illustrated by the fact that, though now small, the main union, the GMB, has a full-time convenor (but, as we will see, union involvement in day-to-day issues has been reduced). Some training courses in team building were held, symbolically, at GMB training centres. The contrast with Scott's (1994) frozen food case is instructive, for here there were also strong work groups but the shopfloor climate was one of hostility and suspicion, and it proved impossible to generate acceptance of change.

The next section shows in detail how far workers accepted teams. An important pre-condition was the continuous process technology. As in industries such as chemicals, even before teamworking, most production workers worked in groups which were responsible for specific operations such as tapping the pots to remove the molten aluminium. This team orientation was encouraged by the long service of most employees. Again like chemicals plants, labour turnover had always been very low. As we will see, workers felt that the old way of working had been associated with an autocratic management style and an unwillingness by managers to trust workers. Teamworking fitted well with existing work patterns.

RESPONSES TO TEAMWORK

Benefits

There are strong indications among the workforce of a positive response to teamworking. Employees generally expressed favourable opinions about the abolition of the supervisory tier and the introduction of team leaders. There are also signs of improved worker job satisfaction. Table 18.1 provides some evidence for this. Asked specifically about changes since teamworking was introduced, workers reported an increased level of interest in their job, more ability to take decisions, and better work relations with their peers. The reported increase in skill is consistent with this. We would not necessarily argue that workers were genuinely more skilled in the sense of having new technical abilities. What most workers mentioned was an increase in the number of tasks they performed, which was underpinned by a systematic approach to training (*see* Wright and Edwards, 1996, for details). Workers felt better equipped to perform a range of tasks. Eighty-eight per cent of respondents said that they had a great deal or some influence over day-to-day production decisions, as shown in Table 18.1.

Table 18.1 Effects of new work organisation

Level of interest in job	2.11
Stress/pressure	3.31
Ability to take decisions	2.20
Relationships with other workers	2.10
Percentage of respondents reporting:	
Increase in skill levels	83
No change	17

Note: N = 31 for Tables 18.1, 18.2, 18.3 and 18.4
Mean scores: 1 = a lot better; 3 = no change; 5 = a lot worse

Interview comments tend to confirm these observations. One TL argued that teamworking is a 'much better system'; another said it 'has worked very well, much better than I ever thought'. Production had improved once TLs took over. Follow-up interviews, almost one year later, suggest the enthusiasm for teamworking remains undiminished. The plant manager and union convenor noted the more consensual management style. Shopfloor operatives reported ongoing satisfaction with teamworking, compared with the close supervision which preceded it. Teams have maintained a high degree of independence from management over job rotation and the training of team members. New recruits have been trained in all operations, and enjoy equal access to preferred job tasks, such as crane driving.

The interference of supervisors under the previous system was strongly resented. Supervisors 'used to be directive' and 'treated you like school kids'. They were 'the main reason the plant went downhill'. Their role entailed inspecting all 176 pots, three times per day, along with administering all holidays, checking work was completed, and on-the-job watching. It was, admitted a former supervisor, 'close supervision', conducted in an 'atmosphere of conflict'.

One indicator of the positive response to teamworking is the performance of the night and day shifts. The night shift was largely self-supervising. Most of the pot room management were on days. Two GLs were on night duty, but they were frequently occupied in other parts of the smelter. Despite the general lack of a management presence, there are, it was claimed, no noticeable differences between the performance of night and day shifts.

There was also an appreciation of the enhanced job autonomy which teamworking allows. For example, production operatives were now able to summon a craft worker without authorisation from a supervisor. It was generally agreed that this promoted a closer sense of shared understandings between production and craft groups. This was illustrated by regular production meetings in some plants, which were chaired by a production worker rather than a manager and in which all functions set out to resolve problems as they were identified.

Tensions

Numerous points of tension remained. First, there is the issue of work loads. Existing critical studies of teamwork routinely report increased levels of work effort and management by stress. As might be expected from the advanced form of teamwork at Lynemouth, the position here was not this stark. Table 18.1 has shown that there was some sense that stress had risen, though this was felt to have been only a modest increase. Table 18.2 reports workers' views on effort levels and their perceptions of these. As can be seen, workers certainly felt that they were working harder, a finding that is very commonly reported (Collinson *et al.*, 1997). But in general, workers felt that they could tolerate the current situation, though several said that they could feel signs of strain creeping in.

Table 18.2 Effort levels

		Percentage
Change in work effort:	A lot harder	27
	Harder	50
	Same	17
	Less hard	7
Effort level is:	Always too demanding	7
	Sometimes too demanding	29
	Generally OK, sometimes too intense	19
	OK	32
	Variable or fluctuating	13
Percentage (as per cent of those working harder) *identifying source of pressure to be:*		
Achieving targets		79
Pace of work		62
Number of hours a week		33
Working from start to finish time		33
Time for training and development		25
Time for rest breaks		23

Interviews substantiate these data. Stewards maintained that staff were working harder, and spent longer on the shopfloor and less time in the restroom. Craft and white collar stewards especially complained that the system was being run 'close to the bone'. Two out of 36 workers represented by the white collar union APEX were off work with stress. Some managers acknowledged increased effort and stress levels. These stresses, it was argued, are exacerbated by an ageing work force being asked to learn different tasks, and to take on the work which other team members are not picking up. One pot room TL noted that formerly there were easier jobs, such as janitor, which older workers could go to. These 'light jobs' have now disappeared. Tight staffing levels became the focus of overt resistance in July 1996, when members of one pot room team briefly 'downed tools', and sat in the restroom, claiming to be short of manpower. Many senior managers, however, argued that workers would naturally complain about changes. When presented with our own findings, they recognised the picture but also claimed that there remained plenty of slack that could be squeezed further.

Second, work groups did not take on all new tasks readily. We observed a dispute over the taking of samples of metal for testing. This was normally the job of a technician but it was suggested by management that, on night shift when there was no one else available, production workers should do the job. This was refused, using the time-honoured argument that it was not within operators' job descriptions. There were thus limits to flexibility.

Third, though we have stressed work group solidarity, this was not complete. A few workers complained of being unable to influence their TLs and of finding it hard to gain access to the benefits in the hands of TLs, notably the allocation of overtime. These workers tended to come from small and specialised activities and it seems that the team structure did not wholly prevent their being neglected by TLs from larger groups.

The fourth issue concerns management support for teamworking. It was felt by some interviewees that management did not fully support teamwork. One shop steward reported the pot room manager expecting standards to fall when supervisors were initially removed; another noted that the pot room manager 'doesn't trust us'. As already noted, our management interviews indicated that plant managers had initially been at best cool towards teamwork, and there seemed to be some remaining doubts on the shopfloor as to how far plant managers had been fully persuaded. Tensions generated by the employee relations style of certain sections of management were ongoing at the time of our follow-up research. The union convenor felt that management 'were not listening' to employees' views on problems with process quality. One manager commented on the essentially autocratic attitudes of some GLs and plant managers, which group members also cited as a source of resentment.

Fifth, the limits to team autonomy were contested. Time-keeping was a particular point of conflict in summer 1996. The plant has a long-standing custom and practice of team members leaving work early, once their number on the opposite shift has arrived on site. It was generally agreed that this practice was nowhere near as prevalent as in the late 1980s, but senior management remained opposed to it. One manager stated that TLs and GLs were responsible for running the shift but they did not have the right to determine all work practices, and 'job and finish' would not be tolerated. Team members complained that they leave early only when every task is complete and there is nothing extra to be achieved by waiting for the official end of their shift.

Teamwork and commitment

These results point to a mixed picture in which there is a welcome for teamwork and a perception that workers have more skills and autonomy but also a concern about stress and workloads. A change in worker attitudes was acknowledged but was not thought to entail high commitment. One shop steward noted that, under the supervisor system, workers would do only what they were formally obliged to. If a shortage of carbon anodes arose due to management error, the team would sit around. Now, they would search for the required carbons. They 'like to go out to work'. Similarly, in the past when relations were tense, pot room operators would refuse to operate vehicles with very minor faults, such as oil leaks. Operators are now more prepared to drive vehicles with minor faults, and were 'more helpful' in providing information.

GLs agreed that there is a problem of resistance among a minority, and a failure to take sufficient responsibility among the majority. One GL observed that '10 per cent of staff are a problem', and there were 'still niggles'. More generally, workers were not sufficiently conscientious, and did not adopt high standard work practices. A GL commented: 'There is a perception of a job and knock mentality still', of workers 'getting the job done as quickly as possible'. For example, where pot hoods are bent, dangerous gases escape. Too often, this was considered 'someone else's job' and workers just walked past.

Follow-up interviews indicate that labour attitudes remain a cause for concern among management. The personnel manager noted a recent fall in the quality of housekeeping but team members were frequently to be seen in the restroom when tidying work could be done. GLs often indulged this behaviour. More broadly, process improvement initiatives were still felt to be largely management driven.

Worker carelessness, according to a number of interviewees, was partially a response to 'dictatorial' managerial methods. For example, the number of pot 'bursts', which reduces the yield of aluminium, rose sharply in the summer of 1996. Management attributed this to workers' failure to follow procedures but workers highlighted management attitudes of 'not sharing' and 'not listening'. These tensions were compounded by one inherent weakness of teamworking in continuous process operations: the lack of opportunity for workers to reflect on daily operations.

Table 18.3 presents some questionnaire data about worker–management trust. There was an almost equal split between those workers having 'complete', a 'fair amount' and 'little trust' in management. This question was the same as that used in an earlier study, of workers in four firms, conducted between 1987 and 1990 (Edwards and Whitston, 1993).

Table 18.3 Trust in management

Percentage	Alcan	Four other cases
Complete/most of time	32	37
Fair amount	29	30
Not much/none	39	31
Don't know/other	0	2

Source: Edwards and Whitston, 1993
Reproduced with the permission of Basil Blackwell © 1993

None of these firms had advanced HRM systems and yet trust levels were similar to those for Alcan. A typical Lynemouth respondent expressed enthusiasm about teamworking, but qualified this by adding, 'I'm not a company man'. Some workers had an underlying feeling that they could not trust management, even though they found it hard to identify specific problems. Others admitted, despite signs of new investment, to an abiding sense that management somewhere above the level of the plant could shift in a new direction. In some ways, plant management was resigned to a lack of high trust. The plant personnel manager claimed that an 'element of them and us' will be ever present 'because there are differences in status and salaries', and there is always the danger of workers 'reverting to type'.

In short, teamwork had not led to a high commitment work system. Nor did it mean that workers were free of external pressures and controls, as we now demonstrate.

PERFORMANCE MONITORING

Much of the rhetoric about teams suggests that workers are now empowered, but, as the critical studies argue, work group autonomy may be greatly constrained through managerial direct observation and monitoring of performance. Lynemouth illustrates the point very clearly.

In contrast to assembly line systems, where there is often direct supervision of work performance, Lynemouth operatives felt that there was little direct surveillance of their work. Table 18.4 shows that the large majority of respondents thought their work was monitored 'not very' closely (39 per cent), or 'hardly at all' (36 per cent).

Table 18.4 Monitoring

		Percentage
Closeness of monitoring by management during work	Very	7
	Fairly	19
	Not very	39
	Hardly at all	36
Measurement against targets	Very tight	14
	Fairly tight	59
	Not very tight	14
	Hardly at all/no targets	14

Although there appeared to be little direct observation of the work process at Lynemouth, demanding targets were set. Table 18.4 shows that the large majority of respondents thought that targets were either 'very' or 'fairly' tight. For example, the garage has 15 objectives set by the senior maintenance engineer. A key objective was 85 per cent of all vehicles fully operational at any time. The data in Table 18.2 also support the role of indirect targets: the main source in working hard was felt to be the achievement of targets (mentioned by 79 per cent of those identifying pressures to work harder).

Employees were also acutely conscious of the product market pressures discussed here. Fifty-three per cent stated that the extent of competition faced by the company was 'very severe', a high percentage. In addition to in-company performance targets, there was awareness of external pressures to be efficient.

TEAMWORK AND TRADE UNIONS

It is generally agreed that, since 1991, a marked change in the climate of industrial relations had taken place. Collective industrial action has been absent. Pay negotiations are now much more speedily resolved. Shop stewards stated that industrial relations had 'changed dramatically' since 1991. Now, relations between unions and management were 'more stable'.

In general, workers considered that unions remained effective in representing their interests (70 per cent of the questionnaire sample considered them to be very or fairly effective). When asked why the union had been effective, most Lynemouth respondents cited managerial willingness to involve unions in discussions and a similar attitude on the part of the unions. However, workers also felt that union influence had declined (77 per cent said this). In discussing union influence over pay, for example, many felt that, though the bargaining process was reasonable enough, the union was unable to exercise any real leverage. There seemed to be few concrete issues over which the union was felt to have any leading role. Stewards were prepared to concede a lowering of union influence and activity. Members had 'lost interest', according to one steward. In several parts of the site, it was hard to find people who wanted to be stewards.

Thus the overall picture of unionism has two elements:

1 Workers retained a strong commitment to their unions and felt that a good job had been done in representing their interests.
2 Members and stewards recognised a decline in influence. Unions were co-operating with managerial initiatives but seemed unable to shape the agenda on such issues as training or the pay structure.

DISCUSSION AND CONCLUSION

We have argued that teamwork did, indeed, work in increasing workers' sense of involvement in their jobs, widening responsibilities and increasing flexibility by encouraging job rotation and more co-operation between operatives and craftsmen. It also worked in being associated with some clear output measures. First, accident rates fell. Second, we obtained data on various labour productivity and efficiency measures. These generally show higher levels than in the era before teamwork. Third, absence statistics are more ambiguous, but they point in a similar direction (*see* Wright and Edwards, 1996). As to the mechanisms by which such results could have come about, it is, for example, now formally agreed that shifts will start with whatever labour is available, although in practice any shortfall is usually made up by overtime from other shifts. Previously, a fixed number of operatives was required before a shift could start.

However, there are several qualifications to this picture. First, we obtained accident data back to the early 1980s and productivity figures from the plant's opening in 1970. In both cases, there is a steady improvement, and not a step change, with the introduction of teamwork. The productivity series can be explained in terms of the way in which a smelter works. Though the basic technology is fixed, it is always possible to juggle the mix of raw materials and to vary the amperage at which a pot runs. We talked in some detail with technical staff, who explained their role as being to find new ways to coax better running from the equipment. The job was as much art, or more precisely craft, as it was pure science. Teamwork may have contributed to this endeavour in reducing some rigidities, but to suppose that it can be starkly contrasted with prior inflexibility would be wrong. Thus we would agree with those who deny any sharp break between HRM as a whole and personnel management. Ideal types such as those produced by Guest (1987) and Storey (1992) are potentially useful in indicating dimensions on which the two may differ, but to suppose that HRM is all about commitment and flexibility while personnel management is bureaucratic and rigid is far too simplistic.

Second, evidence for high commitment was distinctly absent, as indicated by the data on trust, a continued willingness to dispute job duties and a belief that unions remained a necessary bulwark against management. This is to criticise a certain model of HRM, but does not condemn the Lynemouth experiment as a failure. As argued elsewhere in relation to TQM, proponents and critics alike tend to operate with an unrealistic benchmark of deep empowerment: a study of six firms shows that managerial and worker expectations were more limited and realistic than claims about empowerment imply (Collinson *et al.*, 1997). In the same way, Lynemouth managers were seeking practical solutions. Why would one necessarily expect high commitment to emerge? To the extent that true high-commitment systems exist, they are likely to operate in very special circumstances.

This links to the third point, which relates to the conditions for successful teamworking. We have seen that the strength of teamwork in this case reflected the structural context (the continuous process technology with its pre-existing use of groups of workers, the long service and solidarity of the workers, and the shock of a product market crisis), the 'fit' between teamwork and Alcan's overall view of HRM, and the way in which teamwork was introduced (including a step-by-step approach, a strong emphasis on training and working with and through the union structure). As critical commentaries on HRM make plain, such conditions are unlikely to hold generally (Legge, 1995; Storey and Sisson, 1993). In relation to debates in strategic HRM, on whether certain HR strategies fit certain environments or whether there are, as the lean production writers would have it, universal best practices, we plainly take the former view. Teamworking seems to be dependent on a specific environment and also an external stimulus, for there was nothing in the technology itself which prevented teamworking in 1970: it is the technical and market conditions together which seem to have been critical.

The argument about fit is one part of the implications for strategic HRM. A closely linked theme concerns the fit between HR and business strategy. Teamworking plainly fitted within Alcan's wider goals of retaining its position in the world market by using its resources more skilfully. The firm focused on core operations and disposed of downstream businesses, and within the core aimed to maintain its position as a low-cost producer. Given the capital-intensive and long-term nature of its activity, it could scarcely have adopted a short-term policy of sweating its assets. That said, there was no direct chain running from business strategy to an overall HR strategy of teamworking and thence to implementation at plant level. The linkages were more indirect. This illustrates the active role of HRM practitioners, for if the connections were really tight, their role would merely be to read off a policy from the business strategy. In firms like Alcan, the HR role in teamworking seems to be an active and creative one. In short, the Lynemouth case illustrates flexibility through teamwork and the ways in which HR initiatives can contribute to performance. However, it does so precisely because of the distinctive conditions in which it operated, and the general lessons have to be seen in this context.

Note

This chapter is part of the programme of IRRU's Centre for International Employment Relations Research, funded by the ESRC. It also draws on joint work with Jacques Bélanger, Département des relations industrielles, Université Laval, Quebec.

19

Flexibility: the gift-wrapping of employment degradation?

KAREN LEGGE

Lancaster University

INTRODUCTION

In the heady days of the 1980s, when the 'loadsa money' enterprise culture was alive and well and even respectable academic commentators believed in the so-called Thatcherite 'economic miracle' (Metcalf, 1988; 1989; 1993; cf. Layard and Nickell, 1988; Nolan and Marginson, 1990), it was a managerialist dictum that increased organisational and employment flexibility was both inevitable and a 'good thing'. It was inevitable due to increasing globalisation and the associated intensification of competition that demanded greater customer responsiveness (better quality of products and services, their more frequent updating in the light of technological advance or fashion changes, shorter delivery dates) and, given low labour costs in the developing world, decreased costs. Employment flexibility was a 'good thing', not only because it had the potential to deliver lower unit labour costs, but because, in theory, it gave employers and employees alike more choice. Thus, for example, the growth in part-time and temporary jobs gave employment opportunities to those who, due to other role commitments (as parents, students), were unable to enter full-time employment. Functional flexibility, implying multiskilling and polyvalency, in theory at least, offered skill enhancement and even 'empowerment' to employees. Flexibility allowed employers the choice of achieving versatility via outsourcing (of goods, services and labour) or through tapping the skills, adaptability and creativity of the workforce.

The 'feel good' factor associated with employment flexibility was promoted, consciously or not, by such influential 1980s writings as Atkinson's (1984) discussion of the prescriptive validity of the flexible firm model; Guest's (1987) harnessing of 'flexibility' with such virtues as strategic integration, commitment and quality in his presentation of a 'soft' model of human resource management; and even in Piore and Sabel's (1984) image of flexible specialisation resulting in policies of decentralisation, participation and involvement, encouraging the high-trust ideologies that might result in the generation of a 'yeoman democracy' to replace the alienated workforce of Fordism. Even the cold breath of scepticism that emerged from the writings of Pollert and her Warwick colleagues (1988a; 1991), Hakim (1990), Hunter and colleagues (1993) tended to concentrate on such issues as whether any increase in employment flexibility reflected employers' conscious strategic pursuit of flexibility or short-term expediency or whether any really significant increases could be observed at all. Although both Pollert (1987; 1988a; 1991), Hyman (1991) and Garrahan and Stewart (1992) raised ideological misgivings about employment flexibility, this was not echoed in the bulk of managerialist writings, such as the 'excellence' school of North American writers (Peters, Waterman, Moss Kanter, Hammer and Champy – not to mention our own Peter Wickens and Charles Handy).

The purpose of this chapter, in light of the empirical evidence of the 1990s, is to issue a counterblast against the assumption that employment flexibility is necessarily a 'good thing' and, with less conviction, to query its inevitability. Rather than being even handed, I intend to be polemical.

LIFE IN THE 1990s

Leaving aside the issues of delayering and downsizing that very directly affect the security of employment (*see* Chapters 1 and 8), the evidence of the 1990s suggests that, in the UK, employment that is classified as non-standard (i.e. not permanent full-time employment) is not only becoming more prevalent but is increasing at a much faster rate than permanent full-time employment (*see* Chapter 15 and for example, Beatson, 1995; Colling, 1995; Dex and McCullough, 1995; Gregg and Wadsworth, 1995; Hutchinson, 1996; Purcell and Purcell, 1996). As other chapters in this book summarise many of the empirical findings of the 1990s in relation to employment patterns, I shall highlight only a few of the indicative trends that emerge largely from the UK Labour Force Survey (LFS) data.

- The proportion of the working population in full-time permanent employment fell from 55.5 per cent to 35.9 per cent between 1975 and 1995.
- Over the period spring 1984 to spring 1996 the number of part-time workers rose by 31 per cent compared to a rise of just 3.2 per cent in the number of full-time workers.
- Almost a quarter of the workforce now works part time and the Institute of Employment Research at Warwick University forecasts that the number working part time could rise to 32 per cent of the working population in the next five years.
- Between summer 1984 and summer 1995 the number of male part-timers has more than doubled compared to only a 20 per cent increase for women.
- Since 1984 the number of temporary jobs has increased by almost 31 per cent, compared to a 0.5 per cent increase in that of permanent jobs. Most of this increase has occurred since 1992, reflecting greater use of fixed-term contracts (often a result of rising outsourcing) and, increasingly, of agency staff (insourcing). The latter involves, as a rule, not just supplying emergency cover, but contracting to supply and manage large numbers of workers on relatively long-term supply contracts.
- There is evidence of increases in the incidence of shiftworking, annual hours working and job sharing since the 1980s.

On the basis of evidence from the Cranet-E survey, these trends toward non-standard employment contracts in the UK appear to be matched by equivalent flexibility in working time and contractual arrangements in continental Europe (*see* Chapter 16, and Brewster, 1996). Leaving aside these examples of what Atkinson (1984) termed 'numerical flexibility' (i.e. the use of non-standard employment contracts to enable an organisation to adjust labour inputs, and cost, to fluctuations in output, and budget), there is case study evidence for some increases in functional flexibility (i.e. the organisation's ability to deploy employees between activities and tasks to match changing workloads, production methods or technology) (*see* Legge, 1995, for a summary of such evidence). Are these changes a 'good thing'?

COSTS AND BENEFITS

As suggested earlier there may be positive benefits in these changes to employment contracts and practices, even for the employed. Part-time working can offer opportunities otherwise unavailable to people with competing role commitments and may indeed reflect supply side factors (i.e. preferences of employees or potential recruits). Indeed, evidence from the LFS (spring 1996) shows that 72 per cent of part-time employees work part time because they do not want a full-time job (compared to 62 per cent in 1984) and only 13 per cent because they cannot find a full-time job. There again, nearly 90 per cent of part-time jobs are permanent, reflecting the fact that their growth matches sector change rather than any new and malevolent employer strategy. Indeed, most women part-timers appear to be in stable and relatively secure employment (*see* Hutchinson, 1996). If employing part-timers is a strategy of job sharing to avoid redundancies, it may have positive advantages for those who might otherwise be unemployed (*see* Jenkins in Chapter 17). If carefully matching employees' hours to their other commitments (term-time only contracts, evening employment and so on) takes place there are clear advantages to the employee, even if this may be colluding with an unequal distribution of domestic and childcare tasks (*see* the discussion of the psychological contract in Chapters 6 and 7). If work and employment contracts are organised to optimise unit labour costs, and by so doing competitive advantage is maintained and with it stable or increasing employment levels, there are benefits to employees as a category, if not necessarily to individual employees.

But against this, part-time employment can inflict costs on the employee. If an individual accepts part-time employment because other commitments render full-time employment impractical, the individual is hardly a free agent or a powerful bargainer in the labour market. It is not surprising then that the vast bulk of all part-timers' work is in the service sector and that, with some exceptions (until recently, financial services), this sector is notorious for low pay. Most part-timers in the private service sector are located in work classified as unskilled or semi-skilled. Even in the public sector, where nominally skilled jobs are available, part-timers tend to be clustered in the lower grades of such skilled and professional work as is available to them (Hutchinson, 1996). The evidence of Hunter *et al.* (1993) is supportive of this conclusion. Employers appear to regard part-timers as less suitable for promotion or for use in positions of authority. A further downside to part-time employment is when part-timers are allowed differential access to non-wage benefits such as occupational pensions, sick pay or even holiday entitlement. Presently, TUC research suggests that 60 per cent of part-timers in the UK do not get the same contracted rights, such as paid holidays, sick leave and occupational pensions as full-timers. However, following an agreement in Brussels on 6 June 1997, between European employers and trade unions under the Social Chapter, all part-timers, except those casually employed, will have equal legal rights vis à vis sick leave, pensions, holidays, staff discounts and share option benefits within two years. The UK is on the verge of signing the Social Chapter and then more than 90 per cent of British part-timers, in theory at least, can expect full equal rights with full-timers, by the end of the century (see the *Guardian*, 7 June 1997). In the experience of the author, it is not unknown in the retail trade for part-timers to be employed for only such number of hours per day that fails to trigger paid refreshment breaks.

A paradox emerges with regard to male potential part-timers. It is not surprising given their generally fewer childcare responsibilities combined with possible greater financial responsibilities and generally greater earnings potential, that more men in part-time work say they could not find a desired full-time job than do women (LFS, spring 1996). However, the proportion who say they could not find a full-time job is still less than the proportion who say they do not want a full-time job (Hutchinson, 1996). Nevertheless men are becoming increasingly disadvantaged at work because employers prefer to create part-time jobs which more women than men apply for and get. It is suggested that men are not willing to apply for jobs in the expanding service sector because they perceive them to be 'women's work' (and low paid) (Hutchinson, 1996). Employers, in turn, are reluctant to employ men part-timers in such jobs because they too operate with the stereotypes that it is 'women's work' and that most men prefer full-time permanent work and are more likely to leave other jobs if such work becomes available (Hunter *et al.*, 1993). Hence, it might be said that the 'flexibility' embodied in part-time employment could just as well be expressed as a rigidity presenting barriers to male employment.

Turning to temporary employment (fixed-term contracts, agency contracts), while there is plenty of evidence of their benefit to employers there is little evidence to suggest they offer anything but second-class employment to the employee. Employers benefit for three major reasons. First, fixed-term contracts are often the only practicable option (short of incurring 'unnecessary' redundancy costs) in the public sector, where funding may be dependent on fixed-term research grants or a limited period, renegotiable competitive tender or where government funding is uncertain and/or on a downward curve in real terms. Second, temporary contracts allow the employer formally to reduce headcount. Third, the employer may use agency staffing to reduce employment costs directly, by negotiating a contract for long-term supply that delivers agency-employed staff at a cheaper rate than their directly employed equivalents (Hunter *et al.*, 1993; Purcell, 1996; Purcell and Purcell, 1996).

For employees, temporary employment has little to recommend it. First, for those on fixed-term contracts there is the insecurity of contract renewal and the frustration that the conditions of contract renewal (awarding of research grants, school budgets, successful competitive tendering, upturn in the economy) are largely out of the employee's hands. Second, there are the costs of unemployment if there is discontinuity between contract renewal or the securing of another job/contract with another employer. Third, those on fixed-term contracts, in a similar manner to part-timers, generally have differential access to fringe benefits and employment opportunities than those on full-time permanent contracts (e.g. in academic life, no entitlement to sabbaticals; generally poor access to promotion opportunities). Fourth, there is the disruption to professional and personal life by frequent, often forced, moves between organisations and, possibly, geographical areas. Of course, in an enterprise culture, this can be presented as both an outcome and re-inforcement of one's 'employability' and hence, for the macro-economy, a 'good thing'.

If such costs are evident for employees whose fixed-term contract is held with the employer of the organisation for which and in which they work, they become enhanced for employees working within an organisation but whose contract of employment is with an agency (i.e. 'insourcing'). Purcell and Purcell (1996) point to added drawbacks. First, agency staff rarely receive the same pay, let alone fringe benefits, as the non-agency staff alongside whom they often work and at the same task. Sometimes such workers may be receiving as little as half the hourly rate. Indeed, this can present a problem for the employer. Geary's (1992) study of the relationship between temporary and permanent employees, working on the same task, reported frequent animosity between the two groups and it does not need a formal knowledge of Adams' (1965) equity theory to under-stand why. The indirect costs to the employer that this may incur (e.g. time-consuming intervention from supervision, taking them away from more productive tasks) can lead to such strategies as separating temporary staff into a distinctive unit (with a distinctive uni-form) to avoid problems between the two groups, thereby, no doubt, highlighting the second-class status of this group of employees.

Second, according to Purcell and Purcell (1996) agency contracts are frequently more concerned with cost rather than quality (hence minimal investment by agency or client organisation in training) and there is a real pressure for cost reduction. A worst case sce-nario is where the client organisation's labour procurement function (I hardly like to call it 'personnel' or 'HRM') itself becomes outsourced and needs to prove its worth by securing a reduction of agency charges in order to secure its own contract renewal. Further, because contracts between agencies and a client company are rarely longer than a year, the agency cannot offer its employees more than one year's contract at a time. Hence, many agency contracts of temporary work are doubly insecure. Not only can an agency employee's contract often be terminated at an hour or a week's notice, with no fringe ben-efits or compensation, but the agency as employer cannot offer any type of long-term security since the commercial contract can be and often is terminated at the end of the con-tract period of usually one, at most two years. Purcell and Purcell (1996) cite the example of NatWest Bank switching contract from Brook Street to Adia Alfred Marks in January 1996. The employee's 'employability' is not obviously enhanced as the insecurities that sur-round such contracts do not encourage the agencies (let alone the organisation in which the agency employee works) to invest in anything more than minimal training.

Where the nature of a skill is generic (e.g. word processing, telephonist, cashier, telesales operators), where there is head office pressure to reduce headcount (*see* Geary, 1992), or where there is pressure to cut labour costs by employing labour on cheaper contracts, temporary contracts appear to be becoming an attractive option to (increasingly) large organisations – whether through agency 'insourcing' or through conventional 'outsourc-ing'/sub-contracting. If the latter involves contracts placed overseas in developing countries, labour cost reduction is secured through paying local (developing country) rates; for example, British Airway's use of an Indian computer firm for their ticket pro-cessing facility.

It is in this context that one can only concur with the trenchant words of an employment agency director (cited in Purcell and Purcell, 1996):

There is a close relationship between E and F in the alphabet. E is for exploitation and F is for flexibility.

I have concentrated here on the downside of numerical flexibility. Similar reservations (which I have made elsewhere, *see* Legge, 1995) might be expressed about so-called functional flexibility. Paul Edwards considered this issue in relation to team working in the previous chapter. All that can be said is that the bulk of the empirical evidence suggests that, rather than involving multiskilling, upskilling and empowerment much that passes under this label more closely resembles job enlargement, an elimination of the porosity of labour, and the assertion of managerial prerogative in the face of the (erstwhile) recession, plant closure and union emasculation. In managerial-speak the working practices and ensuing flexibilities involved may be presented as a 'tripod of success' (flexibility, quality and teamwork) (Wickens, 1987; 1993); for leftward leaning commentators (notably Garrahan and Stewart, 1992) they more aptly represent a 'tripod of subjugation': flexibility equating with labour intensification and 'management-by-stress'; quality with control and 'management-through-blame'; teamworking with peer surveillance and 'management-through-compliance'. (For a summary of evidence to support these assertions, *see* Legge, 1995).

In briefly describing such trends in employment and working patterns today – and I have not mentioned the evidence of a massive rise of overtime working, much of it unpaid, between 1984–94 (*see* Casey *et al.*, 1997) – the words that come to my mind are insecurity, stress, labour intensification. Although this volume considers three issues (psychological contracting, partnership and flexibility), much of the debate about changing working patterns in the UK has been structured around the single concept of 'flexibility'. Why?

WHAT'S IN A WORD?

In Chapter 16 Chris Brewster examined some of the theoretical underpinnings of flexibility. When I read the word 'flexibility', whether I realise it or not, I am confronted by an epistemological dilemma. Do we acquire language through which to represent exactly our experiences of and discoveries about the world, or does language acquire us, as available discourses position us in the world in a particular way before we have any choice (Alvesson and Deetz, 1996)? Is it a question of us working through language or language working through us (Burrell, 1996)? Or might it be a bit of both? In other words, those with the power in society might, through language, frame discourses which those without power allow to work through them, unconsciously structuring their perceptions and mindsets. I am reminded of Berger and Luckmann's (1967) pithy comment: 'He who has the bigger stick has the better chance of imposing his definitions.'

These thoughts came to me when I considered how the word ' flexible' is used in everyday conversation and when I first heard it used in relation to economic life. In everyday life, flexibility is a property of materials, time, space and their use. In relation to all three the conventional definition, in true Derridean fashion, follows from assumptions about what flexibility is *not* – it is the opposite of rigid, unbending, fixed, unyielding and so forth and, hence, it is about adaptability, movement and change. As such, flexibility, in a western culture at least, tends to be associated with positive things. Who wants to be assessed as rigid when it comes to muscles and bones and movement? To have a flexible body is generally considered a good thing judging by the prevalence of aerobics classes and fitness videos. Videos, of course, are sold on the virtues of flexibility, capable of being seen at a time and in a manner convenient to the consumer, their images capable of being moved backwards or forwards or frozen in time, according to taste.

But the very word 'taste' takes me away from realms of production to those of consumption. Way before the word 'flexible' was in regular use with reference to patterns of production and employment it was used to refer to a new technology of consumption – the credit card, the 'flexible friend'. (Remember, incidentally, how in the 1960s with the prevalence of unionised manufacturing employment there was not so much talk about 'flexible working' as about 'productivity bargaining' and the 'relaxation of demarcation lines' – while 'short-time working' might have been recognised, 'flexible' employment for a male worker would be a puzzling category.) The 'flexible friend' was marketed as a ticket to instant gratification and shopping convenience. For the 'flexible friend' puts us in the driving seat, because in essence its use is about gaining some mastery over time and space. And who can resist enjoying the company of a 'friend'?

Yes, the associated language and imagery is persuasive. The 'flexible friend' is a 'credit' card, not (more accurately for the positivists among us), a 'debt' card. Think of all the positive associations with the word 'credit'. It reminds me of exam passes and, even in our first years at school, little golden and silver stars that rewarded good work. It is about recognition and praise and a 'feel good' factor. By association it is linked with what is now a major leisure, indeed, tourist activity: shopping. As I write this, coaches will be swelling the car park of the K-Village in Kendal – a heritage centre (shoe museum) combined with a shopping mall. And this is hardly a Metro-Centre or Meadowhall, the massive shopping malls and tourist attractions of the North East and Sheffield/Doncaster respectively.

In Chapter 1 it was noted that HRM practitioners cannot avoid dealing with issues of work and its role in society. The masking of a degraded employment relationship in the language of flexibility is not surprising – indeed a master stroke – when we recognise and explore its relationship with consumption. For what seems to be occurring is that our roles as producers and employees (with the increased labour intensification and insecurity attached to both) are being packaged (gift-wrapped?) in the language that we associate with pleasure and gratification, the language of consumption. Hence, as producers, we have been converted into 'internal' customers; towards employees, the increasingly confident exercise of managerial prerogative and control can be re-represented as management through customer responsiveness, for 'customers are made to function in the role of management . . . as customer satisfaction is now defined as critical to success' (du Gay and Salaman, 1992). Further, as 'waste' (such as 'unnecessary headcount', 'overhead') is a product that a consumer, by definition, has rejected or does not want, how can the producer/employee, who is *also* a consumer who wants products/services of the best possible quality *and* at the lowest price, reject the logic that this has for employment contracts (i.e. lower their costs/employment contracts responsive to [consumer] market demands)?

And here we come to the crux of the argument. Which groups have a vested interest in translating words such as 'insecurity' into 'flexibility' or 'stability' into 'rigidity'? Richard Hyman's (1991) comments seem very much to the point when considering this question:

> *To define certain social realities as rigidities (rather than points of stability) and others as flexibilities (rather than areas of uncertainty) is to impose a particular evaluation, to commend a particular distribution of options and constraints, and hence to propose a particular structure of social power . . . Here the ideological dimension is of crucial importance, for a key influence on the discourse of flexibility is **who gains or loses** from a particular set of institutional arrangements, and **whose interests** would benefit or suffer from their alteration.* (original emphasis)

In my view 'flexible' employment patterns largely benefit the employer at the expense (with a few exceptions) of the individual *employee*, if not at the expense of *employment* in general. So, let us paint a different scenario of employees and employment, and see if we might offer a 'better' alternative.

TWO CHEERS FOR BUREAUCRACY?

In a capitalist society, it is natural to see the purpose of organisation in terms of accumulation and wealth creation and, hence, to prioritise ownership/shareholders as the stakeholders-in-chief. Suppose we take a different view and ask what the experience of organisation is for most people? For most people, the most intimate contact with any organisation is as employee or client/customer. As employees we spend most of our working day within the physical confines of organisations and our activities within organisations have a great influence on what we do when living our so-called private lives. Suppose then we consider that the primary function of an organisation is to provide the best possible work experience for its employees consistent with the organisation remaining economically viable. Suppose we promote the employee to be stakeholder-in-chief, what sort of organisational form might be consistent with delivering a high quality of working life?

At one level the answer is easy. Organisations that offer real empowerment and rewards according to collectively agreed contributions, *prima facie*, in a democratic society, would appear to offer an environment that is consistent with quality of working life (QWL) objectives. The sorts of organisational forms that might be preferred are partnerships or employee collectives (*see* Chapters 9 and 14). Here we have a problem. Leaving aside such examples as the John Lewis Partnership (where the conception of partnership seems somewhat tenuous given inequalities of power and reward between so-called 'partners'), true 'partnerships' seem to work best in knowledge-intensive professional organisations (e.g. law or accountancy firms) and in relatively small, decentralised organisations. This is not to deny, though, that working in a partnership can be uncomfortable for the less able or for those whose face does not fit. The well-known dictum of partnerships – 'up or out' – can put great pressure on both those who do as well as those who do not, make the grade. Nevertheless, given the growth in knowledge-based private sector service industries in western economies, this may be an increasingly viable form of employment in the 21st century. As for employee collectives, certainly in relation to manufacturing industry, their history is of small organisations, often born out of an earlier bankruptcy, and of questionable economic viability (e.g. Meriden co-operative).

It is in this context, that the ideal may not be attainable, that I wish to re-examine the case for bureaucracy, in terms of the employment experience it can offer. Bureaucracy has had an undeniably bad press. Leaving aside the classic studies of the dysfunctions of bureaucracy (trained incapacity, displacement of ends for means, vicious circles of control, rigidity and unresponsiveness and, at the very worst, the enabler of the Holocaust) (*see* for example, Bauman, 1989; Gouldner, 1964; Merton, 1957; Selznick, 1949), in the 1960s and 1970s it was conventional to identify bureaucracy with its machine-like forms and to link it with the supposedly alienating working conditions of mass production, the assembly line, Taylorism, Fordism and so forth (*see*, for example, Blauner, 1964). Even in this context, there was and still is a tendency to ignore the benefits machine bureaucracy and mass production brought to the employee: full-time, more or less permanent employment up to 65 years of age; a steadily increasing standard of living; and often friendships borne of long, uninterrupted association with workmates. Even the monotonous, hard and repetitive work might contain some intrinsic satisfactions, if we are to believe Baldamus' (1961) analysis of the rhythms of 'traction and tedium'. Indeed, bureaucracy lay at the heart of the post-war Keynesian settlement of full employment and a social wage (Harvey, 1989).

But if we go back to Weber's (1947) original formulation of the ideal model of bureaucracy, it was rooted not in manufacture, but in the office, in administration, or what we might call today the (largely public) service sector. And what contract of employment was on offer? Full-time, lifelong employment with an emphasis on the development of expertise and specialist skills, recruitment of personnel on the basis of ability and specialist knowledge, promotion on the basis of seniority combined with merit, and rules and procedures aimed at establishing, not only rationality and efficiency, but fairness. In terms of the experience of employment, behaviours that today are commonly presented as dysfunctions of bureaucracy (rigid demarcation lines, lack of flexibility in behaviour and response, over-possessive 'ownership' of a job) can be seen as having positive benefits for the employee: protection against labour intensification and rewards and celebration for developing in-depth, if narrow expertise, and the psychological security that may result. Mintzberg (1979) too recognises that professional bureaucracies, at least, have the virtues of being highly democratic structures, given the power held by the operating core and the opportunities it allows for the (admittedly professional) operator to maintain control over his or her own work and the decisions that affect it.

Of course, there is a downside to all this. I would argue that, in contrast to today, bureaucracy's first concern was to protect production and the producer, regarding this as ultimately in the best interests of the consumer. It might be argued that mass production, both allowing and depending on mass consumption, did just this. In contrast, it might be argued that where bureaucracy was most protective of the rights of producers – in professional bureaucracies – consumers were less well served, given the essential unresponsiveness of such structures to client individuality and variation and their reliance on, sometimes arrogant and flawed, professional judgement.

CONCLUSION

I have argued that flexibility in employment contracts in not necessarily a 'good thing' from the point of view of the employee-as-producer, even if it does have advantages for the employer and the employee-as-consumer. Is it inevitable? A fashionable argument, echoed even by the leadership of the Labour Party, is that the intensification of competition consequent on globalisation makes such employment practices inevitable if organisations are to survive. Even Japan's dual economy points to the relevance of flexibility in employment contracts as a cornerstone of economic success. In Germany too there is evidence of increases in part-time and temporary working (Brewster, 1996). Fair enough, perhaps international competition will dictate strategies to minimise unit labour costs. But, it should be noted that in the EU (including the UK) the bulk of part-time, fixed-term and temporary contracts occurs in the service sector. How many of these jobs, particularly in the public sector services and in personal services such as hotels, restaurants, leisure activities, and so on, are really at threat from international competition? How many of these jobs can be realistically exported? Yet it is the private personal services sector that contains some of the most insecure and least well-paid jobs in the UK. In the public service sector, arguably fixed-term contracts are not inevitable but a result of conscious decisions about levels of public sector spending and direct taxation that are not immutable.

The language of flexibility may persuade us that the growth in non-standard contracts is both 'inevitable' and a 'good thing'. After all, it speaks to us and benefits us in our role as consumers. And, as Keenoy and Anthony (1992) remind us:

> *Once it was deemed sufficient to redesign the organisation to make it fit human capacity and understanding: now it is better to redesign human understanding to fit the organisation's purpose.*

The worry is, however, that those employees most likely to 'enjoy' a flexible non-standard contract are precisely those least likely to 'enjoy' their roles as consumers, given the association of employment flexibility with low pay.

20

Re-engaging the HRM function

Rebuilding work, trust and voice

PAUL SPARROW

Sheffield University Management School, University of Sheffield

MICK MARCHINGTON

Manchester School of Management, UMIST

The arrival of a new government in May 1997 certainly signalled the beginnings of an alternative HRM agenda in the UK. Anticipated developments include legislation to address age discrimination, implementation of working time directives which will have a marked effect on paid vacation provision and unpaid leave, a minimum wage, and a 'new deal' for the unemployed with changes in welfare provision and recruitment subsidies as part of a welfare-to-work programme (Incomes Data Services, 1997a). However, as this book has demonstrated, these are mere 'tilts at the windmill'. A far more fundamental revision of the field of HRM, the contribution it makes, and its ability to influence the work and society agenda is needed. In this last chapter, we address five critical questions:

1 Is HRM in crisis or not?
2 What are the requisite fields of knowledge that HR academics need to understand and HR practitioners need to develop, and what lessons do these fields suggest for the contribution of HRM in the future?
3 How do we understand and manage the concept of trust, when we have to trust in the transitions taking place in work, but see that trust itself is also in transition?
4 How do HR practitioners cope with the problems created by institutional behaviour and break the cycle of continued breach of trust?
5 How should we continue to unravel the HRM contribution?

NO CRISIS, JUST DECISIVE TIMES?

Only when they have earned and rebuilt trust will HR practitioners be in a stronger position to exert their authority and contribute to what are decisive times within organisations.

In the opening chapter we pointed out that crisis comes from the Greek word *krînein*, a decisive moment or turning point and asked if decisions made today about the shape of HRM policies and practices will prove to be a turning point in terms of what is feasible after the millennium? In analysing the torments of transition in European patterns of HRM, Sparrow and Hiltrop (1994) argued that the actions of today's HR practitioners in dealing with issues of productivity, flexibility and performance management would determine the aspirations of a generation. We have argued that we do not face a crisis, but the field of HRM is clearly at a significant juncture. The problems and dilemmas discussed in Chapter 1 and faced worldwide are not going to go away of their own accord. As noted in Chapters 1 and 4, even the ability of Japan to withstand some of the pressures is questioned. The tensions continue to mount and the various dilemmas grow in their potential to create a future crisis of affairs.

To what extent do the various authors in this book feel that the field of HRM is in crisis? A range of positions is taken by the contributors. The first perspective characterised by David Guest in Chapter 3 is one of *phased evolution*. He is sceptical of the idea of crisis. He feels that we can manufacture the argument that there is a crisis, but in so doing we are making assumptions that HRM is both a coherent concept and a widely applied framework (both of which assertions he refutes). More tellingly, he makes the point that HRM is only in crisis if there is a powerful and competing orthodoxy to take its place. He does not believe there is an alternative to challenge the centrality of HRM ideas about the generation of high commitment and high performance. The contracting culture does not provide a strong challenge. To Guest, we are moving into a period in which we return to a previous way of thinking about co-ordination and control. The short-term, insecure contract culture is subject to strong market forces, and will inevitably trigger a reawakening of historical concerns about the need for hierarchy. We are moving around a non-ending loop. The need for more co-ordination, the end of careers and the desire to opt-out of the 'employment game' have been discussed throughout all phases of personnel and development.

Whether this argument holds or not depends on the view taken on the three scenarios highlighted by Paul Sparrow in Chapter 8. He takes a different view, and argues first that shifts in the pattern of work and society fundamentally influence HRM by shaping the perceptions that employees have of work (and therefore conditioning their psychological contract). They also alter the economics of labour, and, further the incentive and need for organisations to build high-commitment or high-trust systems. He also argues that we face three possible scenarios, derived from the work–leisure literature of the 1960s, each of which presents varying degrees of concern for the HR practitioner. The first would not present a crisis, just a busy agenda. This is the scenario in which we assume that people are 'self-correcting animals'. The various challenges to HRM and to levels of commitment and trust, outlined throughout this book, serve to move the majority of people to lower and more transactional levels of commitment and trust, but essentially all people make this adjustment once they realise that the days of the post-war full employment contract have gone.

The second scenario takes on the form of a short-term crisis in that it assumes people actually have 'limited capacity'. The pressures and changed demands of work mean that many reach their finite ability or desire to cope. We therefore see HRM tools losing relevance and motivational potential for many segments of the workforce. The third scenario is more disconcerting. For this we have to assume that we are witnessing 'discontinuities' in the psychological make-up of employees, especially across the generations, and that people start playing to 'new rules of the game'. This latter scenario suggests possible crisis, but also opportunity for HR practitioners to engage people in new ways, once the behaviours are understood. The evidence to date suggests that the first scenario is most applicable to today, the second is a distinct influence, and the third is a future possibility.

The 'new rules of the game' assumption also pervades Ian Beardwell's analysis in Chapter 13. Here HRM is not in crisis, but is rather in uncharted territory. HR practitioners have to manage a world in which individuals may be conscious accepters of the new deal, placing their trust in the ability of globalisation to deliver the goods they want; or may perceive themselves as being victims of this; or may just be unwitting accomplices. Beardwell admits that in a world in which flexibility and insecurity affect a wide range of jobs, the role of 'accomplice' best fits the patterns of union recognition, membership and employee behaviour. This takes us into uncharted territory because HR practitioners now have to manage high-discretion, non-qualified and low-involvement managers and unwitting employees. This is very different territory from managing the traditional post-war employment relationship exchange, which was based on a more favourable balance of power as far as employees were concerned. Under these new 'structural conditions' the employee contribution is limited to the job in which they find themselves, and what they make of this job. However, as we saw in Chapter 8, what now constitutes a job is in question. Recharting the HRM contribution in this environment is seen as a critical task by Ian Beardwell. He is optimistic about the potential outcome, because we are not really in a period of totally arbitrary managerial discretion. We are in a true 'black hole' i.e. something about which we know little but which has a profound influence on the environment around it. There is compelling evidence that the HRM process can reconfigure the new employment relationship in ways that are attractive to both employer and employee, but with increasing irritation at the inability to re-establish a sense of employee voice.

For some contributors, such as Chris Brewster in Chapter 16 and Derek Torrington in Chapter 2, there is some strategic threat to the HR department. Brewster considers the threat to HRM in the context of the flexibility debate and the transfer of both costs and risks from the organisation to the individual and the state that is taking place. He argues that if the HR department's raison d'être is dealing with *employment* issues, then increasingly it is going to become less relevant to the overall costs and output of the organisation. Outputs are going to be linked more commonly to options outside employment or at least to options outside the standard employment package, and if the HR department is not involved in managing these transactions, it will face a reduced workload. There is also opportunity in taking on the workload associated with repositioning the HR department and the HR practitioner as managers of the way in which the organisation works, but this means the development of different knowledge, different attitudes and different skills. Unless the function and the people in it are prepared to change to meet the circumstances and requirements of the new labour market, HRM will indeed be in crisis, he argues.

Derek Torrington examines the issue from the perspectives of confidence, identity and direction. The position facing the field of HRM is not one of crisis, but one of lost nerve and focus. He sees the main challenge to the field in terms of a loss of its operational and strategic implementation expertise. There is a crisis of confidence, understandably given the developments outlined in this book, but then there always has been such a crisis. The crisis in identity is not helped by books such as this, because most academics set up too wide and too ambitious an agenda for HR practitioners. There is a crisis of direction, which is a more serious charge, but he argues that much of this results from too much control and knowledge being handed over to consultants and line managers.

However, there is every reason to believe that this process of devolution and outsourcing will continue. In outlining the recent turnaround at Continental Airlines, the Vice President, global human resources, describes a process in which a significant HRM agenda was delivered by a department that has undergone a 30 per cent cut in staffing (Carrig, 1997). The HR department operated with a ratio of one HR employee for every 300 staff, three times the spans of control afforded by their sector rivals. Despite significant outsourcing of the existing HRM process, there is room for yet more activity to follow the same route. Carrig (1997) concludes that 'the transactions handled by many HR departments are still mostly routine and trivial, amounting to an expensive use of the HR department's own human resources'. Continental Airlines is pursuing a policy of creating strategic partnerships with many outsourced HR service providers. However, in addition to outsourcing the simple and most transactional HR functions of benefits administration, record keeping and employee services, in future the *provision of many more field administration tools and the design of traditional HR interventions* will also be targeted for outsourcing. The line of argument put forward by Carrig (1997) is that as more design, development and implementation work associated with the *transactional functions* of performance management, training, recruitment, compensation, labour relations and management development is outsourced, the in-house HR function will be able to concentrate on *transformational functions* of strategic planning, organisation development, knowledge management, contracting and trust building. Given the developments in the field of HRM outlined in this book, this would seem to be a likely routemap for HR functions at the millennium.

REQUISITE FIELDS OF KNOWLEDGE

Common to all these positions is the stress placed by contributors on the need for HR practitioners to develop new areas of knowledge for the millennium. Before detailing these, we begin with two caveats. First, it is all too easy to become fixated on the importance of new fields of knowledge, when in some cases, what is needed is a simple dose of effective management skill. Seitchick (1997) draws attention to the need for HR practitioners to take a leaf out of their own teachings, and to learn how to become effective followers (Kelly, 1988), not just strategic partners and leaders. HR practitioners often find themselves in a dilemma, operating in a 'brave new world where leaders must be followers and followers must also lead' (Seitchick, 1997). While their organisations are asking them to become leaders and partners in running the business, as several chapters in this book remind us, they are often asked to implement initiatives and programmes over which they have no formal authority, or with which they disagree on professional grounds. The programmes may be based on a poor or non-existent diagnosis of the problem, may be in opposition to the stated values of the culture or organisational design, or may be seen as a superficial reaction to what they know is a deep-seated human problem. Managers from all specialisms find themselves in this position, and so have to learn how to think for themselves, be committed to the organisation's greater purpose, hold onto standards that are higher than the immediate work environment requires, and have the courage to challenge leaders. Only a crisis of confidence and contribution stands in the way of doing this, not a crisis in the relevance of the field of HRM.

Second, in reassessing the contribution to be made by HR practitioners, the chapters in this book have also moved us towards some deeper philosophical issues which present both future opportunities and new sources of identity for HR practitioners. It is not just a question of new techniques and new knowledge insights. In Chapter 7 Peter Herriot argued that HR practitioners must come to terms with the reality of continuous transition and that we can no longer expect periods of preparation and stabilisation. Yet an overriding set of conclusions from the ESRC workshops was that HR practitioners are searching for new sources of continuity. Given that massive change within organisations seems to be unavoidable, some areas of stability and new perspectives on basic HRM principles are emerging. What are the new frames of reference or fields of knowledge that HR practitioners should bring to bear? Eight priority areas have been highlighted:

1 **Strategic management:** The nature of human resources as a source of competitive advantage.

2 **Business process, organisation structure and organisation design linkages:** In Chapter 5 Mike Oram draws attention to the need for HR practitioners to develop new skills and competencies associated with understanding the operation of process-driven or parallel forms of working. At the most obvious level this places the onus on HR practitioners to guide the organisation on how best to develop – and more importantly for Oram, how best to recruit and select – behavioural skills such as teamworking, listening, and telephone communication. Non-behavioural capabilities such as time-management and quality-management methods are areas HR practitioners must learn about. In Chapter 8 Paul Sparrow identifies four fields of knowledge that HR practitioners need to master if they are to influence the linkage between business processes, organisation structure and organisation design. First, they need to comprehend the various components that are bundled together into definable 'jobs' (through the tasks, operations, work elements and duties that are deemed still necessary). Second, they need to be able to redesign the context into which jobs are placed and the position of the new job in the broader organisation design (through knowledge of the family of jobs to which it is deemed to belong, the occupation of the job holder, the career stream to which jobs belong, and the work process of which it forms a part). Third, they need to understand the way in which jobs relate to, and interact with, each other (through the roles assigned to jobs, the information and control systems, and the relative levels of power they possess). And finally they need to understand the way in which HRM systems integrate the new bundles of jobs into the strategic process (through the way in which employee contributions to the jobs are co-ordinated, controlled and committed to).

3 **Interdependencies of HR systems:** Point 2 stimulates us to understand the interdependencies of HR systems, rather than being experts in each separate system. For Mike Oram, the central areas of knowledge need to be concentrated on understanding the consequences of misaligning core HR processes: job analysis and job definition, recruitment, monetary and non-monetary rewards, organisational learning, technological learning, involvement and participation, communication, benchmarking and internal consultancy support.

4 **Transition management:** We need to understand the individual outcomes, options, justification, skills and competencies, and flexibilities associated with the existing labour market dynamics. Peter Herriot argues that HR practitioners have to understand how to manage a range of transitions in employment without relying on the luxury of preparing for the transition or regaining a sense stability. The way people encounter and make adjustments to major transitions in trust and role becomes a central field of knowledge for HR practitioners. This knowledge needs to be applied to transitions from employment to unemployment, across roles within the organisation, changes to enlarged roles, and changes across the various forms of atypical employment.

5 **Psychological contracting:** This means we need to educate HR practitioners about the processes of psychological contracting – managing socialisation, feelings, commitment and trust – and not just the techniques of doing it (the reward and performance management systems, training techniques and so forth). An area of clarification is the need to understand whether the *content* of the contract is the most predictive of employee behaviour, i.e. whether the different 'contractual stances' noted in Chapter 8 are in fact associated with different HRM preferences, or whether the *process through which it is negotiated,* as highlighted in Chapter 7, is more important and predictive of eventual outcomes.

6 **Motivational processes:** This forces a rethink and reappraisal of the basic motivational processes. How do people develop identify with the organisation, or its sub-units? What are the implications of the recent studies on attitudinal change, commitment and motivation for organisational behaviour?

7 **Marketing principles:** The fragmentation of HRM also highlights the need for HR practitioners to learn the basic principles of marketing and consumer behaviour. How to sell the HR function and its technical offerings to an increasingly individualised, selective set of consumers (employees) will become a key skill for HR practitioners.

8 **Trust and partnership building:** This is the most fundamental area of knowledge of all. We outline the most important aspects of this requirement later in the chapter.

RETHINKING THE BASIC HRM ROLE AND CONTRIBUTION

All these fields of knowledge highlight the need to rethink the basic contribution that is made by the HR function. In considering the fields of knowledge that are now central to the role and contribution of HR practitioners, we would make two observations.

First, this knowledge has to be developed through the interventions that HR practitioners are encouraged to make in their organisations; the knowledge inputs that are built into their professional education, such as the IPD syllabus; and through a refocusing of the academic agenda over the coming years. What does it mean to study HRM? A refocusing of the professional syllabus should call into question some of the fads of the 1990s. For example, the recent attention to benchmarking – which often directs attention to the content of HRM – may be ill founded, because it serves the purpose of external satisficing rather than internal critical evaluation.

Second, HR practitioners need to be helped, and HR academics need to be encouraged, to see and manage the individual psychological contract in the context of other contracts (for example, social and cultural). The 'new deal' or contract must reflect the reality of how people behave and has also to limit disruption to the broader community group. The contracting role also has to bind people culturally into the group. What is the interface between the creation of a series of individual psychological contracts and the avoidance of any perceived violation of communal assumptions? A rethink on how to create a sense of community outside the organisation, through the operation of local labour markets, will be an area in which HR practitioners might need to become involved. One of our problems is that we have little understanding of the way in which local labour markets provide long-term stability to organisations, even during periods of rapid change, through their possession of skills, work cultures, employment mindsets and attitudes, and networks of relationships. David Guest argues that the concept of community goes beyond the organisation, but an understanding of it will provide useful managerial insights for large organisations, networked or telecottage work arrangements, and even individual small teams.

In Chapter 1 Derek Torrington noted that personnel professionals are unique in having a syllabus dictated by academics. Nevertheless, historically the syllabus has provided professionals with considerable product knowledge and prescriptions. It provides little sociological or psychological insight into the workings of people and organisations, nor does it provide practitioners with organisation development process skills or the basic tools for how to develop business process knowledge. In Chapter 7 Peter Herriot draws attention to the need to consider the process of contracting – as an action verb – rather than getting too hung up on its content. Judge HRM practices against their ability to deliver a deal, not against the deal they deliver, is his message. This has significant implications for the role of HR practitioners.

Moreover, the ESRC workshop dedicated to the psychological contract raised deep questions about the role and education of HR practitioners. It suggested that continued conflict can be expected in their role. Are HR professionals the brokers of the deal? Are they again the 'fair-play' representatives of the employer and employees? This issue of *representational focus* has existed since the beginning of the profession, but the recent redefinition of the employment relationship has brought it back to centre stage once again. It becomes an issue because there are hidden costs in having to manage careers as psychological contracts. These added costs come through having to supervise the psychological contract (which has to act as an alternative to internal career management structures). Many of the costs of contracting may not yet be understood, but still have to be managed. There is an educational aspect to any full 'contracting' approach and this has implications for management competencies. Line managers have to be educated about both the 'hard' and 'soft' contract issues that are needed to maintain effective management. Paradoxically, it is the so-called 'soft' issues that are the hardest ones to crack, and this is most evident with the issue of trust.

TRUST IN TRANSITION

One of the enduring messages of the book is that we need to rethink the nature of trust both in organisations and in the nature of HRM. The ability of organisations to re-establish trust has to be questioned. In a theoretical analysis of the basis of trust and the consequences of violation of the psychological contract, Morrison and Robinson (1997) argue that:

We (also) caution organisations against misrepresenting purposeful reneging by trying to convince the employee that it was due to either uncontrollable factors or incongruence. Although in our model we suggest that this behaviour may minimise violation, it is highly risky and may backfire if employees fail to accept the explanation and consider it as one more act of deception. This perception will further undermine, and perhaps even destroy, the trust that is critical to the maintenance of the psychological contract.

Some indication of the transactions in which trust has to be re-established at the individual level can be gleaned from the recent study of the content of the psychological contract by Herriot, Manning and Kidd (1997). Organisations had seven categories of obligation expected of employees:

- to work contracted hours
- to do a quality piece of work
- to deal honestly with clients
- to be loyal and guard the organisation's reputation
- to treat property carefully
- to dress and behave correctly
- to be flexible and go beyond one's job description.

It is input, not just output, that matters most to the employer, whereas: 'for employees, the preference was for a basic transaction of pay and a secure job in return for time and effort' (Herriot *et al.*, 1997). What does the employee expect of the employer? Twelve constructs were revealed:

- to provide adequate induction and training
- to ensure fairness in selection, appraisal, promotion and redundancy procedures
- to provide justice, fairness and consistency in the application of rules and disciplinary procedures
- to provide equitable pay in relation to market values across the organisation
- to be fair in the allocation of benefits
- to allow time off to meet family and personal needs
- to consult and communicate on matters that affect them
- to interfere minimally with employees in terms of *how* they do their job
- to act in a personally supportive way to employees
- to recognise or reward special contribution or long service
- to provide a safe and congenial work environment
- to provide what job security they can.

This high level of agreement about the nature of the contract means that it shall be easier for both parties to establish what is a 'fair exchange deal'. It also suggests a simple basis for restoring employee trust. Employers have a long hard slog ahead of them, and need to focus their attention on delivering these simple, basic and transactional constituents of the psychological contract if they are to restore mutual trust and commitment (Herriot, Manning and Kidd, 1997).

Flexible resources need managing and to do this effectively HR practitioners need better insights into the nature of trust and the role of social capital if they are to re-engage enough people. The paradox facing HR practitioners is that they are asking employees to trust *in* transition at the very time that employee trust *is itself in* transition. The concept of trust has become central to the field of HRM at the millennium.

So what exactly is trust? For Clark and Payne (1997) trust is best seen as a willingness to rely or depend on some externality (an event, process, individual, group or system). It is defined as the specific expectation that the actions from such externalities will be beneficial rather than detrimental (Gambetta, 1988) and is therefore buttressed by the ability (rightly or wrongly) to take for granted many features of the social order (Creed and Miles, 1996). HR practitioners need to distinguish between the influences on employee well-being that accrue from trust as a *state of mind*, and the actions and overt behaviours that result from the *process of trusting*. This means that they have to understand the factors that contribute to trust, what is involved in the act of trusting, and the outcomes of high and low trust (Mayer, Davis and Schoorman, 1995). Creed and Miles (1996) distinguish *three* different types of trust:

1 **Process-based trust:** personal experience of recurring exchanges which create ongoing expectations and norms of obligation about what is felt to be fair treatment (e.g. I have come to trust . . .).
2 **Characteristic-based trust:** beliefs about another's trustworthiness that results from a perception of their expertise, intentions, actions, words and general qualities. Trust is associated with clearly defined social groups based on the attitudes and behaviour they possess (e.g. I trust a doctor because . . .).
3 **Institutional-based trust***:* trust in the integrity and competence of informal societal structures (e.g. I have trust in the independence of the press . . .).

Clearly, we need to relate our understanding of these three facets of trust to the field of HRM, specifically in terms of how each form of trust is breached and how it may be rebuilt. Many chapters in this book demonstrate how the basis of each of these three facets of 'trust' have been challenged by changes in work and society:

1 **Changes to the shape and design of organisations and jobs** have either designed in or designed out trust. Specifically, this occurs through the choices made by managers about empowerment and the design of control systems, co-ordination systems and associated business processes. This was highlighted by David Guest in Chapter 3, Mike Oram in Chapter 5 and Paul Sparrow in Chapter 8. Trust is also designed in through the levels of information sharing and shape of reward systems associated with the operation of teamworking, as argued by Mick Marchington in Chapter 14 and Paul Edwards in Chapter 18.
2 **Challenges to the psychological contract.** The lack of mutuality has broken both the expectations and norms that are expected at work and there has been a perceived breach of trust in many sectors. This was noted by Steve Bendall, Chris Bottomley and Pat Cleverly in Chapter 6, Peter Herriot in Chapter 7 and Paul Sparrow in Chapter 8. Expectations of employment security have been severely tested over the last decade, and it is proving very hard for managers to convince their staff that they can be trusted to make decisions which promote continuity and long-term goals rather than short-term expedients, as argued by John Monks in Chapter 11.
3 **Social groups and the trusted divisions and behaviours expected from them.** Many expected divisions have been thrown into confusion. The HRM philosophy challenges

age-old and trusted divisions between employer and employee or between managers and unions. However, the trust that employees put in the HRM paradigm and their belief that it would deliver greater benefit than a reliance on voice achieved through more formal union–management partnership has been questioned. There are new social groupings of what Ian Beardwell in Chapter 13 calls 'victims', 'accomplices' or 'conscious believers'. The pursuit of flexibility has broken the assumptions about behaviours that managers have come to trust as characterising full-time workers or part-time workers, older employees or younger employees, men or women, as noted by Mike Emmott and Sue Hutchinson in Chapter 15. Even in high-trust environments dependent on teamwork, as described by Paul Edwards in Chapter 18, evidence for high commitment was distinctly absent, as indicated by the data on trust, continued willingness to dispute job duties and a belief that unions remained a necessary bulwark against management.

High trust has been shown to be associated with many of the positive features desired by employers, such as long-term commitment, acceptance of incremental increases in risk and co-operative behaviour, and openness to learning (Creed and Miles, 1996). If we wish to rebuild trust, we should learn from the sociologists and psychologists who have analysed how trust is constructed (Lewicki and Bunker, 1996). A useful reference point for HR practitioners is to consider how trust is built up in professional relationships, where according to Shapiro, Sheppard and Cheraskin (1992), there are three incremental trust processes.

The first aspect of trust creation is actually rather negative and is called deterrence or calculus-based trust. It is developed on the basis of people seeing a consistency of behaviour which shows that people will do what they say they will do. This is sustained by threat of punishment, which is at this stage a more significant motivator than the promise of reward (for example, we learn to trust our enemies because we see evidence that no superpower will really use the nuclear deterrent due to the fear of mutual destruction). The potential loss of future interaction with others must be seen to outweigh the profit potential that comes from violating expectations. In order to control the behaviours associated with trust, deterrence requires a close monitoring and the ability to tell one another when a violation has occurred, and the potentially harmed person must be willing to withdraw benefits or introduce harm to the person acting distrustfully. This shapes the 'upside' and 'downside' calculations made by the trustee. This clearly is the dominant part of the agenda for HR practitioners. We consider the implications of the deterrence or calculus-based aspect of trust building on p.311 when we outline how HR practitioners need to demonstrate their contribution to organisational performance.

The second phase of trust development is the creation of knowledge-based trust. This is grounded in the other's predictability and it relies on information, not deterrence. Regular communication and courtship contributes to the building up of accurate insights that enable the two parties to anticipate one another's wants, preferences and approaches to problem-solving. The partnership debate clearly falls into this second phase of re-establishing trust.

The third phase is identification-based trust. At this stage of the relationship each party effectively understands and is seen to appreciate the others' wants and is prepared to act effectively in one another's interests. Each party is willing to substitute for the other in any transaction and can be confident that interests will be justly served. Each party learns what is required to sustain the other's trust (*see* Chapter 9 by Couper and Stevens, and Chapter 10 by Thomas and Wallis on partnership). This categorisation by Shapiro, Sheppard and Cheraskin (1992) corresponds rather well to the phases that a partnership organisation, such as Welsh Water, actually goes through. This is particularly apparent if there has been a history of poor industrial relations at the organisation, or trust has been shattered by recent management actions. The importance of trust for good management–employee relations is well known; as Brown (1973) pointed out many years ago, in the negotiating process 'without trust you are like a conger eel on ice'.

COPING WITH INSTITUTIONAL BEHAVIOUR

In Chapter 19 Karen Legge questioned the inevitability of many of the changes outlined in this volume, and placed the pursuit of parallel and multiple flexibilities in the context of broader societal changes as employees rebalance their roles as both producers and consumers. Chris Brewster points to the transfer of costs and risks from state and organisation to the individual. One inevitability in such a period is that the HRM agenda continues to be set – and is being increasingly driven – by institutional behaviour at the level above the organisation. John Monks takes issue with the philosophy of corporate governance in Chapter 11. The core problem for HR practitioners is continued evidence of a lack of institutional-based trust. The following stories about General Motors (GM) and Electrolux that featured prominently in the business press in 1997 reinforced the argument that there are now *inherent system faults that blight the ability of HR practitioners to make a useful contribution*. Following the US approach, Britain, the Netherlands and Switzerland have led the trend for laying off staff in Europe. The pressure is now on France, Germany and Sweden to do the same. The situation at Electrolux (responsible also for the Zanussi, AEG and Frigidaire brands) is a classic example. It currently has a 4 per cent margin and provides a return on equity of 8.7 per cent (McIvor, 1997; Moss and Richards, 1997). This is not enough for financial analysts, and below the desired margin of 6.5 per cent to 7 per cent and return on equity of 15 per cent. So the new Chief Executive, Michael Treschow, has announced the closure of 25 plants and 50 warehouses, with the loss of 12 000 jobs (11 per cent of the workforce) at a cost of £197 million. In reacting to the news, a financial analyst at UBS is reported by McIvor (1997) as saying 'a shake-up has been overdue and people are very happy to see it has happened . . . it looks much more comprehensive than anyone dared hope.' Share prices jumped 25 per cent in two days to an all time high, and the Chief Executive pronounced 'in the past we have been most criticised for failing to deliver sufficient profitability. If we don't deliver that, we can't create pride in our business.' Whose pride? Whose price? Affecting how many generations? We noted in Chapter 1 that CEOs are under conflicting pressures from a range of stakeholders and are often guilty of not telling analysts about the difficult people-related, but nevertheless business issues, associated with implementing heightened performance expectations. This runs the risk of creating unrealistic financial expectations among institutions, because the internal problems associated with creating the necessary changes in culture and systems are obscured and glossed over. John Monks considered this issue in Chapter 11.

Meanwhile, in the USA employees of GM went on strike claiming that they are being driven too hard (Waters, 1997). The latest productivity study shows that GM employs

3.47 workers for each car, which though one fewer than five years ago, is more than the 3.29 workers per car at Ford, 3.09 at Chrysler and 2.23 at the best US-based Japanese plant. The latest GM products will require 30 per cent less labour to build. Staff levels have been trimmed and jobs outsourced to lower paying non-union suppliers. Labour agreements mean that the present generation of workers, now aged in their late 40s and 50s, have been virtually guaranteed jobs for life or generous pay-offs. The 1990s have been seen as a period of 'joyless prosperity' and industrial relations have been poor at GM. As one of the picketers complained 'the big thing isn't the money – there's just too many hours. We're not 20 years old any more.' In 18 months GM has seen £920 million in lost profits due to industrial action. It will be early next century before GM rehires large numbers of employees to replace the existing generation who near retirement. Waters (1997) concludes 'in many ways it is over terms and conditions of these jobs that this summer's strikes are being waged.' So are we living through decisive times in HRM? The employees of GM and Electrolux would certainly say so and would not perceive the word 'crisis' to be an overstatement. So how can we match the academic view that there is no crisis with the perception of many employees that something has to change?

BREAKING THE CHAIN: DEVELOPING META-STANDARDS FOR HRM

An important part of the HRM agenda has to be the consideration of new co-operative forms of HRM co-ordinated across whole networks of organisations. Faced with the sorts of events outlined in the previous section, we argued in Chapter 1 that HR practitioners have to help rebuild new structures and processes that set the overall *social contract* (the system rooted in the organisation's practices and culture that shapes the assumptions, beliefs and behaviour of employees) within the organisation. It is this social contract that sets the context for, and increasingly influences the success of, the organisations' HRM policies and practices.

In Chapter 1 we referred to Ghoshal and Bartlett's (1995) call for the development of a 'new moral contract' in HRM, which was based on their insights into innovative IT and service companies such as ISS, Andersen Consulting, Intel and Motorola. They argue that in the context of the current radical change in economic regulation and political and social ideologies, it is the basis of relationships that must change. The new 'contract' will only be successful if organisations develop work methods and redesign work processes that foster the creation of continuous self-development. Citing the example of General Electric's strategic planning process, they note that in the current rapid redesign of organisational processes we should pursue true empowerment. Work designs have to incorporate the ability for employees to switch to and from production and learning activities. This can be achieved by focusing the provision of information and need for decision-making on shopfloor and office employees so that information has to flow through direct relationships at work group level. This would then require organisations to compensate managers for their consequent sense of uncertainty, caused by their reliance on others. One way of doing this is to allow more creative and strategic activities at senior management level, rather than insisting on the more routine monitoring of complex strategic and performance planning and control systems. Pascale (1995) is pessimistic about such solutions and argues that a new social contract predicated on the concept of 'employability' is 'an ill-thought through concept infused with more hope than substance'. There is no painless remedy to replacing the broken psychological contract of the past. Such changes in management philosophy will likely be limited to small and emerging 'communities of practice' or 'post-industrial guilds'. We should not hide from the need to accept a deeper, more realistic understanding of the task that lies before us (Pascale, 1995).

Most post-industrial management philosophies, into which Ghoshal and Bartlett (1995) suggest we place our HRM solutions, would seem to require us to reverse 100 years of industrial and management process evolution, to alter the mechanisms of corporate governance, and reskill a generation of workers. Clearly this is no easy task, but it is one that *is* possible, and one that can be crystallised through each one of the millions of decisions being made today as we redesign our organisations. Ghoshal and Bartlett (1995) and Pascale (1995) argue that the creation of a new moral contract requires a fundamental transformation of a company's management processes and in the mindsets of both its employees and its top management. How do we start to achieve this?

As with many areas of management behaviour, the question is whether changes can be achieved voluntarily and through self-regulation, through persuasion, or through regulation and legislation? The first step is to make the environment for change in the management process more 'receptive'. One option is to take part of the problem out of the hands of individual organisations and HR practitioners, and to develop solutions at a level above the firm. We need to pursue what could be called 'network HRM' and to encourage self-regulation through the adherence to external standards. Increasingly, the social contract has to be applied across the whole network of suppliers and customers – single organisations feel reluctant to attempt to change the rules of the game by themselves. It is, however, possible to alter the dynamics of a system by pursuing external 'meta-standards' (Uzumeri, 1997). Patrick Flood touches on this issue in Chapter 4 when he discusses the performance metrics associated with a total quality HRM philosophy. For example, organisations such as Marks and Spencer realised the importance of gaining control over training standards down the supplier network, and many new foreign direct-invested organisations such as the Japanese car manufacturers have engaged in a process of HRM systems transfer through a local regional network of firms. HR practitioners and academics can learn how this can be used to their advantage.

How can stability and advanced HRM practices be introduced into what is a complex area of management? There are many equally complex areas of management, such as product quality, financial and control systems, crime prevention and security, where managers and individuals (on behalf of the organisation) are now convinced that it makes sense to be regulated by 'meta-standards' (such as ISO 9000). They are more than willing to bear the additional labour costs, changes to their internal control systems and expense to conform to standards. This is particularly so when the reason for standardisation is made meaningful to them (Uzumeri, 1997). There is no reason why HRM systems cannot also be encouraged to conform to new 'meta-standards'.

There is however an important distinction to be made. It could be argued that in countries such as France, or in Germany with its *Sozialpläne*, that the social partnership arrangements and web of legislation provide such meta-standards and regulation of the employment relationship. However, as we saw in Chapter 17 by Alan Jenkins, there are major problems with such an approach, given the issues of competitiveness facing

European organisations. As one German steel employee recently complained: 'We don't want any social plans, we want work!' Indeed, throughout much of Part Two of the book where the issue of partnership was considered, there was a reluctance to seek externally imposed institutional solutions of almost any kind.

What is needed is a series of meta-standards that *regulates the internal business processes of organisations according to HRM principles*. Such an option will not be easy as this route raises some deep philosophical and strategic conflicts within organisations. For example, the philosophy of creating customised and devolved HRM systems on the back of a psychological contracting process – which as we saw in Chapter 6 is currently seen as being a hopeful development by many organisations – stands in conflict with the need to design new centralised or super-ordinate rules that guide the operation of the HRM management sub-systems. The logic and tensions created by such disparate developments will have to be sold very carefully to line managers.

There is reason to believe that this task might become easier. Largely on the back of previous meta-standards in the field of quality, we have seen the adoption of multiple stakeholder strategic performance control systems. The balanced scorecard is a case in point, discussed by Patrick Flood in Chapter 4 and seen in the NatWest case in Chapter 6. The Norton-Kaplan model views strategic objectives from four perspectives: financial, customers, internal processes and organisational learning. It is now adopted by 60 per cent of the top 100 US companies and is used in the UK by organisations such as BT, BUPA, the Halifax, Shell, and Brown and Root (van de Vliert, 1997). As managers are made aware increasingly that the value chain incorporates such elements as service, customised design and response times, largely due to self-imposed regulation through quality meta-standards, they understand the need for a broader view of strategic and competitive performance. Organisations are adapting the basic system to suit their own needs, so that BP Chemicals may consider a category for the environment (van der Vliert, 1997) while Xerox uses its own 'management model' and 'business assessment process'. Indeed, Xerox has adopted a 31-measure system across six categories:

- leadership
- human resource management
- business process management
- customer and market focus
- information utilisation and quality tools
- results.

No crisis in HRM in this organisation, indeed a strong base from which to build up understanding of the contribution of the HR process.

UNRAVELLING THE HRM CONTRIBUTION

Limitations of the HR bundles approach

Before such changes are accepted, and before HR practitioners can re-engage their function and rebuild work, trust and voice in the organisation, for many commentators proving the contribution of the function and understanding its role in the strategic process remains a central task (Guest, 1997; Tyson, 1997). If the HRM contribution is proven, then the case for the application of new more socially inclusive 'meta-standards' to be applied across HRM systems becomes legitimate. However, employers are usually only likely to pursue Ghoshal and Bartlett's (1995) 'moral contract' if they can see a business case. It is our view that much existing research that has tried to demonstrate the links between HRM and organisational performance is not powerful enough to create the first precept of trust – deterrence. For example, the attempt to link 'bundles' of HRM policies with improved organisational performance, though well-intentioned, is a little naive and certainly rather prescriptive. There are many methodological and pragmatic issues that discount certain types of research and while the approach by Huselid and others (Huselid, 1995; Huselid, Jackson and Schuler, 1997) is interesting, it would be subject to much criticism in the UK. The assumptions that have to be built into the bundling of HRM policies and in particular the choice of financial performance measures make the task of showing such linkages impractical. Most 'raw' organisational performance measures are subject to situational manipulation – especially in the UK where return on assets has become a major focus, but is not truly reflective on the inner strength of the organisation. Moreover, simply measuring 'inputs' such as HRM policies and 'outputs' such as broad organisational performance, is likely to 'mask' the sophisticated set of linkages that really exist between HRM and performance. These include various 'time shift' issues. For example, investments may be made in HRM policies which build up into a critical mass over time, with any positive influences not taking hold until two or three years into the process. Moreover, many HR programmes are run 'politically' with clear 'front runner' policies intended to mobilise attitudes and change behaviour, i.e. there is a clear logic to the sequencing of the policies, they do not act as a composite bundle. Any cross-sectional or bundling methodology ignores all of these powerful effects.

The lesson is that academic research should be wary of using cross-sectional research designs which underestimate time lag or political impacts of HRM. Moreover, 'internal' performance, financial or control measures tend not to exist at the level of sophistication needed to conduct simple HRM input–firm performance output type of studies. When researchers tried to link training investments to performance in the late 1980s (Hendry and Pettigrew, 1990) it was clear that the internal budget processes of firms, with their inclusion or exclusion of various costs or activities associated with HRM, were so variable that comparing one firm with another was like comparing apples with oranges. So many assumptions and 'guestimates' have to be made that any analysis is not worth the paper it is written on. If academics are to help HR practitioners, a more qualitative approach is needed.

A number of contingent variables is known to influence the relationship between HRM and performance. HR practitioners have to be aware how their organisations vary in terms of what the HR strategists call 'human asset intensity' (Coff, 1997). In many cases the link between HRM and performance depends on the centrality of HRM issues to the core business process. This clearly varies across sectors. For example in retail, despite the rhetoric about customer service, only marginal gains are likely to be made by a high staff retention rate and good customer service skills. More money can be made by effective use of EPOS technology, branding and store location. Linking effective HRM to performance in such sectors is a harder and more sophisticated task than doing so in a sector in which people represent a higher proportion of the costs or have more ability to add value to the core business process.

Another problem faced by the 'bundles' approach becomes clear if we consider the challenge created by the drive for flexibility. As was made clear in Chapter 1, in trying to link HRM activities to firm performance, HR practitioners need to be aware that their organisations are seeking *seven* discrete flexibilities and may choose to pursue one of the flexibilities for one job, a different combination for another, or be attacking the whole organisation across a series of fronts. Each flexibility tends to be associated with a different set of contentions, type of struggle or 'battle' which requires the HR practitioner to command very different sets of expert knowledge and business arguments. When faced with such a range of flexibilities a 'one best way' HRM approach is misguided. Yet success or failure in delivering each different form of flexibility can be linked clearly to a series of contingencies: the range of difficult choices that have to be made about associated people management issues, the consequences of poor decision-making in the design and delivery of flexibility, or the knock-on benefits that accrue to the organisation from well-implemented interventions.

Deterrence-based insights into the HRM contribution

The issue facing HRM professionals at the millennium is then how to untangle what they know is an 'act of faith' logic. Of course the well-equipped and business-minded personnel and development specialists should be able to persuade managers to adopt or negotiate HRM interventions on the basis of clear business benefit. The problem is that the linkages between good HRM and good performance are becoming harder to prove in the devolved, deregulated and redesigned organisation of today. To do so requires skills, knowledge and insights that the HR specialist does not always have. How do you advise an organisation, for example, on which forms of flexibility are best suited to which operations, with what risks and benefits? Who has this knowledge? It increasingly resides in a range of stakeholders, including the HR specialist, the designers of the corporate control systems, the customers and the employees. The challenge is to capture the organisational learning that resides in such people.

In order to reconceptualise the contribution that HRM makes to organisational performance, HR practitioners will need to reinforce the deterrence-based trust arguments mentioned earlier in this chapter. We have to unravel the contribution that HRM makes to the process of organisational performance to show how the potential loss of future interaction with employees outweighs the profit potential that comes from violating expectations. In establishing the link we need to identify which indicators need close monitoring and provide HR practitioners with the ability to advise other stakeholders when a violation has occurred. We need to understand exactly how the potentially harmed person is likely to withdraw benefits and show how they do introduce harm for the person acting distrustfully. This requires the provision of information relating to every stage of the process that will enable organisations to shape their upside and downside calculations about change.

This suggests that HR practitioners need to find new 'handles' on which to build the arguments. There seem to be a series of fruitful arguments. A central task is to demonstrate the *cost of trust deficits*. One relatively unexplored area is in terms of the conflict between the organisation design decisions and the requisite levels of trust needed to make them effective. There are 'measurable dollar costs associated with the failure to meet minimal trust requirements' (Creed and Miles, 1996). These are incurred in several ways:

1 Through the higher transaction and control costs associated with organisation designs that operate on low levels of employee trust.

2 Through miscalculations about employees' level of capability and potential for exercising responsibility and self-direction (task reliability) or their ability or desire to apply a dominant philosophy based on operating logic values that are congruent with the organisations' design (value congruence). The rework that becomes necessary through the failure of employees to deliver these two qualities now bears significant cost.

3 Through the lost opportunity costs of operating with a low trust workforce in a world of increasingly high-risk–high-trust business relationships. There are costs associated with failures in strategically important inter-firm relationships (such as joint ventures, strategic alliances, collaborative arrangements), and evidence to link these failures to people-related problems.

Trust deficits are also seen in the hidden costs associated with downsizing and poor psychological contracts.

Proving the case

But how should HR practitioners prove this new contribution? Taking a leaf out of the strategists' book, they could employ cognitive mapping and causal analysis methodologies. We argued earlier that quality meta-standards make managers more familiar with:

● the input and output standards that guide the management process
● the design rules that guide the operation of the relevant management sub-systems
● the cause and effect consequences of altering key parts of the management process.

Once managers have this broader understanding, the case for external meta-standards becomes easier to accept. Therefore, if we wish to demonstrate the same contribution of HR considerations, we need to reveal the linkage between a series of core business processes, the resultant HRM choices and policies, and the impact on performance. In short, we need to map out the *process through which the* HRM contribution links to organisational performance. Rather than argue that a bundle of HR practices (point A) is linked to financial output measures (point B) through the statistical control of various factors, we need to 'join up the dots' and show the causal linkages between a complex set of factors.

Social and behavioural scientists began to take an interest in these sorts of research problems in the 1970s but it was only in the 1990s that the technique was used in the field of strategic management. Cognitive dimensions in part, therefore, represent core beliefs and assumptions that can be used to bind people together and explain events/actions of individuals and organisations in terms of implied cause and effect relationships. Different writers have given different names to these cognitive dimensions, such as dominant logic, myths, paradigms, belief systems, belief structure, schema, schemata, scripts, recipes, artificial intelligence, cognitive maps, influence diagrams or mindsets.

The strategic management literature emphasises the challenge faced by managers in this process of 'managerial sense-making'. They are assumed to be 'information workers' who spend most of their time absorbing, processing, and disseminating information about organisational issues, opportunities and problems as they see them. This is as true for HR practitioners as it is for the CEO pursuing the management of change. All specialists employ particular frames of reference to represent their information world and thus facilitate information processing and decision-making by others. Cognitions are seen as the specific belief systems of individual decision-makers, who draw upon various sub-sets of available knowledge in both formulating their expectations of, and in making choices about, organisational strategies. The challenge is to show how managerial cognition is linked to performance (Jenkins and Johnson, 1997). The investigation into managerial cognitions has naturally become more important in the context of the contemporary business environment as it helps researchers gain an understanding of the strategy of organisations and the dynamics of industries from the view point of managers. By analysing these dominant logics, the determination of organisational decisions – such as investments in HRM – and associated performance outcomes can become more predictable in an uncertain environment. Cognitive mapping techniques have been used in management research to gain insight into the belief systems of managers. Maps have been used to represent the causal assertions that are embedded in the policy arguments forwarded by decision-makers, and also to reveal the internal logic, constructs and belief systems that individuals use to solve organisational problems, i.e. how managers make sense of and explain their problems. We might expect such developments to move into the HRM field given the need to unravel their contribution.

CONCLUSION

Whatever methodologies and approaches are eventually adopted to help unravel the HRM contribution, our conclusion must be that it is clear that this task will not be one of 'defending the territory' and justifying the continued existence of large specialised internal HR departments. The task is to prove the contribution of an effective HRM process, not of HR departments. How an effective HRM process is organised becomes a subsequent decision once employers are convinced that it is something worth pursuing. Much of the evidence in this book shows that effective HRM processes can be delivered through HR departments that are organised and staffed in very different ways than we see at present. Patrick Flood and Mike Oram make this argument in Chapters 4 and 5. The NatWest case in Chapter 6 also describes the delivery of a major change programme through an HR function considerably reduced in numbers but with a sizeable influence over key strategic decisions and organisational cultures. There are plenty of examples of effective HRM transformations being delivered through radically redesigned HR functions. There is no reason to assume that the resumption of a new social contract in the field of HR and proof of significant contribution will mean that HRM specialists will continue to be employed *in-house* in large numbers. That is an option, however desirable or not to the field, that was designed out of the HRM process in the early 1990s.

The key task, therefore, for HR practitioners and HR academics within this new agenda is to find ways of ensuring that proper notice is taken of the employee contribution to organisations, and that short-term financial solutions are not allowed to dominate management decisions. As we have repeatedly stressed, trust is not something which senior managers can turn on and off like a tap, and organisations which allow such thinking are deluding themselves. Commitment to a professional and proactive HR philosophy, whether through a specialist department or not, is a central feature of the new agenda.

REFERENCES

Abbott, A. (1988) *The System of Professions: An Essay on the Division of Labour*, Chicago, IL: University of Chicago Press.

Academy of Management Survey (1995) *Corporate Downsizing, Job Elimination and Job Creation*, New York: AMA.

Adams, J.S. (1965) 'Inequity in social exchange', in Berkowitz, L. (ed.) *Advances in Experimental Social Psychology*, Vol. 2. New York: Academic Press.

Advisory, Conciliation and Arbitration Service (1988) *Labour Flexibility in Britain*, ACAS Occasional Paper 41, London: ACAS.

Ahlstrand, B. (1990) *The Quest for Productivity: A Case Study of Fawley after Flanders*, Cambridge: Cambridge University Press.

Al-Dosary, A.S. and Garba, S.B. (1997) 'Inter-organisational co-ordination', *Human Resource Planning*, Vol. 20, No. 1, pp. 10–2.

Allcorn, S. and Diamond, M.A. (1997) *Managing People During Stressful Times: The Psychologically Defensive Workplace*, Westport, CT: Quorum Books.

Alvesson, M. and Deetz, S. (1996) 'Critical theory and postmodernism: approaches to organizational studies', in Clegg, S. R., Hardy, C. and Nord, W. R. (eds) *Handbook of Organization Studies*, Beverly Hills, CA: Sage.

Amadieu, J-F, and Cadin, L. (1995) *Compétence et Organisation Qualifiante*, Paris: Vuibert.

Amit, R. and Schoemaker, P.J.H. (1993) 'Strategic assets and organisational rent', *Strategic Management Journal*, Vol. 14, pp. 33–46.

Andrews, G. (1994) 'Mistrust; the hidden obstacle to empowerment', *HR Magazine*, Vol. 39, No. 9.

Appelbaum, E. and Batt, R. (1994) *The New American Workplace*, Ithaca: ILR Press.

Argyris, C. (1960) *Understanding Organisational Behaviour,* Homewood, IL: Dorsey.

Armstrong, P.J. (1984) 'Work, rest or play? Changes in time spent at work', in Marstrand, P. (ed.) *New Technology and the Future of Work and Skills*, London: Frances Pinter.

Armstrong-Stassen, M. (1993) 'Survivors' reactions to a workforce reduction: a comparison of blue collar workers and their supervisors', *Canadian Journal of Administrative Sciences*, Vol. 10, No. 4, pp. 334–43.

Arthur, J.B. (1994) 'Effects of human resource systems on manufacturing performance and turnover', *Academy of Management Journal*, Vol. 37, pp. 670–87.

Atkinson, J. (1984) 'Manpower strategies for flexible organizations', *Personnel Management*, Vol. 16, No. 8, pp. 28–31.

Atkinson, J. (1985) 'Flexibility, uncertainty and manpower management', *IMS Report,* No. 89, Brighton: Institute of Manpower Studies.

Atkinson, J. (1986) *Changing Working Patterns: How Companies Achieve Flexibility to Meet New Demands*, London: National Economic Development Office.

Atkinson, J. (1987) 'Flexibility or fragmentation? The United Kingdom labour market in the eighties', *Labour and Society*, Vol. 12, No. 1, pp. 87–105

Atkinson, J. and Gregory, D. (1986) 'A flexible future: Britain's dual labour market force', *Marxism Today*, April, pp. 12–17.

Atkinson, J. and Meager, N. (1986) *Changing Working Patterns: How Companies Achieve Flexibility to Meet New Needs*, London: National Economic Development Office.

Atkinson, J. and Rick, J. (1996) *Temporary Work and the Labour Market*, Institute of Employment Studies, Report 311.

Aubry, M. (1991) *Changer le Travail,* Paris: Ministère du Travail.

Bacon, N. and Storey, J. (1993) 'Individualization of the employment relationship and the implications for trade unions', *Employee Relations*, Vol. 15, No. 1, pp. 5–17.

Bacon, N. and Storey, J. (1996) 'Individualism and collectivism and the changing role of trade unions', in Ackers, P., Smith, C. and Smith, P. (eds) *The New Workplace and Trade Unionism: Critical Perspectives on Work and Organization*, London: Routledge.

Bain, G. and Price, R. (1983) 'Union growth: dimensions, determinants and destiny', in Bain, G. (ed.) *Industrial Relations in Britain*, Oxford:Blackwell.

Baird, L. and Meshoulam, I. (1988) 'Managing the two fits of strategic human resource management', *Academy of Management Review*, Vol. 13, No. 1, pp. 116–28.

Baird, L., Meshoulam, I. and De Give, G. (1983) 'Meshing human resource planning with strategic business planning: a model approach', *Personnel*, Vol. 60, No. 5, pp. 14–25

Baldamus, W. (1961) *Efficiency and Effort,* London: Tavistock.

Barney, J. B. (1991) 'Firm resources and sustained competitive advantage', *Journal of Management*, Vol. 17, pp. 99–120.

Bartlett, C.A. and Ghoshal, S. (1989) *Managing across Borders,* Boston: Hutchinson.

Bartlett, C.A. and Ghoshal, S. (1992) 'What is a global manager?', *Harvard Business Review*, Vol. 70, No. 5, pp. 142–52.

Batstone, E. and Gourlay, S. (1986) *Unions, Unemployment and Innovation*, Oxford: Blackwell.

Batstone, E., Gourlay, S., Levie, H. and Moore, R. (1987) *New Technology and the Process of Labour Regulation*, Oxford: Clarendon.

Bauman, Z. (1989) *Modernity and the Holocaust,* Cambridge: Polity.

Beardwell, I. (1997) 'Into the black hole: an examination of the personnel management of non-unionism', *New Zealand Journal of Industrial Relations*, Vol. 22, No. 1, pp. 37–49.

Beatson, M. (1995) *Labour Market Flexibility*, Employment Department Research Series, No. 48, Sheffield: DfEE.

Beaumont, P. (1985) 'Trade union recognition and the recession in the UK', *Industrial Relations Journal*, Vol. 16, No. 2, pp. 34–41.

Becker, B. and Gerhart, B. (1996) 'The impact of human resource management on organizational performance: progress and prospects', *Academy of Management Journal*, Vol. 39, No. 4, pp. 779–801.

Beer, M., Eisenstat, R. A. and Spector, B. (1990) 'Why change programs don't produce change', *Harvard Business Review*, Vol. 68, No. 1, pp. 158–66.

Beer, M., Spector, B., Lawrence, P., Quinn Mills, D. and Walton, R. (1985) *Human Resource Management: A General Manager's Guide,* New York: Free Press.

Bélanger, J. (1996) 'Alcan: market pressure and decentralization of labor regulation', unpublished draft book chapter, *Département des relations industrielles*, Université Laval: Québec.

Bélanger, J., Dumas, M. and Monette, I. (1995) 'Implication négociée et régulation du travail: étude du processus d'innovation à l'Usine Isle-Maligne', *Cahiers du GRT*, 95–01. Département des relations industrielles, Université Laval: Quebec.

Benkhoff, B. (1997) 'Ignoring commitment is costly: new approaches to establish the missing link between commitment and performance', *Human Relations*, Vol. 50, No. 6, pp. 701–26.

Bennis, W.G. (1966) *Changing Organizations,* New York: McGraw-Hill.

Berger, P. and Luckmann, T. (1967) *The Social Construction of Reality*, Harmondsworth: Penguin.

Berggren, C. (1993) 'Lean production: the end of history?', *Work, Employment and Society*, Vol. 7, No. 2, pp. 163–88.

Bertrand, H. and Azoulay, M. (1996) 'Aménagement du temps de travail et négociation', *Travail et Emploi*, p. 64.

Beuve-Méry, A. (1997) 'Des conflits sociaux éclatés et radicaux', *Le Monde*, 18 February, pp. 1, 15.

Bevan, S. (1996) *Who cares?: Business Benefits of Career-Friendly Employment Policies*, Brighton: Institute for Employment Studies.

Bielenski, H. *et al.* (1993) 'New forms of work and activity: a survey of experiences at establishment level in eight European countries', *European Foundation for the Improvement of Working and Living Conditions*, Working papers, Dublin.

Blain, C. (1994) 'Assurance-qualité et autonomie au travail: une étude de cas dans l'industrie chimique', *Formation-Emploi,* No. 48, October.

Blauner, R. (1964) *Alienation and Freedom*, Chicago: University of Chicago Press.

Blinkhorn, S. and Johnson, C. (1991) 'A response to personality tests: The great debate', *Personnel Management*, Vol. 23, No. 9, pp. 39–40.

Blyton, P. (1992) 'The search for workforce flexibility', in Towers, B. (ed.) *Human Resource Management*, Oxford: Blackwell.

Blyton, P. and Trinczek, R. (1997) 'Renewed interest in work-sharing? Assessing recent developments in Germany', *Industrial Relations Journal*, Vol. 28, No. 1, pp. 3–13.

Boisard, P. (1996) *L'Aménagement du Temps de Travail*, Paris: PUF.

Bosch, G. (1992) *Retraining – not Redundancy: Innovative approaches to industrial restructuring in Germany and France*, Geneva: International Institute for Labour Studies.

Boxall, P.F. (1991) 'Strategic HRM: beginnings of a new theoretical sophistication?', *Human Resource Management Journal*, Vol. 2, No. 3, pp. 60–79.

Boxall, P.F. (1994) 'Placing HR strategy at the heart of business success', *Personnel Management*, Vol. 26, No. 7, pp. 32–5.

Bradach, J.L. and Eccles, R.G. (1989) 'Price, authority, and trust: from ideal types to plural forms', *Annual Review of Sociology*, Vol. 15, pp. 97–118.

Bradley, K. and Nejad, A. (1989) *Managing Owners: The National Freight Consortium in Perspective*, Cambridge: Cambridge University Press.

Brannen, P. (1983) *Authority and Participation in Industry*, London: Batsford.

Braverman, H. (1974) *Labour and Monopoly Capital*, New York: Monthly Review Press.

Brewster, C. (1996) 'Working time and contract flexibility in the EU', paper presented at the ESRC/IPD Seminar on *Flexibility in Employment*, Manchester Metropolitan University, 27 September.

Brewster, C. and Bournois, F. (1991) 'Human resource management: a European perspective', *Personnel Review*, Vol. 20, No. 6, pp. 4–13.

Brewster, C. and Hegewisch, A. (1994) *Policy and Practice in European Human Resource Management*, London: Routledge.

Brewster, C. and Smith, C. (1990) 'Corporate strategy: a no-go area for personnel', *Personnel Management*, Vol. 22, No. 7.

Brewster, C., Gill, C. and Richbell, S. (1983) 'Industrial relations policy: a framework for analysis' in Thurley, K. and Wood, S. (eds) *Industrial Relations and Management Strategy*, Cambridge: Cambridge University Press.

Brewster, C., Hegewisch, A. and Mayne, L. (1993) 'Trends in HRM in Western Europe', in Kirkbride, P. (ed.) *Human Resource Management in the New Europe of the 1990s*, London: Routledge.

Brewster, C., Hegewisch, A. and Mayne, L. (1994) 'Flexible working practices: the controversy and the evidence', in Brewster C. and Hegewisch A. (eds) *Policy and Practice in European Human Resource Management: the Price Waterhouse Cranfield Survey*, London: Routledge.

Brewster, C., Mayne, L. and Tregaskis, O. (1997) 'Flexible working in Europe: a review of the evidence', *Management International Review*, 1/97.

Brewster, C., Mayne, L., Tregaskis, O., Parsons, D. and Atterbury, S. (1996) *Working Time and Contract Flexibility in Europe,* Report prepared for the European Commission, DGV.

Brewster, C., Tregaskis, O., Hegewisch, A. and Mayne, L. (1996b) 'Comparative research in human resource management: a review and an example', *International Journal of Human Resource Management*, Vol. 7, No. 3, pp. 585–604

Brewster, C. *et al.* (1993) *Flexible Work Patterns in Europe*, Institute of Personnel Management, Issues in People Management Series, No. 6, London: IPD.

Bridges, W. (1994) *Jobshift: How to Prosper in a Workplace Without Jobs*, Reading, MA: Addison-Wesley.

Brockner, J. (1992) 'Managing the effects of layoffs on survivors', *California Management Review*, winter, pp. 9–28.

Brockner, J., Greenberg, J., Brockner, A., Bortz, J., Davy, J. and Carter, C. (1986) 'Layoffs, equity theory and work performance: further evidence of the impact of survivor guilt', *Academy of Management Journal*, Vol. 29, No. 2, pp. 373–84.

Brockner, J., Grover, S., O'Malley, M., Reed, T.F. and Glynn, M.A. (1993) 'Threat of future layoffs, self-esteem and survivors' reactions: evidence from the laboratory and the field', *Strategic Management Journal*, Vol. 14, pp. 153–66.

Brown, W. (1973) *Piecework Bargaining*, London: Heinemann.

Bruining, J. (1992) *Management Buy-Out*, PhD dissertation, Erasmus University, Rotterdam.

Buchanan, D.A. (1997) 'The limitations and opportunities of business process re-engineering in a politicized organizational climate', *Human Relations*, Vol. 50, No. 1, pp. 51–72.

Buchanan, D. and McCalman, J. (1989) *High Performance Work Systems: The Digital Experience*, London: Routledge.

Buchanan, D. and Preston, D. (1992) 'Life in the cell: supervision and teamwork in a manufacturing systems engineering environment', *Human Resource Management Journal*, Vol. 2, No. 4, pp. 55–76.

Burrell, G. (1996) 'Normal science, paradigms, metaphors, discourses and genealogies of analysis', in Clegg, S. R., Hardy, C. and Nord, W. R. (eds) *Handbook of Organization Studies*, London: Sage.

Business Strategies (1996) *Labour Market Flexibility and Financial Services*, London: Business Strategies.

Cabanes, P. (1997) *Inégalités d'Emploi et de Revenu: les Années Quatre-vingt-dix*, Paris: CSERC.

Callon, M. (1986) 'Some elements of a sociology of translation: domestication of the scallops and the fishermen of St Brieuc Bay', in Law, J. (ed.) *Power, Action and Belief: A New Sociology of Knowledge?* Sociological Review Monograph 32, London: Routledge.

Campion, M.A. (1994) 'Job analysis for the future', in Runsey, M.G., Walker, C.B. and Harris, J.H. (eds.) *Personnel Selection and Classification*, Hillsdale, NJ: Erlbaum.

Cardy, R.L. and Robbins, G.H. (1995) 'Human resource management in a total quality organizational environment: shifting from a traditional to a TQHRM approach', *Journal of Quality Management*, Vol. 1, No. 1, pp. 5–21.

Carley, M. (1995) 'Talking shops or serious forums', *People Management*, Vol. 1, No. 7.

Carrig, K. (1997) 'Reshaping human resources for the next century – lessons from a high flying airline', *Human Resource Management*, Vol. 36, No. 2, pp. 277–89.

Carroll, S.J. (1991) 'The new HRM roles, responsibilities, and structures', in Schuler, R.S. (ed.) *Managing Human Resources in the Information Age*, Washington, DC:Bureau of National Affairs.

Carroll, G.R., Delacroix, J. and Goodstein, J. (1990) 'The political environments of organisations: an ecological view', in Staw, B.M. and Cummings, L.L. (eds.) *The Evolution and Adaptation of Organisations*, Greenwich, CT: JAI Press.

Casey, B., Metcalf, H. and Millward, N. (1997) *Employers' Use of Flexible Labour*, London: Policy Studies Institute.

Charpentier, P. (1991) 'Le travail dans une organisation en juste-à-temps', *Lettre de L'ANACT*, Vol. 177, pp. 19–25.

Clark, M.C. and Payne, R.L. (1997) 'The nature and structure of workers' trust in management', *Journal of Organisational Behaviour*, Vol. 18, No. 3, pp. 205–24.

Claydon, T. (1989) 'Union derecognition in Britain in the 1980s', *British Journal of Industrial Relations*, Vol. 27, No. 2, pp. 214–24.

Claydon, T. (1996) 'Union derecognition: a re-examination', in Beardwell, I.J. (ed) *Contemporary Industrial Relations: A Critical Analysis*, Oxford: Oxford University Press.

Claydon, T. and Green, F. (1994) 'Can trade unions improve training in Britain?' *Personnel Review*, Vol. 23, No. 1, pp. 37–51.

Clegg, S.R. (1989) *Frameworks of Power*, London: Sage.

Clement, B. (1997) 'Public sector scraps job demarcation', *The Independent*, 10 March.

Coff, R.W. (1997) 'Human assets and management dilemmas: coping with the hazards on the road to resource-based theory', *Academy of Management Review*, Vol. 22, No. 2, pp. 374–402.

Cole, R.E. (1989) *Strategies for Learning*, Berkeley: University of California Press.

Coller, X. (1996) 'Managing flexibility in the food industry: a cross-national comparative study in European multinational companies', *European Journal of Industrial Relations*, Vol. 2, No. 2, pp. 153–72.

Colling, T. (1995) 'From hierarchy to contract? Subcontracting and employment in the service economy' *Warwick Papers in Industrial Relations*, No. 52, IRRU, University of Warwick.

Collinson, M., Edwards, P.K. and Rees, C. (1997) *Involving Employees in Total Quality Management*, London: Department of Trade and Industry.

Collomp, F. (1995) 'L'Alsace-Lorraine à l'heure du taylorisme japonais', *L'Expansion*, No. 493, 23 January.

Commission of the European Communities (1990) *Employment in Europe*, Brussels: Directorate-General V.

Commission of the EC (1992) 'The position of women on the labour market: trends and developments in the 12 member states', *Women of Europe Supplements*, No. 36, Brussels, EC.

Conference Board (1997) 'Implementing the new employment compact', *HR Executive Review*.

Cooke, W.N. (1989) 'Improving productivity and quality through collaboration', *Industrial Relations*, Vol. 28, No. 2, pp. 219–31.

Coupar, W. (1997) *Towards Industrial Partnership: New Ways of Working in UK Companies*, London: Involvement and Participation Association.

Coutrot, T. (1995) 'Gestion de l'emploi et organisation du travail dans les entreprises innovantes', *Premières Synthèses, INSEE*, No. 84, 18 April.

Creed, W.E.D. and Miles, R.E. (1996) 'Trust in organisations: a conceptual framework linking organisational forms, managerial philosophies and the opportunity costs of control', in Kramer, R.M. and Tyler, T.R. (eds) *Trust in Organisations: Frontiers of Theory and Research*, London: Sage.

Cressey, P. and Scott, P. (1992) 'Employment, technology and industrial relations', *New Technology, Work and Employment*, Vol. 7, No. 2, pp. 83–94.

CSC Index (1994) *State of Re-engineering* (Report), London: CSC Index.

Cutcher-Gershenfeld, J. (1991) 'The impact on economic performance of a transformation in workplace relations', *Industrial and Labor Relations Review*, Vol. 44, No. 1, pp. 241–60.

Cutcher-Gershenfeld, J. *et al.* (1994) 'Japanese team-based work systems in North America: explaining the diversity', *California Management Review*, Vol. 37, No. 1, pp. 42–64.

Daft, R.L. and Lewin, A.Y. (1993) 'Where are the theories for the "new" organisational forms?', *Organisation Science*, Vol. 4, pp. 513–28.

Davidow, W.H. and Malone, M.S. (1993) *The Virtual Corporation: Structuring and Revitalising the Corporation for the 21st Century*, London: Harper Business.

Dawson, P. and Webb, J. (1989) 'New production arrangements: the totally flexible cage?', *Work, Employment and Society*, Vol. 2, pp. 26–39.

Department of Employment (1989) *People and Companies: Employee Involvement in Britain*, London: HMSO.

Dex, S. and McCullough, A. (1995) *Flexible Employment in Britain: A Statistical Analysis*, Manchester: Equal Opportunities Commission.

Dickens, L. and Hall, M. (1995) 'The state: labour law and industrial relations', in Edwards, P. (ed.) *Industrial Relations*, Oxford: Blackwell.

Dodgson, M. and Martin, R. (1987) 'Trade union policies on new technology: facing the challenges of the 1980s', *New Technology, Work and Employment*, Vol. 2, No. 1, pp. 9–18.

Doherty, N. and Horsted, J. (1995) 'Helping survivors to stay on board', *People Management*, Vol. 1, No. 2, pp. 26–31.

Donovan, the Lord (1968) *Royal Commission Report*, Cmnd 3623, HMSO.

Drucker, P.F. (1955) *The Practice of Management*, London: Heinemann.

Drumm, H.J. (1994) 'The paradigm of a new decentralisation: its implications for organisation and HRM', *Employee Relations*, Vol. 17, No. 8, pp. 29–45.

du Gay, P. and Salaman, G. (1992) 'The Cult(ure) of the Customer', *Journal of Management Studies*, Vol. 29, No. 5, pp. 615–33.

Dumoulin, E. and Lombard, D. (1995) *Le Guide de l'Aménagement du Temps de Travail*, Paris: Editions d'Organisation.

Dunn, S. (1985) 'The law and the decline of the closed shop in the 1980s' in Fosh, P. and Littler, C. (eds) *Industrial Relations and the Law in the 1980s*, Aldershot: Gower.

Dunn, S. (1990) 'Root metaphor in the old and new industrial relations', *British Journal of Industrial Relations*, Vol. 28, No. 1, pp. 1–31.

Dunn, S. (1993) 'From Donovan to . . . wherever', *British Journal of Industrial Relations*, Vol. 31, No. 2, pp. 169–87.

Dyer, L. and Reeves, T. (1995) 'Human resource strategies and firm performance: what do we know and where do we need to go?', paper presented to the 10th IIRA World Congress, Washington, 31 May–4 June, 1995.

Edwards, P.K. (1995) 'The employment relationship' in Edwards, P.K. (ed.) *Industrial Relations: Theory and Practice in Britain*, Oxford: Blackwell.

Edwards, P.K. and Whitston, C. (1993) *Attending to Work: The Management of Attendance and Shopfloor Order,* Oxford: Blackwell.

Edwards, P.K., Ferner, A. and Sisson, K. (1996) 'The conditions for international human resource management: two cases', *International Journal of Human Resource Management*, Vol. 7, No. 1, pp. 20–40.

Ehrlich, J.C. (1994) 'Creating an employer-employee relationship for the future', *Human Resource Management*, Vol. 33, No. 3, pp. 491–501.

Eichinger, R. and Ulrich, D. (1995) 'Are you future agile?', *Human Resource Planning*, pp. 30–41.

Employment Department Group (1991) *The Government's Expenditure Plans 1991–1992 to 1993–1994*, Cm 1506, HMSO.

European Industrial Relations Review (1996) No. 273, p. 11.

Eustache, D. (1996) *Les Nouvelles Politiques de Rémunération des Entreprises et Les Réactions des Salariés*, Marseille: Cereq.

Evans C. (1995) *The Challenge of Managing the Part-Time Workforce,* Roffey Park: Management Institute.

Fernie, S. and Metcalf, D. (1995) 'Participation, contingent pay, representation and workplace performance: evidence from Great Britain', *British Journal of Industrial Relations*, Vol. 33, No. 3, pp. 379–415.

Flanders, A. (1964) *The Fawley Productivity Agreements*, London: Faber.

Flanders, A (1967) *Collective Bargaining: Prescription for Change*, London: Faber.

Flanders, A. (1970) *Management and Unions*, London: Faber & Faber.

Flood, P. and Olian, J.D. (1995) 'Human resource strategy for world class competitive capability', in Flood, P., Gannon, M.J. and Paauwe, J. (eds) *Managing Without Traditional Methods: International Innovations in Human Resource Management*, Wokingham: Addison Wesley.

Flood, P. and Toner, B. (1995) 'Managing without unions: a pyrrhic victory?' in Flood, P., Gannon, M.J. and Paauwe, J. (eds) *Managing Without Traditional Methods: International Innovations in Human Resource Management*, Wokingham: Addison Wesley.

Flood, P., Gannon, M.J. and Paauwe, J. (1995) *Managing Without Traditional Methods: International Innovations*, in *Human Resource Management*, Wokingham: Addison Wesley.

Flood, P. and Toner, B. (1997) 'How do large non-union companies escape a catch-22?', *British Journal of Industrial Relations*, in press.

Flood, P., Fong, C., Smith, K.G., O'Regan, P., Morley, M. and Moore, S. (1997) 'Pioneering and the top management team: a resource-based view', *International Journal of Human Resource Management*, June.

Flood, P., Smith, K. and Derfus, P. (1996) 'Top management teams: a neglected topic in human resource management', *Journal of Irish Business and Administrative Research*, Vol. 17, No. 1, pp. 1–17.

Fombrun C., Tichy, N.M. and Devanna, M.A. (1984) *Strategic Human Resource Management,* London: John Wiley.

Fox, A. (1974) *Beyond Contract: Work, Power and Trust Relations*, London: Faber.

Francis, D. (1987) *Unblocking Organisation Communication*, Aldershot: Gower.

Freedman, A. (1986) "Jobs: insecurity at all levels", *Across The Board*, Vol. 23, Iss. 1, pp. 4–5.

Freeman, R.B. and Medoff, J. (1979) 'The two faces of unionism', *The Public Interest*, Vol. 57, pp. 69–93.

Freyssenet, M. (1995) 'The origins of team work in Renault' in Sandberg, A. (ed) *Enriching Production*, London: Avebury.

Gadbois, C. *et al.* (1995) 'Union assimilation of the ergonomic approach and the transformation of social relations', *Relations Industrielles*, Vol. 50, No. 4, pp. 852–72

Gall, G. and McKay, S. (1994) 'Trade union derecognition in Britain, 1988–1994', *British Journal of Industrial Relations*, Vol. 32, No. 3, pp. 433–48.

Gallie, D. and White, M. (1993) 'Employee commitment and the skills revolution: first findings from the Employment in Britain survey', London: Policy Studies Institute.

Gambetta, D. (1988) 'Can we trust trust?' in Gambetta, D. (ed.) *Trust: Making and Breaking Co-operative Relationships*, Oxford: Basil Blackwell.

Garrahan, P. and Stewart, P. (1992) *The Nissan Enigma: Flexibility at Work in a Local Economy*, London: Mansell.

Geary, J. (1992) 'Employment flexibility and human resource management', *Work, Employment and Society*, Vol. 6, No. 2, pp. 251–70.

Geary, J. (1993) 'New forms of work organisation and employee involvement in two case study sites: plural, mixed and protean', *Economic and Industrial Democracy*, Vol. 14, No. 4, pp. 511–34.

Geary, J. (1995) 'Work practices: the structure of work' in Edwards, P.K. (ed.) *Industrial Relations*, Oxford: Blackwell.

General, Municipal and Boilermakers' Union and Union of Communication Workers (1990) *A New Agenda: Bargaining for Prosperity in the 1990s*, London: General Municipal and Boilermakers Union/Union of Communication Workers.

Gennard, J. and Kelly, J. (1994) 'Human resource management: the views of personnel directors', *Human Resource Management Journal*, Vol. 5, No. 1, pp. 15-32.

Gennard, J. and Kelly, J. (1997) 'The unimportance of labels: the diffusion of the personnel/HRM function', *Industrial Relations Journal*, Vol. 28, No. 1, pp. 27–42.

Gershuny, J.I. (1983) *Social Innovation and the Division of Labour,* Oxford: Oxford University Press.

Ghoshal, S. and Bartlett, C.A. (1995) 'The new moral contract: guaranteeing employability', Paper for *20th Anniversary Euroforum Conference*, 15–16 September, Strategic Leadership Programme, London Business School.

Ghoshal, S. and Moran, P. (1996) 'Bad for practice: a critique of the transaction cost theory', *Academy of Management Review*, Vol. 21, No. 1, pp. 13–47

Gilbert, R. (1993) 'Workplace industrial relations 25 years after Donovan: an employer view', *British Journal of Industrial Relations*, Vol. 31, No. 2, pp. 235–53.

Gillen, D.J. and Carroll, S.J. (1987) 'Relationship of managerial ability to unit effectiveness in more organic versus more mechanistic departments', *Journal of Management Studies*, Vol. 22, pp. 351–9.

Godfrey, G. (1994) *Shop Stewards in the 1990s*, MSc dissertation, Manchester School of Management, UMIST.

Godfrey, G. and Marchington, M. (1996) 'Shop stewards in the 1990s', *Industrial Relations Journal*, Vol. 27, No. 4, pp. 339–44.

Goffee, R. and Hunt, J. (1996) 'The end of management? Classroom versus the boardroom', *Financial Times*, 22 March.

Gold, M. and Hall, M. (1992) *European-level information and consultation in multinational companies: an evaluation of practice*, Dublin: European Foundation for the Improvement of Living and Working Conditions.

Gold, M. and Hall, M. (1994) 'Statutory European works councils: the final countdown?', *Industrial Relations Journal*, Vol. 25, No. 3, pp. 177–87.

Gomez-Mejia, L.R. (1992) 'Structure and process of diversification, compensation strategy, and firm performance', *Strategic Management Journal*, Vol. 14, pp. 381–97.

Goold, M., Campbell, A. and Alexander, M. (1994) *Corporate-Level Strategy – Creating Value in the Multibusiness Company*, New York: John Wiley.

Gorgeu, A. and Mathieu, R. (1995) *Recrutement et Production au Plus Juste: Les Nouvelles Usines d'Equipement Automobile en France*, Noisy-le-grand: Centre d'Études de l'Emploi.

Gottlier, M.R. and Conkling, L. (1995) *Managing the Workplace Survivors: Organisational Downsizing and the Commitment Gap*, Westport, CT: Quorum Books.

Gouldner, A. W. (1964) *Patterns of Industrial Bureaucracy*, New York: Free Press.

Grant, D. (1994) 'New style agreements at Japanese transplants in the UK. The implications for trade union decline', *Employee Relations*, Vol. 16, No. 2, pp. 65–83.

Grant, D. (1996) 'Japanization and the new industrial relations' in Beardwell, I.J. (ed.) *Contemporary Industrial Relations: A Critical Analysis*, Oxford: Oxford University Press.

Grant, R.M. (1991) 'The resource-based theory of competitive advantage: implications for strategy formulation', *California Management Review*, Vol. 33, No. 3, pp. 114–35.

Gratton, L., Hope-Hailey, V., McGovern, M., Stiles, P. and Truss, C. (1996) 'Delivering short-term and long-term business strategy through people processes: a description of the findings', Working Paper 2, Centre for Organisational Research, London Business School.

.Gregg, P. and Wadsworth, J. (1995) 'A short history of labour turnover, job tenure and job security 1975–93', *Oxford Review of Economic Policy*, Vol. 11, No. 1, pp. 73–90.

Grint, K. and Willcocks, L. (1995) 'Business process re-engineering in theory and practice', *New Technology, Work and Employment*, Vol. 10, No. 2.

Guéganou, Y. (1997) *Le Bilan du Temps Partiel*, Paris: Ministère des Finances.

Guest, D.E. (1987) 'Human resource management and industrial relations', *Journal of Management Studies*, Vol. 24, No. 5, pp. 503–21.

Guest, D.E. (1989) 'Personnel and HRM: can you tell the difference', *Personnel Management*, Vol. 21, No. 1, pp. 48–51.

Guest, D.E. (1990) 'Human resource management and the American Dream', *Journal of Management Studies*, Vol. 27, No. 4, pp. 378–97.

Guest, D.E. (1991) 'Personnel management: the end of orthodoxy', *British Journal of Industrial Relations*, Vol. 29, No. 2, pp. 149–76.

Guest, D.E. (1992) 'Employee commitment and control', in Hartley, J. and Stephenson, C. (eds) *Employment Relations: The Psychology of Influence and Control at Work*, Oxford: Blackwell.

Guest, D.E. (1994) 'Organizational psychology and human resource management: towards a European approach', *European Work and Occupational Psychologist*, Vol. 4, No. 3, pp. 251–70.

Guest, D.E. (1995) 'Human resource management, trade unions and industrial relations', in Storey, J. *Human Resource Management. A Critical Text*, London: Routledge.

Guest, D.E. (1997) 'Human resource management: a review and research agenda', *International Journal of Human Resource Management*, Vol. 8, No. 3, pp. 263–76.

Guest, D.E. and Hoque, K. (1993) 'The mystery of the missing human resource manager', *Personnel Management*, June, pp. 40–41.

Guest, D.E. and Hoque, K. (1994a) 'The good, the bad and the ugly: employment relations in new non-union workplaces', *Human Resource Management Journal*, Vol. 5, No. 1, pp. 1–14.

Guest, D.E. and Hoque, K. (1994b) 'Yes, personnel does make a difference', *Personnel Management*, November, 40–44.

Guest, D.E. and Hoque, K. (1995) 'Personnel management and performance' in *The contribution of personnel management to organisational performance*, Issues in People Management, Report No. 9, London: Institute of Personnel and Development.

Guest, D.E. and Hoque, K. (1996) 'Human resource management and the new industrial relations', in Beardwell, I. (ed.) *Contemporary Industrial Relations*, Oxford: Oxford University Press.

Guest, D.E. and MacKenzie Davey, K. (1996) 'Don't write off the traditional career', *People Management*, Vol. 2, No. 4.

Guest, D.E. and Peccei, R. (1994) 'The nature and causes of effective human resource management', *British Journal of Industrial Relations*, Vol. 32, No. 2, pp. 219–42.

Guest, D.E. and Peccei, R. (1996) 'A test of the feasibility of changing organizational commitment', *Department of Organizational Psychology Working Paper*, London: Birkbeck College.

Guest, D. *et al.* (1996) 'The state of the psychological contract in employment', Institute of Personnel and Development, *Issues in People Management*, No. 16.

Guzzo, R.A. and Noonan, K.A. (1994) 'Human resource practices as communications and the psychological contract', *Human Resources Management*, Vol. 33, pp. 447–62.

Hage, J. and Alter, C. (1993) *Organizations Working Together*, Newbury Park, CA: Sage.

Hakim, C. (1990) 'Core and periphery in employers' workforce strategies: evidence from the 1987 ELUS survey', *Work, Employment and Society*, Vol. 4, No. 2, pp. 157–88.

Hall, L.A. and Torrington, D. P. (1997) *Developments in the Personnel Function*, London: Pitman Publishing.

Hall, M. (1992) 'Behind the European Works Councils' directives: the European Commission's legislative strategy', *British Journal of Industrial Relations*, Vol. 30, No. 4, pp. 547–66.

Hall, M., Carley, M., Gold, M., Marginson, P. and Sisson, K. (1995) *European Works Councils: Planning for the Directive*, London/Coventry: Eclipse Group/Industrial Relations Research Unit.

Hambrick, D. (1994) 'Top management groups: a conceptual integration and a re-consideration of the "team" Label' in Staw, B.M. and Cummings, L.L. (eds) *Research in Organisational Behaviour*, Vol. 16, Greenwich, CT: JAI Press.

Hamel, G. and Prahalad, C.K. (1991) 'Corporate imagination and expeditionary marketing', *Harvard Business Review*, Vol. 69, No. 4, pp. 81–92.

Hamel, G. and Prahalad, C.K. (1994) *Competing for the Future*, Boston, MA: Harvard Business School Press.

Hammer, M. and Champy, J. (1993) *Reengineering the Corporation: A Manifesto For Business Revolution*, New York: Harper Business.

Hammer, M. and Champy, J. (1995) *Business Re-engineering*, New York: Harper Business.

Handy, C. (1995) 'Trust and the virtual organisation – how do you manage people whom you do not see?' *Harvard Business Review*, May–June, pp. 40–50.

Hart, T. J. (1993) 'Human resource management: time to exorcise the militant tendency', *Employee Relations*, Vol. 15, No. 3, pp. 29–36.

Harvey, D. (1989) *The Condition of Postmodernity*, Oxford: Blackwell.

Hay Group (1990) *The Hay Human Resource Forecast 1991–2000: Trends Shaping Organisations in the Next Decade*, New York: The Hay Group.

Heery, E. (1996) 'The new new unionism', in Beardwell, I.J. (ed.) *Contemporary Industrial Relations: A Critical Analysis*, Oxford:Oxford University Press.

Hendry, C., Bradley, P. and Perkins, S. (1997) 'Performance management: missed a motivator?', *People Management*, Vol. 3, No. 10, pp. 20–5.

Hendry, C., Pettigrew, A.M. and Sparrow, P.R. (1989) 'Linking strategic change, competitive performance and human resource management: results of a UK empirical study', in Mansfield, R. (ed.) *Frontiers of Management Research*, London: Routledge.

Hendry, C. and Pettigrew, A. (1990) 'Human resource management: an agenda for research', *International Journal of Human Resource Management*, Vol. 1, No. 1, pp. 17–43.

Hepple, B. (1983) 'Individual labour law', in Bain, G.S. (ed.) *Industrial Relations in Britain*, Oxford: Blackwell.

Herriot, P. and Anderson, N. (1997) 'Selecting for change: how will personnel and selection psychology survive?' in Anderson, N. and Herriot, P. (eds.) *International Handbook of Selection and Assessment*, Chichester: John Wiley.

Herriot, P. and Pemberton, C. (1995a) *New Deals: The Revolution in Managerial Careers*, Chichester: John Wiley.

Herriot, P. and Pemberton, C. (1995b) 'A new Deal for middle managers', *People Management*, Vol. 1, No. 12, pp. 32–5.

Herriot, P. and Pemberton, C. (1996) 'Contracting careers', *Human Relations,* Vol. 49, No. 6, pp. 759–90.

Herriot, P. and Pemberton, C. (1997) 'Facilitating new deals', *Human Resource Management Journal,* Vol. 7, No. 1, pp. 45–56.

Herriot, P., Manning, W.E.G. and Kidd, J.M. (1997) 'The content of the psychological contract', *British Journal of Management*, Vol. 8, No. 2, pp. 151–62.

Higgs, F. (1994) *Transport and General Workers,* Union Supplementary Submission on Union Recognition and Collective Bargaining Rights (Companies in the Oil Industry), Evidence to the House of Commons Select Committee on Employment, 6 January.

Hill, S. (1995) 'From quality circles to total quality management', in Wilkinson, A. and Willmott, H. (eds) *Making Quality Critical*, London: Routledge.

Hiltrop, J.M. (1995) 'The changing psychological contract: the human resource challenge of the 1990s', *European Management Journal*, Vol. 13, No. 3, pp. 286–94.

Hirsh, W. and Jackson, C. (1996) *Strategies for Career Development: Promise, Practice, and Pretence,* Brighton: Institute for Employment Studies.

Hirschhorn, L. and Gilmore, T. (1992) 'The new boundaries of the "boundaryless" company', *Harvard Business Review*, Vol. 7, No. 3, pp. 104–15.

Hoffman, R. and Lapeyre J. (1995) *Le Temps de Travail en Europe: Organisation et Réduction*, Paris: Syros.

Holder, G. (1986) 'Human resource professionals: adaptations to changes in function', paper presented at the 18th annual meeting of the Personnel section of the Personnel Management Association, Key Biscayne, FL, 10 February.

Holland, J.L. (1976) 'Vocational preferences', in Dunnette, M.D. (ed.) *Handbook of Industrial and Organizational Psychology*, Chicago: Rand McNally.

Howard, A. and Wellins, R. (1994) *High-involvement Leadership: Changing Roles for Changing Times,* Pittsburgh PA: Development Dimensions International, Leadership Research Institute.

Huiskamp, R. (1995) 'Regulating the employment relationship: an analytical framework' in van Ruysseveldt, J., Huiskamp, R. and van Hoof, J. (eds) *Comparative Industrial and Employment Relations*, London: Sage Publications.

Humes, S. (1993) *Managing the Multinational: Confronting the Global-Local Dilemma*, Hemel Hempstead: Prentice-Hall.

Hunter, L.W and McKersie, R.B. (1992) 'Can "mutual gains" training change labor – management relationships?', *Negotiation Journal*, Vol. 8, No. 4, pp. 319–30.

Hunter, L.W., McGregor, A., MacInnes, J. and Sproull, A. (1993) 'The "flexible firm": strategy and segmentation', *British Journal of Industrial Relations*, Vol. 31, No. 3, pp. 383–407.

Huselid, M.A. (1995) 'The impact of human resource management practices on turnover, productivity and corporate financial performance', *Academy of Management Journal*, Vol. 38, No. 3, pp. 635–72.

Huselid, M.A. and Becker, B.E. (1996) 'Methodological issues in cross-sectional and panel estimates of the human resource–firm performance link', *Industrial Relations*, Vol. 35, pp. 635–72.

Huselid, M.A., Jackson, S. and Schuler, R.S. (1997) 'Technical and strategic human resource management effectiveness as determinants of firm performance', *Academy of Management Journal*, Vol. 40, No. 1, pp. 171–88.

Hutchinson, S. (1996) 'The changing nature of employment in the UK: employment flexibility', Paper presented at the ESRC/IPD Seminar on *Flexibility in Employment*, Manchester Metropolitan University, 27 September.

Hutton, W. (1996) *The State We're In*, London: Viking.

Hyman, R. (1991) 'Plus ça change? The theory of production and the production of theory', in Pollert, A. (ed.) *Farewell to Flexibility?*, Oxford: Blackwell, pp. 259–83.

Ichniowski, C., Shaw, K. and Prennushi, G. (1994) *The Effects of Human Resource Management Practices on Performance*, Working Paper, Columbia University.

Income Data Services (1997a) *The New Agenda*, London: IDS.

Income Data Services (1997b) *IRS Employment Trends No. 631*, London: IDS.

Inns of Court Conservative and Unionist Society (1958) *A Giant's Strength*, London: ICCUS.

Institute of Management and Manpower (1995) *Survey of Long Term Strategies*, October, London: IMM.

Institute of Personnel and Development (1995) *People Make the Difference*, London: IPD.

Institute of Work Psychology (1996) *Study of Corporate Performance in the UK Manufacturing Sector*, University of Sheffield: Mimeo.

Involvement and Participation Association (1992) *Towards Industrial Partnership*, London: IPA.

IRS Employment Trends (1990) 'The Japanese in Britain: employment policies and practice', *Industrial Relations Review and Report*, 470, August.

IRS Employment Trends (1996) December 1996.

James, B. (1977) 'Third party intervention in recognition disputes: the role of the commission on industrial relations', *Industrial Relations Journal*, Vol. 8, No. 2, pp. 29–39.

Jenkins, A. (1994) 'Teams: from ideology to analysis', *Organisation Studies*, Vol. 5, No. 6, December.

Jenkins, C. and Sherman, B. (1979) *White Collar Unionism*, London: Routledge.

Jenkins, M. and Johnson, G. (1997) 'Linking managerial cognition and organisational performance: a preliminary investigation using causal maps', *British Journal of Management*, Vol. 8, No. 2, pp. S77–S90.

Johansson, H.J., McHugh, P., Pendlebury, A.J. and Wheeler, W.A. (1993) *Business Process Reengineering: Breakpoint Strategies for Market Dominance*, Chichester: John Wiley.

Jones, K. (1995) *Dwr Cymru/Welsh Water: Involvement and Change, the DCWW Partnership Agreements*, London: Involvement and Participation Association.

Kahn-Freund, O. (1954) 'Legal framework', in Flanders, A. and Clegg, H.A. (eds) *The System of Industrial Relations in Great Britain*, Oxford: Blackwell.

Kalleberg, A.L. and Reve, T. (1993) 'Contracts and commitments: economic and sociological perspectives on employment relations', *Human Relations*, Vol. 46, No. 9, pp. 1103–32.

Kamoche, K. (1994) 'A critique of a proposed reformation of strategic human resource management', *Human Resource Management Journal*, Vol. 4, No. 4, pp. 29–43.

Kaplan, R.S. (1988) *Sources of value in Management Buy-Outs*, PhD dissertation, Harvard, Cambridge.

Kaplan, R.S. (1989) 'The effects of management buy-outs on operating performance and value', *Journal of Financial Economics*, Vol. 24, pp. 217–54.

Kaplan, R.S. and Norton, D.P. (1993) 'Putting the balanced score card to work', *Harvard Business Review*, Vol. 71, No. 5.

Kaufman, R. (1992) 'The effects of IMPROSHARE on productivity', *Industrial and Labor Relations Review* Vol. 45, pp. 311–22.

Keenoy, T. and Anthony, P. (1992) 'HRM: metaphor, meaning and morality', in Blyton, P. and Turnbull, P. (eds) *Reassessing Human Resource Management*, London: Sage.

Kelly, J. (1996) 'Union militancy and social partnership', in Ackers, P., Smith, C. and Smith, P. (eds) *The New Workplace and Trade Unionism: Critical Perspectives on Work and Organization*, London: Routledge.

Kelly, J. and Heery, E. (1994) *Working for the Union.:British Trade Union Officers*, Cambridge: Cambridge University Press

Kelly, J. and Kelly, C. (1991) '"Them and Us": social psychology and the "new industrial relations"', *British Journal of Industrial Relations*, Vol. 29, No. 1, pp. 25–48.

Kelly, R.E. (1988) 'In praise of followers', *Harvard Business Review*, December, pp. 142–8.

Kessler, I. and Purcell, J. (1996) 'The value of joint working parties', *Work Employment and Society*, Vol. 10, No. 4, pp. 663–82.

Kessler, I. and Undy, R. (1996) *The New Employment Relationship: Examining the Psychological Contract*. London: Institute of Personnel and Development.

Kessler, S. (1995) 'Trade union recognition: CIR and ACAS experience', *Employee Relations*, Vol. 17, No. 6, pp. 52–66.

Kets de Vries, M.F.R. and Balazs, K. (1996) 'The human side of downsizing', *European Management Journal*, Vol. 14, No. 2, pp. 111–20.

Kets de Vries, M.F.R. and Balazs, K. (1997) 'The downside of downsizing', *Human Relations*, Vol. 50, No. 1, pp. 11–50.

Kinnie N. *et al.* (1996) *The People Management Implications of Leaner Ways of Working*, Institute of Personnel and Development, *Issues in People Management*, No. 15, London: IPD.

Klein, J. (1989) 'The human costs of manufacturing reform', *Harvard Business Review*, March–April, pp. 54–62.

Klein, J., Edge, G. and Kass, T. (1991) 'Skill-based competition', *Journal of General Management*, Vol. 16, No. 4, pp. 1–15.

Knights, D., Morgan, G. and Murray, F. (1992) 'Business systems, consumption and change: personal financial services in Italy', in Whitley, R.D. (ed.) *European Business Systems: Firms and Markets in their National Context*, London: Sage.

Koch, M.J. and McGrath, R.G. (1996) 'Improving labour productivity: human resource management policies do matter', *Strategic Management Journal*, Vol. 17, pp. 335–54.

Kochan, T.A. (1995) 'HRM: an American view', in Storey, J. (ed.) *Human Resource Management: A Critical Text*, London: Routledge.

Kochan, T.A. and Useem, M. (eds) (1992) *Transforming Organizations*, Oxford: Oxford University Press.

Kochan, T.A. *et al.* (1986) *The Transformation of American Industrial Relations*, New York: Basic Books.

Konovsky, M.A. and Brockner, J. (1993) 'Managing victim and survivor lay-off reactions: a procedural justice perspective', in Cropanzano, R. (ed.) *Justice in the Workplace*, Hillsdale NJ: Erlbaum.

Korten, D.C. (1993) *When Corporations Rule The World*, New York: Berrett-Koehler.

Kossek, E.E., Huber-Yoder, M., Castellino, D., Heneman, R.L. and Skoglind, J.D. (1997) 'The working poor: locked out of careers and the organisational mainstream?', *Academy of Management Executive*, Vol. 11, No. 1, pp. 76–92.

Krafjic, J. (1988) 'The triumph of the "lean" production system', *Sloan Management Review*, Fall, pp. 15–28.

Kramer, R.M. and Tyler, T.R. (eds) (1996) *Trust in Organisations: Frontiers of Theory and Research*, Newbury Park, CA: Sage.

Labour Force Survey (various), *Labour Market Trends*, Department of Education and Employment.

Lane, C. (1989) *Management and Labour in Europe*, Aldershot: Edward Elgar.

Lansbury, R.D. and Marchington, M. (1993) 'Joint consultation and industrial relations: experience from Australia and overseas', *Asia Pacific Journal of Human Resources*, Vol. 31, No. 3, pp. 62–82.

Lapperousaz, P. (1990) 'Grandes ou petites séries; l'intéret du juste-à-temps', *L'Usine Nouvelle*, 2286, pp. 44–52.

Lawler, E.E. (1994) 'From job-based to competency-based organisations', *Journal of Organisational Behaviour*, Vol. 15, pp. 3–15.

Layard, R. and Nickell, S. (1988) 'The Thatcher miracle?', LSE Centre for Labour Economics, Discussion Paper 343, London.

Lécluse, M. (1997a) 'Le CSERC conseille une flexibilité négociée dans les entreprises', *Les Echos*, 8 January.

Lécluse, M. (1997b) 'Temps de travail: pressions dans la majorité pour modifier la loi Robien', *Les Echos*, 28 January.

Lécluse, M. (1997c) 'Chômage, retraites et sécurité: les hantises grandissantes des Français', *Les Echos*, 14 October 1996.

Legge, K. (1978) *Power, Innovation and Problem Solving in Personnel Management*, London: McGraw-Hill.

Legge, K. (1995) *Human Resource Management: Rhetorics and Realities,* Basingstoke: Macmillan.

Lehrman Brothers (1994) *Jobs Study*, Paris: OECD.

Lemaître, F. (1996a) 'La réduction du temps de travail s'étend peu à peu dans les entreprises', *Le Monde*, 26 March.

Lemaître, F. (1996b) 'Le temps partiel subi se développe et accrôit la précarité', *Le Monde*, 18 May.

Lenglet, F. (1996) 'Emploi: pourqoui le grand ménage continue', *L'Expansion,* No. 523, 18 April.

Lengnick Hall, C.A. and Lengnick Hall, M.L. (1988) 'Strategic human resource management: a review of the literature and a proposed typology', *Academy of Management Review*, Vol. 13, pp. 454–70.

Levine, D.I. (1995) *Reinventing the Workplace: How Business and Employees Can Both Win,* Washington DC: Brookings Institution.

Levine, D.I. and Tyson, L.D. (1991) 'Participation, productivity and the firm's environment', in Blinder, A. (ed.) *Paying for Productivity* , Washington, DC: Brookings Institution.

Levinson, H. (1962) *Organisational Diagnosis,* Cambridge, MA: Harvard University Press.

Lewandowski, J-C. (1996) 'Les DRH condamnés à innover', *Les Echos Management*, 20 February.

Lewicki, R.J. and Bunker, B.B. (1996) 'Developing and maintaining trust in work relationships', in Kramer, R. and Tyler, T.R. (eds) *Trust in Organisations: Frontiers of Theory and Research*, London: Sage Publications.

Lewis, R. (1983) 'Collective labour law', in Bain, G.S. (ed.) *Industrial Relations in Britain*, Oxford: Blackwell.

Liaisons Sociales (1996a*)* 'Incitation collective à la réduction collective du temps du travail', A2 No. 7479.

Liaisons Sociales (1996b*)* 'Incitation à l'aménagment et à la réduction conventionnelle du temps du travail', A2 No. 7542.

Littlefield, D. (1996) 'Quarter of staff ready to resign', *People Management*, Vol. 2, No. 24, p.11.

Lucero, A.M. and Allen, E.R. (1994) 'Employee benefits: a growing source of psychological contract violations', *Human Resource Management*, Vol. 33, No. 3, pp. 425–46.

MacDuffie, J.P. (1992) *Human Resource Bundles and Manufacturing Performance*, Mimeo, Wharton School: University of Pennsylvania.

MacDuffie, J.P. (1995) 'Human resource bundles and manufacturing performance: organisational logic and flexible production systems in the world auto industry', *Industrial and Labour Relations Review*, Vol. 48, pp. 197–221.

MacDuffie, J.P. and Krafcik, J.F. (1986) 'Integrating technology and human resources for high performance manufacturing: evidence from the international auto industry', in Kochan, T. and Useem, P. (eds) *Transforming Organizations*, New York: Free Press.

Mackay, L. and Torrington, D.P. (1986) *The Changing Nature of Personnel Management*, London: Institute of Personnel Management.

Macy B. and Izumi, H. (1993) 'Organizational change design and work innovation: a meta-analysis of North American field studies 1961–1991', in Woodman, R. and Passmore, W. (eds) *Research in Organizational Change and Development,* Vol. 7, Greenwich, CT: JAI Press.

Manufacturing, Science and Finance Union (1989) *The Way Ahead Training Initiative*, London: MSF.

Marchington, M. (1992) *Managing the Team*, Oxford: Blackwell.

Marchington, M. (1994a) 'Trade unions: partners in competitive success', presentation *to* IPD Annual Conference, Harrogate.

Marchington, M. (1994b) 'The dynamics of joint consultation', in Sisson, K. (ed.), *Personnel Management in Britain*, Oxford:Blackwell

Marchington, M. (1995) 'Involvement and Participation', in Storey, J. (ed.) *Human Resource Management: A Critical Text,* London: Routledge.

Marchington, M. and Armstrong, R. (1981) 'A case for consultation', *Employee Relations*, Vol. 3, No. 1, pp. 10–16.

Marchington, M. and Loveridge, R. (1979) 'Non-participation: the management view', *Journal of Management Studies*, Vol. 16, No. 2, pp. 171–84.

Marchington, M. and Parker, P. (1990) *Changing Patterns of Employee Relations,* Hemel Hempstead: Harvester Wheatsheaf.

Marchington, M. and Wilkinson, A. (1996) *Core Personnel and Development*, London: IPD.

Marchington, M., Goodman, J., Wilkinson, A. and Ackers, P. (1992) *New Developments in Employee Involvement*, Employment Department Research Series, London: HMSO.

Marginson, P., Armstrong, P., Edwards, P., Purcell, J. and Hubbard, N. (1993) 'The control of industrial relations in large companies: an initial analysis of the second company level industrial relations survey, *Warwick Papers in Industrial Relations No. 45,* Coventry: IRRU Warwick University.

Mayer, R.C., Davis, J.H. and Schoorman, F.D. (1995) 'An integrative model of organisational trust', *Academy of Management Review*, Vol. 20, No. 3, pp. 709–34.

MacLachlan, R. (1996) 'Liberté, egalité and now employabilité', *People Management*, Vol. 2, No. 24, p. 16.

McGregor, A. and Sproull, A. (1991) *Employers' Labour Use Strategies: Analysis of a National Survey*, Employment Department Research paper No. 83, London: DfEE.

McIvor, G. (1997) 'Electrolux to shed 12 000 jobs in sweeping shake-up', *Financial Times*, 13 June.

McLean Parks, J. and Schmedemann, D.A. (1994) 'When promises become contracts: implied contract and handbook provisions on job security', *Human Resource Management*, Vol. 33, pp. 403–23.

Merton, R.K. (1957) *Social Theory and Social Structure*' (Rev. edn) Glencoe, IL: Free Press.

Metcalf, D. (1988) 'Trade unions and economic performance: the British evidence', LSE Centre for Labour Economics, Discussion Paper 320, London.

Metcalf, D. (1989) 'Water notes dry up: the impact of Donovan reform proposals and Thatcherism at work on labour productivity in British manufacturing industry', *British Journal of Industrial Relations*, Vol. 27, No. 1, pp. 1–31.

Metcalf, D. (1991) 'British unions: dissolution or resurgence?', *Oxford Review of Economic Policy*, Vol. 7, No. 1, pp. 18–32.

Metcalf, D. (1993) 'Industrial relations and economic performance', *British Journal of Industrial Relations*, Vol. 31, No. 2, pp. 255–83.

Metcalf, D., Fernie, S. and Woodland, S. (1994) 'What has HRM achieved in the workplace?', *Employment Policy Institute Economic Report No. 8*, London: Employment Policy Institute.

Miles, R.E. and Snow, C.C. (1984) 'Designing strategic human resource systems', *Organizational Dynamics*, Summer, pp. 36–52.

Miller, P. (1987) 'Strategic industrial relations and human resource management: distinction, definition and recognition', *Journal of Management Studies*, Vol. 24, No. 4, pp. 347–61.

Millward, N. (1994) *The New Industrial Relations*, London: Policy Studies Institute.

Millward, N., Stevens, M., Smart, D. and Hawes, W.R. (1992) *Workplace Industrial Relations in Transition*, London: ACAS.

Milne, S. (1997) 'Part-time workers gain equal rights', *Guardian*, 7 June.

Miner, J.B. (1976) 'Levels of motivation to manage among personnel and industrial relations managers', *Journal of Applied Psychology*, Vol. 61, pp. 419–27.

Mintzberg, H. (1979) *The Structuring of Organizations*, Englewood Cliffs, NJ: Prentice-Hall.

Mintzberg, H. (1983) *Structure in Fives*, Englewood Cliffs, NJ: Prentice-Hall.

Mintzberg, H. (1994a) 'The rise and fall of strategic planning', *Harvard Business Review*, January-February, pp. 107–14

Mintzberg, H. (1994b) *The Rise and Fall of Strategic Planning*, New York: Free Press.

Mirvis, P.H. (1997) 'HRM: leaders, laggards and followers', *Academy of Management Executive*, Vol. 11, No. 2, pp. 43–56.

Mirvis, P.H. and Marks, M.L. (1992) *Managing the Merger,* Englewood Cliffs, NJ: Prentice-Hall.

Miyake, D., Enkawa, T. and Fleury, A.C.C. (1995) 'Improving manufacturing systems performance by complementary application of JIT, TQC and TPM paradigms', *Total Quality Management*, Vol. 6, No. 4.

Monks, K. (1992) 'Models of personnel management: a means of understanding the diversity of personnel practices?', *Human Resource Management Journal*, Vol. 3, No. 2, pp. 29–41

Morrison, D. (1994) 'Psychological contracts and change', *Human Resource Management*, Vol. 33, No. 3, pp. 353–72.

Morrison, E.W. and Robinson, S.L. (1997) 'When employees feel betrayed: a model of how psychological contract violation develops', *Academy of Management Review*, Vol. 22, No. 1, pp. 226–56.

Morse, D. (1969) *Peripheral Worker*, New York: Columbia University Press.

Moss, N. and Richards, H. (1997) 'Mike The Knife cuts deep', *The European*, 19 June.

Mroczkowski, T. and Hanaoka, M. (1997) 'Effective rightsizing strategies in Japan and America: is there a convergence of employment practices?', *Academy of Management Executive*, Vol. 11, No. 2, pp. 57–67.

Mumford, E. (1995) 'Creative chaos or constructive change: business process reengineering versus socio-technical design?', in Burke, G. and Peppard, J. (eds) *Examining Business Process Reengineering*, Cranfield: Kogan Page and Cranfield University.

Mumford, E. and Hendricks, R. (1996) 'Business process re-engineering: RIP', *People Management*, 2 May.

Murakami, T. (1995) 'Introducing teamwork: an automobile industry case study from Germany', *Industrial Relations Journal*, Vol. 26, No. 4, pp. 293–305.

Naudin, T. (1997) 'Flexibility can bend job rules', *The European*, 19 June.

New Ways to Work (1995) *Flexible Working in Local Government*, London: New Ways to Work.

Nicholson, N. and West, M.A. (1988) *Managerial Job Change: Men and Women in Transition*, Cambridge: Cambridge University Press.

Noer, D.M. (1993) *Healing the Wounds*, San Francisco, CA: Jossey Bass.

Nolan, P. (1989) 'Walking on water? Performance and industrial relations under Thatcher', *Industrial Relations Journal*, Vol. 20, No. 2, pp. 81–92.

Nolan, P. (1996) 'Industrial relations and performance since 1945', in Beardwell, I. (ed.) (1997) pp. 99–120.

Nolan, P. and Marginson, P. (1990) 'Skating on thin ice? David Metcalf on trade unions and productivity', *British Journal of Industrial Relations*, Vol. 18, No. 2, pp. 225–47.

O Neill, H. and Lenn, J. (1995) 'Voices of survivors: words that downsizing CEOs should hear', *Academy of Management Executive*, Vol. 9, No. 4, pp. 23-35.

OECD (1986) *Flexibility in the Labour Market: The Current Debate*, Paris: OECD.

OECD (1989) *Labour market flexibility: Trends in Enterprises*, Paris: OECD.

OECD (1991) *Employment Outlook*, Paris: OECD.

Olian, J.D., Durham, C., Kristof, A., and Pierce, R. (1993) 'Training and development in world class companies', *Mimeo*, University of Maryland.

Oliver, N. (1991) 'The dynamics of just-in-time', *New Technology, Work and Employment*, Vol. 6, No. 1, pp. 2–16.

Oliver, N. and Wilkinson, B. (1992) *The Japanization of British Industry: New Developments in the 1990s*, Oxford: Blackwell.

Oliver, N., Delbridge, R., Jones, D. and Lowe, R. (1994) 'World class manufacturing: further evidence from the lean production debate', *British Journal of Management*, Vol. 5, Special Issue, pp. S53–S65.

Oram, M. and Wellins, R. (1995) *Re-engineering's missing ingredient – the human factor*, London: Institute of Personnel and Development.

Ouchi, W.G. (1980) 'Markets, hierarchies and clans', *Administrative Science Quarterly*, Vol. 23, pp. 293–317.

Overholt, M.H. (1997) 'Flexible organisations: using organisational design as a competitive advantage', *Human Resource Planning*, Vol. 20, No. 1, pp. 22–32.

Paauwe, J. (1995) 'Personnel management without personnel managers', in Flood, P., Gannon, M.J. and Paauwe, J. (eds) *Managing Without Traditional Methods: International Innovations in Human Resource Management*, Wokingham: Addison Wesley.

Pahl, R.E. (1984) *Divisions of Labour*, Oxford: Basil Blackwell.

Pahl, R.E. (1995) *After Success: Fin de Siècle, Anxiety and Identity*, Cambridge: Polity Press.

Parker, S.K. and Wall, T.D. (1996) 'Job design and modern manufacturing', in Warr, P. (ed.) *Psychology and Work* (4th edn), London: Penguin Books.

Pascale, R. (1995) 'In search of "The new employment contract", Paper for 20th Anniversary Euroforum Conference, 15–16 September, Strategic Leadership Programme, London Business School.

Peters, T.J. and Waterman, R.H. (1982) *In Search of Excellence*, New York: Harper and Row.

Pfeffer, J. (1992) *Managing With Power*, Boston: Harvard Business School Press.

Pfeffer, J. (1994) *Competitive Advantage Through People: Unleashing the Power of the Work Force*, Boston: Harvard Business School Press.

Pfeffer, J. (1995) 'The basis for competitive success: people and organisational culture', Investors in People Conference paper.

Pinnington, A. and Woolcock, P. (1995) 'How far is IS/IT outsourcing enabling new organisational structure and competences?', *International Journal of Information Management*, Vol. 15, No. 5, pp. 353–65.

Piore, M. and Sabel, C. (1984) *The Second Industrial Divide*, New York: Basic Books.

Plewes, T.J. (1990) "Labor force in the next century", *Monthly Labor Review*, Vol. 113, Iss. 4, pp. 3–8.

Pollack, M.A. and Bernstein, A. (1986) "The disposable employee is becoming a fact of life", *Business Week*, 15 December, pp. 52–6.

Pollert, A. (1987) 'The "flexible firm": a model in search of reality (or a policy in search of a practice)?', *Warwick Papers in Industrial Relations*, No. 29, Coventry: IRR, University of Warwick.

Pollert, A. (1988a) 'Dismantling Flexibility', *Capital and Class*, Vol. 34, pp. 42–75.

Pollert, A. (1988b) 'The "flexible firm": fixation or fact?', *Work, Employment and Society*, Vol. 2, No. 3, pp. 281–316.

Pollert, A. (1996) 'Team work on the assembly line: contradiction and the dynamics of union resilience', in Ackers, P., Smith, C. and Smith, P. (eds) *The New Workplace and Trade Unionism*, London: Routledge.

Pollert, A. (1991) (ed.) *Farewell to Flexibility?*, Oxford: Blackwell.

Pontusson, J. (1992) 'Unions, new technology and job redesign at Volvo and British Leyland', in Golden, M. and Pontusson, J. (eds) *Bargaining for Change*, Ithaca: Cornell University Press.

Poole, M. (1986) *Towards a New Industrial Democracy: Workers' Participation in Industry*, London: Routledge and Kegan Paul.

Prahalad, C. and Hamel, G. (1990) 'The core competencies of the corporation', *Harvard Business Review*, May/June, pp. 79–91.

Purcell, J. (1979) 'A strategy for management control in industrial relations', in Purcell, J. and Smith, R. (eds) *The Control of Work*, London: Macmillan.

Purcell, J. (1981) *Good Industrial Relations*, London: Macmillan.

Purcell, J. (1991) 'The rediscovery of the managerial prerogative', *Oxford Review of Economic Policy*, Vol. 7, No. 1, pp. 33–59.

Purcell, J. (1995) 'Corporate strategy and its links with human resource management strategy', in Storey, J. (ed.) *Human Resource Management: A Critical Text*, London: Routledge.

Purcell, J. (1996) 'Contingent workers and human resource strategy: rediscovering the core/periphery dimension', *The Journal of Professional Human Resource Management*, No. 5, October, pp. 16–23.

Purcell, J. and Ahlstrand, B. (1994) *Human Resource Management in the Multi-divisional Company*, Oxford: Oxford University Press.

Purcell, J. and Sisson, K. (1983) 'Strategies and practice in the management of industrial relations', in Bain, G.S. (ed.) *Industrial Relations in Britain*, Oxford: Blackwell.

Purcell, K. and Purcell, J. (1996) 'Responding to competition: insourcing, outsourcing and the growth of contingent labour', paper presented at the conference on the Globalization of Production and Regulation of Labour, University of Warwick, 12 September.

Ramsay, H. (1991) 'The community, the multinational, its workers and their charter: a modern tale of industrial democracy', *Work, Employment and Society*, Vol. 5, No. 3, pp. 541–66.

Reed Personnel Services (1995) *The Shape of Work to Come*, London: Reed Personnel Services.

Reed, R. and DeFillippi, R.J. (1990) 'Causing ambiguity, barriers to imitation, and sustainable competitive advantage', *Academy of Management Review*, Vol. 15, No. 1, pp. 88–102.

Rees, B. and Brewster, C. (1995) 'Supporting equality: patriarchy at work in Europe', *Personnel Review*, Vol. 24, No. 1, pp. 19–40.

Rees, C. (1996) 'Employee autonomy and management control in the quality organisation', Paper to International Labour Process Conference, Aston University.

Rioux, O. (1989) 'L'ascension des DRH', *Liaisons Sociales, Mensuel*, No. 36, February.

Rivest, C. (1996) 'Voluntary European works councils', *European Journal of Industrial Relations*, Vol. 2, No. 2, pp. 235–53.

Robinson, S.L. and Morrison, E.W. (1995) 'Psychological contracts and organisation citizenship behaviour: the effect of unfulfilled obligations on civic virtue behaviour', *Journal of Organisational Behaviour*, Vol. 16, pp. 289–98.

Robinson, S.L. and Rousseau, D.M. (1994) 'Violating the psychological contract: not the exception but the norm', *Journal of Organisational Behaviour*, Vol. 15, pp. 245–59.

Rojot, J. (1992) 'Flexibilité de la main d'oeuvre dans les entreprises, expériences nationales', in Durand, M. (ed.) *Politiques Economiques et Sociales en Europe*, Paris: L'Harmattan.

Rousseau, D.M. (1990) 'New hire perceptions of their own and their employer's obligations: a study of psychological contracts', *Journal of Organisational Behaviour*, Vol. 11, pp. 389–400.

Rousseau, D.M. (1995) *Psychological Contracts in Organisations: Understanding Written and Unwritten Agreements*, Thousand Oaks, CA: Sage.

Rousseau, D.M. and Greller, M.M. (1994) 'Human resource practices: administrative contract makers', *Human Resource Management*, Vol. 33, pp. 385–401.

Royal Commission of Trade Unions and Employers' Associations (1968) *Report*, London: HMSO.

Royal Society of Arts (1995) *Tomorrow's Company*, London: RSA.

Rubery, J. and Fagin, C. (1993) 'Occupational segregation of women and men in the European Community', *Social Europe*, 3.

Rubery, J., Smith, M., Fagin, C., Almond, P. and Parker, J. (1996) 'Trends and prospects for women's employment in the 1990s', *Report for DGV of the European Commission*, Manchester: UMIST.

Ryf, B. (1993) *Die atomisierte Organisation: ein Konzept zur Ausschöpfung von Humanpotential*, Wiesbaden: Gabler.

Ryland, E. (1997) Review of 'When corporations rule the world', by D.C. Korten, *Academy of Management Review*, Vol. 22, No. 1, pp. 298–301.

Sako, M. (1996) 'The effects of supplier relationships and worker involvement on corporate performance', in Westall, A. (ed.) *Competitiveness and Corporate Governance*, London: Institute for Public Policy Research.

Salaman, G. (1996) 'Indian snacks: change and continuity', in Storey, J. (ed.) *Blackwell Cases in Human Resource and Change Management*, Oxford: Blackwell.

Scali, S. (1997) 'Blue Circle Cement', *Towards Industrial Partnership Putting it into Practice*, Case Study No. 6, London: IPA.

Schein, E.H. (1978) *Career Dynamics: Matching Individual and Organisational Needs*, Reading, MS: Addison Wesley.

Schein, E.H. (1992) *Organizational Culture and Leadership* (2nd edn) San Francisco: Jossey Bass.

Schneider, B. and Bowen, D.E. (1993) 'The service organization: human resource management is crucial', *Organizational Dynamics*, Vol. 21, pp. 39–52.

Schuler, R.S. (1989) 'Repositioning the human resource function: transformation or demise?', *Academy of Management Executive*, Vol. 4, No. 3, pp. 49–60.

Schuler, R.S. and Jackson, S.E. (1987) 'Linking competitive strategies with human resource management practices', *Academy of Management Executive*, Vol. 1, No. 3, pp. 207–19.

Schulten, T. (1996) 'European works councils: prospects for a new system of European industrial relations', *European Journal of Industrial Relations*, Vol. 2, No. 3, pp. 303–24.

Scott, A. (1994) *Willing Slaves? British Workers Under Human Resource Management*, Cambridge: Cambridge University Press.

Seitchick, M. (1997) 'Dilemmas in the HR partnership', *Human Resource Planning*, Vol. 20, No. 1, pp. 42–4.

Selznick, P. (1949) *TVA and the Grass Roots*, Berkeley: University of California Press.

Senge, P. (1990) *The Fifth Discipline: The Art and Practice of the Learning Organisation*, New York: Doubleday.

Sewell, G. and Wilkinson, B. (1992) 'Empowerment or emasculation? Shopfloor surveillance in a total quality organisation', in Blyton, P. and Turnbull, P. (eds) *Reassessing Human Resource Management*, London: Sage Publications, pp. 97–115.

Shapiro, D.L., Sheppard, B.H. and Cheraskin, L. (1992) 'Business on a hand shake', *Negotiation Journal*, Vol. 8, pp. 365–78.

Sisson, K. (1993) 'In search of HRM', *British Journal of Industrial Relations*, Vol. 31, No. 2, pp. 201–10.

Sisson, K. (1995) 'Human resource management and the personnel function', in Storey, J. (ed.) *Human Resource Management: A Critical Text*, London: Routledge.

Skinner, W. (1987) 'Big hat – no cattle: managing human resources', *Harvard Business Review*, Vol. 59, pp. 106–14.

Slack, N. (1991) *The Manufacturing Advantage: Achieving Competitive Manufacturing and Operations*, London: Mercury Books.

Smith, A.E. (1994) 'New technology and the process of labor regulation: an international perspective', in Bélanger, J., Edwards, P.K. and Haiven, L. (eds) *Workplace Industrial Relations and the Global Challenge*, Ithaca: ILR Press.

Smith, D. (1997) 'Job insecurity and other myths: the employment climate', *Management Today*, May, pp. 38–41.

Smith, K.A. (1995) 'Managing without traditional strategic planning', in Flood, P., Gannon, M.J. and Paauwe, J. (eds) *Managing Without Traditional Methods: International Innovations in Human Resource Management*, Wokingham: Addison Wesley.

Smith, P. and Morton, G. (1993) 'Union exclusion and the decollectivization of industrial relations in contemporary Britain', *British Journal of Industrial Relations*, Vol. 31, No. 1, pp. 97–114.

Smith, P. and Morton, G. (1994) 'Union exclusion in Britain: next steps', *Industrial Relations Journal*, Vol. 25, p. 1.

Social Europe (1991) *Working Time, Employment and Production-capacity; Reorganisation/reduction of Working Time'*, Supplement 4/91 DGV European Commission.

Sparrow, P.R. (1986) 'The erosion of employment in the UK: the need for a new response', *New Technology, Work and Employment*, Vol. 1, No. 2, pp. 101–12.

Sparrow, P.R. (1994) 'The psychology of strategic management: emerging themes of diversity and managerial cognition', in Cooper, C. and Robertson, I. (eds) *International Review of Industrial and Organizational Psychology*, Volume 9, Chichester: John Wiley.

Sparrow, P.R. (1995) 'Human resource strategy', in Nicholson, N. (ed.) *Encyclopaedic Dictionary of Organisational Behaviour*, London: Blackwell.

Sparrow, P.R. (1996a) 'Transitions in the psychological contract in UK banking', *Human Resource Management Journal*, Vol. 6, No. 4, pp. 75–92.

Sparrow, P.R. (1996b) 'Life after downsizing at Galenco Healthcare Materials: managing change in a difficult climate', in McGoldrick, A. (ed.) *Cases in Human Resource Management*, London: Pitman Publishing.

Sparrow, P.R. (1996c) 'Careers and the psychological contract: understanding the European context', *The European Journal of Work and Organisational Psychology*, Vol. 5, No. 4, pp. 479–500.

Sparrow, P.R. (1996d) 'Linking competencies to pay: too good to be true?', *People Management*, Vol. 2, No. 23, pp. 22–7.

Sparrow, P.R. (1997a) 'Organizational competencies: creating a strategic behavioural framework for selection and assessment', in Anderson, N. and Herriot, P. (eds) *Assessment and Selection in Organisations: Methods and Practice for Recruitment and Appraisal,*Chichester: John Wiley.

Sparrow, P.R. (1997b) 'Job-based flexibility', in Brewster, C. (ed.) *Flexible Working Practices,* London: Croner Publications.

Sparrow, P.R. and Hiltrop. J.M. (1994*) European Human Resource Management in Transition*, London: Prentice-Hall.

Sparrow, P.R. and Hiltrop, J.M. (1997) 'Redefining the field of European human resource management: a battle between national mindsets and forces of business transition', *Human Resource Management*, Vol. 36, No. 2, pp. 201–20.

Stalk, G. Jr, Evans, P., and Shulman, L.E. (1993) 'Competing on capabilities: the new rules of corporate strategy', in Howard, R. (ed.) *The Learning Imperative: Managing People for Continuous Innovation*, Cambridge: Harvard Business School Press.

Steele, C.M. (1988) 'The psychology of self-affirmation: sustaining the integrity of the self', in Berkowitz, L. (ed.) *Advances in Experimental and Social Psychology,* San Diego, CA: Academic Press.

Steinmann, L. (1996) 'Un dispositif ambigu', *L'Expansion*, No. 523, 18 April.

Stephens, C.K. (1994) 'Crossing internal career boundaries: the state of research on subjective career transitions', *Journal of Management*, Vol. 20, pp. 479–501.

Stephenson, C. (1996) 'The different experience of trade unionism in two Japanese transplants', in Ackers, P., Smith, C. and Smith, P. (eds), *The New Workplace: Critical Perspectives on Work and Organization*, London: Routledge.

Stevens, M.J. and Campion, M.A. (1994) 'The knowledge, skill and ability requirements for teamwork: implications for HRM', *Journal of Management*, Vol. 20, pp. 503–30.

Stirk, H. (1996) 'Directive Action', *People Management*, Vol. 2, No. 20, pp. 50–1.

Storey, J. (1989) *New Perspectives on Human Resource Management*, London: Routledge.

Storey, J. (1992) *Developments in the Management of Human Resources*, Oxford: Blackwell.

Storey, J. (1995a) *Human Resource Management: A Critical Text*, London: Routledge.

Storey, J. (1995b) 'Is HRM catching on?', *International Journal of Manpower*, Vol. 16, No. 4, pp. 3–10

Storey, J. and Sisson, K. (1993) *Managing Human Resources and Industrial Relations*, Milton Keynes: Open University Press.

Storey, J., Bacon, N., Edmonds, J. and Wyatt, P. (1993) 'The "new agenda" and human resource management: a roundtable discussion with John Edmonds', *Human Resource Management Journal*, Vol. 4, No. 1, pp. 63–70.

Storey, J., Mabey, C., and Thomson, A. (1997) 'What a difference a decade makes', *People Management*, Vol. 3, No. 12, pp. 28–30.

Streeck, W. (1989) 'Skills and the limits of Neo-liberalism; the enterprise of the future as a place of learning', *Work, Employment and Society*, Vol. 3, No. 1, pp. 89–104.

Susskind, L.E and Landry, E.M. (1991) 'Implementing a mutual gains approach to collective bargaining', *Negotiation Journal*, Vol. 7, No. 1, pp. 5–10.

Taylor, R. (1997) 'Councils and unions close to deal on wages', *Financial Times*, 10 March.

Terpstra, D.E. and Rozell, E.J. (1993) 'The relationship of staffing practices to organizational level measures of performance', *Personnel Psychology*, Vol. 46, pp. 27–48.

Terry, M. (1983) 'Shop stewards through expansion and recession', *Industrial Relations Journal*, Vol. 14, No. 3, pp. 49–58.

Thurley, K. (1981) 'Personnel management in the UK: a case for urgent treatment', *Personnel Management,* August, pp. 24–8.

Tichy, N.M., Fombrun, C.J. and Devanna, M.A. (1982) 'Strategic human resource management', *Sloan Management Review*, Vol. 23, No. 2, pp. 47–61.

Torrington, D.P. and Hall, L.A. (1996) 'Chasing the rainbow: how seeking status through strategy misses the point for the personnel function', *Employee Relations*, Vol. 18, No. 6, pp. 79–96.

Torrington, D.P. and McKay, J. (1986) 'Will consultants take over the personnel function?', *Personnel Management*, February, pp. 34–6.

Tracey, T.J. and Rounds, S.B. (1993) 'Evaluating Holland's and Gati's vocational interest models: a structural meta-analysis, *Psychological Bulletin*, Vol. 113, pp. 229–46.

Trades Union Congress (1990) *TUC Guidance: Joint Action over Training*, London: TUC.

Trades Union Congress (1991) *Collective Bargaining Strategy for the 1990s*, London: TUC.

Trades Union Congress (1994) *Human Resource Management: A Trade Union Response*, London: TUC.

Trades Union Congress (1997) *Partners for Progress: Next Steps for the New Unionism*, London: TUC.

Tranberg, M., Slane, S. and Ekeberg, S.E. (1993) 'The relation between interest congruence and satisfaction: a meta-analysis', *Journal of Vocational Behaviour*, Vol. 42, pp. 253–64.

Transport and General Workers' Union (1989) *Negotiating Training at the Workplace*, London: T&GWU.

Truss, C. and Gratton, L. (1994) 'Strategic human resource management: a conceptual approach', *The International Journal of Human Resource Management*, Vol. 5, No. 3, pp. 663–86.

Truss, C., Gratton, L., Hope-Hailey, V., McGovern, P. and Stiles, P. (1997) 'Soft and hard models of human resource management: a reappraisal', *Journal of Management Studies*, Vol. 34, No. 1, pp. 53–74.

Turnbull, P. (1988) 'The limits to Japanization: JIT, labour relations and the UK automotive industry', *New Technology, Work and Employment*, Vol. 3, No. 1, pp. 3–15.

Turnbull, P. and Wass, V. (1997) 'Job insecurity and labour market lemons: the (mis)management of redundancy in steel making, coal mining and port transport', *Journal of Management Studies*, Vol. 34, No. 1, pp. 27–52.

Tüsselmann, H-J. (1996) 'Progress towards greater labour flexibility in Germany – the impact of recent reforms', *Employee Relations*, Vol. 18, No. 1, 50–67

Tyson, S. (1987) 'The management of the personnel function', *Journal of Management Studies*, Vol. 24, No. 5, pp. 523–32.

Tyson, S. (1995a) *Human Resource Strategy*, London: Pitman Publishing.

Tyson, S. (1995b) 'Human resource and business strategy', in Tyson, S. (ed.) *Strategic Prospects for HRM*, London: IPD Press.

Tyson, S. (1997) 'Human resource strategy: a process for managing the contribution of HRM to organisational performance', *International Journal of Human Resource Management*, Vol. 8, No. 3, 277–90.

Tyson, S. and Fell, A. (1995) 'A focus on skills, not organisations', *People Management*, Vol. 1, No. 20, p. 43.

Tyson, S., Doherty, N. and Viney, C. (1995) 'The contribution of personnel management to business performance', in *The Contribution of Personnel Management to Organisational Performance*, Issues in People Management, Report No. 9, London: Institute of Personnel and Development.

Ulrich, D. (1996) 'Transforming the HR function: interview with Dave Ulrich', *Transformation – Journal of Gemini Consulting Group*, spring.

Ulrich, D. and Lake, D. (1990) *Organisational Capability: Competing From the Inside Out*, New York: John Wiley.

Uzumeri, M.V. (1997) 'ISO 9000 and other metastandards: principles for management practice?', *Academy of Management Executive*, Vol. XI, No. 1, pp. 21–36.

van de Vliert, A. (1997) 'The new balancing act', *Management Today*, Iss. 7, pp. 78–80.

Van Neerven, T., Bruining, J. and Paauwe, J. (1995) 'Managing without traditional owners', in Flood, P., Gannon, M.J. and Paauwe, J. (eds) *Managing Without Traditional Methods: International Innovations in Human Resource Management*, Wokingham: Addison Wesley.

Vesey J.T. (1991) 'The new competitors: they think in terms of "speed-to-market"', *Academy of Management Executive*, Vol. 5, No. 2, pp. 23–33.

Waddington, J. and Whitston, C. (1996) 'Empowerment versus intensification: union perspectives of change at the workplace', in Ackers, P., Smith, C. and Smith, P. (eds) *The New Workplace: Critical Perspectives on Work and Organization*, London: Routledge.

Wall, T.D., Kemp, N.J., Jackson, P.R. and Clegg, C.W. (1986) 'Outcomes of autonomous workgroups: a long term field experiment', *Academy of Management Journal*, Vol. 29, pp. 280–304.

Wally, S., Carroll, S.J. and Flood, P. (1995) 'Managing without traditional structures', in Flood, P., Gannon, M.J. and Paauwe, J. (eds) *Managing Without Traditional Methods: International Innovations in Human Resource Management*, Wokingham: Addison Wesley.

Walton, R.E. (1985) 'From control to commitment in the workplace', *Harvard Business Review*, March–April, pp. 76–84.

Walton. R.E and McKersie, R.B. (1965) *A Behavioural Theory of Labor Negotiations*, New York: McGraw-Hill.

Wareing, A. (1992) 'Working arrangements and patterns of working hours in Britain', *Employment Gazette*, March, pp. 88–100.

Warnecke, H.J. (1993) *Revolution der Unternehmenskultur: Das Fraktale Unternehean*, Berlin: Springer.

Warr, P.B. (1987) *Work, Unemployment and Mental Health*, Oxford: Oxford University Press.

Waters, R. (1997) 'We're driven too hard, say car strikers', *Financial Times*, 12 June.

Watson, T.J. (1977) *The Personnel Managers*, London: Routledge and Kegan Paul

Weber, M. (1947) *The Theory of Social and Economic Organization,* translated by Parsons, T. and Henderson, A. M., New York: Free Press.

Welch, J. (1997) 'Intel faces fight over "termination quotas"', *People Management*, Vol. 3, No. 13, p. 9.

Welch, R. (1994) 'European works councils and their implications: the potential impact on employer practices and trade unions', *Employee Relations*, Vol. 16, No. 4, pp. 48–62.

Wellins, R.S., Byham, W.C. and Wilson, J.M. (1991) *Empowered Teams – Creating Self-directed Work Groups that Improve Quality, Productivity and Participation*, San Francisco: Jossey Bass Publishers.

Whipp, R. (1991) 'Human resource management, strategic change and competition: the role of learning, *International Journal of Human Resource Management*, Vol. 2, No. 2, pp. 165–91.

Whitley, R.D. (ed.) (1992) *European Business Systems: Firms and Markets in Their National Context*, London: Sage Publications.

Wickens, P. (1987) *The Road to Nissan*, London: Macmillan.

Wickens, P. (1993) 'Lean production and beyond: the system, its critics and the future', *Human Resource Management Journal*, Vol. 3, No. 4, pp. 75–90.

Wild, A. (1996) 'How to set up a European works council', *People Management*, Vol. 2, No. 19.

Wildermann, H. (1994) *Die Modulare Fabrik: Kundennahe Produktion durch Fertigungs-segmentierung*, München: TCW.

Wilkinson, A., Marchington, M., Goodman, J. and Ackers, P. (1993) 'Refashioning industrial relations: the experience of a chemical company over the last decade', *Personnel Review*, Vol. 22, No. 3, pp. 22–38.

Wilkinson, B. and Oliver, N. (1988) *The Japanization of British Industry*, Oxford: Blackwell.

Williams, A.R.T. and Guest, D.E. (1971) 'Are the middle-classes becoming work-shy?', *New Society*, No. 457, 1 July.

Williamson, O.E. (1975) *Markets and Hierarchies: Analysis and Anti-Trust Implications*, New York: Free Press.

Williamson, O.E. (1985) *Economic Institutions of Capitalism*, New York: Free Press.

Willmott, H. (1994) 'Business process reengineering and human resource management', *Personnel Review*, Vol. 23, No. 3, pp. 34–46.

Wilsher, P. (1996) 'Flexible workers of spare bodies', *Human Resources*, July/August, pp. 37–9.

Wilson, M., George, J., Wellins, R.S. and Byham, W.C. (1994) *Leadership Trapeze – Strategies for Leadership in Team-Based Organisations,* San Francisco: Jossey Bass.

Winterton, J. and Winterton, R. (1994) *Collective Bargaining and Consultation over Continuing Vocational Training*, London: HMSO.

Womack J.P., Jones D.T. and Roos, R. (1990) *The Machine that Changed the World*, New York: MacMillan.

Wood, C. (1994) *The End of Japan Inc,* New York: Simon and Schuster.

Wood, S. (1995) 'The four pillars of human resource management', *Human Resource Management Journal*, Vol. 5, No. 5, pp. 49–59

Wood, S (1997) *Statutory Union Recognition*, London Institute of Personnel and Development.

Wood, S. and Albanese, M.T. (1995) 'Can we speak of high commitment management on the shopfloor?', *Journal of Management Studies,* Vol. 32, No. 2, pp. 215–47.

Wright, M. (1996) 'The collapse of compulsory unionism? Collective organization in highly unionized British companies, 1979–1991', *British Journal of Industrial Relations*, Vol. 34, No. 4, pp. 497–513.

Wright, M. and Coyne, J. (1985) *Management Buy-outs,* London: Croom Helm.

Wright, M., and Edwards, P.K. (1996) 'Does teamworking work and, if so, why?', Paper to Employment Relations Unit conference, Cardiff Business School.

Wright, P.M. and McMahan, G.C. (1992) 'Theoretical perspectives for strategic human resource management', *Journal of Management*, Vol. 18, pp. 295–320.

Wright, P.M., McMahan, G.C. and McWilliams, A. (1994) 'Human resources and sustained competitive advantage: a resource based perspective', *The International Journal of Human Resource Management*, Vol. 5, No. 2, pp. 301–27.

Zipkin, P. (1991) 'Does manufacturing need a JIT revolution?', *Harvard Business Review*, January–February, pp. 40–52.

NAME INDEX

COMPANY NAME INDEX

SUBJECT INDEX